Psychic Self-Defense and the Zodiac

Y.S. Yacoubian

Copyright Y.S.Yacoubian, 2024

All Rights Reserved

Without limiting the rights reserved above under copyright, no part of this publication may be reproduced, stored in, or introduced into a retrieval system, or transmitted in any form or by any means (electronic, mechanical, photocopying, scanning, recording or otherwise), without written permission from both the author and the publisher, except in the case of brief quotations embodied in reviews and articles.

The scanning, uploading and distribution of this book via the Internet, or via any other means, without the written permission of the publisher is illegal and punishable by law. Please do not encourage electronic piracy of copyrighted materials.

ISBN: 978-0-86690-691-3

Cover art: K.J. Ten Cate

Requests and inquires may be mailed to the publisher:

American Federation of Astrologers, Inc.

6553 S. Rural Road

Tempe, AZ 85283

www.astrologers.com

Acknowledgments

My deepest gratitude goes to the following people for contributing to this work, both directly and indirectly. Special thanks to my husband Kevin, for his Leonine encouragement and unwavering support during the entire process of writing this book, from its conception to its completion. To those involved in my book at American Federation of Astrologers; in particular to Deborah, for her cheerful correspondence in editing and wonderful sense of humor, and to Celeste for proofreading and formatting. Both were delightful to work with.

I want to express my gratitude to my incarnate "archangel" Michael, an Aquarius, for helping me out of more predicaments than I can count, and for making me laugh with his wildly irreverent mannerisms. I thank my Oma, who tested my mettle sometimes but always out of love.

To the Sagittarius friends in my life who have shared so much power and wisdom with me: Marta, who long ago inspired me to become an author. Alex, for all of his spot-on intuitive insights, martial arts lessons, and alchemical magick.

I am thankful to the friends and earth angels who showed great kindness toward me and encouraged my healing path in different ways, including Ann, Priscilla, June, Kenny, Bonnie, and the Ewert family. There is not enough room to name all of them here. I give thanks for all of the talented healers, astrologers and teachers I have known, several of whom shared their unique gifts with me, for the great work that is dedicated to our spiritual understanding and liberation.

Last but not least, I am grateful to my enemies. Dealing with spiritual attacks was also a blessing in a disguise, because I learned firsthand how to counteract malignant forces, even though it took many arduous years of trial and error.

Contents

Introduction	vii
~PART ONE~	1
Chapter 1 Psychic Attack and Self Defense	3
Chapter 2 Categories and Divisions of the Zodiac	7
Chapter 3 Psychic Self Defense and the Signs	17
Chapter 4 Decans of the Zodiac: The Three Temperaments of Each Sign	81
Chapter 5 Emotional Reactivity Throughout the Zodiac: The Signs Acting Out	89
Chapter 6 Self Defense Tools and the Zodiac – Correspondences and Perspectives	97
Chapter 7 Planetary Influences on the Soul's Journey	109
Chapter 8 Aspects of Power, Danger and Potential	125
Chapter 9 Mars and Jupiter The Inner Warrior and the Inner Protector	131
Chapter 10 Coping with Eclipse Season	149

~PART TWO~ 157

Chapter 11
The Astrology of the Spirit World and Psychic Phenomena 159

Chapter 12
The Ascendant and Descendant 187

Chapter 13
Tips, Tools and Timing for Empaths, Psychics, and Healers 201

Chapter 14
Protective Remedies for Signs and Transits 215

Chapter 15
Elemental Well-being: Psychic Protection for Body, Emotions, Mind, Spirit 233

Chapter 16
Self-Empowerment Affirmations and Meditations for the Signs 245

~PART THREE~ 253

Chapter 17
Adversarial Groups by Sign 255

Chapter 18
Astrological Cycles and Historical Events 267

Conclusion 287

Appendix 289

Introduction

Have you ever wondered why some people seem to have it made while others struggle with ongoing hardships? What makes some people immune to common troubles and others easy targets for almost any negative influence that comes their way? Spiritual seekers often turn to religion to make sense of it all. Some have chalked up so-called good and bad luck to karma or fate, while others with a nihilistic view just figure that life is all one big gamble and there is no purpose behind it. What I am attempting to do is to take the reader on a journey of exploration into the reasons for, as well as the possible solutions to much of our human suffering, through an astrological lens.

Astrology has often been used to help us to understand our psychology, revealing both our weaknesses and strengths. By itself, the study of psychology can be triggering for most people, as it is commonly used as an aid to categorization rather than healing. The study of astrology can become a very practical and empowering self-help tool. In astrology, the natal chart serves as an inner map of the heavens above us, indicating the relationships we each have to both inner and outer influences. Within every chart lies the formula for protecting the psyche and increasing resilience.

People of all zodiac signs and planetary configurations struggle occasionally with a feeling that they are being tested and opposed, whether by seen or unseen forces. Some seem particularly affected by psychic phenomena while others have found themselves repeatedly drawn into a number of situations or relationships that left them feeling drained and victimized. For many it is a combination of both, for we are both physical and spiritual beings.

Like many other subjects of widespread interest, astrology has often been infiltrated with certain ideologies and world views, leaving little room for different opinions on these matters. In addition, many descriptions have been categorized in such a way that discourages alternative interpretations. Some people don't mind the sting of such punitive terms as are commonly used in this field of study and others who might benefit from it are repulsed by a set of beliefs that may actually have no bearing on reality.

The terminology used by astrologers of the Middle Ages was appropriate for the times they were in, but as humanity evolves, so should our descriptions expand based on new developments and outlooks that have grown out of our present-day environments and experiences. We can take the best of what we have learned from those who have come before and add to our knowledge base what we are currently learning to leave behind for future generations.

It is by no means an easy task for any astrologer to maintain the timeless coherence of particular sets of symbols and patterns that have indeed been proven to work, while also remaining flexible enough to broaden the scope of understanding and different angles of perception about such symbols and patterns. We all know the simple math of adding two plus two to make four. When it comes to astrology, other details that must be accounted for in order to gain full understanding of this math equation are the precise objects or areas being added, their overall conditions, their location, the time of their being added, and so on. This two plus two, or other number additions, can become very layered and complex, just like the human psyche. In other words, certain parts of astrology are very specific, but when it comes to interpretation, very nuanced, and they should be.

After all, there is nobody in the world – not even the greatest astrologer out there who can know another person better than they know themselves. A hard aspect between so-called malefic planets such as Mars and Saturn has a decidedly challenging tone about it, but it will mean slightly different things in different natal charts. Many aspiring astrologers do not yet grasp this fact, but the advanced practitioner is well aware of it.

It's often been stated that the aspects made from one planet to another must be harmonious in order for them to yield positive results. That is not necessarily true, but a simplistic take on a very complicated subject. Some hard aspects give greater incentive to change, and some soft ones don't stimulate enough activity. Much depends on what the soul of the individual is choosing to accomplish in their lifetime, and sometimes that focus changes. A chart should always be read with the individual in mind, and not only on what you know the aspects mean according to classic definitions. This is where intuition and astrology combine for a practical and well-rounded interpretation. It has become an internet trend for people to repeat verbatim what some other astrologer has said, circulating words and ideas that may not even be accurate on the whole. Therefore, I have made every effort to include various possibilities of each of the sign's expressions in simple and accessible terms, knowing full well that there are probably millions of others that had not occurred to me at the time of writing them.

Although typically viewed as an alternative profession, astrology as a whole is much more utilized in a serious fashion than most of us have been lead to believe. Some of the world's most influential and wealthy people, including some politicians use astrology for their investments and other actions. America's founding father, George Washington was an astrologer and he left behind a memoir in which he regularly tracked astrological transits. Fellow founding father and freemason Benjamin Franklin published the yearly Poor Richard's Almanack, which in 1733 he accurately predicted the time of death of a friend using astrology. It is also no secret that U.S. president Ronald Reagan and his wife Nancy often planned the timing of events based on advice from an astrologer. It was specifically Nancy who consulted astrologer Joan Quigley for scheduling special events. President Abraham Lincoln's wife Mary also brought astrology into the White House. Princess

Diana consulted the astrologer Debbie Frank for astrological advice. Queen Elizabeth 1 consulted her astrologer, the occultist John Dee on major decisions.

The saying "Beware the Ides of March" associated with the Roman general and statesman Julius Caesar bears astrological relevance as many significant political events throughout history have occurred during this month, coinciding with the March Equinox. I began to write the material for this book in March of 2019 and it was March of 2020 when the world began to be faced with many shocking events unlike those we have ever experienced before.

To be clear, in this book I am not promoting any particular political ideology, social movement or spiritual belief system other than the existence of a spiritual reality that includes all kinds of entities. As has become increasingly clear on a worldwide scale in recent years, many people suspect now more than ever before that there exist certain billionaires, who instead of using their wealth only to benefit society as a whole as they claim to, rather seem to aim toward fulfilling their own greed and lust for power. The general population has been impacted by what specific individuals and groups are funding and promoting with their wealth. Although several of these individuals neglect its mention, they are well aware of how astrology works and they use it in the timing of important events. Our past ignorance about this has allowed for their ongoing success. There is a famous quote attributed to American banker J.P. Morgan (April 17, 1837 – March 31, 1913) which states that:

"Millionaires don't use astrology; billionaires do."

During these unprecedented times, it has become apparently more critical now than ever before for us to recognize the tyranny that we are being faced with. No matter what political side one takes, if any, there exists the danger of our words being hijacked, censored or used against us. The system of currency that governs our material world is used to enslave rather than to set people free. Our beautiful mother earth and all living beings who dwell upon and within it have endured massive attacks from all angles. Surely some of this can be traced to our own actions and reactions, but from my perspective the worst harm has been grossly manufactured and enabled by those who wield more than their fair share of power and influence in world affairs. Many of our so-called leaders have collectively failed us and therefore it is impossible for *them* to save us from ultimate ruin. We are in the midst of a great crisis that appears to threaten the very fabric of our existence. This might sound pessimistic, but the truth can ultimately set us free. My hope in the goodness of humanity is actually what motivated me to write this book. We are not doomed unless we believe ourselves to be, and unless we give up.

Each one of us is so much more than a physical body, and our minds extend far beyond the mazes of our gray matter, far beyond the imprints shown in our natal charts. In the modern world where materialism and the fear of lack seems to prevail it can benefit us to be reminded of who we really are at the core of our being. For some of us, it is not just mere chance, skill, or a positive outlook that steers us clear of danger and destruction but a certain kind of willpower, combined with what may be termed *divine providence.* The saying that "God helps those who help themselves" is ever so true when viewed from this angle. Those who follow a path with heart, and one that strengthens the resolve to both better themselves and to be kind and just toward others seem to gain a certain kind of psychic protection around themselves. Acting with integrity is by no means a foolproof buffer against earthly hardships but its buffer exists nonetheless, especially in a spiritual sense.

As for the zodiac, it should be borne in mind that all of us contain characteristics of all of the astrological signs within our consciousness but some are highlighted more than others, and at certain times more than others. There is no single sign that represents evil or its opposite. Each has positive and negative expressions. These are archetypal symbols and energies that may be seen to exist in all things manifest on the earth in various measures. This is reflected in the fact that nobody is inherently all good or all bad, but each of us contains elements of harmony and discord within our being.

There is a broad spectrum of certain ideas that each individual adheres to, based on their particular chemical, mental, and emotional makeup, including their personal moral compass. These ideas and their degrees of significance are based on such factors as age, early life conditioning, cultural background, religious orientation, major life events and personal values to name the obvious ones.

Is it not amazing how certain people have overcome terrible setbacks, losing a limb in war or their loved ones to catastrophe and yet somehow, despite all odds, went on with their lives, performing tasks that ordinary people with more advantages only wish they could accomplish? In each case it was not their flesh but the power of their spirit that enabled them to conquer their earthly challenges. It is the spirit, not the brain of the person who is reading that I am addressing in this book.

Some people might be particularly opposed to the idea that so much time should be spent looking on the dark side and defending ourselves on a psychic level because to them, merely giving this subject attention would feed negativity. This entire book and what it implies would seem morose. My response to this is that self-defense, going hand-in-hand with self-respect, is a critical aspect of survival and the human species has collectively forgotten how it works. That is precisely why we have gotten ourselves into the current state of affairs that we find ourselves in today, with our home planet being trashed and our civil liberties being stripped away. In this sense, we are not owed anything by humankind or by nature, but must earn our own rights, and in some cases we must fight for them.

With regard to hostility, humanity has cyclically arrived at some place and point when counterattack became necessary, because choosing submission would mean no uncertain death. Historically, in times of war there has always been one group or nation that made the first move to attack another. It never began with mutual attacks at the same time. The group that was first attacked struck back and possibly tried to negotiate in order to end the war. Until recently, there was no nation of people on earth, ever, who threw their arms up into the air and said "Okay, you got us. We give up. Finish us off. Let our children perish." Instead, they did what all of us are still wired to do on an instinctive level, which is to engage in self-defense, even when our modern-day attempts at this are futile. It was in many instances also a moral and spiritual obligation to defend one's family and community. In today's Western civilization, self-defense has become a touchy subject and is not valued as important by society. Yet people continue to war with each other on psychic levels and to fall prey to forces that they cannot see or comprehend.

To suggest that the ideals of equality, peace and tolerance are the answers to all of life's problems can be ineffectual and a form of bypassing in the midst of devastating crimes and misfortunes. Loving one another, although wonderful in theory, is not only easier said than done but does nothing to protect us from danger. A rhetorical question to ask ourselves is: how do we actually *arrive* at the state of genuinely caring for each other despite our differences? Unlike our other human emotions, love is a power that is cultivated within. It is never propagated from without. The word love is both overused and misunderstood for what it is. Love can never be genuine when *respect* is absent.

Ponder all the times, if any, when so-called love was a concept shoved into your face while you were being mistreated. If this happens to someone frequently enough, a revelation eventually makes itself known to them, even if late in life, blaring its truth like a trumpet at full blast: *It is no virtue to allow others to walk all over you, to cheat you, and violate you repeatedly.* By choosing the route of passivity and tolerance of mistreatment, one actually feeds the monsters that they have grown to fear, despise, and feign respect toward. This is evident in today's widespread social conflict and collapse.

It is often a lack of discernment combined with some type of early negative imprint that grants what we have come to define as evil a clear passage into our hearts, minds and homes. Taking a firm stance in our own self-preservation in addition to honoring what we deem as sacred starves energy vampires and stops those in their tracks who would otherwise slip in during the silence of the night when our guard is down. By respecting our own boundaries, we also tend to raise the standards of our own general conduct toward others. We become more conscientious overall, and our generosity and assistance are naturally directed toward those who will appreciate and make use of what goodness we have to offer instead of those who will take advantage of us. We no longer give endlessly of our time, energy and resources to "takers" and "dumpers" and those whose emotional needs are like bottomless pits. We wave goodbye to those troublemakers who appear to be lost causes so that they may go on and find themselves instead of going out of our way for them whereby losing ourselves in the process. In short, we stop enabling others in ways that disable ourselves. Help is given where it is truly needed and not where it will spiral into oblivion.

Although all of us experience trials and attacks both obvious or covert against us we were never given a manual on how to defend ourselves in the midst of such a chaotic, cruel and competitive world. The point here is not to walk around with armor around ourselves at all times, expecting the worst from everyone and everything, for that would be exhausting and self-defeating. It is to live with fewer regrets and more gratitude. This book not only describes the qualities of the signs in people in detail but also the zodiacal influences that all of us get to experience each year, and those that become highlighted during certain peak experiences. It includes specialized methods of building and sustaining psychic immunity, and how to counter various types of attack, both to and from each of the signs.

My wish is that this information based on the wisdom gained from experience may embolden you to relate to others and yourself with greater clarity, dignity and effectiveness than ever before. The way I see it, the most scary thing that any of us could come to terms with during the course of our lives is the degree to which we are capable of influencing the world around us. It has already been said many times before, but it is true that we are each far more powerful than we know.

Part One

Chapter 1

Psychic Attack and Self-Defense

Everyone knows what self-defense means when it comes to the physical body. Psychic attack has become sort of an umbrella term for several types of harmful thoughts, actions and energy that are either directed or received. Some attacks are obvious, and others are hidden from view. In some cases, they are accompanied by physical acts of violence. Whether is it conscious or unconscious in nature, psychic attack is basically defined by the onslaughts, manipulations and intrusions of either a psychological or spiritual nature which can have detrimental effects on physical health over time.

One might wonder just who is generating all of this negative energy so often anyway? In truth, it is *almost* each and every one of us, each and every day to some degree. We have each been guilty of sending negativity to another or others on a psychic level at some point in our life, although not necessarily on purpose. Attacks may also be self-inflicted. Such actions are and have always been a widespread phenomenon. Unfortunately, being impacted by the not-so-kind intentions of others has become all too common in our modern world. Usually, we are not consciously aware of the kinds of negativity we are spewing forth, let alone that which escapes our lips in conversations. However, not all of this bad invisible stuff is equal or lasting in its impact. It does not affect all of us in the same exact ways.

Psychic attack does the most damage to those who are already vulnerable. It is less likely to affect adults who are vibrant, happy and strong, but with enough repetition it can bring anyone down. The aura, which is the energy field surrounding the physical body, has its own immune system and can suffer from certain types of illnesses just like those of the physical body. The aura is actually where many types of diseases have their origins. Once an opening has been created within it, it becomes easier for negative forces to seep into and infect that person's energy matrix.

Some attacks are inflicted by physical beings that are readily seen and noticed and others are from the spirit realm. Psychic attack may occur in the form of verbal abuse, or through something as cryptic as psychic vampirism, which indicates leeching of the energy of others in ways that are extremely toxic. The effects of psychic attack can be mild and fleeting or binding, with crippling effects. Conscious types of psychic attack include the use of black magic spells.

I used to be skeptical in my youth of the effects of black magic, until I began to run into people who practiced it in addition to those who were being victimized by it. It was always more frustrating than frightening to me because I couldn't understand why people would ever fall prey to something so silly. I wanted to help them to realize that they could free themselves from these "cursed" experiences they were having. Apparently, I had to go through some cursed trials of my own in order to understand their source of power.

There are very different reasons why people attack others on a psychic level. These reasons include jealousy, lust, hatred and revenge. Others stem from a desire for power and domination. Excess worry about a person, although not a true form of attack, can worsen their condition because it reinforces their own fear, which in turn can interfere with either their health or some of their activities. Since the year 2020, I have witnessed an increasing number of people attacking each other in a psychic sense while driving their vehicles in the United States. The number of impatient, reckless, and lawless drivers on the roads reveals much about the psychic disturbances and stress levels that have affected life on our planet lately. Psychic attacks are not only executed by individuals but also by groups both small and large, from mundane cliques to occult circles, and from snobby towns to massive institutions and governments.

Sadly, for many of us the worst adversaries that we have faced happen to be our own blood relatives. It is especially devastating for a child to be born into a situation where they experience both abuse and neglect, and literally have no choice in the matter. These children then go on and continue the cycle of abuse, passing on what they have learned to their own children, until or unless there is something inside of them, some awareness that causes them to break the cycle. Then, they will be the ones to rise up, to change the course of their own destiny and to uplift their fellow humans in the process.

As a result of experiencing so much vulgar behavior from others, a person may begin to change inside. Anger is a completely natural response to being attacked or witnessing violence and injustice, and it is a sign of being alive. However, anger becomes toxic when it is internalized, allowed to collect and churn within us over time. It can later become a highly explosive and destructive force, when we least expect it. The key is to find healthy outlets for anger, which eventually transmutes its energy into even more powerful reserves that can be used for problem-solving, healing and creative endeavors for oneself and others. Astrology can provide the kinds of insights that can aid us in moving more quickly through psychological pain and anger, and to become more of who we truly are without the baggage.

In order to properly guard oneself against psychic attack it is important to understand both overt forms of attack and covert maneuvers. Even more valuable than this is an improved understanding of oneself. This implies delving into what may be perceived as dangerous psychic territory. The more we look at the forbidden aspects of ourselves the more uncomfortable we may feel, and yet this discomfort can be incredibly insightful. Pain and discomfort are part of what makes us human and ironically a huge part of what enables us to heal, evolve and become greater than what we were before. If we pay attention to the message that our pain is trying to communicate to us, then we can grow in both wisdom and compassion for ourselves and others.

Some people seem to always be caught up in unconscious acts of self-sabotage while others appear to get away with bringing misery to so many lives around them, who revel in their ability to sway and influence others with their fame, status or fortune. Then there are those who serve as constant do-gooders, who never appear to have any lasting enemies. The ability for fair self-appraisal and self-corrective behavior is implied in becoming stronger in a psychic sense. This includes being able to recognize and reflect upon the not-so-flattering aspects of one's own character and to make conscious efforts to improve. Having patience with ourselves, knowing that we have each carried on an ancient ancestral chain of habit is the key to breaking it. The results of doing this are many, but they can include the development of various abilities, enhanced creativity, deeper and more meaningful relationships, expanded perception and a greater enjoyment of life in general. The ability to help others is also increased exponentially.

We are each comprised of energetic juxtapositions visible within our natal chart. For example, the chart may reveal a conflict between the Sun, the symbol of one's inner essence and the Ascendant, which represents the face one shows to the world, or some other conglomeration of diametrically opposed archetypes. The combined placements of the signs and planets point out whether one tends to be one's own worst enemy or seems to be a constant target for outside attacks from others, and whether the native is a fighter, pacifist, or neither – and why. A chart may reveal a proclivity to dominate or to be dominated. All charts reveal certain types of potentials that may be directed toward helpful or harmful purposes, so one should be careful not to rely on the birth chart alone in making the assessment. How a person is actually conducting themselves overall must be taken into consideration, and in most cases intuitive hunches about people should be confirmed with legitimate evidence before taking action accordingly.

Astrologers often carry a heavy burden of responsibility for their use of the knowledge of symbols and timing of certain events. Those of us who perform astrological and intuitive readings for others know how important it is to choose certain words carefully as some recipients of readings tend to deeply internalize and even obsess over what was said or not said to them during a session, sometimes to their detriment.

In reading through the chapter Psychic Self Defense and the Signs, the faces of certain people might pop into your mind. They could be teachers, lovers, parents, siblings, public figures or acquaintances. You may or may not have knowledge of their Sun signs or natal charts. Please use discernment when linking up the following attributes with people that you know who were born under a certain sign. These attributes may or may not apply in the ways described. It is recommended that you spend some quiet reflection on the comparison between the elements of discord and harmony that you experience first with yourself and second with the person in question. If the good outweighs the bad, then with your newfound knowledge, you may have discovered a way to better cope with minor relational tension and make the best of the connection that you share. If, however, the bad outweighs the good it would be wise to seriously consider a method of extricating yourself from such a negative tie. If it doesn't end with you taking a firm stance that connection might suck you dry until you have no choice. In some cases, it may be you who needs to reconsider your treatment of another.

Some people are so egotistical they believe it to be within their authority to derail others whom they despise or envy. Turning away from or completely severing ties with such individuals is one of the most effective forms of self-defense. It deprives them of the satisfaction of eliciting the types of reactions that can ultimately be used against you. Only if they make violent threats or become aggressive should other protective measures be taken.

Lastly, here is an insight that can aid in a quick process of elimination for many people. Those who make the loudest noise about their pain and misfortunes often turn out to be bullies, competing for attention by becoming strong victims. This becomes their own justification for victimizing others. This does not mean that everyone who talks about their pain or shares their stories of abuse are the types of people I'm referring to. This is really a matter of *how* people share their experiences rather than what they are saying about them that reveals their intentions.

It just so happens that some of the kindest people are some of the most deeply injured, having been taken for granted and used by others, and sadly, they are often silent in their suffering. If you are one of these people and bad things keep happening to you by others, this book is especially meant for you. It is not meant to harden your heart but to better understand when and how to set up appropriate boundaries, without guilt or other excuses.

Chapter 2

Categories and Divisions of the Zodiac

The categories listed here may be especially important to read for those who are just beginning the study of astrology. Those who are already familiar with them may like to skip down to the very last category, "Expressions of the Elements", which is one that I formulated and is referenced many times in the following chapter.

Elements

The Elements represent basic types of temperaments within the Zodiac, dividing four groups of three signs of the same element. These include the following:

Fire signs: Aries, Leo, Sagittarius

These signs indicate the presence of energy, enterprise, passion, leadership, and enthusiasm.

Earth signs: Taurus, Virgo, Capricorn

These signs indicate the presence of physical and financial concerns, practicality, and a work focus.

Air signs: Gemini, Libra, Aquarius

These signs indicate the presence of mental stimulation, communication of ideas, and the intellect.

Water signs: Cancer, Scorpio, Pisces

These signs indicate the presence of emotion, intuition, the nonphysical, feelings and sensations.

Triplicities

The Triplicities are four sets of three signs that correspond to each season of the year. There is a Cardinal, Fixed and Mutable sign for every season. Some people also refer to the Elements as Triplicities but for the sake of simplicity, I am reserving the term here for the signs of the seasons, specifically of the Northern regions. In Southern regions, the seasons are reverse but the signs remain the same.

Spring: Aries, Taurus, Gemini

These are the signs that represent new beginnings, acquisition and experimentation.

Summer: Cancer, Leo, Virgo

These are the signs that represent nurturing, growth and personal fulfillment.

The signs of the first two seasons represent youth and growth.

Autumn: Libra, Scorpio, Sagittarius

These are the signs that represent harvest, processing and dispensation.

Winter: Capricorn, Aquarius, Pisces

These are the signs that represent leadership, group purpose and recycling.

The signs of the second two seasons represent maturity and death.

Quadruplicities

Quadruplicities represent modes of activity and behavior. These quadruplicities, also known simply as Modes, include four each of three different types:

Cardinal signs: Aries, Cancer, Libra, Capricorn

These signs emphasize action, initiation, leadership and seeking results.

Fixed signs: Taurus, Leo, Scorpio, Aquarius

These signs emphasize endurance, persistence, stability and long-range vision.

Mutable signs: Gemini, Virgo, Sagittarius, Pisces

These signs emphasize changeability, adaptability, and being able to learn from the past.

Dualities

Dualities represent the masculine and feminine signs and they also. The masculine duality is active, positive and outgoing while the feminine duality is passive, receptive and self-contained. The masculine signs are more impulsive and the feminine signs more pensive. Masculine signs go after what they want, while feminine signs tend to attract what they want and need.

Aries – masculine

Taurus – feminine

Gemini – masculine

Cancer – feminine

Leo – masculine

Virgo – feminine

Libra – masculine

Scorpio – feminine

Sagittarius – masculine

Capricorn – feminine

Aquarius – masculine

Pisces – feminine

Polarities

Polarities represent six pairings of twelve signs which are exactly opposite of each other in the Zodiac.

They are as follows:

Aries/Libra:

Aries is the sign of the self and Libra is the sign of the other in relationship.

Taurus/Scorpio:

Taurus is the sign of personal possessions and Scorpio is the sign of shared possessions.

Gemini/Sagittarius

Gemini is the sign of the conscious mind and Sagittarius is the sign of the super-conscious mind.

Cancer/Capricorn

Cancer is the sign of the home and security and Capricorn is the sign of the public and career pursuits.

Leo/Aquarius

Leo is the sign of personal pleasures and Aquarius is the sign of shared dreams, goals and visions.

Virgo/Pisces

Virgo is the sign of physical work and Pisces is the sign of dreams, delusions, and spiritual realization.

Houses of the Zodiac

Houses represent areas of life where and when planetary themes play themselves out. Their sequence follows the natural order of the horoscope. The entryway into the chart is always the beginning of the first house, called the Ascendant. Its sign and degree at any given time determines the signs governing subsequent houses. The natural order of the chart follows the order of the zodiac, which begins with Aries and ends with Pisces. Whatever the actual sign may be ruling any of the houses, there is always the undercurrent of the original rulers. For example, Taurus on the Ascendant reveals that someone initiates activities (by the influence of the AC's natural ruler Aries and Mars) in an earthy, organized and methodical way. They have an outer appearance or mannerisms that are Venusian, which means that they are somehow attractive, sensual, fashionable or business-oriented.

First House – ruled by Aries and Mars

Modality – Angular, cardinal and leadership oriented

This is the house of personal identity and physical appearance. If the Sun is here one tends to have a strong sense of self. As the first of four cardinal houses this is the "Spring" area of the chart where new beginnings take place.

Second House – ruled by Taurus and Venus

Modality – Succedent, fixed and security oriented

This earth house is concerned with personal values, security and attainment. It relates to material belongings as well as self-worth. Those with an emphasis in this house may prioritize acquisition and financial success in some way.

Third House – ruled by Gemini and Mercury

Modality – Cadent, mutable, and service oriented

This air house represents conscious awareness and knowledge, and how we communicate with others in general. It emphasizes useful education on the one hand and trifle subject matters on the other. The Sun in this house reveals eagerness to learn and a sociable nature overall.

Fourth House – ruled by Cancer and the Moon

Modality – Angular, cardinal and leadership oriented

This is the water house, symbolic of "Summer", where certain things begin to blossom and come to fruition. It corresponds to family life, the home, and close-knit community. It is the house of the early beginnings as well as the conditions around life's endings.

Fifth House – ruled by Leo and the Sun

Modality – Succedent, fixed and security oriented.

This house, like the first fire house is related to personal identity but additionally, the products of one's creative fire, whether in the form of offspring or art. This is also the house of love affairs and strong desires.

Sixth House – ruled by Mercury and Virgo

Modality – Cadent, mutable, and service oriented

This earth house is based on work, service to others, daily routines and health in general. People with the Sun or another kind of emphasis in this house often go out of their way for others. It is a very busy type of house, indicating menial work and movement.

Seventh House – ruled by Libra and Venus

Modality – Angular, cardinal and leadership oriented

The house of the Other is directly opposite the house of the Self. It is about contracts and commitments, and the influences that others may have upon us, especially when their actions reflect something about ourselves. It represents the "Autumn" of life, and the harvest of that which was planted and nurtured earlier, revealing cause and effect.

Eight House – ruled by Scorpio and Mars

Modality – Succedent, fixed and security oriented.

This is the water house associated with shared assets, legacies, and major life changes. It tends to highlight taboo subjects such as sex, death and the occult. It may also give a glimpse into psychic abilities.

Ninth House – ruled by Sagittarius and Jupiter

Modality – Cadent, mutable, and service oriented

This is the fire house of travel, exploration and higher learning. Any emphasis in this house points toward the bigger picture in life, and a desire to understand one's purpose in it all. It is house of both seeking for and teaching greater truths.

Tenth House – ruled by Capricorn and Saturn

Modality – Angular, cardinal and leadership oriented

This earth house relates to authority, profession, and high standards. Those with the Sun in this house tend to reach for and attain high levels of responsibility. They may become the corporate leaders or the statesmen of the world. This is the "Winter" area of the chart where things have reached a pinnacle and a new cycle of growth awaits.

Eleventh House – ruled by Aquarius and Saturn

Modality – Succedent, fixed and security oriented.

This air house relates to group endeavors, friends and the hopes, goals and wishes kept near and dear to our hearts. The Sun or any other strong emphasis in this house indicates a draw toward groups and humanitarian pursuits. It represents one's personal ideals whether or not they are actively pursued.

Twelfth House – ruled by Pisces and Jupiter

Modality – Cadent, mutable, and service oriented

The twelfth is the last of the three water houses and the final house of the wheel. It is associated with endings, privacy, and spending time alone. This is the place where we withdraw from the hustle and bustle of society or do something important behind the scenes. In the worst case scenarios it is the house of imprisonment and silent suffering.

Expressions of the Elements

Below is a list of descriptions relevant to the qualities of each of the elements as they pertain to the signs. These descriptions are referred to in the chapter Psychic Self Defense for the Signs but make sure to note that, unlike the official categories listed above, these are not standard descriptions used by other astrologers. You may consider them as poetic filters on the elements.

Fire: Aries, Leo, Sagittarius – "Force"

The Force corresponds to the element of Fire. It is passionate, flaming energy that can be used as fuel for movement and major accomplishment. Within the force there is an inherent resistance to stress and disease. The force is self-animated with a visible pulse. This is life *force* energy, libido and willpower. It implies the capacity to take on huge challenges as well as the ability to cause them. Even when Force is coming from unseen dimensions it can have a huge impact upon the physical body. It can erupt like a volcano in full view or hit like an invisible sledgehammer. Some things in life simply must be destroyed by it in order for new growth to occur.

Earth: Taurus, Virgo, Capricorn – "Containment"

Containment corresponds to the element of Earth. It can be extremely suffocating or stabilizing and supportive, depending on the situation at hand. On some occasions, earthly containment such as self-restraint can work in one's favor instead of against it. Containment is a method of keeping things, energy or ideas organized and accessible for the times when they are needed for some purpose. It enables one to conserve energy and to carefully "choose one's battles". Containment is steady, sustainable, and unwavering. It holds certain things together, as if by glue. Its metaphorical function is helping to us stay connected to *terra firma* so that we don't float away aimlessly like feathers in the wind.

Air: Gemini, Libra, Aquarius – "Speech"

Speech corresponds to the element of Air. It is usually audible but sometimes it's all in the mind, or transcribed onto paper in the form of written words. Its trajectory can be as quick as lightning or as slowly meandering as the steam rising from a cup of hot tea. Speech can be confusing or clarifying, just as thoughts can be. It can be excessive and meaningless or inspirational, even deeply moving to the soul. Speech may be directed at someone to hurt them, or as a balm that helps their heart to heal. It can expose buried lies and fiercely uphold the truth. Speech is one of the most misused and misunderstood aspects of human existence, for if people truly knew its power they would use it more wisely.

Water: Cancer, Scorpio, Pisces – "Permeation"

Permeation corresponds to the element of Water. It knows no bounds and because of this can be the most powerful and frightening expression of all. Through permeation, we discover what lies on the other side of what had previously been a shield or barrier. Permeation can bypass containment and lead to sickness, by spreading bacteria and fungi through surfaces. Sometimes it is that which liberates us from the sensation or reality of being confined. Permeation introduces us to the limitlessness of our existence. It illustrates how certain things merge into and with one another, transmuting into different substances altogether.

Quick Guide to Relationships between Signs

Did you ever wonder why you have "great chemistry" with some people and clash horribly with others? It might be due to the elemental interactions between you, among other things. Elemental interactions exist between signs in any type of relationship. Those elements of the greatest prominence are those of the Sun to Sun, Ascendant to Ascendant, Moon to Moon, Sun to Ascendant and Moon to Sun. For the full picture of relationship interactions it is most helpful to employ a combination of synastry and composite charts. Synastry entails overlaying one chart upon another and Composite entails joining the midpoints of each person's planets and key placements to make a single chart.

Fire and Fire: Fire sign interactions with each other tend to be harmonious, passionate, and exciting. They favor movement and change.

Earth and Earth: Earth to Earth sign interactions are harmonious, supportive, and grounding. They favor prosperity and manifestation.

Air and Air: Air signs interact with each other harmoniously. They favor mental stimulation, education, conversation and change.

Water and Water: Water sign interactions are harmonious, inspirational, and emotional. They tend to emphasize family matters, creativity or emotional cycles.

Fire and Earth: Fire signs and Earth signs interact in contrasting ways, for better or worse.

Air and Fire: As signs of masculine polarities Fire and Air signs complement each other well.

Fire and Water: Fire interacts with Water in contrasting ways for better or worse.

Air and Earth: Earth sign and Air sign relationships interact in contrasting ways for better or worse.

Earth and Water: As signs of feminine polarities Earth and Water signs complement each other well.

Water and Air: Air and Water signs interact in contrasting ways for better or worse.

Chapter 3

Psychic Self Defense and the Signs

Just as there are both positive and negative attributes of each sign, we each possess certain weaknesses and strengths. Not every person of the same sign will exhibit the same exact characteristics of their sign, just as not every person will realize the wondrous potential reflected in their natal chart and apply themselves accordingly. There is spiritual choice inherent within each sign, and the choices made may result in what is commonly termed the "high" or "low" expressions of the sign. Most of us tend to fluctuate in these expressions depending on astrological transits and interactions with others.

Any of the individual signs may be perpetrators or fall prey to psychic attack, and in both instances, it can be helpful for us to have some background on what makes them tick. This kind of knowledge can make one better equipped to handle many different types of challenges. Individuals are better able to defend themselves when they first understand their own psyche. In other situations, it helps to know why something has happened or what someone's motivation is for their unethical behavior. An interesting and relevant study regarding the interplay between victims and their attackers is called Forensic Astrology and is specifically used to discover the details of a crime scene.

Each Zodiac sign is known to relate to a certain part of the body, so there is some mention made of body parts and bodily functions. These correspondences are explored in more depth in the subject of Medical Astrology. Each sign also relates to different aspects of the psyche and these are described as well. Certain stones and herbs are also suggested with the focus directed on psychic integrity. There are more elaborate descriptions about these in a separate chapter. First, I would like to acknowledge one of the most understated themes in the history of astrology, that which is linked with mythology.

The Ongoing Battle of the Twelve Titans

The Titans were the pre-Olympian gods of ancient Greece, born as twelve children of the sky god Uranus and the earth goddess Gaia. Six of these gods were male and six were female; just as in our modern Zodiac male and female are equally divided. They were Krios – god of stars and constellations, whose name means "ram", Rhea – the fertile mother of the gods, Phoebe – the lunar goddess of oracles and prophecy, Mnemosyne – the goddess of memory and intellect, Hyperion – god of the sun and vision, Tethys – goddess of the waters of life, Themis – goddess of justice, Kronos – leader of the gods, Iapetus – god of crafted metals and of death, Coeus – god of intelligence and rational thinking, Euryphaessa – goddess of heavenly light, and Oceanus – god of the oceans. Many records associated with the Titans have been lost forever in the sands of time, and it is difficult to say exactly who and what they really were.

In the Titanomachy, the great war that occurred between the Titans and the Olympians, a ten-year battle resulted in the defeat of the old pantheon and the establishment of the new one that more of us are now more familiar with. These Greek Olympians are Zeus, Hera, Hestia, Hermes, Demeter, Apollo, Athena, Ares, Artemis, Hephaestus, Aphrodite, and Poseidon, known also under the names of their Roman counterparts. There are a few small differences of opinion as their precise correspondences with the modern-day Zodiac.

The psychologist Carl Jung believed that archetypes (the patterns of behavior or ideas that often resemble religious and other iconic figures), come from the collective unconscious, influencing each of us in a multitude of ways. Although the Titans may have been defeated and banished to the abysmal prison of Tartarus, their archetypal energies continue to live and battle on within our collective consciousness today. It could be said that our subconscious is the symbolic dwelling place for Tartarus, where the Titans continue to exert their influence upon us whether or not we recognize their presence. They live through us vicariously as we embody their essence and continue to fight their battles in human form. Tartarus is the realm of Hades, or the Underworld that we may identify as Pluto. Within the stormy molten lava of our Plutonic subconscious, with all its trauma, brokenness, and defilement we both die and eventually, by some miracle, regenerate.

When we integrate every part of the Zodiac and not just one sliver of it that we identify as our Sun sign, we gain greater access to the full spectrum of our abilities. These are the cosmic influences that live within our psyches, no matter who we are, when or where on earth we were born. You may like to take the signs of the Ascendant and Moon into consideration as being of equal significance.

Aries

Aries is the first of the four cardinal signs, meaning it is the first sign to indicate a seasonal shift. When the Sun passes through this sign, typically from around March 20th to April 20th, life on earth comes under the influence of a potent type of energy. In the Northern hemisphere, Aries brings in the spring season. The days become longer, and the light grows brighter as it gets closer to summer. The Sun is traditionally said to be "exalted" in this section of the sky, which indicates that one with this as their Sun sign is inherently strong and resilient. Under Aries' yearly influence we generally become energized and renewed.

Animated by the fire element, Aries represents the spark of life and starting point in human or animal consciousness. It is just coming into a sense of itself within the immediate surroundings. Some astrologers have assigned the mental age of this sign from birth to around age seven, and some simply to infancy. This is merely a symbolic representation of the sign and is not meant to imply that those born under the sign of Aries are infantile. They are however often enthusiastic as young children tend to be.

Aries Symbolism and Physique

Aries, named after the Greek god of war, is a masculine fire sign ruled by the planet Mars, which is also named after the Roman god of war. At best, this is the sign of the epic discoverer, or the heroic warrior, in defense of the helpless. Passionate, energetic and eager for experience, Aries is the one who, like the Star Trek voyagers, dares to "to boldly go where no man has gone before". This is the sign born to try something new, to make mistakes, to fall, to get up and try again, and to carve new paths for the rest of humanity.

Aries tends to have a strong, sleek build. Whatever their height and weight may be they generally have the physical appearance or at least the habit of being active rather than sedentary. They often enjoy regular involvement in some kind of sport, game, or other exercise program. They also tend to attract and excite others in sexual ways.

The symbol for Aries is the Ram, which is a strong animal eager to explore new territory. Just as thick-horned rams are known for being bold and determined creatures, Aries is the sign that is known for trailblazing. Life force energy is at its peak in this sign, which is why Aries folk tend to be physically robust, active, and outgoing. They are down to challenge themselves in all ways possible, unafraid to take risks. They are not easily discouraged but instead courageous and enterprising. If they want to obtain or do something they will usually not take no for an answer. They go after whatever interests them.

Aries and the First Level of Force

Aries is the first of three fire signs that use what I have referred to in this book as the force in both their method of attack and defense. Force is generally defined as energy that rushes outward or forward, in order to accomplish something with its active power. This may include exerting pressure onto another thing. It implies the fire that force is fueled by, whether this force is applied to the physical, emotional, mental or spiritual levels. Force is born of and generates heat.

We have heard of terms such as "the force of creation", "the force of nature" and the "force of will". "May the force be with you" became a popular expression from the classic Sci-Fi movie *Star Wars*. Basically, the force can be constructive or destructive, for better or worse. The first level of this force is the most raw, basic, and primal, and it is critical to survival. Some refer to this as "life force energy", virility, or the divine spark. It can agitate or inspire. It is the force that eagerly seeks to discover itself and the extent of its powers in the world. It tends to move outward with haste, because it has no sense of reason in and of itself.

Because of these things, this first level of force is utilized in the most direct type of attack which is easy to recognize. The force does not ever beat around the bush. It goes directly for its prey or objective. That doesn't necessarily mean this force is easy to defend oneself against or conquer, but it is very quickly spotted by most people and animals. In fact, it can be directed in such a ruthless manner that many people fall into shock and denial after they have seen it or felt it. It's as though they don't know what hit them and they don't want to know.

At one time upon the earth people had much quicker reflexes and recognized an attack when it came at them. Modern technology has torn humanity away from nature and distracted most people from their deeper instincts and intuition. Now they tend to need training in order to be able to both see and fight their attackers. Aries is a sign that can remind us of how to live life more fully and to defend ourselves more effectively.

Psychic Protection Against Aries

As a cardinal sign, Aries attacks by way of domination, to subdue and lord over either a victim or opponent. They share this in common with Cancer, Libra, and Capricorn, but with their own fiery methodology. An attack of any kind by an Aries is hard to miss. In fact, it is the most direct, blunt, or forceful type of attack you could possibly experience. It is literally in your face and will be no secret to you or anybody in the vicinity. Like a swift blow that knocks somebody stunned and speechless, a hit from Aries is as clear and decipherable as a blaring siren or a searing migraine on a hot day. It's not subtle. This is a highly driven, direct and masculine sign. Any type of attack from them whether physical, mental, emotional or spiritual is or soon becomes obvious. If delivered verbally instead of physically it may emotionally sting or burn. It could possibly have implications that intimidate or infuriate the recipient.

The nature of the attack would be determined by the value system of that person. They can be quick to make assumptions about certain things and people. Unless they have a reflective nature or spiritual orientation, those whose egos have become bloated can seek to dominate others and use them for their own personal ends. When angered, many Aries men in particular do not back down from a fight, and some can be both physically abusive and ruthless. The qualities of swiftness and strength make Aries the ideal candidate to be hired as hitman.

Murderers born under the sign of Aries have been known to inflict highly bizarre and violent treatment on their victims, and to display insane behavior in general. It is as if many of them got a thrill out of the attention they gained when arrested. Jane Toppin, nicknamed "Jolly Jane" was a serial killer born March 31, 1854. Murders were carried out in homes where she worked as a nurse, in which she administered legal injections of morphine. Pisces was also a strong influence in her chart, with Mercury, Venus and Uranus occupying this sign. She admitted to wanting to kill as many people as possible to satisfy a sexual fetish. Keith Jesperson, an Aries born on April 6, 1955, was known as the "Happy Face Killer" (Aries rules the face) because he often drew smiley faces on his letters to media and authorities. He often took his anger out on animals. Richard Kullinski, born April 11, 1935, was a serial murderer, burglar and convicted for distributing pirated pornography. He proudly described his murders in graphic detail. A movie called The Iceman was based on his character.

Some attacks by Aries are accidental in nature or otherwise the result of reckless behavior. Aries may be self-absorbed to the point of not realizing the effects of both their words and actions on others. Some of them really just love to hear themselves talk, often about themselves, not really pausing to take notice of how they are being received by their listeners. The best way to avoid getting pummeled with their melodrama is simply to refuse to be their mental dumping ground. If you don't have to be there to listen, don't make yourself available. It is easy to dismiss their senseless commands.

Another type of Aries personality can be so fully confident in their assessment of other things and people that they quickly project their ideas onto them, as if they are the true experts, leaving very little room for others' authentic expression. Usually, you will find them in self-employed or entrepreneurial careers because they seldom work for other people. Self-employment is by no means a vice, but this just underlines Aries' existing tendency to take matters in their own hands and do things their own way.

As the sign that initiates new cycles, Aries prefers positions of authority where it is possible to dictate while avoiding getting bogged down in too many of the details of management. In coarse types there can be a strong desire to get noticed, be the leader, and wear the crown without actually having to work to maintain it. Their commands and requests can be nonsensical at times.

They can be lacking in adequate judgment about the character of others, and foolishly place certain people on pedestals while considering those they happened to glance at for a mere moment to be unimportant. In their own desire to elevate themselves to a higher status or move on to greener pastures they can alienate even their closest friends. Well, good riddance; as the saying goes: "with friends like these, who needs enemies?!"

The best way to avoid an attack from the Aries without a rein on their temper is to stay out of their way when they're angry, because their anger is not necessarily rational. If you agitated them then you likely had it coming, as if sticking your finger into a hornet's nest. They have the capacity to cause permanent injuries. To hang around when they are raging is a bit masochistic. If you have been psychically attacked by one for no valid reason, you may find that their view of what happened is very different from yours. Sometimes they just want to be noticed and will do crazy things to gain attention. No matter how hot-headed and aggressive they may seem, after all the struggle and mayhem, they may burn themselves out, and they ultimately want peace like anybody else does.

To avoid or recover from attack by Aries on the metaphysical level, work to develop the power of invisibility or learn to lay low when you need to. Mask yourself in the appropriate method in order to become unnoticed by those who are untrustworthy. In the Middle Ages, the herb Wolf's Bane, also known as Monkshood, was carried as protection against vampires and werewolves and also to become invisible when needed. This herb is used today for similar purposes and can be incorporated into visualizations that make one invisible in the presence of predators or dangerous places. To use invisibility to gain unfair advantages over others is a form of black magic and will backfire.

Psychic Protection for Aries

What makes Aries vulnerable to attack is quite simply when they let their guard down too soon. These people are naturally open and can be very friendly and sociable, even wearing their heart on their sleeve. They are more sincere and less complicated than many of the people that they attract and, at least early in life, they don't automatically expect bad treatment from others. They are shocked when this happens. To some people they may be perceived as naive, but this perception can be a judgment based on Aries' sense of undying youthfulness.

Physically, Aries is associated with the head and all of its orifices which include the eyes, nose, ears and mouth. These are the areas that tend to be most vulnerable to both physical and psychic attack. From a psychic perspective, one reason their head area is vulnerable is because it stands out as being unique. Aries stands out even when trying to blend into a crowd. There's always something about them that is quite noticeable but particularly their face.

If and when they are attacked it may be out of envy and jealousy, or because they are seen as a threat. They may also be attacked for no apparent reason whatsoever. Aries is prone to accidents and attacks by others involving speed, fire and sharp objects. They might inadvertently injure themselves when they are emotionally stressed out or have lost their temper. They should avoid reckless driving, in addition to reckless drivers surrounding them on the road, no matter how irritating and difficult they may be. Being so quick and impulsive, those of this sign might sometimes get themselves into trouble by just being in the wrong place at the wrong time.

The head contains the brain, which serves to maintain overall equilibrium. The brain is just as important to feed and exercise as the rest of the body, to build strength and immunity. Sitting in front of a T.V. screen for too long and too often weakens the body and mind. Surprisingly, many Aries people have an addiction to things such as television programs, social media, video games, pornography, and other types of electronic visual stimulation. The blue rays and other frequencies emit imagery that travels through the eyes, which in Chinese and Eastern medicine are known as the gateways of the liver. The balance of the internal system is upset by the constant barrage of both radiation and negativity that it is subjected to through by television sets, smart phones and other computer devices. Those who frequently use screen technology may benefit from wearing a pair of protective blue screen glasses.

Possible signs of a psychic attack could show up for Aries as repetitive nightmares, suddenly feeling lifeless and drained, blazing head aches and muscle tension. Those of this sign may best protect themselves psychically and energetically by frequently spending time in secluded spots in nature where they can unwind, discharge their pent-up frustrations and gain inspiration. If they do not have physical outlets to express their dynamic energy and passion, they may become destructive to themselves or others. It can help for them to get adequate greens in their diet and to do exercises that keep them physically fit and mentally sharp.

Aries and Physical Strength

Aries is outgoing and inquisitive, serving to remind others that there is always something new to discover about ourselves and the world around us. This sign teaches us that some degree of physical strength is paramount for overall productivity and resistance to attack. The first line of psychic protection actually tends to be physical in nature. When in doubt, it is wise to rule out surface level factors before moving on to metaphysical ones.

One is more quickly victimized on other levels if they are physically weak. Therefore, the best way to avoid this is to strengthen the body vehicle. This can be done by weight resistance training, martial arts, yoga, Pilates or other exercises that build endurance. In the state of weakness and fragility, stress is more likely to become unmanageable and grow into illness. Trauma of almost any kind is easier to recover from and to possibly to avoid when the body has resilience.

Aries motivates us to strive not just for average health but optimal health and fitness according to our own body type. We learn the importance of feeding our visual sense with green nature, adequate sunlight, and beautiful scenery whenever possible which all serve to strengthen vitality.

Taurus

Taurus, the Bull, is the second sign of the Zodiac, following Aries, the Ram. Although Taurus carries a few similar traits as Aries, such as being strong in many ways, it is a world apart in terms of habits and values. Taurus is the first of the four fixed signs, and first of the three earth signs. Physically they are sturdy and mentally they can be very stubborn and set in their ways.

The Sun transits Taurus between April 20 and May 20 and highlights a time of year when people generally become more relaxed and search for pleasure. Taurus represents the still developing state of consciousness in every life cycle that highlights a sense of possessing certain things and qualities. Taurus's symbolic age group is that of the toddler years, during which time most of us begin to identify some of the things we like and don't like through our five senses. Under Taurus's influence we also distinguish what belongs to us and what belongs to others.

Taurus Symbolism & Values

Taurus is a feminine earth sign ruled by the planet Venus, which was named after the Roman goddess of love. This is the planet of not only love, but of beauty, pleasure and money. All of these things are very important to the sign of Taurus which especially thrives on all of the good things that life has to offer.

The Bull which represents Taurus has been revered in many cultures as a sacred animal and symbol, and one that correlates with several goddesses. Ancient Mesopotamians considered it to be the first sign of the zodiac and called it "The Great Bull of Heaven". For some the bull is a symbol of aggressiveness and stubbornness because of the animal's behaviors when provoked. Despite their gentle and unassuming nature, if you keep pushing the buttons of any Taurus you will eventually see the furious side of the bull coming out.

Taurus and the First Level of Containment

Taurus is the first of three earth signs that use what may be referred to as Containment in their methods of attack and defense. Containment implies that a boundary has been made around some thing or situation, which can be protective, binding, or suffocating in its effects. To give a comparative, but metaphorical example of how this works, a classic Aries attack is a swift blow of force, whereas a Taurus attack is the steady grip of a headlock. Think for a moment of the sport of bullfighting which involves humans and animals attempting to subdue a bull before a wide audience. This is an act that is meant to confine the movement of the animal, which is similar to what a Taurus tends to do when their anger is aroused.

Containment takes many different forms, but when it comes to Taurus it can indicate the withholding of energy, information or oftentimes, money. In some cases, Taurus's containment is an act of self-preservation and completely appropriate to the situation at hand. This sign can be acquisitive or stingy, having the ability to make large sums of money but may have many lessons to learn about the management of it.

Taurus's most prized possessions may become great blessings or heavy burdens to maintain. These people should be careful to avoid giving things away with strings still attached to them.

This doesn't always happen but if it does, it is usually done out of an insecurity that can be traced to not having their early needs met.

Psychic Protection Against Taurus

As a fixed sign Taurus attacks by stealth, and clamps down heavily upon its catch. When it comes to psychic attack, the wrath of Taurus tends to sneak up slowly like the kind of muscle pain that occurs the day after a workout or injury. It's the kind of sting that occurs if you realize you've been stuck in a dreadful dead-end job where you never got the raise you were repeatedly promised, when one day you find out that everyone else had. That is to say, if it seems to come out of nowhere, it is just that you didn't anticipate or see it coming hours, days, or maybe years ago. You weren't paying attention when it moved toward you until it burned like hot lava upon arrival. Somehow, you failed to read the small but sure warning signs right up in your face, at eye level.

Psychic attack by Taurus can be a rather painful, unforgettable experience that leaves a lasting impression in one's life. It may be physical, financial, or verbal in nature, or some odd combination of things. Frequently it does involve something relative to values and personal belongings, but not in the way one might expect. They might not necessarily steal money or objects blatantly, but if triggered they would find some way to undermine someone's worth or abilities, or to exploit them selfishly for their own gain and purposes. Due to greed, they may seek to dominate others through monetary means. They are not always above lying and cheating in order to get their way. They can actually be the most convincing BS artists when they really want something.

Being so obstinate and determined to maintain their own status and possessions, those types who are not really tuned in to the subtle nuances in life prefer to keep their own company and do not care much about whatever is going on in the outside world. Something in their environment could be crumbling to bits, infested with mold, or in some other state of malfunctioning and it wouldn't matter much. Most important to them in the moment is that they know it well enough. They rarely choose to engage in conflicts. Taurus is a sign that typically minds its own business, but if their own personal sense of order is threatened by another person, they could attempt to derail them in some way, narrowing the scope of their worth in the eyes of others, such as in some form of public humiliation; influenced people might stop doing business with the unfortunate target. Another act of spitefulness by Taurus is to belittle another person's experience of having been victimized. This is an inconspicuous form of bullying that ultimately tears down the other through marginalization. Once they have held someone hostage or tagged them like cattle, they won't let them or the issue go until they get what they want out of it. They tend to find out sooner or later, but typically much later in life when they are in distress and at wits' end, that what goes around comes around.

The lowest possible expressions of Taurus are those of hedonism and gluttony combined with total disregard for the welfare of others. If refinement is lacking, those of this sign can behave in ways that shock and disgust those in their presence. There is a degree of ingrained selfishness that literally destroys relationships and brings ruin to social settings.

In order to avoid psychic attack by the questionable type of Taurus, make sure that you have a solid sense of what your role is in any given situation that involves them. That means being extra clear about what you are selling, what you represent overall, what you will and won't tolerate, and whether you specifically own something, are borrowing or representing it. If you look like an easy target don't expect them to have mercy on you just because you're in harm's way. To them, everyone has a sob story, and theirs is always worse than yours. They will push your limits unless you stand your ground.

Due to their good looks, alluring voices or overall sex appeal, Taureans can easily seduce people into doing or buying things. This may be done either consciously or unconsciously and their approach in any given situation may be innocent, noble, or cunning depending on their overall character. When they are agitated or excited, they can easily *bulldoze* a conversation, leaving very little room for the other person to be able to speak.

It would be wise to be very cautious about accepting any favors or lavish gifts from Taurus unless you them very well and trust their motives. When angered they may later turn around and claim that you are a taker. They will remind you of all the nice things they have done for you. They may try to convince you that if it were not for them, you would have had nothing and you would have failed without their great generosity.

In most situations pulling away is the best way to avoid further obstacles posed by Taurus. These are generally not the kinds of people who will chase after you in order to get revenge. They only make a scene while it's relevant to them and then move on when they feel done. You can rest assured that they have much better things to do after they are done being the "Bull in a China shop".

Grounding techniques such as laying on the sand or allowing your bare feet to touch the earth can help discharge and transmute psychic attack and interference from Taurus. Taurus is an earth sign so it can be helpful to use stones and crystals that are clarifying to recover. Black Tourmaline and Black Kyanite may be especially helpful for doing this. Stones are especially helpful when combined with strong visualizations and the vocalization of your intentions for clearing your space.

Psychic Protection for Taurus

Taurus is not known to be an aggressive sign but those who are born under it are obviously not at all weak. On the contrary, they are extremely resilient, can take a great deal of wear and tear in life and still be standing. Generally, these people are often peaceful, fairly quiet and slow to anger. They are handsome and well liked in their family or community. There is always something charming in their nature that endears them to others. They make highly skilled artisans and successful business owners.

Taurus may not adapt well to large scale change and viewpoints contrary to their own because of their tendency to cling to the familiar and comfortable. They tend to feel that they must maintain their position at any cost, but sometimes the cost is just too high. They are known to get stuck in a rut every now and then, but when they realize there are solutions or better options available than what they are working with, they begin to wiggle themselves out and onward. However, it might take a while for that realization to dawn on them.

Taurus benefits from taking a little stand back from a relationship or situation every once in a while, to assess what is really going on and how they and the others around them truly feel about it. Maybe it's all really wonderful, but maybe it's far from that. They could be kidding themselves that something is working out just fine, because the alternative is too scary to consider. When they are willing to take that risk toward a more fulfilling career, location or some other endeavor, they can amaze themselves with their own incredible breakthroughs and achievements.

Taurus's polar opposite sign is Scorpio, which reflects their more secretive and intuitive side. Taurus is both instinctive and naturally tuned in on a psychic level, but when in conflict with their polar opposite nature they may reveal their stubbornness in combination with a lack of discrimination which becomes a problem in their daily affairs. Trusting the wrong people can drain them of huge amounts of money which can take a lot of time and effort to replace.

Some Taureans can be prone to being plagiarized, used for sexual purposes, taken advantage of for their kindness or otherwise ripped off. They may be victims of theft or false accusations that get them into legal difficulties. Taurus rules the throat, neck and vocal cords and these areas may be especially vulnerable to psychic attack and disease. Those of this sign may struggle with thyroid imbalances, depression, and troublesome fluctuations in weight.

Taurus is a highly determined earth sign, so whatever happens, they will likely find a way to succeed. They tend to attract some degree of wealth but should be careful not to let it slip right through their fingers and into someone else's hands. Many are fortunate when it comes to regaining what they lost and then some. Returns may come through gifts and aid from others who feel sympathy and adoration for Taurus and all of their endearing Venusian qualities.

Taurus may gain solace and psychic protection by taking long nature hikes, tending a garden, and sitting beneath trees. Adorning their homes with plants and their bodies with flowing fabrics and fine jewels helps to calm them and deflects negative energy. They are adept at creating their own sanctuary wherever they may be and they thrive in beautiful, well-kept environments. Creating appropriate boundaries helps them feel more secure. They need plenty of time away from crowded environments to regain equilibrium and hear their own thoughts versus the thoughts and demands of others.

Taurus replenishes their energy reserves by confining themselves to some place where they cannot be disturbed until they are ready to come out and play again. These people often have a great sense of taste when it comes to food, clothing and décor, but they can easily overdo it on the pleasure principle. Their love of beauty and luxury runs so deep that it remains a priority for them, which may be good or bad depending on circumstances. For some, their extravagance or sensuality can lead them into some rather dangerous and sticky liaisons.

Taurus should make sure that they are engaged with a worthy partner, or they will deeply regret the interaction. Not only is this sign highly sexed but can also be very loving and very hurt when their heartfelt care and kindness for loved ones is not reciprocated. The food they eat should be enjoyable, but not too heavy, which could both cause stagnation and exacerbate psychic disturbances. They may choose to walk off their extra caloric intake after large meals or otherwise engage in some regular form of exercise which helps them to find balance.

Taurus and Self Esteem

Taurus teaches us that we protect our bodies, minds and spirits from harmful influences by developing a greater sense of self-respect and self-esteem. Taurus has much to give and to receive, and when those of this sign have self-respect as well as some measure of security within their own lives they are quite happy to share their wealth with others with no strings attached. We also learn from Taurus that we cannot give of ourselves or give anything of value if there is no "Self" to give. This is the sign that relates to self-worth, personal values, money, and possessions. Those who are lacking in self-worth fall prey to all kinds of misfortunes and attacks in life. Building it can be easier said than done, but one thing is sure. True self-esteem has nothing to do with how much money one has, the size of one's home, what kind of car one drives, or the genetic properties that give someone a certain type of appearance. It is based on the awareness of being a spiritual being, having a human experience, upon personal sovereignty, knowing one's unique worth in any number of ways, and being as respectful toward oneself as toward others. On the spiritual level Taurus also teaches that life is both fragile and precious, and points our attention to the present moment where true joy is to be found.

Gemini

Gemini is the third sign of the Zodiac, masculine in nature (with an androgynous undertone), ruled by the planet Mercury. This is the first of the four mutable signs and the first of three air signs, indicating an inherent flexibility, excitement and desire for change, with some type of variety in life. The air element rules the mental plane of existence and communication in general. That is why those of this sign seem to frequently live in their heads.

The Sun transits through Gemini between approximately May 21 and June 20, signaling a time that becomes very busy for many people. Gemini represents the youthful state of consciousness that is focused on childhood with all of its combined learning curves and playfulness. Under Gemini's influence we learn how to communicate through words and expressions. We crave both information and mental stimulation in the forms of games, studies, or conversations. There is so much to explore and do that we do not wish to remain still.

Gemini Symbolism and Wit

The Latin translation of Gemini is the Twins, which refers to the twin brothers Castor and Pollux in Greek and Roman mythology. These twins came to be regarded as the patrons of athletes, sailors and travelers in general. Gemini's ruling planet Mercury was named after the Roman god of commerce, communication, travel, trickery and theft. This clues us into the very changeable and restless nature of the sign. With mischievous Mercury as their leading influence, it should be no wonder that Gemini is considered to be the joker of the Zodiac.

Gemini's sense of humor and off-beat goofiness is often un-paralleled by that of the other signs, although Sagittarius and Pisces definitely have their moments too. Fun and funny, Gemini has a natural ability to get people laughing any place, any time, for the most ridiculous reasons. This is all fine and dandy until the jokes, pranks and sarcasm go too far. Just how far is too far may be up for debate in today's "politically correct" world. One indicator that the humor has gone south is a devil-may-care attitude causing other people to feel alienated, belittled, or mocked which creates unnecessary rifts in relationships. Not everything is meant to be taken lightly.

Generally speaking, Gemini is one of the most openly friendly signs to relate to, and they are very family oriented. They are the best kind of company to keep when you want to forget your troubles, kick up your heels, shoot the breeze, or learn some new and interesting things about the world you live in. They make great orators and lively conversationalists. In sports, dance and many types of physical activities those of this sign are often exceptionally gifted.

Those who are seriously down and out, heartbroken or emotionally battered would probably do better keep it to themselves or to find someone more sympathetic and to talk to who will lift their spirits, such as a gentle nurturing Cancer or highly affectionate Leo. Gemini won't ever make things worse on purpose, but their way with words tends to be best suited toward other things than cheering people up who don't wish to laugh. They may however find non-verbal ways to do offer their support.

Gemini and the First Level of Speech

Gemini is the first of three air signs that generally uses what may be referred to as speech in both its methods of attack and defense. Speech typically relies on the voice which has the ability to project sound into the atmosphere using one's vocal cords. This is something that both humans and animals use, often in very unconscious ways. Within the sign of Gemini, the voice, speech or any method of communication will be emphasized. The first level of speech is the most raw and primitive, so to speak. It may or may not be intelligent. It may be coherent or nonsensical, verbal or wordless. Thus, many Geminis are experts at mimicking sounds with their voices. Many of them like to talk…a lot, for God's gift to them has long been the gift of gab. In several cultures and creation myths, the Bible included, the voice is said to be the source of Creation itself.

For these reasons Geminis make excellent writers, authors, or journalists. They make ideal comic strip columnists and comedians. They know how to captivate an audience and string together random bits of information in ways that somehow make sense. These are the expert collage artists of the zodiac, who can frame images and concepts together in brilliant ways.

Gemini, like their polar opposite sign Sagittarius can make a fine teacher, especially if the subject matter is related to language, trivium, or skills requiring mental prowess. They can make difficult words more accessible and easier to understand. This is one reason why Geminis work so well with children and young people in particular. They are also the eternal student, eager to add to their mental storage base of information.

Psychic Protection Against Gemini

As a mutable sign Gemini's attacks tend to involve swift acceleration, whether of plans, words or actions. Due to a constantly curious mind, Gemini can sometimes appear to be nosy or invasive. If found prying into the affairs of others, bear in mind that this is done rather openly and often out of a genuine desire to get to know someone or be helpful. Depending on who they are seeking to help and how, their efforts may be greatly appreciated or abhorred. What others may find offsetting and annoying about Gemini's random "helping hand" is that after they've gotten the information that they sought to gain from you, they've already moved on to the next question or subject, which happens to be about something completely irrelevant to the previous one. They might enjoy the idea of helping, but they are not known to be particularly patient regarding the troubles of others.

So don't worry, they're not holding on to your secrets, unless of course they happen to have a strong Scorpio influence in their charts, in which case they could be double agents. There are simply no guarantees. In many instances though they will forget what you wanted them to remember and recall in detail what you wish they hadn't. Gemini's general attention span often leaves much to be desired, which is that it's not only short, but it doesn't always meet the standard requirements for being applicable to the situations at hand.

Gemini is the sign most likely to engage in psychic attacks that involve gossip, fraud and scams. They make adept storytellers, easily separating their own emotions from facts. When they want to, they can be the expert liar, with total ease and lack of guilt. Their particular motives may be centered around stealing objects or information for their own personal use. They know how to casually "sweet talk" others in order to get their way.

In other situations, they use words in such a way as to completely throw someone off course. This may come in the form of the retraction of an important agreement or offer, constant verbal interruptions, or public accusations that lead to legal difficulties and slander. It can also take the form of weaponized humor that diminishes the validity of another person's experience. One of the most insidious methods of invalidating someone is to completely ignore what they have said or what they feel, even when Gemini has been directly addressed as the cause of the injury. They can be quick to conceal their behavior by claiming that they did what they thought was in everyone's best interest. This happens especially when their own self-interest is their obvious priority.

One example of a very well-known and exploited Gemini is the past U.S. president Donald Trump. His manner of speech has been one of the most hotly debated aspects of his overall character, by both his followers and critics. Some people have found his social media retorts and remarks hilarious, and others found them to be offensive. It's clear that Donald Trump has had a tremendous impact on others, which has at times been positive and at other times quite negative. Most people cannot seem to ignore what he says but they have a definite reaction to it. This is largely due to the compelling power of his speech.

One of the problems in dealing with the shifty sort of Gemini is that you never know which Twin you're going to be faced with on any given day. One day you are greeted by the honest, loving Twin and on another day you could be met by the dark half who is both egocentric and unscrupulous. These types of people can be deceitful, two-faced, and irresponsible when it comes to affections and business agreements. At their worst they can be completely amoral.

An example of Gemini gone south is the serial killer Danny Rolling, who was known as the Gainesville Ripper in Florida in the year 1990. The horror movie Scream was based on true accounts of his murders. Rolling was born on May 26, 1954, and his death was in the month of October of 2006. He had claimed that a demon named Gemini appeared to him and caused him to commit heinous acts of rape and murder. Like so many Geminis he was versatile and had a knack for rhymes and drawing. He drew the demon that possessed him, which reflected his mental schism. He even wrote a poem about his victims: "tonight…in the arms of Gemini….a captured butterfly will die." The full version of this poem can be found on the internet.

Get to know the two Twins or double personalities before agreeing to make any solid contracts with them or entrusting them with something important to you. As a reminder, Geminis are usually harmless and even tempered, even if at times they are a bit capricious. Their tricks often appear in pairs, which is something to look out for. One thing is placed in front of you to divert your attention while they get past you with another. They may also tend to enlist a third party as a distraction while they go off performing their various misdeeds. Or they may cheat on their spouse with their spouse's so-called best friend.

In other cases, there are no words at all being used by Gemini when they execute an attack out of nowhere, with a sudden strike or movement that was completely unexpected. Then they quickly scurry away, out of view and dodge any counterattacks.

The way to recover from psychic attack by a Gemini is to first take a moment to mentally recount what happened and to validate your own experience because it was mostly likely shrugged off or scoffed at while it happened. "Oh well, such is life!" would be their nonchalant response. "It happens to the best of us." If deception was involved, recognize and accept that you have been deceived. Gemini was probably convincing even to themselves. If this is a person you must continue to face or work with, simply place them in the category of persons not to be taken seriously.

One of the more peculiar habits that seem to exist only in certain Geminis is an ease and comfort in lying about their progress in areas where they pretend to have expertise. It's like a game for some of them. They may read a book or attend a seminar and the next day suddenly begin charging services for the subject matter that recently inspired them. They could become plagiarists who rely on the genius of others to gain them an audience. They show no visible shame for donning a spiritual costume. The sad part of this is, they may have a genuine talent for something that never gains them recognition because they looked for it in all the wrong places.

All things considered, one of the surest ways to avoid becoming injured by any sort of reckless Gemini is to lower your expectations of their morale altogether. The less you expect from them the less disappointment you will experience, especially since they really tend to move on quickly after doing or saying untoward things. A rather salty interpretation of the situation is that there is no need to forgive Gemini for their sins because they've already gone and forgiven themselves. They got over it, "so you should too". You might as well.

On a metaphysical level, if you need to discern whether or not Gemini is being truthful, wear or carry a clear, quality piece of Aquamarine for a few weeks and see if the truth is revealed, either directly, in dreams or in the form of a psychic impression.

Psychic Protection for Gemini

Gemini may experience psychic attack when there is a lack of discrimination regarding friends, hangouts or habits. The ironic thing is that they often are very intuitive people but may have selective viewing on certain things that they are attached to being a certain way, perhaps a carryover of Taurean stubbornness. Even those Geminis who are disciplined and highly evolved can become overstimulated by psychic impressions, both their own and those of others.

Sometimes, being too open-minded and accepting can lead to serious problems.

Since they are so friendly, they can get along with those from all walks of life. They can sometimes wind up being blamed for things they did not do, because they were caught in the crossfire of some situation. Remember that this is an air sign ruled by swift moving Mercury, which makes Gemini prone to mental upsets and miscommunications, but this is especially so for this sign when it comes to family members. Their issues with family can flare up like tornadoes of destruction, sucking them into some very confounding spins.

Even though they have a need for human warmth and interaction, Gemini is a mentally oriented sign and often has difficulty drawing the line between thoughts and feelings, or relaxing their minds for that matter. They can suffer from insomnia because their thoughts are on overdrive. Mental exhaustion can leave them open to suggestion which means easily swayed and taken over by various types of mental implants and programming. Such suggestions may come in the form of advertisements or subliminal messages. In extreme cases they may even begin to hear the voices inside their heads having arguments. Gemini may be targeted because they are seen as a useful tool in some situations, in which they are unaware of the way they are being used toward some end.

Their curiosity about certain things or people can sometimes lead them into danger zones. When curiosity knows no bounds, it can obviously be an invitation to all sorts of mischief and mayhem. They can turn this tendency around by asking how things can improve instead of constantly investigating how bad they are. This also brings a bit more peace of mind to themselves and those around them.

Physically Gemini rules the lungs and upper extremities: the arms, hands and fingers. Energetically, this sign rules the first layer of the mental body and its activities. These areas are the most prone to ailments, injury and attack, but also areas typically advanced in their capacities. Those of this sign are dexterous with their hands, with an excellent sense of coordination in their bodies overall. They can be very inventive and come up with all sorts of clever and genius ideas. They should be careful to guard their inventions until they are ready to fully disseminate. This is to prevent others from snatching up their ideas for their own profit. They would also do well to have back-ups of their most important written work and files, just in case of unexpected losses.

Geminis can protect themselves by choosing to limit contact with certain things, people and places that bring upset into their lives. What they need are appropriate outlets for expression. They tend to need to either communicate their thoughts or release their excess nervous energy by doing something with their hands. If they do not have the appropriate outlets their innate desire to creatively express themselves may turn into nervous anxiety and depression, which also lowers their defenses to outside attacks. It is as though they experience an implosion of energy.

The phrase: "the devil finds work for idle hands" is particularly true for this sign. They could engage in unconscious acts of self-sabotage when they become bored, restless or overly stressed. They can use their voices beneficially in creative ways such as singing, teaching, speaking, or chanting. Writing or drawing tend to be great activities of mental release for them and helps them to tune in to their intuition. They also greatly benefit from deep breathing exercises which help to quiet their minds and bring overall equilibrium.

Gemini Perspectives

We learn from Gemini that there is always another side to the story, another angle from which to perceive any given thing or situation, and another option available to us that is not obvious on the surface. We become less attached to stubborn viewpoints and grow open to new possibilities. Gemini teaches that the best method of protecting one's mental space is to consciously choose what to focus on instead of just taking every noticeable word, image, idea, and statement at face value. Many things in this world are simply not what they seem. That need not become a burden for the one who is aware of this fact and decides not to give him or herself over to the superficial side of life. For the person who is observant and open to change, fear is replaced with a sense of wonder and adventure. A spirit of playfulness does much to support health and deflect negative energy overall.

Cancer

Cancer is the fourth sign of the Zodiac, feminine in polarity and ruled by the Moon. It is the first of the three water signs and is very emotional in nature. Cancer, being associated with motherhood and birth, also represents something new being birthed into the world, or into our life. The Sun transits Cancer between around June 21 and July 22 and as the second cardinal sign it brings us into a new season, which is summer in the Northern hemisphere.

Cancer represents a turning point not only in seasons but in consciousness, specifically the still young and tender stage that is focused on discovering where and to whom we belong. The focus is on family and connecting more to others while maintaining a sense of security. It is here that we tend to learn that the world is not always kind, and can sometimes even be a harsh place. We become aware of our basic needs for nourishment and shelter, and for personal time-outs.

Cancer Symbolism and Sensitivity

The symbol of the Crab illustrates why generally those of this sign are said to need a protective shell to retreat into when feeling threatened. Just as the crab moves sideways, Cancer moves sideways and even backward when they don't like the energy of a place. They are known to be one of the most if not *the* most vulnerable to attack of all kinds. There are various reasons for this, which will become evident as we continue this exploration.

In the ancient Temple of Dendera in Egypt the symbol for the sign of Cancer was depicted as a scarab beetle and not a crab. The scarab was a sacred creature to the Egyptians and was an emblem of the soul, and Cancer is the sign that represents the soul's entry into the earth plane. Cancer's planetary ruler has always been the Moon which exerts its powerful influences over the physical body and emotions.

Cancer is the first sign that brings us into the realms of the unseen where we may encounter bogeymen, goblins and things that go bump in the night. Not surprisingly, many who were born under it are known to be highly psychic, although some are also fearful and superstitious. The same applies for those with an emphasis on this or any other water sign in their birth chart. Imagination is greatly heightened here, which can make for amazing storytelling, poetry and artistic expression. A flair for mystical pursuits and musings is also enhanced.

Feelings run deep but are not necessarily outwardly expressed within this sign. Major actions and decisions are often based on security. Part of feeling secure might be wearing a mask to camouflage the inner goings-on. That mask could be placid, non-emotional, joyous or even stern. This is not a mere mask but a survival mechanism.

Cancer and the First Level of Permeation

This is the first of three water signs, which uses permeation in both their methods of attack and defense. This permeation is akin to that of the moisture that seeps through hard cracks and penetrates soft surfaces with its vapors. Permeation does not operate by force, it often escapes confinement, and has no need for speech. This makes the water element the most unpredictable, dangerous and difficult to subdue. Also, it is easy to be overtaken by the emotions which water represents. That is obvious when you consider that many people dread the impact of a torrent of tears more than they do a stormy temper.

No matter how wise and mature, there is often something childlike in Cancer's nature, an aspect to them that remains youthful and innocent, that may come across as a bit naive. They equally express the opposite of the childlike state and tend to be very nurturing in a maternal or paternal sort of way. Some may seem to alternate between the archetypal Great Caregiver and the one who needs to be taken care of. They can also be extremely hard-working, loyal and devoted to worthy causes. Many have also been called crabby, cry-baby, moody, irrational and even raving lunatics at times. The word lunatic originally meant "moon-struck" and came to be associated with insanity that was triggered by the changes of the moon.

Here is a quote regarding two words (including lunacy) that have come to some ironic usage in our modern vocabulary:

> "The word "idiot" comes from a Greek root meaning private person. Idiocy is the female defect; intent on their private lives, women follow their fate through a darkness deep as that cast by malformed cells in the brain. It is not

worse than the male defect, which is lunacy: they are so obsessed by public affairs that they see the world as by moonlight, which shows the outlines of every object but not the details indicative of their nature."

- Rebecca West, *Black Lamb and Grey Falcon*

In an attempt to comfort and nurture others, they may come across as overbearing and excessively concerned with safety. Some Cancerians exhibit an obsessive-compulsive desire to control their environment, because of a deep-set insecurity. They can be great organizers when it comes to large tasks but with minor ones they seem to lose sight of the details.

One of Cancer's greatest struggles is their propensity to live in the past. It can be hard for them to let go of anything, both physically and emotionally. They remember every wrongdoing toward them, every boon and favor granted. This means that they can play stories over and over like a broken record until it drives them and those around them crazy. It is painful for them and is a habit they often just can't seem to ditch. On occasion it borders on being masochistic. More than any other sign, they tend to take offense when none was intended.

Psychic Protection Against Cancer

Cancer seldom truly desires to harm anyone but when they do happen to get under somebody's skin, it's often done in very unconscious, immature and insidious ways. Their method is to come at someone from an unexpected angle, like the crab moving itself sideways. Once they clamp down with their pincers, they grip tightly to maintain control, and like the movie character Edward Scissorhands they might wind up snapping something in two, much to their chagrin.

An example of what they might do is to lay the infamous guilt trip on someone without directly saying what the underlying issue is. They're so afraid of confrontations, and yet they pout until they are noticed, and howl like wolves to inform others when they are neglected. Coherent speech may be lacking the entire time. In a worst-case scenario, they may go around expressing their discontent until their childish needs are both properly deciphered and then addressed.

The ill-natured Cancer can abuse others through emotional blackmail, manipulations conducted through food and eating. Complaining, repeating bad news or frequently generating needless fears as a mealtime conversation while someone eats causes the victim digestive upset or malfunctioning over time. This could be done by the overly protective mother that clings to her child but never lets them grow and learn by mistake. She retards their development by coddling them after every perceived injury, trying to become their shield from every outside danger, but simultaneously filling the child's mind with ideas, blown up way out of proportion, about all the horrible violence in the world.

All the while, she may be completely ignorant of the emotional violence she is inflicting upon her young. She is driven by worries and fears based on her own memories of failure to meet her challenges with courage. In her most cruel manifestation, she could limit food or withhold it altogether, causing starvation. Or, as in the case of Munchausen syndrome by proxy she could cull attention from others by fabricating sickness in the child she is supposed to be taking care of.

When seeking to psychically defend yourself against Cancer, it is important to remember that this sign inherently fears conflict and prefers to side-step issues. No matter how incredible their actions are, they probably feel more threatened or stressed by you than you fear them, which is why those who are off kilter have a penchant for avoiding direct conflicts. How quickly they shift into victim mode when they're called out on their behavior. Some Cancerians may not respond well to plain facts and logic, and it is best to deflect their tactic of permeation by choosing not to react. This means that you are not using force, entrapment or intellect but you are simply letting their psychic garbage "roll like water off a duck's back" as the saying goes.

Don't internalize it. You may politely indicate to them that you've reached your limit, because yelling would cause them to become startled and defensive, or even to be fueled by your fire. Some may actually provoke arguments because they feed on the emotional drama, caring little for the subject matter itself. They may do this because they're lonely and it brings a little excitement into their otherwise bland routines. Give them the indication that if they continue you will have to take the next measure to protect yourself, which might mean taking time away from them either temporarily or permanently. Give them a chance to exhibit a change before you make your decision. It would be fair to say that this technique is akin to the act of disciplining an unruly child.

Another form of perceived attack that may be executed by those of this sign is that of mirroring. When Gemini mimics others it's done for laughs. For Cancer is it is method of being able to relate to others. Again, we often see this behavior in small children who are just learning how to speak and walk, which is perfectly natural. Cancer sometimes loses sight of what they are even doing because they are taking on the qualities of all of the people and things that surround them. It may even seem that they have no mind of their own, but actually they are just reflecting back to others their interpretation of things, which at times can seem to others as bothersome.

On a metaphysical level, if you know or suspect that you are being attacked in a psychic way by Cancer, keep cactus plants in your home, especially near the front of the house or where you spend the most time. Wear or place a charm somewhere made of the thorns of any type of plant or flower of choice when you are in their presence. This sends out the psychic message that you are not to be messed with in any way.

Psychic Protection for Cancer

As mentioned before, Cancer is often found to be the most vulnerable sign of the Zodiac.

This implies that hurt has already been experienced and as a result there exists a default shield that helps to prevent further damage from reaching their core. The reasons why Cancers are such targets for outside forces has always seemed a great mystery, both to themselves and others. Part of it could be because of their appearance, which may be stoic, tough and unruffled by outside circumstances but hides their truly delicate interior. There is something both strong and fragile about them, as though they are paradoxically both tenacious yet easily shaken. There is also a certain degree of melancholy that many Cancerians carry and have a difficult time hiding from their facial expressions.

Cancer is most vulnerable to misfortune and attack right within their own dwelling space. This is perhaps because of how much time they spend there. Those of this sign may benefit from ensuring all levels of security both within and around their home and property. The home is more than a place of shelter for them. It is a sanctuary, a refuge, and ideally, the place to let down their guard. They crave the domestic comforts such as soft fluffy blankets, potted plants, sentimental art pieces, and home-baked desserts. Weighted blankets may be especially helpful for those who have difficulty sleeping at night due to anxiety or night terrors. Triple locks with an added chain on their front door may help give them a little peace of mind at night but it doesn't rid them of general anxiety. That would best be addressed by creating a soft atmosphere where they can truly relax.

In relationships they may be used for various purposes and then abandoned after the other has exploited and extracted all that they can from them. Many Cancers have a deep psychological wound that repeatedly gets punctured or sliced, as if salt has been poured onto it. This does not help to overcome their tendency to live in the past or wallow in sadness.

They are often very kindhearted and gentle souls, with much sympathy for those less fortunate than themselves. They may have deep and profound insights that make them excellent counselors. Their natural inclination is to give or do something for others that makes them more comfortable and secure, such as feeding them, offering shelter or provisions for survival. They are easily taken advantage of when they extend their generosity too far to those who prove to be undeserving, which can make them enablers of destructive personalities.

Even skeptical Cancers will admit to being psychic from time to time. Cancer's intuitive faculties are very acute and they should trust their first impression about a person, place or thing. When they ignore this initial hit, they often deeply regret it later on. The reason that they so quickly dismiss their intuition is that they become easily swayed by emotion including the emotional manipulations of others, especially when they feel sorry for them.

Cancer best protects him or herself first by bringing full awareness to their body and emotions in relation to their living situation and daily environment. They are often too deeply empathic with others and sensitive to their surroundings. It seems that the females have more difficulty with their sensitivity levels than the males. They mentally and emotionally internalize their settings in a very automatic way and this pattern is very difficult for them to break.

They pick up "vibes" wherever they go which tend to have swift and direct influences upon their overall health. They can counteract some of this vulnerability by tapping into the qualities of the first Cardinal sign, Aries. Working out at the gym, engaging in some form of weight resistance exercise and building their physique is an important step for their immunity. They tend to have sensitive stomachs, so they need to watch what they eat but not in an obsessive-compulsive way. They should simply be aware of how the food they eat affects them and adjust accordingly. Other areas of vulnerability in women include the breasts and womb.

Dissociation and spaciness can manifest in Cancers when they are being attacked by psychic forces. The worst-case scenario is when they themselves become a host for harmful entities. They can defend themselves by regularly clearing their space with the use of such agents as burning resins, essential oils, and keeping a salt lamp on during times of great fear or stress. Perhaps, even more importantly, they should be mindful of the things that they allow to accumulate in their homes because some of these things can become the warehouse for bad memories negativity to nest itself.

Cancer and Emotional Boundaries

The astrological sign of Cancer teaches us the importance of maintaining proper emotional boundaries between ourselves and others. There is a strong radar on any approaching impositions of the body, mind and spirit. We learn the true meaning of the term "psycho-somatic" as we observe the effects that our emotions have upon our overall health. Cancer is inherently a private sign, and it reminds us that everyone has a right to their own private domain in which to process deep thoughts and feelings, just as almost everyone needs a bed to sleep in at night to recover from the day's stress. This privacy should be kept sacred, meaning that we should honor the privacy of others as well as our own.

Leo

Leo is the fifth sign of the Zodiac and ruled by the Sun itself. As the natural domicile of the Sun; those born under its influence tend toward having a strong and robust constitution overall. The keywords for this sign are creativity, willpower and love. Leo is the second of three fire signs, and the second of the four fixed signs. Unlike Aries, which is a cardinal sign and an initiator, Leo is fixed in nature and tends to be set in its ways.

The Sun transits through Leo between July 21 and August 22. Leo represents the still fairly young but now maturing phase of consciousness, from late teen years into early twenties. It highlights the span of time that we tend to experiment with different styles of clothing, artistic expression, and relationships to others. We leave the nest of our comfort zone in order to experience more that life has to offer. During these years many people have a first sexual experience of some kind, and in some cases may begin to procreate.

Leo Symbolism and Strength

As the second fire sign of the Zodiac ruled by the central star of our solar system, Leo is filled with a sense of importance, which may or may not be obvious on the surface. The passions run very high and this is why Leo is linked with romance, sexual desire and offspring.

Leo is a masculine fire sign, symbolized by the fierce Lion which represents strength in many cultures, and its regal, proud and commanding presence is initially quite off-putting to any would-be predators. In fact, most would seriously think twice before approaching those of this sign with less than noble motives. The two main reasons for attacking a Leo with any forethought would either be that the attacker does not realize who they are dealing with or that they are seeking revenge against something that Leo has done to them.

Once their trust has been earned and you have found a place in their heart, no one serves as a better champion of his or her loved ones than does Leo. When they see the truth of who you are, they will defend your honor unlike anyone else has or ever will. The tendency to protect and uplift their closest associates is a unique trait of this sign. Their natural sense of leadership brushes off any attempts at subversive dominance while creating a sense of safety for others who are less likely to stand up for themselves.

You can count on Leo to deliver their opinions straight. Not necessarily in a rude way but just clear and completely honest without any frilly nonsense. In the spiritual battlefield, one is fortunate to either be Leo or to have Leo's assistance. That is because they direct themselves fully into any meaningful engagements without holding themselves back.

Leo and the Second Level of Force

Within the sign of Leo, the second level of Force comes into play. This is the force of the will, emanating from the heart. This force is no longer raw but has become strongly defined. It is directed toward very specific pursuits and it does not easily waver. Let this be a clue as to just how dangerous this sign can be under certain circumstances.

Being heart-driven, Leo's force can move others emotionally, through words, actions, music, and the arts. This is also the sign of the love affair so those of this sign are known to be both romantically inclined and appealing to the opposite sex or to others in general. They can be well-loved and popular overall.

Generally speaking, Leos have a magnanimous disposition and tend toward either spoiling their children and other loved ones or being very generous toward them. In their worst moods some would take their anger out on loved ones in the form of dictatorship, breaking objects, harsh rejection or criticism. This would all be done with great force!

Like their preceding sign Cancer, they will fiercely defend their loved ones against any outside attacks, like the father lion looking out for his cubs. Leo mothers may also train their children in the arts of war and self-defense, or they may be more actively involved in showing their children the ways of the world in creative ways.

Psychic Protection against Leo

The greatest vice of Leo can be a subtle yet pervasive form of spiritual arrogance. This is when either their confidence in their abilities or the lack thereof causes them to subconsciously or blatantly treat others as inferior to their "greatness". It is true that Leo is able to lift others up like no other sign can, but when they deem fit, they are also capable of taking them right back down, even further down than before, giving both the best praise and the worst criticism possible. This form of dominance is based on Leo's own self-importance. The results are particularly disastrous in situations of arrested development. With this knowledge, one would better know how to approach or deal with an unstable or juvenile sort of individual who is not operating with much awareness. Another way of saying this is *don't take the bait*.

Leo can love and hate with so much intensity which is what makes it incredibly awful and unfortunate to be on their bad side. If they lack self-control, they will strike another person's areas of weakness with such force that others may be completely shocked at their words or actions. The reasoning behind such an attack could be a case of projection, having little or nothing to do with the target of anger.

Those who dabble in the occult for selfish purposes would not be above using black magic in their attempts to harm someone. In this extreme scenario measures must be taken to counteract their curses, especially for those who are highly suggestible and susceptible to psychic energy.

Some Leos can be sex addicts, so unless one is also a sex addict it may not be wise to enter into a romantic relationship with one if this is a concern. Although fixed in nature, this type of Leo can quickly become a stray cat when they're no longer satisfied in the bedroom with someone. They won't necessarily come out in an obvious way with how they feel, but the truth will emerge sooner or later.

When Leo gets angry, the first thing they tend to do is verbally steam about it, whether that's under their breath, through texting, or aloud to a close friend. Better yet, this energy will be channeled and transmuted through an artistic medium of some kind, or as a spiritual aspirant they will go into meditation to seek clarity and resolution. That way they don't stoop to the level of attacking anyone. Leo knows there is tremendous power in passion of any kind, so they usually don't act on it right away. They typically believe themselves to be above brutish behavior. They have to be seriously and repeatedly provoked into acting on a negative impulse.

However, if they have reached the breaking point of what they can tolerate, they will cave in to the dictates of their anger and when that happens, run. You don't want to be around to see what unfolds. To say that Leo would be losing their cool is an understatement. For this reason, it would be wise not to incur their wrath. Although it takes much before they finally snap, they can be one of the most ruthless signs when they are not acting in accordance with their own conscience.

It is worth taking note of *why* Leo buttons are even pushed to this point. The first reason is that they have been hurt, their pride injured, and possibly their love betrayed. They may feel unappreciated and taken advantage of; whether in their own perceptions or in actuality they have been cheated, stolen from and lied to, not just once or twice, and not in any small way. It usually takes a lot of deep betrayal and many years for a build-up to occur in which Leo finally explodes or goes off the deep end. At that point, if they haven't dealt with their feelings of heartache, Leo may dump onto a person who does not even deserve it, due to a hugely inflated sense of self-pity. This is a fixed sign and when ego doesn't run the show, loyalty is as steadfast as can be. When overtaken by lower impulses, Leo shocks everyone.

Then again, in yet other situations Leo will have internalized all of the pain they have experienced, which erodes their health and vitality. Not all Leos have a love of attention and drama. Some are truly humble and would rather hide behind the scenes. It is always obvious in dealing with those who have no doubts whatsoever about their personal talents and would prefer that the world knows full well about them.

More than the other signs, Leo is known to break things and punch holes into walls when angry, but this is more common in the men than women, and this is only true when they lack self-control. It's a good idea to move any heated arguments with them as far away from the China cabinet as possible. However, in defending yourself against psychic attack from Leo, the number one area to look out for is not material but your own sense of dignity. When a Leo is your friend, partner or loved one they will adore you like no other and lift your spirits high. If you're no longer special to them or when you have aroused their anger you may be the target of their accumulated grievances, insecurities, and projections. They could drop someone like an old rag because at the time of their being triggered, they just happened to be in the way.

A minor attack from a mildly annoyed Leo would be that they rather unknowingly belittle or dismiss you, your title, your experiences or your worth. Don't take such condescending behavior to heart because usually it will soon pass with an apology given or exchanged. You'll know the difference between this and a major attack in which Leo goes out of their way to downgrade a person and their life. Pray this never ever happens because that's where multiple forms of self-defense would become necessary in body, mind and spirit.

A deliberate psychic attack from Leo may require a full on magickal ritual to adequately put to an end. Of course, this all depends on the person who is attacking and being attacked. If you notice their sway taking hold, you may benefit from the herbs and stones that are very powerful against the negative energy being sent to you. These may include Bay Laurel, St. John's Wort, Galangal root, Black Tourmaline and Goldsheen Obsidian.

Psychic Protection for Leo

Although Leo is known to have a love of the spotlight, the early Leos, having certain Cancerian leanings, tend to be more interested in having a strong home base with solid connections to friends, children and other loved ones. They crave security more than attention and large social events. They're content with life's simple pleasures and they know how to enjoy themselves. From time to time they can sink into a mood of sulking, but they do not stay in that state very long.

Since Leo has such a big heart, at least metaphorically, they are prone to overextending in the way of charitable deeds, giving too much, and sometimes to the wrong people. They search for the good in everyone, and while this is a wonderful way to view others it can lead to trouble when it goes too far. Not everyone is worthy of Leo's generosity, second chances and favors. The time comes when something feels *off* and that feeling must be heeded by this feline before it becomes the source of excess stress.

One of the greatest challenges of Leo is that of the struggle that is experienced with their ego. Whereas their preceding sign Cancer may feel easily hurt and affected by negativity, Leo may be easily offended. As humans in general we tend to struggle with the feeling of being either too small or too big in comparison to our peers and environment. Leos are especially sensitive to the significance of their egos, which are often quite fragile and easily bruised. They may compensate for this by putting on huge displays of some kind, to make sure that everyone sees them as being mighty and strong, and pretty darn sexy to boot.

Then again, some Leos know with total confidence that they're hot, strong, talented or all of the above, and they have no problems reminding those around them of the special position they hold within their family, community or society. Usually this is harmless. Narcissistic behavior is only exhibited in extreme types.

The issue of ego may have nothing whatsoever to do with wanting to be the center of attention, but rather a desire to prove something to close family members or childhood friends that have underestimated Leo's intelligence and abilities. Those of this sign really hate to be misrepresented and misunderstood, so they may go out of their way to clarify their position and to bolster their worth in the eyes of others. It can be extremely difficult for them to let go of the feeling that they've been slighted by someone they cared about, and they may in some cases spend the rest of their lives driving themselves toward feats and accomplishments based on what others said they could not, or would not ever do. "Oh yeah!?" says indignant Leo... "Watch me!"

The correct way for Leo to defend him or herself against psychic attack would of course depend upon the severity of it. Over time some of the wildest cats have become tamed and domesticated creatures. Leo can be like a cat that has been tamed but still has the potential to shred something to pieces with its claws. Leo inherently knows the damage they are capable of so they hold back. They despise pettiness and instead of squabbling over spilled milk and small upsets they would rather be engaged in very big issues and problems to solve. After all, this is a royal sign and Leo has a kingdom to look after. That means that they frequently take on far more than they can handle, and their strenuous efforts may eventually take a toll on their health.

The body parts ruled by Leo are the heart and spine and these are the areas that Leo needs to watch out for when they are under prolonged stress. They also need to guard their hearts in an emotional sense and when they fall in love they should maintain their wits and not sacrifice themselves just to please another.

The loss or betrayal of love deeply impacts Leo because they of all signs tend to give love and to give others their all. When what they give is not reciprocated or when it has been taken for granted their whole world seems to turn inside out. In some cases that so-called love can suddenly sour, and they can become strong victims of the one who they feel has crushed their heart and trust. It can take them a while to finally move on.

Leo most often falls prey to psychic attacks by others when they are weakened somehow, such as by illness, either mental or physical, or when they have unconsciously given themselves away. Minor, indirect psychic attacks against Leo are the most common, and these are performed by trying to "one-up" them, in order to arouse their jealousy and hostility. Another common form of attack against Leo is that of theft. Some people mistake Leo's generosity and kindness for weakness or mistakenly view them as a source of energy and other goods, so they try to snag up some of that goodness for their own use. All the while, Leo is sitting there watching with alert cat eyes, shocked in the beginning, with smoke coming out of his or her ears.

When the reason for Leo being attacked is due to revenge, Leo may or may not recognize the reasons at hand. It must be underlined that it is not an easy thing to defeat a member of this sign, which is why their position or health would have to be heavily compromised before they would make an easy target. They would have to be born into a situation of slavery to ever submit to it and even then, they would find some way to rebel against it and become masters of their domain, or to escape.

On the other hand, some Leos who complain of being psychically attacked are making a bigger deal out of what was said or done than what actually occurred. They tend to dramatize things, and this is what can get them into even more trouble down the line. Whatever the situation may be, it is part of Leo's spiritual task to become more aware of their abilities and to channel their power wisely.

Leo and Self-Mastery

From the sign of Leo we learn the importance of focus and self-mastery. Leo knows about their innate strength which is what they fear the most until they have faced their inner dragons. The cruelest beast one will ever have to face in life and to tame is the self. We also discover the power that true love has to heal and uplift hearts and minds. Leo also teaches us genuine self-worth. Everyone has a unique energetic signature that is unlike any other, and a purpose to fulfill in life. This purpose should not be ignored but honored. This sign reminds us that "when there is a will there is a way" to overcome some of the most stubborn obstacles and to actualize many of our heart's desires. Leo does not back down just because something looks or feels difficult. By example they show the world that it takes a combination of focus and strong will to tackle certain hardships. Love is their fuel, and their prime motivation for doing so.

Virgo

Virgo is the sixth sign of the Zodiac and the second sign after Gemini to be ruled by the planet Mercury. A feminine earth sign, Virgo is concerned with everyday earthly matters and has a pragmatic approach to solving problems. It is hard working and service oriented. The Sun transits this sign between August 22 and September 22.

Virgo represents the passage into an adult state of consciousness that leads toward the Saturn Return that occurs at around age twenty-eight. Our worldly responsibilities begin to grow. During these years many people go to college and experiment with menial jobs before settling into a career. At this time we realize we are not going to be young forever, so we put more effort than ever before into maintaining our health and appearances. We are still learning a lot about the world and our place in it, so we keep our options open.

Virgo Symbolism and Virtue

Virgo is a mutable earth sign, feminine in polarity and represented by a young woman or an angel in female form. She is often depicted holding an ear of corn or a sheaf of wheat which symbolizes the beginning of the harvest season. There have many religious implications tied into this sign through the centuries, in connection with the Blessed Mother, nunnery and celibacy. That doesn't mean that Virgos lack sensuality or that they have a religious mindset. In fact, they may be extremely sensual and many even shun religion altogether.

One of the deeper meanings of this sign is that of personal sovereignty. Virgo has many fine qualities and is first and foremost concerned with the goal of wholeness, whether that is on a physical, mental or spiritual level. Those of this sign are natural helpers and tend to be humble, at least early in life, as they seek to aid others in all ways that they can and to make the best out of whatever life has given them. Often, they are willing to do the dirty work that nobody else does, because to them cleanliness is godliness. They have a natural kinship with animals and are drawn toward ecology, natural healing methods and dietary programs.

At first glance, Virgos are very unassuming and do not appear at all combative or disagreeable. There is a natural sweetness to them that is immediately disarming to those around them.

However, when their temperament has gone sour in some way, they can be sharply critical. If there is any great flaw that those of this sign carry, it would be their fussiness and propensity to magnify flaws in general.

Virgo and the Second Level of Containment

As the second earth sign, Virgo's method psychic attack and self-defense is conducted by the second level of containment. Taurus separates their things from others and Virgo separates themselves from the pack. They can show much self-restraint and they feel that they are special, like Leo but for different reasons. Leo wants to be the boss, while Virgo wants to be the best. This is why those of this sign are known to be perfectionists. Although talkative and friendly enough on the surface, they may be rather solitary in many ways, like the Hermit shown on the card of the Major Arcana, which is ruled by this sign.

Virgo are known to be highly skilled at organization. It is easy for them to discard what has become obsolete or does not serve an immediate purpose. They are often said to label and categorize things on a nearly constant basis, creating an environment of total order and neatness wherever they may be. That is because those of this sign may quickly sift through information, things, and people in their assessments. Some of them can become stressed out when a person or thing does not fit neatly into one of their conceptual boxes. This is not true for all Virgos, for some of them manifest more of the qualities of their opposite sign Pisces and are a bit random or even sloppy in their habits. This is not to say that Pisces is always sloppy, but the comparison is that Virgo forms a container and Pisces energy does not want to be contained or limited in any way.

Virgo is adept at separating the "wheat from the chaff" in many situations. Often, they are able to discipline themselves internally instead of allowing their emotions to dictate their actions, at least for a while. They do not usually open up easily about their feelings which run very deep, although their expressions say enough without needing explanations. Talkative as they may be, they tend to skirt around their real feelings or motivations, not revealing too much of what is truly going on with them.

Mercury as their ruling planet indicates an intellectual orientation and highly nervous energy that must have physical outlets for creative expression, exercise or work. Virgos are acute observers who pick up all manner of details that have gone completely unnoticed by others, and this makes them expert supervisors.

Psychic Protection Against Virgo

Virgo is a very complex sign because a native born under it is often concerned with things of the world while also trying to maintain a certain level of coolness and control over him or herself within it. The outer pride of the preceding sign Leo is replaced with a kind of inverted pride that is displayed as humility. This is revealed by their frequent desire to either be virtuous or very skilled in some way, but especially in regard to serving others. Where this leads to trouble for others is when their drive for perfection becomes so strong that they may reject or try to tear down anyone who does not live up to their own ideas of what is acceptable or desirable. More than anything, they pride themselves on being *correct*, and they go out of their way to ensure their own correctness in the areas of importance to them.

Although usually accurate in their assessments they occasionally make false assumptions which means wrongly interpreting their gathered data or jumping to conclusions. Because they prize the virtues of keen perception and accuracy so highly, they may hate to admit when they are wrong. They sometimes rely too heavily on logic and not enough on their own intuition, which they sometimes fight. In their ultra-pragmatic outlook, they may risk shredding things to bits in their analysis of words, relationships, and situations. It becomes very difficult for some of them to be silent about what they observe. They may blame and complain to the point of exhaustion for everyone involved, including themselves. The tendency to quarrel or constantly draw attention to the shortcomings of others can wear on friends, family and coworkers, not to mention the intimate partner.

Virgo's outward projections can lead to all sorts of bickering and animosity both to and from others. Their bitter wrath can be like that of an avalanche of petty, verbal complaints that come down in the tone of a negative feminine manner of nitpicking. When they get on a tangent, they accuse others of what they themselves are doing. They might twist others' words around making it seem as though they have said the exact opposite thing.

In trying to reform others or give help where it is not requested, even if their intention is good, they eventually push them away. Those of a grumpy disposition are notorious for pointing the finger at others and making quick enemies. Their tendency to gather data on others is very similar to that of Scorpio's, but the methods of attack are different and more socially oriented.

Since Virgo is a feminine earth sign, an attack by them will be subtle and covert, on the mental and emotional levels rather than overt or outright physical ones. As acute observers they will already know all of your weaknesses long before a conflict arises. They use this information primarily as some sort of intellectual leverage. Understanding where they are coming from helps to dissipate the air of defensiveness that may arise, but it may well be best to decline further engagement.

The conscientious Virgo can make a wonderful companion, but one who has chosen the route of blame can seem rather cold in their manners of punishment. Don't let them drag you into a whirlpool of their own agitation and crisis. Inwardly they can be equally critical of themselves whether or not they reveal this habit to the world. If they perceive someone as beneath them, they can easily cast them aside as if they were some filthy rag that is no longer of use to them. Their disdain for their fellow humans and their flaws can grow as they age.

Like the other mutable signs, Virgos have often been known to cheat on their spouses. While there have certainly been people of all signs guilty of cheating, Virgos are probably some of the least expected to engage in this type of activity. Their reasons for doing this typically include dissatisfaction in some area with their mate, and looking elsewhere to make up for deficits. Judgments and expectations may run high. Indications that Virgo is cheating may show up in the forms of them being both extra critical and less available than usual. The person they are most likely to cheat with is usually someone they see regularly, such as a physician, colleague, or even someone they connect with in a spiritual setting such as a church.

If deliberate psychic attack is coming from Virgo, just remember it is likely being directed to an area where you are already weak rather than strong. Visualize that aspect of your body, life or emotional reality to be glowing with golden light, growing in strength, and becoming impervious to any and all forms of intrusion. See your whole entire body, your endeavors and life as being held in the highest and holiest of divine light. Choose an affirmation, poem or song that uplifts your soul and gives you the sense of being invincible.

Psychic Protection for Virgo

Psychic protection may be very important for Virgoan people to learn because they can be too open and giving, especially when they are young. They assume that other people will meet them halfway, pick up where they left off or will thank them for their contributions. When these behaviors are not forthcoming, they can become despondent.

To protect themselves psychically they need to prioritize their physical health with adequate nutrition, rest and exercise. They may also need some assistance with calming their anxieties at times. Their minds can be over-active, and they are often better off if they have some kind of outlet for their ideas in the form of speaking, journaling or blogging. They can be very eloquent and well-spoken, with an admirable sense of detail, grammar and expression. Those who are not particularly focused on writing and speaking tend to find they have the gift for details when it comes to music or other arts and crafts.

Due to being so observant in an almost superhuman way, Virgo may suffer both mentally and physically from the state of hyper-vigilance, being overly tuned in to details that distract from rather than enhance the quality of life. This state may be triggered by traumatic events or excessive fearfulness. They benefit from relaxing techniques such as yoga, meditation or from long nature walks and birdwatching. This is the sign that rules pets and small animals, and they may find much peace and joy by working with and being around them. They also tend to be protective of animals and may often feel closer to them than they do humanity.

The body parts ruled by Virgo are the liver, intestines and the nervous system. Just as the major organs help to eliminate toxins from the body, Virgo seeks to eliminate them from the psyche. This is one reason why they can make great nurses or healers. However, when they become weighed down with toxicity of any kind, it can become difficult for them to maintain composure because they can be very prone to nervous exhaustion. Virgo needs plenty of quality time in nature, in the woods or by the seaside, or with their hands in the earth helping things to grow. They thrive in all kinds of elements and climates as they are adaptable to change.

Virgo's planetary ruler is Mercury which gives them a sharp, analytical mind that is great for many tasks but also lends itself toward mental obsessions and anxiety. They can become high strung and worn out from overthinking, or experience acute random panic episodes when their thoughts literally seem to be running away with them. In these types of scenarios, they need space to calm down, and deep breathing can assist them in unwinding. Quiet reassurance and a shoulder to lean on may help, but don't ask them too many questions which will only intensify their anxious feelings.

Consider the hard work that many Virgos have chosen to take on in their lifetime. They ultimately seek to upgrade the conditions of their body, mind and environment, and by doing this they may contribute to the betterment of conditions for many others. In order to do so they must relinquish some aspect of the demands of their ego in the process. This is a lot easier said than done. It can be painful and tedious, yet they are willing to do it. Although they may start and stop again several times, they will eventually chip away at a particular task until it has reached completion, owing to the consistency of the earth element assigned to them.

Virgo and Psychic Integrity

The sign of Virgo teaches the significance of maintaining one's integrity instead of squandering precious life-force energy. This sense of integrity could be related to work, health, sex, or other practical matters. Under Virgo's influence we are guided to stand back, look at ourselves honestly, and to make improvements in our character rather than self-sabotaging ourselves. We also learn how to stop expecting too much from others and to take certain matters into our own hands, engaging in the process of self-sufficiency.

This sign also encourages us to become more mindful about the substances and influences that we allow into our bodies, minds and spirits, as they affect our health in various ways. Virgo raises the bar for humanity, so that we become inwardly inspired to excel beyond what we thought was possible, making ourselves and the world a better place, even if just one little bit at a time.

Libra

As the seventh sign of the Zodiac, Libra, being exactly opposite of the first sign Aries, marks a shift in focus from personal concerns to outer matters. Its season begins around September 23 and lasts until October 22. This is the second of the three air signs, bringing us into the third season of the year, which is Autumn in the Northern hemisphere.

The stage of development represented by Libra is the period of time that leads up to what is commonly referred to as the mid-life crisis. Typically, between the ages of thirty and forty, we begin to slow down and take inventory of what we have been doing so far and how we feel overall. Our focus is no longer about our own needs and desires, but about sharing what we have and know with those who are important to us and taking responsibility for the impact that we have in the world. Familiar roles tend to shift, leaving a person wondering who they really are and what they are doing with their life. This phase represents the reflective and thoughtful qualities of the sign of Libra.

Libra Symbolism and Charm

This is a masculine air sign ruled by the planet Venus and is the only one represented by neither beast nor human form. Its symbol is the scales, which stand for balance and justice. One matching archetype for this sign is the Egyptian goddess known as Ma'at, who is often depicted holding the scales weighing the human heart against a feather of truth to determine the virtues of the deceased. It is as if Libra is constantly engaged in the weighing between two opposites or choices, and between wrong and right, self and other, yin and yang, good and bad, male and female, this and that.

Libras are known for their charm and social graces, ever seeking balance in relationships to others. They are generally easy-going and search for ways to beautify their environments every chance they get. That all seems like a good thing until you get into a skirmish with one of these folks, in which case all hell may break loose. Libras desperately want to live a peaceful and harmonious life, but the truth is that they seldom attain peace of mind until they have tamed their inner aggressiveness and sometimes combative nature which is typically well-hidden and tucked away from the average person's view.

Though not seething with anger, they often have a hard time acknowledging that anger is even there until situations have escalated, which forces them to reconcile with their darker emotions. Delayed reactions are common. Standing up for themselves and being truthful with others about how they feel is sometimes a challenge.

Libra and the Second Level of Speech

As an air sign Libra is mentally oriented and smart. In this sign the mind has become more serious than it was in Gemini. The second level of Speech is the first means by which Libra attacks or defends themselves. This level of Speech is focused primarily on two-way communications, and especially the making or breaking of deals and contracts. All forms of communication are highlighted, but Libra usually seeks creative forms of expression. In a heavily imbalanced state, speech is used to manipulate others and promises are made that cannot be kept. Libra can be superficial, glossing over important matters with glib terms and blanket statements. As with all other signs, much depends on the other influences in their natal chart combined. Libras have become infamous for being flaky and unreliable.

Behind the cute dimples and neatly combed hair, Libra is a sign of sharp, surprising contrasts and juxtapositions. It is as much warfare as it is compromise. Their minds can be overflowing with contradictions. This is the first sign of the Zodiac to symbolically exit the inner domain of the self and family and to enter the world at large. Because of this, Libra is the most polarized sign of all and one that can cause much stress for those born under it. A paradoxical nature can at times cause the native to be torn in radically different directions during which they seem to be suspended in a sort of limbo, where they feel unable to act. Their process of weighing on the scales of duality is ongoing. Although they are known as the diplomats and peacemakers, they somehow also wind up stirring up a lot of animosity at times in their attempts to restore balance where things are off. They especially struggle to form solid decisions, from fear of making the wrong choices and upsetting the apple cart. Procrastination appears to be a Libran vice tied in with their dislike of commitments, mistakes, conflicts.

One of Libra's hardest lessons in life is that they cannot please all people or avoid conflicts. They either positively attract or negatively repel others, with seldom a neutral effect. Everyone knows that conflicts and disagreements are inevitable. What matters ultimately is how they are dealt with. Libra can get so caught up in other people's points of view that they sometimes lose sight of their own personal philosophy and values. They must come to terms with the fact that they *will* either upset or disappoint some people with their words and choices. Therefore, they should strive to let go of the false notion of being a friend to everyone or of being liked by all.

Psychic Protection Against Libra - Male and Female Differences

There are notable differences that are observable between the males and females born under any sign, but the contrast is especially acute and easy to spot when it comes to Libra. Because we are dealing with a sign that involves opposites and duality, the differences between the sexes here are quite profound and ironic. There are exceptions to the rules and roles can reverse in those who are attracted to the same sex.

Libra is a masculine air sign ruled by a feminine planet. Libran women tend toward being classy, sleek, or fashionable but they have a distinctly masculine type of mind. Their quick wit and sharp intellect are shocking to certain people who didn't expect such strong words from such soft-looking ladies. Ironically, for a sign that is known for being so indecisive, Libra enjoys taking on leadership roles. They have a natural take-charge attitude which is why you find that many of them become business owners, lawyers, activists, politicians, and entrepreneurs.

An inordinate number of Libran women as well as those born under Aquarius and the fire signs can be found working in military positions or other Martian occupations dealing with the law. Overall, they can be both outwardly driven while also being drawn toward partnership with another. Many Libra women are lone wolves, but a great deal more also find pleasure in married life, to which they are also well suited.

If and when a Libra woman strikes out for any reason, it's likely to burn from the force of a verbal whip. She won't necessarily do it right away because Libra always gives others the benefit of the doubt, usually for longer than is warranted. If immediately, you were a notably bad egg. Both men and women Libras tend to beat around the bush before drawing a conclusion and getting to the point. She waits for enough evidence to back up her final decision. When judgment day finally comes, watch out. She prepares for her aim like an archer or shooter and hits her target with stunning precision. The analogy of the "iron fist in a velvet glove" is especially relevant here.

By comparison, many Libran men look the part of the ideal male on the surface. They are well-proportioned and many of them can make great models if they so choose. They might even have manly professions or be involved in sports. However, many of them fool others with their alpha male appearance. Libran men can be prone toward vacillation and feminine evasiveness because of how much they hate conflict. They seek to remain on an even keel even when situations indicate that's not going to happen. Mohandas "Mahatma" Gandhi, the immortalized Indian lawyer who led civil rights movements and pushed for the seemingly impossible ideal of world peace was a Libra.

Some Libra men use their charm to get their way with women, the more the better. These are the types of men who drive women crazy with their non-committal attitudes but who also fear hurting anybody's feelings, so they leave things unresolved and never throw down a strong answer. Their frequent phrases are "Maybe" and "I'll think about that" or the all-famous line "Tomorrow!" Tomorrow for many can be a torturous place to be left hanging. Especially when tomorrow is stretched out over weeks, months, or years. Libra eventually starts either agreeing with or saying yes to too many people and before he knows it, he's in a really tight position that forces him to choose his sacrifice. Constantly rescheduling or postponing of plans is often evident in both sexes.

In a worst-case scenario, a Libran man may be more concerned with his public image than with taking care of his family. He avoids facing his problems behind the scenes. Gandhi actually provides us with an example of some of this type of behavior. His interpersonal relationships did not reflect the peaceful appearance that was presented to the world at large. Some biographies claim that he had neglected his wife and children in order to fulfill what he believed to be his purpose in life. Many Libra men and women have been found guilty of roundabout speech and misplaced anger. This is when lovers, friends and would-be allies become enemies. If only they would muster the courage to be upfront, they would avoid so much opposition from others. Libra man typically attacks under the radar rather than outwardly in plain sight. His stance may be wishy-washy, and he may offer no explanation for his actions, which keeps others forever guessing at his motives. This is because he himself isn't sure of his own position.

Positively, Libra is intelligent and a fine conversationalist. If others view him as some kind of information guru, he gladly assumes the role. He should be aware of this so as not to come across as arrogant. Many internet figureheads with large followings happen to be Libran men.

Both male and female Libras have a hard time with formulating their own opinions at times. They are so open to the thought pools of others that they can find themselves swimming in a sea of others' ideas, losing themselves in the mix. This is a dangerous situation both for themselves and those who depend on them for various purposes. Their Venusian tendency toward comparison may be weaponized, in that the lesser of two choices gets a worse wrap than deserved, or else doesn't get an honest enough review. These people can drive others mad by frequently playing the role of Devil's advocate. Too frequently, procrastination appears to be a Libran vice that seems tied in with their huge dislike of mistakes and conflicts. There is a propensity for telling little white lies when telling the truth gets too uncomfortable. Affections can also be easily faked.

Libra's polar opposite sign, Aries, is outwardly aggressive. Libra is calm on the surface but when provoked by another is likely to push back with equal force. This is done on an intellectual level while maintaining a certain degree of coolness and detachment which unnerves some people. This behavior can both wear themselves out and make enemies unnecessarily. Many Libras have a built-in defense mechanism which makes them excellent in competition or in occupations that require short bursts of energy and sharp mental focus. In other situations, their hidden anger eventually explodes like a volcano, leaving everyone in their midst completely bewildered. Every now and then you may also come into contact with a Libra who is mean-spirited, whose surface-level, sickly sweet mannerisms do little more than infuriate those whom they betray.

The subjects that you are most likely to find Libra engaged in fights over involve issues surrounding personal relationships, whether their own or others, or over injustices in general. Some can get very upset about things going on in a way that shifts attention from the subject matter of importance onto themselves, revealing an undercurrent of egotism.

In dealing with a lop-sided Libra, prepare yourself for possible arguments and spiels that go nowhere but in circles very fast. The quickest exit is a verbal halt will counteract the unpleasant atmosphere of suspense that has been created. Libra abhors a fork in the road, but they clearly understand and obey a stop sign when they see it. Another approach is to offer them love and kindness, which if genuine can dissolve their anger just as quickly as it came.

Unless there are other factors that cause them to be introverts or private, there are not many secrets that Libras keep to themselves. They have just enough class to prevent them from oversharing. For those concerned about their social status in relation to this sign, cloves have long been used in spells for spiritual protection, and they have been burned as an incense to prevent others from gossiping about oneself. Libra is not a sign that deliberately sets out to harm others though, because that would highly disturb their own psyche. In most cases their attacks are counterattacks, and if you study them closely you will see the scales in action.

Psychic Protection for Libra

Libra is often victimized by people who take advantage of their kindness and think that there is a never-ending supply of energy and goodwill to draw upon from them. If their upbringing was dysfunctional, it can be difficult for them to develop their own capacity for self-preservation. They may waste too much precious time and energy giving to others who have already, long ago, many times over, proven themselves to be untrustworthy or disrespectful. They make good listeners, which is why others find it so easy to confide in them, but also why others find it so easy to dump on them. They are exceedingly patient and often generous in their dealings with friends, family, and associates.

However, even Libra has limits to what will be tolerated. When very tired their naturally cheerful demeanor may get buried behind a grumpy expression that is unbecoming of them. When they lay down boundaries instead of letting people walk all over them, they are often met with dismay and hostility. This is when they are forced to face the music and recognize that they cannot make everyone happy or continue to compromise themselves to the point of total exhaustion.

The best way for Libra to defend themselves against psychic attack is to strike a balance of alone time and socializing. That is much easier said than done, for even when Libra is not looking for interaction, he or she attracts all kinds of people who want to engage in all kinds of ways with them. They can't seem to help how magnetic and popular they are, but they can decide to take healthy time-outs long enough to hear themselves think. If they do this, they will make better choices and avoid a lot of heartache and unnecessary drama overall.

Libra will finally learn to close the books on unhealthy attachments and to walk away before these things have a chance to erode their self-confidence and energy. Then they can give of themselves to those who are truly deserving instead of *"casting pearls before swine"*.

The Sun in Libra is said to be in its fall, which is one reason why it is not considered to be a vital sign. Physically, Libra rules the kidneys which is where life force energy is stored and from where it gets depleted. This is why Libras should pay extra attention to their diets and to make sure that they stay well hydrated. Electrolytes or a tiny pinch of Celtic Sea salt in each glass of drinking water has been used for this purpose. Their health seems to suffer most when they have become emotionally affected by perceived injustices and unfairness in the world. Exercises that help them to remain calm and to gather their internal reservoirs of energy are especially helpful. These may include yoga, qi gong and deep breathing.

Libra and Equilibrium

Libra is a sign that exemplifies harmony, tactfulness and poise. It is quite seldom that a Libra will completely give in to their tempers or any other occasional state of extremes. Their ability to step back, use reason and remain objective is what helps them to regain their footing after a disagreement or chaotic event. Libra also leads by example what is taught in the ancient adage "as above, so below". They are always seeking balance in their expression of contrasting energies. Libras often serve as mirrors for others around them. Some will like what they see and others will be upset by it. They teach us about the effect that others have on us and vice versa. There is a time to speak and a time to listen, just as there is a time observe and a time to be seen. Libra is here to both learn and teach how to master the art of relationships to others in general.

Scorpio

Scorpio is the eighth sign of the Zodiac, and is associated with healing, transformation, and death. This is the sign that represents a deepening of awareness and a desire to pierce the veil of life's many illusions. It is the second of the three water signs and highly sensitive in nature.

The Sun passes through Scorpio from October 23 to November 21. The developmental stage represented by this sign spans the midlife ages, when much of life's deepest introspection begins.

There is so much potency at this time as there is in this sign in general. Middle age is when people begin to think more about their mortality and the legacy they will leave behind them when they go. This clues us in to the urgency that lies dormant within this sign, which is to *change* what we fear changing and to let go of that which no longer serves a beneficial purpose.

Scorpio Symbolism and Complexity

Scorpio is a complex sign and one that has long been maligned and misunderstood. It is symbolized by several creatures which reflect various stages of its evolution. The first and most obvious symbol is the stinging scorpion, after which Scorpio is named. The second is the snake which sheds its entire skin to allow for new growth. Its third symbol is the eagle of freedom, or alternately, the legendary phoenix rising from the ashes.

At some point in every Scorpio's life, there is at least one major and symbolic death of the personality that occurs which makes way for a new expression to emerge. The person could be young, middle aged or elderly when it hits, and this symbolic death could occur for any number of reasons. Most Scorpios experience them many times in their lives. One could experience a gradual and natural shift from one specific mode of operation to another. This shift could be the result of leaving an old career that one had always identified with, or moving to another state or country different than one has always lived in, or a divorce.

Negatively, one could be catapulted into a new direction via shock, trauma and grief. These shocks and jolts to the personality may involve common occurrences or more extreme experiences such as drug trips, personal assaults or other ego-shattering events. This sign represents sex, death, transformation and all of the aspects of life that are fearsome and taboo.

Scorpio is a fixed water sign, so major life changes are not taken lightly. It is the second of the three feminine water signs and was ruled originally by the planet Mars. Later, it came to identified with Pluto, the small but potent planet named after the God of the Underworld. It has been said that Pluto is a higher or intensified expression of Mars, as both of them can be forceful in nature. The passionate aspects of Mars are very much alive in Scorpio, as are the transformative elements of Pluto.

As a general rule, Scorpios are physically strong but emotionally sensitive. Their very strong body chemistry tends to excite and attract others on unconscious levels. Like Aries, also ruled by Mars, they are also known for having a high libido. Whether or not they act out their sexual impulse, they are also likely to channel or sublimate it some other way, such as through artistic mediums.

By nature, Scorpios are known to be reserved although many of them are quite outgoing and talkative on the surface. If you observe closely, however, the things they talk about are broad in context, and often allow them to wheedle the secrets out of other people while they actually reveal very little about themselves. They are sharply intuitive and always gathering information about the things and people in their environment, storing it away in their mental filing cabinets for some future use.

There are generally three types of Scorpios, counting those who fluctuate in behavior between two basic types. In short, one is the very sweet and conservative type, and the other is overpowering and intense. Both tend to be emotionally sensitive and physically sensual. One may be the angel, seer or medicine man or woman who is able to see deep into the souls of others, to facilitate healing and release.

Whether or not they are spiritually oriented, they use their knowledge for the good of others. They may be exceptionally creative, using their gift of perception to translate the world around them into powerful works of art, to serve as catalysts or to maintain a healing oasis. The Scorpio operating from their lower nature may be vindictive, jealous, cunning and opportunistic. They use the secrets of others against them when least expected and they can be relentless in their pursuit of revenge against those they feel have done them wrong.

Due to powerful inner reserves of energy Scorpio has the capacity for both large-scale healing and destruction. This is one reason why those of this sign can make great surgeons. Destruction may be harmful or beneficial and even necessary in certain situations.

These people have a fixed disposition with strong likes and dislikes, and they tend to make solid decisions in general. They tend to take an immediate position on something of importance to them, whether it's good or bad. They have instinctual responses to people and events which can make others around them feel uncomfortable at times. They are extremely passionate about what they believe in.

Scorpio and the Second Level of Permeation

The mode of psychic attack and self-defense used by Scorpio is that of permeation. This is the second level of permeation which is even more insidious than the first one, assigned to the sign of Cancer, in the way that it affects others. Permeation is generally a silent type of action which goes unseen and unheard in many cases. It is watery, invisible, and reaches far and wide. Scorpio's permeating presence contains within it a certain type of force similar to that of Aries. It is assertive in its methods of occupying space.

Because Scorpio is a fixed sign its watery permeation can sometimes lead to stagnation and infection. This is when boundaries and purification become necessary. For some this would mean general space clearing, for some it would mean removing harmful spiritual attachments, and for others it would mean literal physical detoxification.

Psychic Protection Against Scorpio

A psychic attack by Scorpio can linger for a very long time. It stings bitterly, in many cases leaving an energetic mark or infection. They know where your weaknesses lie and that is exactly where they strike. There is a noticeable streak of sadism in those who would attack others. Scorpio on his or her worst behavior exemplifies the classic description of the "psychic vampire". This is a person who extracts energy from others by manipulating their emotions. They can be brooding, envious or even psychotic. They can be needy, always with some problem or habit that becomes everybody else's problem too because they need more than anybody can ever give them. These types of behavior are extremely toxic and can do immense damage to individuals and to large groups. They may use covert methods of gaining control over others. If they are operating from their lower drives, they will spy and eavesdrop so that they can use what they know about a person or situation to their own advantage. They are also not above lying, stealing or cheating if it serves their purpose.

Scorpio's sometimes enormous displays of jealousy are one of their most widely discussed behaviors. Not every Scorpio acts in this way, but in those who do, there is no mistake about what is taking place. They can be very possessive and have a double standard when it comes to fidelity. They may demand it from a partner while secretly being unfaithful to their significant others. Those with integrity are extremely loyal and devoted. They use what they know and intuit in order to help others instead of trying to tear them down.

Scorpios are often projected upon and may carry a lot of subconscious guilt from childhood, which is sad and difficult for many of them to overcome. They frequently feel taken for granted or misunderstood and it's not their fault. Those who have not taken an honest enough look into their motivations can be the worst projectors of all kinds of muck that lurks in the shadows of their own bad secret behavior as well as those around them. They may point the finger at someone else instead of taking responsibility for what they did wrong, or they may actually project their own base flaws onto others. If they repeatedly choose this route of coping with an inner sense of inadequacy it becomes a pattern, and theirs is one of the most bitter life lessons of all: being forced to accept that they are the ones who are responsible for destroying relationships and burning bridges. Loneliness is the end result.

Because of Scorpio's capacity to bleed into others' space in such a subtle and intrusive manner it may become very important to establish both physical and psychic boundaries when these behaviors arise. To purify the infection and toxins they have left behind may take a greater length of time than seems fair and a lot of elbow grease to scrub away, figuratively speaking. Some of their habits can also literally be filthy, leaving traces of scum and dirt in the most unexpected places. It could, of course, be the reverse situation, in that Scorpio is the one cleaning everyone else's messes.

The best way to avoid an attack from Scorpio is not to reveal too much about yourself to them unless you absolutely trust them, and they have proven themselves to be worthy of your friendship, time or energy. Guard your heart, privacy and personal possessions.

If Scorpio is deliberately attacking you through occult or psychic means, you will probably need powerful protection against them. I have found this to be the case for all of the fixed signs (Taurus, Leo, Scorpio, Aquarius – but Aquarius less so than the others) when they are engaged in the dark arts or otherwise very negative people who entrap others in their toxic energy. It can be harder and take longer to rid oneself of their influences. A lot of prayer, meditation, burning of white candles, and protective amulets are advised.

Psychic Protection for Scorpio

Those Scorpios with a strong sense of morality and respect would not dream of betraying your trust but instead do everything they can to protect you from harm. Actually, they would never so much as even step on an ant if they could help it. What makes them vulnerable to attack is ironically when they have not taken proper measures to protect their own hearts, plans or private property from the invasions of others. It's a strange thing that despite their strong intuition overall many of them wind up with partners of questionable character. They can be very giving, and it seems to be the case for many that at least once in their life when they fell in love with someone they later found out that the other person was not truly faithful or worthy of all that they had to offer. Where some of them also go wrong is when they confuse their fear and paranoia with psychic perception and make judgments or decisions that turn out to work against them.

Since they are often right in their assessments about people and situations, they may assume that they know what is going on and what is best for all involved. They need to frequently stand back and detach themselves from something they have become overly attached to being a certain away, whether positive or negative. Otherwise, due to their stubborn nature they can get themselves into a lot of needless trouble, heartache and disappointment with others.

Physically, this sign is associated with the reproductive organs and the function of elimination through the rectum. These are the areas where Scorpio tends to be most vulnerable to malaise or attack. It is important that they protect all of the delicate areas of their body and skin overall to keep them functioning well. When it comes to sex, they should be very careful to make sure to take protective measures. They would also do well to make sure that their partner is truly compatible with them on an energy level because otherwise they may develop an unhealthy attachment that turns out to be the cause of their unhappiness.

Those of this sign may either be obsessed with cleanliness, somewhat like Virgo, or conversely, they can let many things go for too long.

Like their sister water sign Cancer, they can become collectors of clutter. Cancer's clutter is for security and sentimental reasons, but Scorpio's is often to feel a certain measure of control within their environment, or in some cases to make a home décor fashion statement. The clutter is comprised of many beautiful, interesting and useful things which are not necessarily well categorized.

Because of their intense emotional nature, Scorpio can evoke equally intense emotions and reactions in others. Others may retaliate against Scorpio because they've been extremely triggered by them. The reasons tend to trace back to something that is intangible, invisible or subconscious. Some self-reflection could be necessary when this happens, for the reason that Scorpio might not have thought things through enough to realize what they were getting themselves into.

In order to protect themselves physically and psychically, Scorpio craves deep interactions with nature and those who are closest to them. When they learn about a healing tool or scientific discovery, they may take a great interest in using it to their utmost abilities. When something bad happens in their community they want to know what's really going on, so rather than reach for a radio or the local paper they are more likely to reach for a pair of binoculars or a drone. They might ask the neighbor what they know. If they're more attuned to psychic currents they'll skip all that stuff and go straight into remote viewing.

Scorpio may benefit from intense weightlifting, yogic workouts, bicycling and forms of exercise such as Pilates and belly dancing that focus on the lower torso, hips, genital region and spine. They should remember to detoxify both their emotions and bodies regularly with herbs and other methods. Lightly salted baths with essential oils, steam rooms, and infrared saunas may be effective methods of purification for them.

Scorpio and Psychic Purification

Scorpio teaches us the importance of staying vigilant when we need to and heeding our intuition in general which is constantly speaking to us whether we pay attention or not. Scorpio shows us how to set our priorities straight by reminding us how fragile life is and that it should not go to waste. Disinterested in small talk and frivolous matters Scorpio shows us how to stay aligned with a greater sense of purpose in life. Because of its emphasis on transformation this sign reminds us that physical life and life as we know it is transitory and will be replaced by some other thing or some other state of being. We learn from Scorpio how to purify ourselves, surroundings and our psyches on the deepest levels of being instead of just skimming the surface or using metaphorical band-aids. Getting to the root cause of a problem is the only way to truly solve it. Last but not least, Scorpio models for us the importance of wisely directing our sexuality, also known as our vital essence. We were conceived by it and with conscious effort may direct it into avenues for creative expression, healing and manifestation.

Sagittarius

Sagittarius is the ninth sign of the Zodiac, blazing forth with bright intensity and light, ready for anything that life throws its way. It is the third mutable sign and the third out of three fire signs. This is the one that naturally deflects many types of psychic attack due to a generally carefree and optimistic attitude.

The Sun transits Sagittarius from November 21 to December 21. This sign represents the mental stage of development associated with that period of time that leads us toward the so-called golden years. At this point, as long as we have not fallen ill or succumbed to other misfortunes we still have energy to move about and may even be at our ultimate peak.

We no longer feel weighed down by emotional patterns and now we want to extract whatever good things we can from life. Because we have learned so much from past experiences, we make wiser choices in life. We gain a new sense of mental and emotional freedom.

Sagittarius Symbolism and Wisdom

Sagittarius is a masculine sign ruled by the planet Jupiter. It is symbolized by the Archer and his arrow, pointing toward the heavens. The archer is a centaur – half-horse, half-man who is often associated with Chiron, the beloved healer of Greek mythology. This can explain both why those of this sign are often drawn to horses, large dogs and animals of all kinds, and why they have such an avid love for travel and freedom overall. Sagittarians generally have a strong physique and take an interest in sports or outdoor activities. They work hard but gravitate toward professions that allow them plenty of room to move around in. Many of them make highly skilled architects, artisans, and physicians. Due to their combined stamina, depth of perception and constant eagerness to learn, they make some of the most powerful and versatile healers of the zodiac.

The spontaneity, jovial nature and wisdom of Sagittarius natives has made it difficult for many astrologers to find fault in them. But as with every sign, their faults surely exist, of course in some more than others. One of these lies in the fact they are often so blunt in their speech, so matter-of-fact and flippant around certain subjects that others can easily feel hurt by their words. Belittling the problems of others is a common occurrence for many with this Sun sign.

On the other hand, their candor may put people at ease, because they are so open. Sagittarius does not take life's troubles too seriously and those of this sign are not even above making fun of themselves at times. They seldom hold grudges.

Sagittarius and the Third Level of Force

Sagittarius is the third fire sign that uses Force in both its method of attack and defense. This is third level force that motivates Sagittarius to explore distant horizons and to challenge themselves in many creative and physical pursuits. This is a tough sign, often perceived to be rough around the edges. Those with an emphasis of planets in Sagittarius are quickly able to find the humor in things that others get stuck in. They instead philosophize and look toward "the bigger picture" of how and why certain things happen the way that they do. Always eager for knowledge, their broad sense of understanding is often achieved through an auto-synthesis of facts and ideas stored in their subconscious mind, that serves as a bridge to their intuitive faculties. They know many things before they consciously know that they know. With Jupiter as their ruling planet, they can go overboard with any of their interests and activities, becoming fanatical about special diets or exercise routines, or simply their beliefs in general.

When angered, Sagittarius can respond swiftly, with aggression that seems out of proportion to what has been done or said. They are easily triggered but they transition quickly after the fireworks. Fast and furious, they have already moved on by the time the other has begun to recover from their reactions. The problem is no longer theirs but belongs to the person whom they may have unintentionally inflicted psychological pain upon.

Psychic Protection Against Sagittarius

Sagittarius is a highly intuitive sign, and although those born under it may see into you, they may not give regard to your sensitivities. They can say things that seem careless, opinionated or rude. They seldom mean any harm but many of them lack a certain type of discretion and respect for the privacy of others. It can be difficult for them and their polar opposite sign, Gemini, to hold the secrets of others in confidence, because they don't have much of a filter on their thoughts to begin with. Knowing this, just be careful how much personal information you divulge in their company.

Because of Sagittarius's loftiness and grand sense of vision, they may look down on those who are not at their level and may either make callous remarks toward them or push them beyond their means. Ironically, this behavior tends to be amplified if they have any sort of religious background. The ideologies of religion and its terminologies are interjected into their outpouring of righteous reform, which can be a most obnoxious form of that neologism termed *virtue signaling*.

According to them, they are right and you are wrong, period. They know what they know, which in their book is more than you know. Argue with this and you'll be taken on a long literary journey filled with all of the explanations and anecdotes that prove your ineptitude on a given subject. They often have this in common with Aquarius. Latent within the disturbed sort of Sagittarian there lurks a very insidious form of spiritual narcissism and megalomania. The more they brag about how evolved they are, the more unstable their personality is likely to be. The spiritual downfall of Sagittarius occurs when spiteful intolerance replaces their higher sense of knowing and desire to be helpful to others.

Instead of acknowledging that everyone has different levels of ability, some high and some low, they may in the heat of the moment, without careful calculation, take that person and their entire situation superficially at face value. Quick, surface level judgments can compete with their otherwise strong intuitive abilities. It's also easy for them to brush off another person's problem as insignificant while they themselves are living in a state untouched by any of the other's concerns. Judgments and expectations are widely based on their own abilities and access, not those of others. If a person is struggling with something such as finances, they may blurt out: "Why don't you just go get a job?" The recipient who may in fact already have one is left to think sarcastically to themselves, "Brilliant. Gee, why didn't I think of that before?"

This kind of attitude is not only directed toward others but sometimes involves reckless actions that put their own lives at risk. They give the impression that they have some kind of death wish, but this is usually not on a conscious level. Their ruling Jupiter can cause them to overdo many things, both good and bad. They may be prone toward excess drinking, reckless driving, overwork, dangerous thrill seeking, and promiscuity.

In the act of creation Sagittarius can swiftly design and artfully piece things together, as if they are "channeling". In a bad mood, they can even more quickly and savagely take things apart. This ability of skillful precision that they possess can make them dangerous enemies. A psychic attack by Sagittarius is as swift as a ninja star wherever least expected, and cuts extremely deep.

If challenged mentally, they may become exceedingly agitated and difficult to be around. The irony in Sagittarius is that as much as they hate drama and pettiness in others, they can at times engage in much exaggeration and dramatization of their own problems. They can produce energy bursts resembling poltergeists that assume lives of their own to attack people at random. This is a result of their becoming unable to assume responsibility for their own rage, so it seems to detach from their own bodies, henceforth going after others.

One famous Sagittarius to name as an example of one who exhibited unexpected behavior was the Prime Minister of the UK, Winston Churchill (born on November 30, 1874), who remains a historical figure that is glorified rather than scrutinized. Churchill, along with U.S. president Franklin Roosevelt (an Aquarius) approved of the plan to bomb Germany, as a way of "breaking her will". The explosives wound up killing and injuring countless thousands of innocent people including women, children and animals as it caught them completely off guard in the middle of the night. The entrance to an office building called the Bracken House in London features an astrological clock with Churchill's face in the middle of it. It would make sense if Churchill was found to have used astrology.

Another Sagittarius that was known to act in sudden, unpredictable violence was a young Polish man named Karol Kot, born on December 18, 1946. He murdered random victims who were usually either children or the elderly. He enjoyed watching animals suffer and drank their blood. He was nicknamed the "Vampire of Krakow" and was executed at the age of twenty-one.

You can easily avoid conflict with a Sagittarius by understanding a fundamental difference in their approach to life from that of the other signs. They take their problems and themselves less heavily and this is what makes them impervious to many forms of suffering at the same time. They are passionate about life, self-expression and beauty and seek for ways to create and experience as much as they can.

One may be special to Sagittarius in a romantic sense, yet someone else could easily become equally special the next day. The trait of inconsistency is negated when Sagittarius has a fixed Ascendant or a strong focus in cardinal and fixed signs which tend to be more loyal overall, or simply when they have grown to dislike the wanton way of life. After a period of time some no longer find satisfaction in living so loosely. Once they find the right person to settle down with, they are extremely devoted to them.

Sagittarius is a strong sign both physically and mentally and can do a lot of damage when angry. What to do if you are in a situation in which such a person is threatening your well-being or livelihood? Leave or force them to leave if possible. Don't engage with them anymore. If you had a particularly bad encounter, it would be wise to immediately clear your space with the cleansing herbs that are available and compatible with you. These may include such herbs as sage, cedar, juniper, palo santo or pine resin. Place quartz crystal clusters at your window, bedside and close to a doorway. Wear Black Tourmaline which helps to deflect negativity instead of absorbing it. Stay active instead of sedentary in their presence if possible, so they cannot locate and hook into your weakness.

Psychic Protection for Sagittarius

Sagittarius is most vulnerable when they feel heart-broken by a family member or significant other. This is their one psychic weakness and seems contrary to their youthful and free-spirited nature. The truth is that many of them do long for that special someone to be with, and when the one they thought was true to them actually betrays them, it can really bring them down for a long time. This is when they often turn to things that will distract them such as alcohol, rebound dates and partying late at night. An excess of these things makes them even more vulnerable to stress and psychic attacks.

The body parts ruled by Sagittarius are the hips and thighs, which generally enable us to move forward and symbolize our ability to move through life's ups and downs, gaining new perspectives along the way that add to our wisdom as we age. When Sagittarius is moving too quickly, over-lifting or overdoing any type of activity they can become injured in either of these areas which thwarts their ability to move with ease. They can develop severe pain such as sciatica or in a worst-case scenario even become crippled. When their lower chakras (the energy stored in their lower organs and hips) are blocked, their attention floats on up toward their head area where they may spend the majority of their time. This also makes them vulnerable to outside influences.

Innately they know how to protect themselves from psychic intrusions, but when they're depressed, they will sometimes put themselves even more in harm's way, because strangely it can make them suddenly feel more alive. This means that ironically, although they are quite capable and strong enough to fight anything that comes their way, they are interested in the danger that it implies. Their thrill seeking can be admirable sometimes but cringe-worthy at other times.

Sagittarius usually does not need any help from others in defending themselves other than making a quick reality check and honest assessment of their situation. They are their own worst enemy and their own best friend, so ultimately, they get to decide when it's game over in a battle that they find themselves engaged in. They need space to move around in, preferably outdoors in a wild and colorful setting. They should remember to get adequate exercise and choose to eat foods that are invigorating instead of indulging in sugary, fatty and salty ones which can pack on the weight and lead to heart issues.

Sagittarians can get too heady and intellectual sometimes even though they are a fire sign. Grounding stones like Obsidian, Jasper, Agate, and Onyx can help them come back down to earth and settle into their bodies. Any of these may be good choices for them to wear during work hours. They can get very wrapped up in their projects and like the other fire signs have a tendency to neglect or push themselves to the max on a physical level. If they are always on the go, they might need to eat food that is more nutrient dense. Protein shakes can be helpful.

Sagittarius and Expanded Awareness

Sagittarius is self-sufficient by nature with a philosophical outlook on life. Those born under this sign are so interested in culture and adventures that they seldom sit around just thinking about their own unhappiness or miserable affairs. This means that even if they slip from time to time, they tend toward optimism overall.

Sagittarius teaches us to be less attached to our own precious problems and to find both the humor in life and the courage to do things that scare us just a little and make our hearts beat with anticipation. They lead by example how to move out of our comfort zones when we feel stuck, in order to experience different things and reach new horizons. We learn from this sign that there is spiritual protection in evolution and movement rather than in remaining static and comfortable. We learn to confront our fears head on and become stronger, wiser versions of ourselves.

Capricorn

As the tenth sign, Capricorn is a cardinal earth sign ruled by the planet Saturn, which is associated with life's many tests, challenges and limits as well as the kind of wisdom and experience that can only be gained over time. At the zenith of the Zodiac, Capricorn represents a turning point in consciousness that has completely shifted from personal concerns to learning the appropriate uses of power in the world. It is the sign that relates to authority in outer-world responsibilities.

The Sun transits this sign between December 21 and January 20, making the winter season in the Northern hemisphere. Opposite of lunar-ruled Cancer, which represents birth, entry and earthly life, Capricorn, with its stern Saturnian influence, represents death, exits and a portal to divinity. The age symbolism of Capricorn is general old age, the time period when we are no longer young or even youthful but have become elders in our families and community.

There is a marked stability in our presence and our position within society may be more respected than it ever was. Capricorn represents a position of leadership that each of us has the opportunity to express in life at some point.

Capricorn Symbolism and Power

Capricorn's symbol is the sea-goat, which incorporates both water and earth elements, signifying mastery over emotions in the reach toward goals and higher pursuits. The earthly goat is observed to climb steadily up the mountain, which is the way that those of this sign tend to move and undertake matters of importance to them. The goat grazes the edge of a steep cliff one moment and reaches the peak of the mountain the next, because he doesn't listen to the chattering of the wind. Focused on the matters at hand, Capricorn is pragmatic, hard-working and generally unmoved by emotional displays. Those of this sign can operate under enormous amounts of pressure that would crush others. They are not easily sidetracked but disciplined toward their chosen pursuits. Patience is one of the great keys to their success.

Capricorn can be a reliable friend or a formidable foe, no matter how rugged and scarred by the rigors of life. This sign reflects maturity and responsibility at best, but total ruthlessness at worst. Those born under it tend to make some kind of grand impression upon others with their natural leadership abilities. On a neutral level, they are the ones who keep things going with their sense of discipline, duty and ability to delegate tasks.

As status-seekers, they particularly enjoy the company of those who are of noble birth, associated with the law, are corporate business owners or are pioneers and leaders in their chosen field, including the literary arts and music. These people may wind up as their allies and this is because they have earned their deep trust.

Capricorn and the Third Level of Containment

This is the third earth sign that uses Containment as a method of psychic attack and self-defense. The first level is executed by Taurus, and includes such tactics as clutching, hoarding and keeping something locked into place. The second level of Containment is most often performed by Virgo and entails compartmentalization, separation, and sometimes overly obsessing over details that create unnecessary drama and limitations or curtail the free-flowing expression of others.

In Capricorn, the Containment may take the forms of order, precision and heightened focus, or conversely domination, dictatorship, censorship, in some cases punishment. There is a certain level of expertise latent within the sign that gives rise to an often rightful air of authority. Capricorns do not back down from a challenge with other authority figures when they see holes in performance and integrity. They use factual evidence as their arsenal, backing up the research and productivity of many years of experience, whether their own or those they themselves look up to in some way.

It is possible that the worst personalities falling under this sign completely cut off the power supply of another person or people, which could mean many different things at different times. Their reasons for cutting off the supply of another do not necessarily stem from cruelty but are sometimes due to fear or negligence. The total person, along with their personal history and legal records, must be taken into consideration in order to discern the reasons behind their words and actions.

Psychic Protection Against Capricorn

Psychic attack by those of this sign tends to have a lasting impact on the recipient. Capricorn has a unique ability to shut off emotion in many social situations, despite how emotionally unstable they may be behind closed doors. They can become heartless, so to speak, not feeling the least bit affected by their own meanness or by the reactions of others. There are plenty of Capricorns who do not act, nor would they ever act in this way because they have been through a lot and learned from the mistakes of others; they do not wish to inflict harm upon anyone. Some of them can actually be quite empathic as is their polar opposite sign Cancer, and they nurture those around them with both a loving and authoritative sense of care.

In psychic self-defense against Capricorn, it is important to know first their motivations toward you. If they are well-meaning but simply coarse in their manner of showing affection, there is less need to defend oneself and more of a need to appeal to their logic. In some situations, they neither wish you harm nor care for your welfare but consider you a useful source of energy or information for their purposes. These are the types you are much better off without, because they only wind up becoming leeches who refuse to pay you genuine respect.

With Capricorn, what you see is often exactly what you get. Many Capricorns naturally lean toward dark and forbidden topics. It is Capricorn and not Scorpio who stands out as the darkest among the so-called "dark lords and ladies". Like Scorpio, many of them also take an interest in the occult. An attack will be obvious for the most part, as anything done to bring another person down tends to involve some degree of domination. They can be given to large displays of ego and power. They may enjoy putting on airs in order to receive recognition, and paint themselves as the expert even when they are far from it. Just as Cancer has trouble concealing their personal discontent and inner woes, there is a self-righteous undercurrent that some Capricorns find impossible to hide from their facial expressions and voices. They simply cannot mask their true intentions, which are revealed sooner or later. One example of a cold-blooded Capricorn was the Chinese communist dictator, Mao Zedong, born on December 26, 1893. Countless millions died under his reign, due to his influence and cruelty.

Capricorn can be highly meticulous in the ways of planning and organization, leaving little to no room for failure. Attacks will always be well thought out and usually effective. There was a British physician named Harold Shipman who killed an estimated 250 victims under his care. He was a Capricorn, born January 14, 1946. He died in his prison cell by suicide, hanging himself close to his birth date on January 13, 2004.

This is a sign that adheres to old ways and traditions and looks mainly toward authority figures in the areas of personal interest. Preserving a set standard of rules and applying methods tried and true are prioritized over experimentation. One should know full well who they are dealing with here. Consider whether the fight is worth it or if the stakes are too high. In matters of war, psychic or otherwise, one ruled by this sign does not back down but calls forth all the resources at their disposal, gathering up all of the strength they have painstakingly gained over time in order to defeat their enemy, or their unfortunate victim.

A highly focused, no-nonsense approach is what enables them to survive their own hardships. Like all Cardinal signs, Capricorn is a warrior and as the final out of four, the most strategic. Due to sheer determination coupled with a highly refined form of intelligence the odds of any fight or struggle are often in their favor.

Like their sister earth sign, Virgo, the ultra-negative type of Capricorn can be quite intolerant and unforgiving regarding the deficiencies of others. They might see too many issues and problems in a person or situation that they are compelled to alter according to their own standards for excellence. Whoever does not meet their personal requirements for optimal performance will be scolded and reformed, if not completely replaced.

Because Capricorn is an earth sign you need earthy, physical protection against them even when their attacks come more from the psychic level. Their attack could be aimed at the structure of your security, which could mean your home base, your physical body, or your career. This would leave you vulnerable and open to all kinds of other intrusions. You will likely need a buffer that prevents them from penetrating your energy field, otherwise you could become seriously ill. Identify the precise method they are approaching you with. If it involves money, then seek a form of financial security that is untouchable by them. If it involves your home, then apply whatever you need to strengthen the security of your home base. In the extreme event that they are stalking you, consider a watch dog or acquiring a bodyguard for some duration of time. The best stone to protect against Capricorn's negativity is Goldsheen Obsidian, which is one of the strongest shields against bullies and those who seek domination over you.

Psychic Protection for Capricorn

Those of this sign are not usually superstitious or prone to attacks of a psychic nature even though they may be very drawn toward metaphysical subjects. They tend to ground and balance themselves through nature and different aspects of corporeal existence. If and when they do find themselves under attack by malignant astral or spiritual forces it may be because they overstepped their boundaries in some way, perhaps without even realizing it. They didn't realize that they marched, with such overconfidence and authority, into a domain that they knew very little about.

That is to say, their own attitude can backfire on them whether based on skepticism, egotism or some other combination of characteristics that elicit a strong reaction from others – others who may even be without physical form. In any case they could benefit from practices such as clearing their space with lighting incense, making grids using protective stones and making sure not to accumulate clutter.

Many Capricorns are capable of making great sacrifices, whether they be for future rewards or for the sake of their loved ones. They often possess the type of quiet focus that is necessary for long-term resullts. Work, power and prestige are very important to Capricorns, and they are deeply dedicated to whatever causes hold importance for them. Sometimes their focus on serious matters gives others the impression that they are cold and uncaring, although this may be far from true. Capricorn actually suffers from a sense of loneliness and alienation from having been misunderstood by family, friends and community. Others may attack them out of revenge, jealousy or sheer misunderstanding of things that Capricorn did or said a long time ago. They are most vulnerable to being attacked while on the job in their career or place of work, especially by authority figures and subordinates.

Due to the influence of Saturn, Capricorn has been known to get more than a little depressed from time to time, or even to sink into despair and a rather morose outlook on life. They can actually build too tall and too strong of a wall of protection around them that nobody else can enter at all. In that kind of situation, they need to learn how to loosen up a little bit and stop arguing with every kind thing that someone says about them or rejecting every gift offered because of their fear that it might be a bribe. They need to stand back and take another look at the other person for who they are, and consider that not everybody is out to get them.

Capricorns can be creatures of habit, locking themselves into routines that may or may not serve them well over long stretches of time. These routines could range from listening to the exact same album day after day to cooking the same meals week after week to visiting the same recreational park, in the same spot, on their days off. They become used to things being a certain way and when new ideas are presented to them, at first they might seem disinterested, because they already know what they like and what works for them. This is usually due to a slight note of caution and not resistance. A little bit of spontaneity goes a long way for them and can greatly uplift their spirits.

Capricorn does best when they are either the boss or able to work in a free-flowing and open environment, whether outdoors or in the privacy of their own home where they can manage their own hours. As employees, they are hard-working but have a way of either working their way to the top or becoming a highly endeared servant or team member. Still, they may find the need to stay on guard from possible traitors or those who would otherwise attempt to undermine their position. It is often tricky for them to find that balance between trusting certain people but staying on guard against others.

The body parts ruled by Capricorn are the knees and joints and these areas are their most vulnerable. They should be careful to avoid remaining sedentary, such as working at a desk for hours without pausing and properly stretching. What is especially detrimental to their health is when they habitually reach for sugary snacks which don't do any good for their teeth and gums. Their ruling planet Saturn rules the teeth. Keeping their circulation going through leisurely walks is beneficial for both their bodies and minds but they may need to be prodded into exercising. No matter what their physical ailments may be, their bodies can often take a lot more abuse than those of the rest of us. They may seem to age in reverse, becoming stronger and more youthful over time.

Capricorn and Focused Energy

Capricorn's influence helps narrow down our focus when we have become too scattered. It highlights a level of persistence combined with patience. A strict sense of order can be of great aid in getting "from point A to point Z", or exactly where one needs to be at the right time. This sign also helps with setting the appropriate boundaries that can be lacking in some of the other signs. In their highest expression, those of this sign model effective social conduct and energy conservation by avoiding a lot of small talk and frivolous activities.

Capricorn is courteous and kind but never excessively nice. They despise gossip and this teaches others to stop frittering away precious life force energy by engaging in it. Efficiency is prized over superficiality and variety. By walking their talk and gaining a clear sense of where they're heading, Capricorn encourages others to do the same.

Aquarius

Aquarius, the eleventh sign of the Zodiac is group-oriented, philanthropic and intellectual in its approach to life. It is the last of the four fixed signs and the third out of the three air signs. Being a masculine air sign with so much mental strength behind it, Aquarius can be the most detached of all when it comes to ordinary human emotions. That is not to say that they don't exist, but feelings are processed much differently here than they are in the preceding signs. They may in fact be first recognized with stark awareness, deeply felt and processed, and then, after being thoroughly analyzed and categorized for future reference, they are discharged and over, with alarming speed. At least when emotions are long-standing for Aquarius, the method of dealing with them is unusual when compared to others.

The Sun is in Aquarius between January 20 through February 18. This sign represents the stage of human development that comes in later years when we find we can get away with acting as weird as we want to be, and nobody gives us a hard time for it anymore. We may decide to dye our white hair hot pink and wear fuzzy yellow shoes. We say whatever we want despite the few people who raise their eyebrows or get offended. We've already lived for ourselves and our families and have hopefully pursued our dreams. We've paid our dues and by now are more concerned with humanitarian causes and the bigger picture. Aquarius represents that point we each eventually reach in which we wish to leave some kind of gift behind to generations after us, while also reserving for ourselves just a little piece of happiness that cannot be argued with or taken away from us.

Aquarius Symbolism and Eccentricity

Aquarius is symbolized by the Water Bearer, pouring life-giving water and spiritual sustenance into the world. The water washes away the weight of the past and beckons us toward the future. This is why the Aquarian is so futuristic and goal-oriented. Individuality, sovereignty and the love of freedom are the hallmarks of this sign. Rebellious and nonconformist, Aquarius is here to shake the status quo and carve new paths, making up its own rules along the way.

Known as the wild bohemian of the Zodiac, this is an intellectual air sign that is both drawn to group pursuits and causes, while being original in manners of dress, lifestyle and relating to others. Having the influence of both Saturn and Uranus provides them with very nuanced personalities. Though their methods of communication may seem odd to others they tend to have others' best interests at heart. To identify whether Saturn or Uranus is the predominant influence in Aquarius check to see which planet has the stronger influence in the natal chart. Either type can have spiritual inclinations, but the Saturnian type is traditional and more likely to be focused on earthly matters while the Uranian is more intuitive, artistic or concerned with technological trends.

This is an air sign with a water vessel as its symbol indicating fluidity, and yet those who were born under it can be icy, crystallized and set in their ways. They know exactly who they are in life and won't be molded by others. Nonetheless they are usually popular and well-liked overall.

Aquarius and the Third Level of Speech

Aquarius is the third air sign of the Zodiac, and the last one that uses speech as its primary methods of psychic attack and self-defense. The first level is associated with Gemini, the second with Libra. This third level of speech is the most opinionated and direct and can make the strongest impact. The intellect has become specialized and laser sharp. In a way that is similar to Sagittarius's communication method, Aquarius does not tend to filter words so sometimes the manner of speech comes across as shocking, strange or extreme. Information may be shared lovingly to benefit their community. Sometimes what Aquarius has to say comes across to others as harsh or TMI (too much information). They can be open books, literally sharing the story of their life as though holding up a diary for public consumption. They may express their views on world events with such conviction that others are left speechless, given much food for thought. At best, Aquarius uplifts and inspires their fellow humans, or aliens, as the case may be, to live life to the fullest. At worst, they are intolerant, rigid and intellectually snobbish, believing that they are helping others when actually they are imposing their will and beliefs onto them.

Justice is just as important to Aquarius as it is to their fellow air sign Libra but their approach to it is much more assertive overall. They are typically not interested in arguments but in dominance. Libra says, "I'm open to debate with you", whereas Aquarius says, "I know what's going on and I'll explain it to you." In some, this mentality leads to the acts of putting other people in check, as if they were the Fact Police. Theirs is the archetypal sign associated with street marches and fights for political causes. Aquarians may enjoy becoming involved in large social events in person or online. They are the ones who encourage others to just be themselves, even if that person is an outcast which they will adore. These are the ultimate "people-persons" who love to be part of something that is larger than themselves. Paradoxically, they don't encourage following the crowd but standing out as unique.

Their emotional nature is an enigma, as they may seem very open about their feelings, which fluctuate or swing from total vulnerability toward total self-control and stoicism, particularly when they are on a mission to accomplish something. They may invite close friends or colleagues to dive into sensitive caverns of their psyche where old memories surface and tears begin to flow...when suddenly, unexpectedly, at the drop of a hat they announce that......their phone is buzzing, they are late for an appointment and must pick up where they left off next time. Cheerio! Enjoy your evening! Carry on with dinner. Relax. Don't take life so seriously because before you know it, it's all over. And just what exactly did you do with your time here on planet earth?

Example of an Aquarian cliffhanger: "It was so intense when I met the brother I never knew that I had. We connected on a deep heart-to-heart level, shared everything with each other including grief over the early loss of our mother." You take a moment to acknowledge this incredible life experience that was shared between sobs. You want to ask questions but don't want to bombard them when they seem so delicate. You nod and share in the amazement of the human journey when suddenly Aquarius indicates that it's time for their daily supplement intake before they attend the board meeting at work, after which they have plans to meet up with the friend they just met two days ago at a local art exhibit. They thank you for caring so much. Kiss kiss, they'll catch up with you soon.

The mysterious thing about it is that it's just so genuine, all of it. Talk about living in the moment. Aquarians can be masters of the art of being present, but it's funny they are the ones who frequently leave you wondering, "What just happened?"

Psychic Protection Against Aquarius

Aquarius is known to be friendly by nature, but when unfriendly can so easily detach from their own immoral behavior. This means that cruel deeds can be performed while Aquarians remove themselves from any sense of guilt regarding the matters whatsoever. They can arrive at a curious state of apathy, not thinking at all about any ramifications that their actions will have on others or even themselves.

A psychic attack by Aquarius seems to come out of the blue, with no forewarning whatsoever. Often it comes in the form of a direct strike against the intelligence or dignity of the recipient. You might notice this similar thread in each of the fixed signs on their worst behavior, the tendency to bring shame and humiliation to their victims.

Their speech may imply that they know more than the other person, and that person is a victim who needs to do some research, figure themselves out or get their lives together. Aquarius seems to have all the answers and tools the other has been searching for. They seem to always know the causes behind the problems that plague humanity, noticing all kinds of imperfections the way that Virgo does, but being more pushy about telling people what to do.

This is a group-oriented sign so in some cases, their methods of bringing someone down involves crowds, a consensus vote, or an army of associates who have been convinced of the reality of some biased or outlandish claim. All the while they are hiding in the background, pretending to blend in somewhere, as if they're not participating in a take-down.

Aquarius is usually not the kind of sign that attacks directly or attacks one person specifically. They would be more likely to attack a group or an idea, or to engage in a group attack against another group. Their method is to stir the "group pot", so to speak, throwing something unexpected at people to see how they will react. Sometimes their intention is not at all to hurt or attack others, but the sheer force of their mental energy, engagement, and their open-book attitude can be overwhelming to certain individuals. One can often reason with Aquarius and let them know what one's stance is and limits are, and they will typically respect them. Emotions will need to be gotten out of the way though, because those won't work as incentives.

Their second ruling planet, Uranus corresponds to computers, the internet and modern technology which can be used for helpful or harmful purposes. The encroaching domination by artificial intelligence that has swiftly crept upon humanity in the twenty-first century is one of the most bizarre and destructive aspects of the lower nature of Aquarius. The irony is that this sign exemplifies all that is humanitarian, and yet without the heart and soul that makes one authentic; the trans-human or perfected clone has been stripped of all that makes him or her truly human. He or she is a soulless creature performing on autopilot, relying solely upon the most advanced forms of technology available to man without concern for physical or spiritual consequences. Aquarius generally likes to stay informed of the latest technological advancements and uses it to their advantage in many areas. In attack mode, this means using the internet to gain the upper hand in social situations. Those of this sign can make expert hackers.

Aquarius acting in aggression can border on or literally become inhumane. If they can separate themselves from their emotions, they separate themselves from caring and there is no limit to what they would be capable of as an abuser or killer. In such extreme situations they would likely have experienced dissociation early on in their life, possibly from some traumatic event. Serial killer Robert Hansen was an Aquarian, born February 15, 1939. He abducted, raped and murdered approximately seventeen women, hunting many of them down in the wilderness in Alaska. His first crime was burning down a school bus garage, for which he got arrested. This was said to be a form of revenge due to his unpopularity in high school.

Aquarius's relationship to time (Saturn) is often very unusual (Uranus) which means that their timing in many aspects of life is different, sometimes seeming to be out of sync with those around them. They may rise and retire long before or after others. They may have a knack for calling you when you're on your way out the door or have a million things to take care of at once, but as fate would have it, they're too busy to chat when you have all the time in the world. These people do not abide by normal clocks and human calendars but according to their own inner compass and rhythms. There's nothing wrong with that but when you know this about Aquarius you can minimize your chances of experiencing challenges and disappointments with them. Don't get your hopes up too high for things going a certain way but always leave room for the unexpected. This can be liberating if you're open to the experience.

An American movie called *Into the Wild* that came out in 2007 was based on a true story of a man named Christopher Johnson McCandless. This man served as a prime, though extreme example of an Aquarius going his own way, on his own watch, who despite his general love for his fellow humans increasingly sought to distance himself from society and immerse himself in nature. He wanted to live life on his own terms and to discover its meaning without indoctrination of any kind. Many times, he created bonds with others but then decided to leave them, exemplifying the Aquarian theme of non-attachment. He was born on February 12, 1968.

If you are being attacked on a psychic level by Aquarius there is also likely to be an invisible army coming after you, analogous to the Wicked Witch of the West's flying monkeys in the *Wizard of Oz*. Fortunately, these typically wind up being silly pests rather than actual threats to your well-being. They hold no power over you and that is what you need to recognize as you zap them out of your way with your clear intentions. You can use powerful herbal disinfectants throughout your home environment which discourage psychic attack. Spices such as garlic and chilis have been used since ancient times to repel psychic attacks, especially when numerous spirits or people are involved.

Psychic Protection for Aquarius

Aquarius often gets him or herself into trouble by association. What makes those of this sign somewhat vulnerable to psychic attack is their open-mindedness, which in itself is not a bad thing, but it can sometimes lead them into dangerous territory. They may be prone to becoming wrapped up in cults and certain wacky New Age ideologies, because these appeal to the Aquarian sense of equality and universal love. They are so friendly that they easily get involved with very shady characters who use them as a sort of cover up for their secret agendas against others, sometimes involving very large groups of people.

Aquarius suffers from psychic attack from very unusual sources and people. It is sometimes due to their own lack of discrimination, and because they are fond of so-called freaks of nature. There is no inherent harm in having a diversity of friends, but being so open can leave one vulnerable to attack because the more popular one becomes it's impossible to know the motivations of each admirer, follower, and friend. Many would be harmless, but there might be at least one, maybe two or three who are scheming and up to no good. Aquarius may suffer from the shocking consequences of placing trust in the wrong acquaintances.

The Aquarian suffers deeply from the harm or worry for their loved ones more than for themselves. By nature, these people are very tough and it takes a tremendous amount of force to take them down, despite how many physical problems they may have. Ironically, those who are closest to the Aquarius person often wind up getting more hurt than the Aquarian does. This illustrates how many forms of psychic attack against them are often either indirect or miss the target, instead falling on those closest in proximity. They are agonized by knowing their loved one was affected in any way. In some circumstances the harm was caused by them. Then they must come to recognize their own conduct as it has affected those around them.

Aquarius rules the ankles and bio-electrical system, and these are the areas where Aquarius may be most vulnerable to physical or psychic disturbances. They benefit from regular exercises that maintain circulation throughout their entire system.

Aquarius gains psychic protection by developing discrimination in their associations and friendships. They are generally popular but must guard against those who would take advantage of them or their loved ones. This goes to show that the general focus of these people is often humanitarian and broad in spectrum, stretching beyond their personal interests. Their responsibility is to a larger number of people than just their own biological family.

Aquarius and the Collective

Aquarius teaches us that we are not just islands unto ourselves but part of a vast family of sentient beings. They exhibit a sense of connection to friends and family in a way that is light-hearted and free. They can be open, outgoing and a bit outrageous all at once, showing us that life is not just for learning lessons but for seizing opportunities. Education becomes adventure. By taking our attention off our own lives and problems and placing it onto the world at large sometimes, we may gain incredible insights into human nature, and into the universe at large. With these insights we may grow in our understanding of our overall purpose here and come closer to fulfilling our divine destiny. This is what the sign of Aquarius can show us how to do.

Pisces

Pisces is the twelfth and last sign of the Zodiac, therefore is the mark of some form of completion in an evolutionary sense. It is the third out of three water signs and the fourth of the four mutable signs, ruled by Jupiter and the later-discovered planet Neptune. Due to its fluid nature, Pisces may be one of the most tricky signs of all to fully understand.

The Sun transits Pisces between February 19 and March 20, putting many of us in a dreamy and receptive state of mind. The stage of development that Pisces represents is the final stage of life itself, as we sense we are moving closer and closer toward what may jokingly be referred to as "God's waiting room", whether that means waiting for a prayer to be answered or for that inevitable ending that awaits us all. There is no exact age assigned to it, but suffice to say Pisces is the last stop before an entirely new cycle begins.

Here, we are finally ready to *let go*. There is far less attachment to people, things and ideas and there is a growing surrender to the great unknown. Important completions are made to the things, activities and people that we once identified with. Life becomes reflective, and for many of us, a lot more peaceful than it has ever been.

Pisces Symbolism and Spiritual Significance

As a feminine water sign Pisces' symbol is two fish, entwined in fluid movement. This is the sign of the poet and the mystic. Is the most associated with the spirit world, the archetype of Christ, and with what many have come to identify with the Eastern concept of karma, stemming from both past lives and present life actions. The ancient Ichthus symbol of two intersecting arcs was adopted by early Christians and has been referred to as the Jesus fish.

The motto of Pisces and its corresponding twelfth house has long been "service or suffering". Service in a general sense, appropriate to the person and situation at hand is considered the key to liberation from worldly strife. However, if one chooses the path of self-gratification or escapism, suffering is said to be the inevitable result. For this reason, many with planets in this sign are so sensitive to earthly problems that they may fall into addictive traps more easily than the others in a subconscious attempt to numb their pain or reunite with an imagined unseen world where all is beautiful and loving.

Pisces bears the burden of a great task, and one that they may or may not feel equipped to deal with in their lifetime. That is the task of clearing house spiritually. They inherently know there is ultimately so much more to release than to gain, so much more to unlearn than to learn and that by letting go of psychic weight or actual garbage the way is cleared for greater things to manifest. When Pisces succeeds in doing this, they become adept minimalists while paradoxically enjoying limitless wealth and abundance.

Pisces people often make great actors and actresses, models and musical performers. Their co- ruling planet Neptune allows them to adopt almost any form that they choose and to embody it completely. Jupiter was the original ruler of this sign, and the general sense of humor that this planet bestows can account for all those Pisceans who are natural born comedians. A few of them will be some of the funniest people you will ever meet. They'll have you rolling over, holding your aching sides and gasping for air. These are the folks who truly understand the meaning of the phrase that "life's a joke.". So why not laugh?

Pisces and the Third Level of Permeation

All water signs are emotional and sensitive on psychic levels. They are a representation of formlessness and all of the mystery and fear that it evokes. These signs and their corresponding houses are known as the most mystical in the Zodiac. While there is some truth to this, mysticism is not automatically implied when dealing with any of them. In the sign of Cancer, negative permeation can be reactive in nature, taking on such expressions as silent treatments, temper tantrums, crying wolf syndrome and guilt trips. In Scorpio, the second level of negative permeation becomes a bit more complex, taking on such expressions as hypnotism, domination, seduction, vampirism and mind games. 0In Pisces, there are no rules and no limitations whatsoever. Borders are dissolved and anything can happen, good or bad. Even the portals to other universes have widened and become more accessible, which means it's easier for humans to exit or entities to enter through, metaphorically or actually. It is not just non-physical entities that enter through these portals but other things invisible to much of humankind, including the invisible factors that cause illness.

Elusive, dreamy and often a bit seductive, Pisceans are some of the most soft and gentle souls among us. Many of them need to learn proper boundaries because they are too open, allowing others into their own space and in some cases bleeding into others' territories without their consent. This is not done in obvious but subtle ways, and they rarely mean any harm by it. This kind of behavior, if and when it exists, is usually a result of not having enough awareness of where their own mental and emotional space ends and another person's begins.

Also, they tend to slip in and out of spaces with the swiftness of sailfish, so that even those who enjoy their company may have a difficult time keeping them in their lives.

Psychic Protection Against Pisces

Pisceans tend to have the appearance of being innocent and pure, with sweet angelic faces. Although this may be an accurate depiction of the kind of person you're dealing with, in many cases it is a mere mask for their secret debauchery and devilish natures. An element of deception is common in this sign, but not always in conscious operation. This can take the form of all kinds of lies and fabrications, in various settings and toward different aims.

The sign of the fish is slippery, so it is not easy to pin them down or even to figure them out. Those with a strong Piscean influence are constant enigmas that others find endlessly fascinating. Sometimes a Pisces will lie simply to cover their back, because in their mind they either don't want to let someone down with the truth or they don't want to deal with the associated repercussions. Note that Libra and Pisces have much in common in this and other ways, with one major difference being that Libra has more of a tough edge and interest in justice being served.

Pisceans tend to be sensitive souls who frequently seek escape from the harsh aspects of earthly reality, including punishment for bad behavior, so it is interesting that prisons and asylums are associated with this sign. Their escapism can entail deceit and denial, to the point that they begin to believe their own fairy tales as facts. When upset, many Pisceans often show it through passive aggressiveness and underhanded criticism. Being upfront would mean they have to come to terms with their own emotions, and they might not feel equipped for that. In the worst-case scenario, who and what you are dealing with is not at all the person you are presented with but some other thing that has taken over the body vessel. This phenomenon can be observed in any of the three water signs when there is extreme imbalance. What leaves them particularly open for co-habitation by nasty forces is alcoholism and drug abuse, which is more prevalent in the signs of Scorpio and Pisces, and in Neptunian types, meaning those with a prominence of this planetary influence in their natal charts. Under the influence of alcohol or drugs their behavior would likely be unpredictable.

The Piscean soul is seldom vindictive or mean but when they fall under the influence of addictive substances their personalities can be masked or influenced by whatever the substance may be. If the substance is something such as marijuana the personality is likely to be docile but if the substance involves excess alcohol or hard drugs these people can seem completely taken over, and therefore exert a strong influence on those around them that can become quite unbearable. In other troublesome situations there is no substance abuse but a kind of psychic permeation that entails fits of crying or sulking or complaining bitterly about things they have no control over such as the state of the world. They may also cry over a feeling of extreme loneliness.

Finally, after so much stress to their delicate system, Pisces may vanish from a scene in which their presence was required in order to fulfill certain commitments or obligations. One example of this could be the father who leaves his wife and kids one day for a so-called business trip, never to return. They may appear to alienate others whose personal drama affects them too deeply, or they may just disappear without notice and reappear years later. The full scope of each situation must be taken into consideration because in some cases they have every right to remove themselves from what has become overly toxic to them. In other cases, they may be evading responsibilities.

To defend oneself against the Pisces who has lost control of their own behavior, first and foremost know that what you see is not necessarily what you get. There is usually an undercurrent, a deeper layer, a secret, a mask, or some kind of deception involved. They can frighten even themselves with what they are capable of. Because of this they will often be the first ones to run away from a difficult relationship. Because of their ability to easily penetrate the auric fields of others the wisest move is to stay as far away from them as you can, although distance will not necessarily protect you in a spiritual sense.

At their very worst, Pisces can be one of the most underhanded and dangerous signs of all when they have cast away their own moral compass in favor of sensual gratification or given themselves over to lower forces. All three water signs can be the most impressionable to psychic influences and statistics have shown that even Pisces is a common sign among serial killers. Among these Piscean criminals have been the infamous Aileen Wuornos, John Wayne Gacy, Randy Kraft, and Richard Ramirez, the "Night Stalker", to name a few. Studies shown on the website *ZodiacSign.com* revealed that forty percent out of about five hundred murderers on file were born under the three water signs. Earth sign Capricorn had the most victims (see Capricorn section for an example), and air sign Aquarius came in second. Other statistics seem to indicate that there are a large percentage of murderers born under the mutable signs.

If caught in some kind of psychic entanglement with a deeply disturbed Pisces, do not believe what they tell you. Intrigue is likely to be involved. File a restraining order if necessary.

You may wish to seek refuge somewhere far away where the attacker cannot track or reach you for a while. Do something to protect yourself spiritually whether it's a spell, lighting a church candle, asking God to intervene. Use anything you own that is imbued with spiritual grace to guide you out of harm's way, and even pray for your enemy to be delivered from ignorance and negativity so that they do not continue to bring harm to so many others.

Psychic Protection for Pisces

Known for their deeply sympathetic nature, Pisceans are known for being kind and receptive, often willing to sacrifice their own needs in order to help others. Martyrdom can be the cause of their own self-undoing. They can be the most passive sign of all when it comes to matters of conflict. At least that is the most common understanding of their subjective nature.

Although they may be agitated just like anyone else at being harmed or violated, they are much less likely to strike back. Unless there are other fiery signs, planets or placements involved they may not have any sort of drive to fight at all. This may be seen by some as desirable, but it has a downside in that it can cause them to be rather crisis prone and victimized often. Others may mistake their kindness for weakness, taking what they can to see how much they can get away with until finally one day…Pisces cannot tolerate being a doormat and decides to walk away.

In order to shield themselves properly, Pisces needs first to recognize when they are in danger, being used, or attacked. There are Pisceans who deceive and many more who unfortunately are the ones being deceived. Sometimes they are used for sex, other times for money, and yet other times for something that is much more obscure and yet valuable. Although they may not be addicted to substances, Pisces may find themselves trapped in a relationship with someone with strong addictions. They can be too trusting and project their goodness onto shady characters. They should especially guard against doing this in religious and cult-like settings for it is all too easy for some of them to place others on pedestals or simply to sympathize with them too much. Many false gurus and messiahs prey on the Piscean soul for they consider him or her to be naive, malleable and an abundant source of energy to draw upon for their "holy" causes.

Some Pisceans are surprisingly skeptical of the spiritual aspect of life and instead focus their idealism on family matters, artistic or even business pursuits. When their strictly mundane attempts at achieving harmony, perfection and their concept of unity fail, they may be overcome with disappointment and sadness.

Pisces is a sign that especially can be vulnerable to psychic attack and intrusion when they are under the influence of alcohol or psychotropic drugs. They should take the necessary precautions to their psychic integrity by making sure they are in a friendly environment before ingesting mind-altering substances. The body part ruled by Pisces is the feet, and it is their feet that may become swollen or injured when they find themselves moving or walking in dangerous territory. It also co-rules the lymphatic system along with Cancer which helps carry toxins and waste out of the body.

It's not that Pisces is sickly by nature, but that their vitality often seems poured into a certain avenue, be it work or play, that leaves them feeling tired and sluggish the rest of the time. Their ruling planet Jupiter expands their senses while the influence of their co-ruler Neptune automatically leaves them open to forces and energies that they may or may not understand. They may be easily taken over by emotion and may seem to burst into tears at the slightest trigger.

Those of this sign tend to envision a world where everybody gets along, and like the nurturing Cancer or peace-loving Libra can be far too generous and forgiving toward those who don't necessarily deserve such treatment or reciprocate the favor. Also, they may expect other people to just patch things up in certain situations where a temporary burst of anger and healthy distancing would be perfectly justified and even necessary for survival.

Their tendency toward martyrdom may lead toward codependent relationships and a sort of Stockholm syndrome with those who either take advantage of them or take them for granted. Instead of "turning the other cheek" some of them need to learn how to stand up and set things straight by being honest about how they feel. Pisces is not a fighter, but this does not mean they shouldn't stand up for themselves. They need to understand their own worth, finding a healthy sense of ego balance instead of just trying to love and forgive all the time. Otherwise, there will be no *authentic* love or forgiveness in their life.

They should be careful about what they eat in general, as their systems can be extra sensitive to what they take in. Whether the cause for discomfort is physical, emotional, mental or spiritual, Pisces is a sign that generally responds well to vibrational medicines such as homeopathy, sound healing, flower essences, Reiki, and certain crystals and gems. They might also gravitate to natural remedies and herbology.

Pisces and the Great Infinite

Pisces reminds us that we are more interconnected than we realize, by heightening the experiences of cosmic signs and synchronicities, telepathy, shared dreams and other invisible aspects of our existence. No other sign so perfectly exemplifies the meaning of universal love more than this one. Pisces also reminds us to trust our intuition and keep up our energetic boundaries and hygiene. This is especially important for those whose primary mode of work is in the Neptunian realm, as it is for many types of healers, psychics and artists.

Healing and divination tools such as crystals and Tarot cards can accumulate heavy energy over time and should be cleansed regularly between uses for best results. Smoking herbs can be burned in the living and working environments or used in the form of essential oils in mist bottles and diffusers. Chanting and the use of chimes and bells can also be helpful in space clearing. Due to its spiritual focus Pisces is the sign that points us on the path Home, to the infinite source of life from which we all sprang.

Chapter 4

Decans of the Zodiac: The Three Temperaments of Each Sign

Each of the twelve signs govern 30 degrees out of the 360 degrees of the zodiac, and these sets of degrees are further divided into three divisions of ten degrees each. These three-part divisions are called the decans or decanates and they represent distinct ten-day sections of each sign. Each of the thirty-six decans has a planetary sub-ruler which falls under the basic rulership of that sign. These sections help to explain why so many people born under the same sign can have such radically different personalities while still maintaining some of the basic qualities of their sign.

The decans reveal various shades of temperaments latent within each sign. After that of the Sun sign, the decan of the Ascendant is considered to be the second most important decan of the natal chart. The decan of the chart ruler adds clarification to the interpretation of the chart as a whole. Every planet in a person's chart falls under a certain decan within a sign, and those should be taken into consideration according to the functions of each planet.

The degrees are actually more important than the dates, because each year there are a few slight fluctuations in the exact timing of the Sun's transits through certain signs. When someone is born on the cusp of a sign it means that they were born in the hours just before or after the Sun entered a new sign. They can only be born under one of the two signs and not both. On the day that the Sun enters Aries, which can take place on the 19th instead of the 20th, there will be those who were born under the last degree (in the last decan) of Pisces and others born later that day under zero degrees of Aries (in the first decan).

Different versions of the decans have evolved over time, including the Chaldean order, the Manilius order, and Ptolemaic order. Ancient Egyptians linked each of the decans with certain gods. Later Greek astrologers came up with their own interpretations of the decans. I tend to view them based on triplicity, in which each decan is linked with signs of the same element. This is the most modern way to use them. Furthermore, each decan also has a constellation connected with it, and within each of these there are fixed stars that bring out certain qualities in particular areas of a sign. I have opted for brevity here, due to the deep complexity of this topic.

Aries Decans

March 20 – 29 (0 -10 degrees) Mars

This decan is the most frank and straightforward of the three. There is often an appearance or countenance that is childlike and sweet while being super fiery in demeanor. There may be athletic abilities. Ambition, enthusiasm and energy levels run especially high.

March 30 – April 8 (10 - 20 degrees) Sun

Ego energies run high in a tug of war between pride and arrogance vs refinement and dignity. The person may actively seek balance in relationships or project outward with little self-awareness. This would depend on other factors in their chart and character overall. They enjoy pushing their own limits to see how far they can go and what they can accomplish.

April 9 – 19 (20 – 30 degrees) Jupiter

These tend to be the most philosophical of the three types and if there are other supporting factors in the native's birth chart, they may also have a strong spiritual orientation. Others can be arrogant and pushy in their views. They can be adventurous with a great love of the outdoors. Luck is often on their side.

Taurus Decans

April 20 – 30 (0 -10 degrees) Venus

Peaceful, beautiful, and elegant, Taurus's first decan produces the most docile of the three types. This type is artistic and has a love of luxury and growing things, from baby creatures to budding flowers. They may have a knack for gardening, cooking, interior design and other domestic activities. Some musical ability is indicated if they choose to develop it. There is a tendency to acquire things of value.

May 1 – 10 (10-20 degrees) Mercury

Curious, friendly and outgoing, those born under the second decan are very active and eclectic. They may have artistic talents or an appreciation for the arts. Due to their communication skills, they may become popular or find themselves on the go often. They don't like to stay in the same place for too long but need plenty of movement and adequate variety in their life to stay inspired.

May 11 – 20 (20 – 30 degrees) Saturn

The third decan is the most serious of the three, denoting a grounded, responsible, and stubborn nature. Those with this decan featured prominently in their chart can be highly creative and driven by their emotions and may have a particularly strong pull toward dark motifs. They can become successful business owners and entrepreneurs if that is their calling. They usually have hardships to overcome.

Gemini Decans

May 21 – May 31 (0 – 10 degrees) Mercury

This is a highly restless placement. Chatty, nervous and eager to explore the world of possibilities, natives are clever and outgoing. They always seem to be either doing things or speaking to others. They can make friends almost anywhere they go. Due to their worrisome natures, they may be the cause of their own exhaustion.

June 1 - June 11 (10 - 20 degrees) Venus

Those Geminis born under the second decan are ruled by Venus, bestowing gentleness and an artistic disposition. Whimsical and fun-loving, these types tend to be well liked and enjoy a certain degree of popularity. They may be business oriented or have a way with money that can make them very financially successful. Love and relationships are very important to them.

June 12 – 20 (20 – 30 degrees) Saturn/Uranus

Those born under the last decan of Gemini are highly intuitive and original in their thinking. They gravitate toward professions where they may take the lead as inventors, authors or teachers, and where they have room to breathe and move around at their own pace. They may have a very wide circle of friends and associates, and are often involved in social events of some kind.

Cancer Decans

June 21 – July 1 (0 – 10 degrees) Moon

The first decan of Cancer has the Moon as its ruler, which doubles the inherent lunar energy of this sign. Those born under it can be very nurturing and sensitive to the moods of others. They are generous and kind and would give another the sweater off their own back. They tend to live a lot in the past, reviewing life's major highlights. They are sometimes crabby and get lost in their emotions. Imaginative or artistic abilities tend to be strong.

July 2 – 11 (10- 20 degrees) Mars/Pluto

There is great intensity of the mind and character, bringing a lot more force to the personality than is present in the other two types. There is an inclination for involvement in mysticism, occult studies and research. Negatively, this one can be obsessive, stubborn and possessive. They have sharp intuitive abilities.

July 12 – 22 (20 – 30 degrees) Jupiter/Neptune

Here there is a highly diffused orientation to life and relationships, with a tendency to drift and dream. The native may be charitable or humanitarian in some way. They gain great enjoyment in connecting with like-minded others and experiencing a sense of community. They may be prone to pipe dreams and disappointment or suffer from relationships with addicts.

Leo Decans

July 23 – August 2 (0 – 10 degrees) Sun

The first decan of Leo is the most sunny of the three, and those born under it may be destined for the limelight. They desire to make a strong impression among peers and authority figures. Their ego seems easily bruised and they may need a lot of reassurance from their loved ones. Although not necessarily combative, being right can be important to them. They tend to be "open books" when it comes to their emotions, opinions and beliefs.

August 3 – 12 (10 – 20 degrees) Jupiter

The native is proud, bold and in some cases a bit conceited. They have a great sense of humor and a love of travel and adventure. They may move far from home when they find their dream job or partner. They are natural leaders who pour a lot of their energy into their work and creative endeavors. They possess great courage and are willing to take risks and to do many things in general that others would shy away from.

August 13 – 22 (20 – 30 degrees) Mars

The last decan of Leo is the most focused and business oriented out of the three. Passionate energy is successfully directed into work or creative pursuits. There may be anger to deal with that should be transmuted through exercise or something else. There may be, in some cases, violent disputes or legal difficulties due to their extreme reactions. Their love life may also be on the stormy side.

Virgo Decans

August 23 – September 2 (0 – 10 degrees) Mercury

The first decan is extra Mercurial, giving an abundance of nervous energy and a heightened intellect. There is a great deal of involvement with family members and a personable manner that attracts many friends and allies. Those of this decan may set higher standards than many people can live up to, which is a cause of stress for both the native and those with certain pressures being placed upon them.

September 3 – 12 (10- 20 degrees) Saturn

The second decan of Virgo is the most serious-minded of the three. Having The Sun or another emphasis here makes one very organized, disciplined and focused on their goals. They can be too hard on themselves when they feel that they have failed and some of them suffer from depression. There is great loyalty and responsibility for loved ones.

September 13 – 22 (20 – 30 degrees) Venus

The final decan of Virgo is ruled by Venus, which bestows of the gift of charm in many areas. The native is artistic, beauty-loving and fashionable. These people are often graceful and influential in their speech, writing or through music. There is often a gentleness in their demeanor.

Libra Decans

September 23 – October 2 (0 – 10 degrees) Venus

The first decan denotes an easy-going personality. Unless there are other planets or signs that indicate otherwise these people are not likely to attack or fight, although they may enjoy a friendly debate on occasion. They are devoted in love and generous by nature and have a strong artistic side. They may suffer from insecurity or a deep personal loss in early life.

October 3 – 12 (10 – 20 degrees) Saturn/Uranus

Although well-mannered and polite, natives can be very set in their ways and others may be frequently taken by surprise at the sharpness of their wit. They may be stubborn, eccentric and unpredictable, with a domineering streak. They can also be very helpful in a pragmatic way. They are natural and effective leaders.

October 14 – 22 (20 – 30 degrees) Mercury

The last decan reveals an academic type of mind which is less emotional and more intellectual in its approach to life and relationships. There may be gifts for speaking, writing and teaching that gain these people a wide audience. Information is constantly being sifted through and sought after. There is a strong determination to succeed. Their true feelings are often hidden from view.

Scorpio Decans

October 23 – November 2 (0 -10 degrees) Mars/Pluto

Emphasis in the first decan of Scorpio equips one with a hypnotic gaze, penetrating mind and formidable willpower. Although the passions run high there tends to be tremendous loyalty in love. One has a highly opinionated mindset that can lead to obsession, but a genuine search for truth may cause those with this influence to shift in some of their views over time.

November 3 – 12 (10 – 20 degrees) Jupiter/Neptune

The second decan of Scorpio is ruled by Neptune, giving the native a deep sensitivity to nuances, vibrations and the world of the unseen. Many of these types often become healers, counselors and therapists of some kind. They can be the most mystical but must guard against escapist tendencies.

November 13 – 22 (20 – 30 degrees) Moon

This can be a very social and magnetic decan. The psychic abilities are very pronounced but not always consciously utilized. There may be strong attachment to family and the native finds it difficult to leave the nest or let go of loved ones. Emotions can go up and down like a roller coaster and there may be both insecurity and reactivity to the emotions of others.

Sagittarius Decans

November 23 – December 2 (0 – 10 degrees) Jupiter

Natives are extremely fond of travel and adventure. There is a great thirst for knowledge, and one spends their entire life acquiring certain skills and adding to their repertoire of wisdom. Although warm-hearted and extremely generous toward their loved ones they can sometimes become scattered and have difficulties committing themselves in relationships.

December 3 – 12 (10 – 20 degrees) Mars

Personal drive and work ethics are very strong here. The person born under this decan is a straight shooter you can count on for an honest opinion. Try not to take offense. They also go the extra mile to let someone know how special and loved they are. Their bright personalities are an inspiration to others. Negatively they can be silent sufferers or sometimes misplace their anger.

December 13 – 22 (20 – 30 degrees) Sun

The last decan in Sagittarius is brimming with vitality and a sense of personal destiny. Whatever life throws this person's way, they are able to learn from it and laugh at it at some point. As with all decans of this sign, there is a love of travel, culture and adventure. They want to be noticed and credited for their achievements, and often they are.

Capricorn Decans

December 23 – January 2 (0 – 10 degrees) Saturn

The first decan of Capricorn gives strong discipline and a marked sense of ambition. The native is well-contained and responsible, functioning well in solitude. Some may perceive them as cold and unfeeling, but they are often actually warm and caring. They make powerful leaders who are content to work behind the scenes.

January 3 – 12 (10 – 20 degrees) Venus

There is a gentleness here that makes this person easy to approach. There is also a highly developed artistic or musical nature, and a great love of beauty. This is the quiet type who does not readily express their thoughts and opinions until they feel they will be well received. Loyalty to their family is very strong.

January 13 – 21 (20 – 30 degrees) Mercury

This Capricorn is quick moving and "thinks on their feet". The native is very hard-working but may go through many relationships, life changes, and travel before they settle down and reach their goals. They may have many friends and close ties with siblings, aunts and uncles. Due to the restless influence of Mercury, they can be the most talkative, or argumentative of the three types.

Aquarius Decans

January 22 - 29 (0 – 10 degrees) Saturn/Uranus

This is the mark of original thinking, strong intuition and quickness of wit. Those born under this decan have a strong independent nature that can cause them to appear detached in their close relationships. They tend to be very popular and influential, while finding others to be a constant source of fascination and entertainment. They may have strong interests in business, science and medicine.

January 30 – February 9 (10 – 20 degrees) Mercury

This person is a strong communicator, having an ability to influence large numbers of people. There is great perception, honesty and an ability to convey profound truths. The mind is eager for new knowledge. Being so outgoing and friendly, others find it easy to relate to them. Travel and foreign languages are strong interests.

February 10 – 18 (20 – 30 degrees) Venus

The third decan of Aquarius bestows tremendous charm on the native, who fluctuates between seeming very relaxed and extremely tense. They may have a flirtatious nature and impulsiveness in seeking after pleasures in general. Artistic expression may be favored over intellectual or business pursuits. Philanthropic work is favored more over time.

Pisces Decans

February 19 – 29 (0 – 10 degrees) Jupiter/Neptune

This is the most dreamy of the three decans, which stirs wistful desires and heightens the imagination. Those with this area highlighted can be very sensual with a love of romance and beauty. They may suffer from disappointments in love due to the influence of Neptune which casts a fog of illusion in some of their relationships. There is a strong artistic flair and a gentle and forgiving nature overall.

March 1 – 9 (10 – 20 degrees) Moon

Those born under this decan are highly perceptive, intuitive and empathic. Being so sensitive to the feelings of others they may go out of their way to help others in need. Old souls with the sense of having been here many times before, they tend to be loners and may have a difficult time finding their match. When they do, it's likely to be a soul-mate experience. They can be very charming and influential with the public.

March 9 – 20 (20 – 30 degrees) Mars/Pluto

This is the most emotionally intense and driven of the three decans. The raw power of feelings must find outlets for expression, often through music or the arts. There tends to be psychic ability or interest in occult subjects. The ability to truly love may be inhibited or universal in nature, given to the world at large. There is seldom an emotional in-between and the love life may alternate in extremes

Chapter 5

Emotional Reactivity Throughout the Zodiac: The Signs Acting Out

One reason why people so often fall prey to psychic attack is that either their past experiences or their emotional imbalances have created psychic holes through which others may enter and draw energy from them. The temperaments and predispositions for certain types of psychic attack can be likened to invisible statements or personal billboards within the body's electrical field. They are usually invisible to the naked eye but perceived by others on instinctual levels. Clairvoyants are able to view them as colors, patterns or areas of blockage. In addition, our body language and energy output speak volumes before our mouths have uttered a single word.

One person's aura may be sending out the signal of something akin to door sign that says, "do not disturb", that may push away potential customers or a romantic partner. The person may spend considerable time alone as a result and may or may not be happy about this. It's not always obvious or easy to understand the invisible messages that others carry, nor is it easy for many people to understand themselves. Another person may put out a non-verbal message that says "I'm happy to help! *Please*, let me help you solve *all* of your problems." They tend to draw to themselves others who are always struggling with some conundrum. Those others take more than they give and have a draining presence because they are always dumping onto the person who will listen. Why people carry this billboard around in their aura varies from case to case. Some feel as though they must atone for something bad they believed themselves to have done and that they owe it to humanity to constantly make up for it. It might sound crazy, but there are many people who carry this tragic complex in their psyche.

It seems easy enough to say to oneself that they have had enough and to remove a sign or burn it and display a new one that says, "I'm confident and deserve respect". Maybe that's all it takes for some people, and it works, mainly because they are ready for it to work. The trouble is that the conscious mind is not in charge of how our invisible messages are received by those around us. The deepest beliefs we hold in our subconscious form the invisible billboards that we cannot replace by any means of force whatsoever. Nothing less than genuine inner trust will do, which can take some time to develop, especially for wounded souls. I don't share in the notion made popular by the New Age movement that it's all easy as pie when you just focus on the positive...and suddenly, like winning the cosmic lotto, you'll be rich, fit as a fiddle, healed of all trauma, connected with your soul mate and have all of your material desires fulfilled. Some things just require effort on our part.

The Sun, Moon and Ascendant all represent some of the most obvious attributes of personal psychology, but none of them in and of themselves fully describe the way that people feel and who they truly are. Astrologers typically take into consideration the two major luminaries for some indications of this. As for our invisible billboards, door signs, flyers and other personal subconscious statements, look to the Ascendant, whatever planet may be close to it (Chapter 11, "The Ascendant and Descendant" explains this more) and the Dispositor of the planet should it be different from that of the sign of the Ascendant. It can help to explain why you tend to attract certain types of people and their responses to you on a regular basis. You gain a glimpse of what someone is putting out there along with the types of responses they generally tend to receive from others as a result.

Below is a list of emotional imbalances and coping mechanisms that have special relevance to certain signs. This does not mean that all people with the sign Aries in prominence are angry by nature, nor does it imply that all who were born under the sign of Pisces on the Ascendant are escapists. When looking for a validation of emotional patterns in your own birth chart, check first to see what kinds of aspects are being made with the Sun, the Moon, Ascendant, and the ruling planet of the Ascendant. This means taking the whole chart into consideration. The more challenging and numerous the aspects being made, the more likely it is that the negative emotional expressions of the signs are in effect.

Aries: Anger

Aries is brimming with energy that must find strong outlets for release. Sports, activities and professions with a bit of risk involved appeal to this sign. They prefer self-employment and having lots of breathing room in their chosen profession, and they actually enjoy problem-solving with exceeding vigor. In some of them there can be black and white thinking and a tendency toward making assumptions. There may not be enough context for Aries to arrive at the correct assessment of a situation unless they take the time to learn more. Irritation surfaces quickly but also disappears quickly and the same goes for impulsiveness. Their anger is not necessarily irrational but one of their lessons lies in refraining from quick, knee-jerk reactions. They should avoid driving or operating heavy machinery while upset, or overworking themselves when they are tired, because this is an accident-prone sign. Anger can be easily transmuted through different channels, but it cannot be suppressed, for held back for too long it could become a ticking time bomb. When loved ones are in need, Aries steps in without hesitation and enjoys playing a heroic role. Being so action-oriented they crave new experiences rather than predictable routines. With all of this physical energy being such a highlight, it may come as a surprise that it is actually a certain kind of mindset that ultimately distinguishes Aries from the rest of the signs. This is the mindset of openness and keen interest, tireless and true, that can last until their very last breath.

Taurus: Denial

Denial is not an emotion but a reaction to a situation in which one feels unable to cope with the emotions that may be brought up by recognizing something for what it truly is. In a highly charged negative situation that needs attention, Taurus may react by going into full-scale denial about it. This is the stubborn nature of the Bull. There may be too much of a threat imposed on either their internal belief system, their home base of security, or some other aspect of life that for them must remain constant at any cost. The further they resist the truth of their reality, the harder they can be hit by it later on, and for a fixed earth sign the effect of this could be absolutely devastating on a number of levels. When the pressure is on and they must act, they are capable of making great strides in matters of importance to them but there is also the possibility that they begin to flounder, feeling at a loss regarding their situation or cause. Though procrastination can be their undoing, Taurus must act upon their own intuition and inspiration, rather than being prodded by outside people or forces. They simply cannot be rushed. Stinginess arises when the fear of certain needs not being met takes over. Prioritizing luxury, beauty and monetary gain can become forms of distraction if underlying problems are allowed to proliferate, as would a destructive kind of fungus. As they come to terms with what is not working, they take charge of their life in a way that greatly inspires others. Taurus can be very demonstrative in their affections but, like Libra also ruled by Venus, should avoid excess so as not to come across as insincere.

Gemini: Scatteredness

Gemini is mutable, mental, and communicative. Alertness and vigilance are its keynotes. Due to its airy nature those of this sign can experience difficulty in settling down in every sense of the word. They are highly energized beings who zip here and there, mentally or physically in a matter of seconds, bringing delight and wonderment as they go along. This talent can be fascinating to behold, but dizzying as well. They often find themselves led by some internal pull toward discovery, or at times the crossroads of terrifying uncertainty. When they feel torn in too many directions, they finally slow down, briefly. It is impossible keep up with Gemini's pace because this is a sign that can barely keep up with itself, so just enjoy their company while you can. Their mind is often miles ahead of their body, which tends to move quickly as well with jerks, twitches, bumps, leaps and bounds. Restlessness or boredom can sometimes cause clumsiness. Multitasking is so tempting for Gemini, but as good as they believe themselves to be at it can result in different types of mental states such as confusion, over-exertion, and an overall mess. They find relief when they have something to focus on, especially if it involves dexterity, writing or speech. Some of them seek too much outer validation among their peers or family members, and just need to be themselves no matter the consequences.

Cancer: Insecurity

Cancer is a complex sign with a composition that is both as enduring as a wall made of stone and as delicate and easy to dissolve as a flower. This paradox is part of what makes life so deeply enigmatic for the Moon Child. Their heart forever holds the history and the poetry of their past, which may be extremely beautiful, or entrenched in too much pain, loss and betrayal. Sensitivities are high, which can be favorable in some instances. They usually do not forget the especially good and bad things that have happened to them, and for some Cancerians, it is their grief that seems to outweigh their happy memories. This tendency can certainly be transmuted through artistic or mystical means, but for those who live without these outlets of expression, a sense of gloom and general defensiveness seems to pervade intimate relationships. It is not wrong to sit in sorrow, as all of us at some point will experience a loss for which to grieve. Cancer may have a specific need to shift out of the drawn-out paralysis of the grieving process and to live their life without so many self-imposed limitations. Cancer's phobias can be crippling in an emotional sense, causing discontent, codependency or neediness. Body movement is helpful for them because the longer they sit, the longer their emotions tend to stew. They benefit from outdoor activities such as gardening and camping, especially near large bodies of water. They can release one insecurity at a time by taking small but frequent leaps of faith. These small steps and the successes that follow begin to assure them of truth of the Shakespearean adage, "The world is your oyster."

Leo: Frustration

Leo is a dignified sign, and has a specific set of standards for both personal performance and treatment from others. At the very least, Leo wants to be granted the same level of respect they have given to others. When their expectations are not being met, there at first arises small disappointment, but eventually, a tremendous, all-consuming frustration. There is a mission to fulfill and when other things or people get in the way of that mission, you will see Leo's not-so-sunny side in full view. You will hear the growls of this regal cat in no uncertain terms. This sign is direct and tells things like they are even when the truth hurts. They will at least state things as they see them and as they believe them to be. Their wordy explosions can be overbearing. Still, Leo may feel that things are unresolved even after they have spoken. They may need additional time and space to be able to vent, to let off steam and to discharge pent up emotions that have accumulated over time. It's more of an ideal situation if this can be done through work or any of the arts instead of unleashing onto inanimate objects of value. Heart-centered Leo hates to be the bad guy or girl or to be seen as less than kind, and always regrets when they have lost control of their tempers in some way. After all, they take pride in their essentially refined nature. For some, frustration is internalized instead of outwardly expressed and in these situations, there is the danger of depression setting in, unless they find some other way to relieve themselves of tension. Speaking to a therapist can be helpful.

Virgo: Dissatisfaction

Along with Gemini who shares the same ruling planet, Mercury, Virgo can struggle with immense anxiety, but for very different reasons. Virgo is both detail-oriented and service oriented and can also be somewhat of a perfectionist at times. Both small and great things are accomplished by them, and none in a careless way. A labor of love is sculpted, chiseled away at and combed through anywhere from hours to years before Virgo feels it is ready to present to others. It has been tended to in a meticulous manner, to the degree that when there is perceived failure, collapse, or results other than those intended, Virgo may experience an acute and extreme form of dissatisfaction. They find it hard to forgive themselves. They might be tempted to do away with everything they've ever done along these lines, because nothing is good enough, and especially because that *one thing* wasn't good enough! The saying "throwing the baby out with the bathwater" has symbolic relevance here. The Virgo who is unsatisfied with the cards that have been dealt to them, or the cake that didn't properly rise in the oven, or the little scratch on the new car, or what So-and-So said on the phone the other day, is convinced of something that doesn't exist, which is human perfection. More specifically they are convinced they should be able to constantly exhibit this trait no matter what, which could possibly be a carry-over of Leo's extra high standards. Positive mantras and affirmations of gratitude can be of assistance in helping Virgo to relax and attune to their finer qualities.

Libra: Overstimulation

Libra is known as the peacemaker, sitting on the fence between two sides of an issue, ever weighing and seeking balance, equilibrium and poise. Although endowed with a marked intelligence, this is not by nature a physically robust sign. Since life tends to throw a lot of different things at all of us, both good and bad, Libra may shut down when overwhelmed by the mad rush. A minor choice to make along the way is but a hiccup, but when faced with a major decision, new and gnarly government mandates, or the inevitable results of human error along with ineptitude, stress levels can skyrocket. Libra is the one in the crowd gulping and exclaiming that this is all just too much and demanding for it to stop. They always find injustice to be unacceptable, whatever the scale. Conflicts, problems, and lots of anything can at some point become unbearable to them. There can also be too much of a focus on petty issues and a need to stand back to assess the whole picture. To some Librans, life is like a roller coaster that never seems to end and makes them more and more queasy as the wheels continue to turn. They need to learn how to get a grip, specifically on their priorities in the moment, not falling too far behind or getting too far ahead of themselves with all the possibilities in the universe. Strength is gained by trusting in their own intuition and decisions instead of remaining trapped in a nauseating state of vacillation. Only then will they find relief from that feeling that everything is caving in on them. Only then can they be as helpful as they have been trying so hard to be toward others, while also being able to enjoy life themselves.

Scorpio: Vindictiveness

Scorpios have always had such a negative stigma placed on them, when they can actually be some of the most caring people you'll ever meet. As a water sign, Scorpio feels deeply and carries much internally that is not always obvious on the surface. Oftentimes, they see clearly through appearances. Those who operate from the lower expressions of this sign are notorious for zeroing in on the weaknesses, insecurities and vulnerabilities in others in order to manipulate or blackmail them. These are the Scorpios who cunningly win the trust of others, collect their personal data, and observe where they appear to fall short, only to later use this combination of trust and information against them. One thing that many a Scorpio also carry around is a long-lasting, profound, nearly immobilizing sense of guilt. The guilt is so embedded in their subconscious mind that they may even have forgotten why they had it in the first place. It can be existential in nature having no purpose other than to weigh down the soul. It may well be due to something they have done wrong and live to regret for the rest of their lives. Conversely, it could rather be the type of guilt that Scorpio carries collectively for all of the sins of the Zodiac, for all earthly crimes, both seen and hidden, known and unknown throughout time. What a burden! When they are able to transform guilt, they are capable of nearly anything they set out to do as they become the best version of themselves. When they are able to transform their pain and despair into inspiration they may become wonderful healers, role models and forces for good in the world.

Sagittarius: Deflection

Sagittarius is the sign that reaches toward the heavens, seeking higher ground and universal knowledge for itself and to share with others. The thoughts both entertain and encompass very large topics. Being so outwardly focused, it is also the sign that tends to have the most difficulty looking at itself in the mirror. Although Sagittarius can indeed laugh at themselves, they tend to have a harder time with deep introspection unless other factors in their natal chart indicate otherwise. They might try to gloss over problems, avoid their inner turmoil with distractions, or in some cases deflect personal responsibility that they had in bringing harm to someone. If they are never wrong in their own eyes, it was the other person's fault or that of some other person who is not present in order to defend their own position. Their opposite sign Gemini can exhibit these similar tendencies except that they explain their own wrongdoings as misunderstood acts of kindness. In contrast, Sagittarius may literally disappear, off into the distance, as far as possible from the situation in order to avoid owning up to either their mistakes, or their interpersonal discomforts. This works temporarily, but they cannot escape the intensity of their emotions or the consequences of their actions forever. At some point the same lessons and issues will resurface sometimes with new and different people in their life. At first they may ask, "Why does this keep happening to me?!" Then they will have to decide whether they are to take responsibility or continue to deflect to their heart's discontent.

Capricorn: Bitterness

Capricorn is known for being forthright, dedicated, and responsible. Emotion exists in this sign but too often gets shoved in the basement in favor of meeting personal ambitions or obligations. There may be hidden fears of failure or even of success. Materialism is an issue to be dealt with, whether Capricorn is in favor of or against it, as they recognize the importance of money. Capricorn loves deeply and can experience inner torment in ways they cannot even describe. Some may wear a hard shell of armor around their heart, just like their polar opposite sign Cancer uses a lot of protective gear for daily routines. They may be calm, quiet people who find difficulty in showing more than surface level responses to others. If they are not in touch with their feelings or decide to drown them in alcohol, Capricorn can grow heavy and somber in spirit. They may lock those feelings into a box and hide it where even they no longer have access. The bitterness they feel or express is not who they really are inside, but is the result of a disconnection from their true self. Their apparent need to keep up with personal appearances is not so much a form of vanity as it is a need to prevent others from seeing into their vulnerability. They may mask themselves behind fame, fortune, work, or some other external factor that keeps a distance between them and their inner reality. For some, there is simply a need to lighten up and enjoy life more because they deserve to. They have earned that right. Traveling tends to help them unwind.

Aquarius: Detachment

Aquarius is the sign of group orientation, networking and philanthropy. As an air sign, Aquarius can frequently feel cut off from certain types of people, and even certain types of emotions, as though their emotions were attached to a dial board from which they could choose from at whim. They greatly enjoy the sampling of various cultural styles, attitudes, vocations and more, whether or not they specialize in one area. An obvious or subtle form of detachment seems to separate many of them from the rest of the perceived herd. They are too cerebral to be getting caught up in complicated entanglements. If they do find themselves all tangled up, they use cerebral rather than emotional means of extrication. Although detachment can be a lifesaver in many instances, it can also be a show of ego, as in being too good for others. Group activity is a highlight for them but not necessarily in the traditional ways.

There are those who would invite the whole neighborhood over for a house party, and those who would lock their doors and mute their phones during the holidays, preferring to delve further into a good read or science project that they have been working on. What the latter Aquarian person may not realize is their impact on those who care for them. Tuning into their thoughtful and giving nature may prove to be healing and unifying in surprising ways. They can thrive in group settings as long as the others share similar goals and values to their own. They naturally take the lead and have much insight to offer.

Pisces: Disarray

Pisces is the sign associated with compassion, spirituality and liberation. It is also the sign of lost vagabonds, beloved martyrs and despised prisoners. Pisces has such a keen sensitivity to the horrors of the world, which is why it is the most notorious for turning to drugs or other forms of escapism. Pisces can *feel* so helpless and so utterly useless to society that all hope becomes lost in a whirlpool of alcohol, video games or some other trivial activity that produces nothing of tangible benefit in their lives. They perceive things very acutely, and without some kind of spiritual faith to lean on, the weight of the world can cause them to become nihilists. Intervals that include silence and solitude are beneficial to them, but if unhappy they may give up, throw in the towel, and just become a hermit without a cause. They do need to be around people, as they have so much to offer and exchange. Some may sacrifice their personal happiness to only serve others. Many Pisceans genuinely gain the greatest personal satisfaction in their service to humanity, and they devote their whole lives to this. When the going gets tough, a little bit of humor helps them go a long way. Innately, they are teachers whose most profound teachings are actually wordless. Pisces holds the key to salvation, if they but understand this. They can use it to unlock, unchain and unshackle themselves and others from pain and darkness and to reach wondrous new heights. They can be prolific artists, entertainers or business leaders. Some of them become the way-showers for humankind

Chapter 6

Self Defense Tools and the Zodiac – Correspondences and Perspectives

This chapter contains a list of the various kinds of tools and methods of self-defense linked to the signs. It also includes basic references to the planetary correspondences within each sign. The generational planets such as Uranus, Neptune, and Pluto are not included because they move so slowly through the zodiac, making their house placements more revealing in an individual's chart than the sign they occupy.

There is an old saying, "Weapons are instruments of ill omen, despised by the Way of Heaven. To use them only when unavoidable is the Way of Heaven."...
Yagyu Munenori, The Killing Sword – The Book of Family Traditions on the Art of War

Aries Self-Defense Tools – Guns, Knives, Sharp Objects

In a perfect world there would be no need for weapons of any kind for any reason, but this world is not perfect. There are weapons meant for hunting or to stop an attacker in their tracks. In some situations, knowing how to use a weapon for self-defense is a matter of life and death. Martial arts train and condition not only the body but the mind in a way that builds strength, immunity and confidence, even if there is never a need to use the methods learned. In fact, most masters of these arts pray that there is never such a need and only engage in combat as a last resort. It is better to be safe than sorry and know what to do should an emergency arise. Fitness training and calisthenics according to one's body type are other great alternatives that give similar results.

Aries placements reveal one's skill and comfort level with physical activities, as well possible interests in competition, military, and the martial arts. They highlight the initiator or warrior side in each of us. Aries is universally known as the go-getter sign.

- **Sun** – The natural warrior, full of life force energy and vitality. Intuitive and impulsive.
- **Moon** – Hidden anger rises to the surface. Energy needs outlets.
- **Mercury** – A quick, sometimes argumentative mind, direct in communication.
- **Venus** – Energetic, friendly and openly expressive. Makes an assertive and strong mate.
- **Mars** – Strong masculine drive, libido and energy. Can be blunt and forceful.
- **Jupiter** – Confident, outgoing, assertive and enterprising. A lively companion.
- **Saturn** – Fierce determination, strong independence. Sometimes too headstrong.
- **North Node** – Learning independence and self-motivation. Experimental nature.
- **South Node** – Self-defined, independent, and capable. Learning cooperation and teamwork.
- **AC** – Strong self-image projected into the world, likely to receive recognition. Quick reflexes.
- **IC** – Challenges and conflicts occur with family or home life. Needs a place to call one's own.
- **DC** – Strongly independent or chooses a strong and independent mate.
- **MC** – Natural leader, entrepreneur, statesman, politician.

Taurus Self-Defense Tools – Money, Assets, Resources

Money has been said to be the root of all evil, and while there may be some truth to this, in today's world, money is a means to be able to purchase and trade essential goods and services. Money may be invested in things that cause great harm or that educate, uplift and heal. It is not how much money someone has that determines their happiness and success in life but how they feel about how and where they have invested the money, time and energy that they do have. This generally has an effect on one's overall self-esteem. Money sometimes reveals how we are rewarded or punished by our own investments. It can be invested in things that protect us and those we care about. Likewise, things and assets can be a blessing or a curse. We either own our things or they grow into such a burden that they own us, taking an inordinate amount of time to organize, monitor, and haul around.

Taurus placements reveal where personal values are placed, and the ability to attain security both in a material sense and emotionally. May indicate business prowess or so-called luck when it comes to money and possessions. Taurus is strong but tries to avoid drama with others.

- **Sun** – Easy-going, dedicated, sensual and attractive. Very acquisitive.
- **Moon** – Artistic ability, focused on money and often fortunate in finances.
- **Mercury** – Business acumen. Slow in major decisions. Stubborn mentality.
- **Venus** – Affectionate, peace-loving, and capable of acquiring great wealth.

- **Mars** – Sensual, resilient, focused on work, money and practical matters.
- **Jupiter** – A desire for security and the ability to acquire wealth through hard work.
- **Saturn** – Tests and learning around self-esteem, personal security and possessions.
- **North Node** – Developing self-worth, building foundations. Inner and outer security.
- **South Node** – Skilled in manifesting. Seeks for stability. Learning to share.
- **AC** – Beautiful, durable, creative, hard-working but prefers a quiet occupation.
- **IC** – Sentimental with family heirlooms or gifts. A custodian and protector.
- **DC** – Dedicated to love and family. Can be stubborn and willful.
- **MC** – The skilled business owner, antique dealer, collector, or gardener.

Gemini Self-Defense Tools – Journals, Libraries, Telephones

Speech and journalism are frequently used to inform and excite readers, and to mislead and manipulate the masses. Words have been used since the beginning of their existence to educate and empower those who are willing to pay attention. When rightly directed, words can alert others of danger in time for them to be able to defend themselves. Communication is one of many things that make the world go around and without it life just wouldn't have evolved to the degree that it has for humanity. There would be no commerce as we know it, and people would not be enjoying any of the modern-day conveniences at our disposal. Information can be a powerful weapon or a form of protection, and as the saying goes, "Forewarned is forearmed."

Gemini placements reveal the way that one communicates, and especially the ways they have been influenced by or interact with family members and loved ones. They are an indication of wit and of mental operations. Gemini is a social sign and can become overly "involved" with others.

- **Sun** – Curious, communicative, and excitable. Youthful and entertaining.
- **Moon** – Intellectual and interested in many subjects. Can be nervous or high-strung.
- **Mercury** – Quick and clever with a keen ability to multi-task. Very communicative.
- **Venus** – Fun-loving, makes for a witty and intelligent mate, and attracted to intelligence.
- **Mars** – Very dexterous with hands, sharp wit, but prone to arguments and conflict.
- **Jupiter** – Super intelligent with a great sense of humor. Guard against scattering forces.
- **Saturn** – Tests and learning around early education. Mental challenges to overcome.
- **North Node** – Learning effective modes of communication. Inquisitive and interested in others.

- **South Node** – Short bursts of energy, need to look beyond the surface, overcome restlessness.
- **AC** – Friendly and talkative, youthful countenance and curious mind.
- **IC** – Much mental activity beneath the surface, restless inner nature.
- **DC** – Tends to choose space from partner, role changes in relationships.
- **MC** – Two or more sides to career or vocation, a variety of skills and worldly interests.

Cancer Self-Defense Tools – Armor, Shelter, Reservoirs

Sometimes the best self-defense is to lay low, stay hidden or inconspicuous so that predators do not notice us. Many animals do this automatically as certain features are built into their very physique that protect their bodies from harm. Depending on the circumstances, a place of refuge can be a home, a cave, some natural oasis or even a state of mind. It can mean silence. Traditionally, there have been many forms of armor used in shielding when battle has become inevitable. In a psychic sense, psychic shielding may take the form of developing a "thicker skin" and learning how to deflect harmful energies that would otherwise negatively impact one's health. Meditation can be helpful in this regard.

Cancer placements reveal early life influences and emotional attachments. They indicate areas of insecurity, where we seek refuge and how we go about nurturing ourselves and those we care deeply about. Cancer retreats from danger when threatened rather than plunges forward.

- **Sun** – Loyal, protective, and sympathetic. Family-oriented and sentimental.
- **Moon** – Attached to family or loved ones. Need for quietude and personal security.
- **Mercury** – Intuitive and emotional rather than logical communicator. Day-dreaming type.
- **Venus** – Protective of loved ones and affectionate. Often needs reassurance.
- **Mars** – Vivid imagination and volatile emotions. Protects loved ones. Needs creative outlets.
- **Jupiter** – Deeply sympathetic and nurturing character. Watch for binge eating or spending.
- **Saturn** – Tests and learning around home life and a struggle with trust issues.
- **North Node** – Tending the hearth fires, family needs, and self-preservation.
- **South Node** – Learning when to hide and when to step out. Step into leadership.
- **AC** – Nurturing and responsive, sensitive to moods and the environment.
- **IC** – Self-preservation is an early life priority. Protective of family.
- **DC** – Hides vulnerabilities. Partner might be overly needy.
- **MC** – Giving love or nurturing to the world at large. Makes a good nurse or chef.

Leo Self-Defense Tools – Candles, Fire Pits, Podiums

Passion is one of the major forces that makes us human. It is the drive to excel, the inspiration that lights our hearts and the attraction and bonding between lovers. The fires of passion can be creative or destructive. The solar radiance of a vital aura automatically deflects energies that would cause it harm. There are many expressions of passion that fuel us. Anger is one that often gets us into trouble, but if consciously directed can be channeled into great works of art. The same goes for lust. Without passion, a person or object becomes inert, and easier to manipulate. When the life-force energy is alive and well, it serves as a powerful buffer against psychic attack, adding a sense of courage and enthusiasm to endeavors.

Leo placements show where there is a great deal of passion, creativity and pride. They indicate areas that stand out from the rest in their uniqueness, and where we want to be acknowledged for something that we either possess or do exceptionally well. Leo is open and direct in their opinions and feelings.

- **Sun** – In its own sign. Creative, ardent, gregarious, sometimes overly proud or reserved.
- **Moon** – Playful, fun-loving, creative, natural performer.
- **Mercury** – Dramatic expression, great public speaker, opinionated.
- **Venus** – Affectionate, artistic, social, romantic, spoils the children.
- **Mars** – Dynamic, impulsive in love, competitive, inclined toward leadership.
- **Jupiter** – Assertive and confident, fortunate in sports or public affairs.
- **Saturn** – Emotionally guarded. Tests and learning around love, children and creativity.
- **North Node** – Becoming more comfortable in the limelight. Turning to artistic expression.
- **South Node** – Growing a greater sense of concern for and inclusiveness of others.
- **AC** – Warm and gregarious, fun-loving and popular.
- **IC** – One who "rules the roost" at home. Creative with design. Generous to loved ones.
- **DC** – Attracted to original and bohemian personalities.
- **MC** – A unique and creative occupation, strong individuality

Virgo Self-Defense Tools – Bathtubs, Healing Tools, Vital Foods

There are many healing tools to address many forms of illness. Some of them are more helpful in the prevention and treatment of disease. Hygiene on both the physical and energy levels is a practice that can help to prevent contamination and infection. Health can be viewed as a barometer. Nothing is found to be in one hundred percent perfect equilibrium in this world, but various degrees of harmony can be attained. The harmonious state seldom lasts for great lengths of time, yet leaves very little room for psychic invasion, and has a built-in system for detoxification. Periodic timeouts or fasting can help to achieve this state. One may use such tools as herbs, essences, and crystals or a combination thereof to help clear and protect personal space.

Virgo placements highlight our relationship to work and how well we take care of ourselves. They may also show interests in healing and medicine, or a service-oriented approach to others. Virgo and Scorpio both share the functions of purging poisons from the body or environment. Virgo attacks mainly through criticism.

- **Sun** – A focus on productivity and efficiency. Strong constitution and multi-talented.
- **Moon** – Helpful, many changes in occupation, prone to stomach problems, stays busy.
- **Mercury** – Literal, analytical, intellectual. Can be exacting with grammar and logic.
- **Venus** – Affectionate and giving mate. Sometimes inhibited, self-critical and overly cautious.
- **Mars** – Dynamic, hard-working, health-oriented. Can be too judgmental of others.
- **Jupiter** – Highly detail-oriented and productive with a strong work ethic.
- **Saturn** – Clean and organized. Tests come through insecurity and excessive habits.
- **North Node** – Practical and hard-working. Learning to let go and trust in life.
- **South Node** – Dedicated and helpful but needs to overcome criticism and perfectionism.
- **AC** – Energetic and youthful. Helpful, detailed and thorough.
- **IC** – Work from home, many home changes. Easily stressed. Nervous temperament.
- **DC** – Change and adventure are priorities in relationships. Prefers a hard-working mate.
- **MC** – Health-oriented profession or professional cleaning.

Libra Self-Defense Tools – Scales, Swords, Voice Recorders

The almighty sword is a prominent symbol in many folk stories, historical accounts and fables. Swords can be physical or metaphorical. They can be used to inflict harm or to cut through lies. The phrase that something is a "double-edged sword" means that it has both positive and negative connotations. A sword can be used in an act of aggression or hung upon the wall as a decoration. It could represent truth which is its own remedy for massive deceit. Such a sword is closely linked with intellect, morals and a strong sense of justice. It may take any number of forms including education, uprising and exposure of non-truths, that if left unchecked would be the cause of great harm. Other forms of the sword could be the skill of reasoning and logic that protects one or many from giving way to destructive emotions mixed with false beliefs. Metaphorically, swords carry words which can be used to clear the air, when the goal is to bring greater understanding where communication has become too muddy or biased.

Libra placements indicate the ways that we relate to others, harmonizing with others or the environment, and where we seek to achieve balance. Weighs between good and bad, masculine and feminine, right or wrong, etc. Libra seeks peace but when opposed will engage in combat.

- **Sun** – Seeks balance and justice. Strong combination of masculine and feminine energies.
- **Moon** – Desires balanced and harmonious interactions with others. Can often be a lone wolf.
- **Mercury** – The mind that constantly weighs and waits before making decisions.
- **Venus** – Fair, loving and kind. Often quite attractive to the opposite sex.
- **Mars** – Strength in legal disputes. Can be argumentative.
- **Jupiter** – Serves as a powerful mediator, benefits through partnerships.
- **Saturn** – Saturn is exalted in Libra, this placement brings mental strength, fairness and focus.
- **North Node** – An increase of cooperation with others, relationships, finding balance.
- **South Node** – Becoming more self-motivated and independent, following one's heart.
- **AC** – Beautiful, decorative in appearance. Social butterfly. Brings balance in social settings.
- **IC** – Brings peace and beauty to the home environment.
- **DC** – Attracts a beautiful, well-loved or popular mate. Enjoys socializing.
- **MC** – A career that is focused on justice or harmony. May be an artist.

Scorpio Self-Defense Tools– Diversion Safes, Magic Wands, Spy Gadgets

With just the wave of a magic wand, the magician can transform their environment. This has been depicted in a fantastical way through cartoons and movies. The wand is really an extension of the mind, and it can be used to focus energy into any area of choice. Combined with intuition, the wand is an incredibly powerful tool. Intuition is the invisible sense that guides us through uncertain times and territories. We all have it but not all of us take heed. It may be closely linked with animal instinct, since many animals sense danger before it occurs, often from miles away. Long ago humans possessed this same ability but became disconnected from it in the modern world. Now we tend to rely on radar and research, which are both helpful in gaining insight into the environment, past events and the intentions of others. In relation to intuition there is manifestation, the ability to bring about desired change by intense focus. Some call this magic. We are all capable of it, but we tend to use it to our own detriment because we are unaware of our abilities. If only more of us knew how to use our powers responsibly.

Scorpio placements indicate areas where there are intense inner battles, a discarding of outmoded ways of being and doing, and some type of transformation. These are areas of keen sensitivity, perception and passion. Scorpio has a reputation for being vengeful but can also be the sign of redemption.

- **Sun** – Plumbing the depths of human experiences, major life transformations.
- **Moon** – Emotionally intense, can be brooding and seething inside, highly intuitive.
- **Mercury** – Sharp-tongued, geared toward research, behind the scenes work, innovation.
- **Venus** – Psychic, emotional and possessive, a need to heal from betrayal or buried guilt.
- **Mars** – Immense power that can injure or heal. Much depends on the rest of the chart.
- **Jupiter** – Strong libido and desire to overcome obstacles. Can exhibit tremendous courage.
- **Saturn** – Tests come through shared resources, sexual involvements or scandals.
- **North Node** – Strengthening personal integrity and a spiritual purpose in life.
- **South Node** – The need to overcome negative habits and possessiveness.
- **AC** – Intense facial expressions and insightful nature. Deep emotional currents.
- **IC** – Highly fixed and set in one's ways. Determined to fulfill personal desires.
- **DC** – Marriage can be stormy. Relationships can be healing and transformative.
- **MC** – Doing the dirty work that others don't want to do. Shedding a light in the dark.

Sagittarius Self-Defense Tools – Arrows, Automobiles, Aircraft

Arrows have been used in hunting, sports and in war. Arrowhead obsidian stones have been worn as amulets, protecting against negativity and evil spirits. The bow and arrow are symbols of the Archer, who aims his arrow high, symbolizing concentration, clear vision, and the pursuit of high knowledge and goals. Psychic arrows may sometimes be directed toward us, causing emotional or mental shock and fatigue. Becoming aware of where they came from and learning how to dodge or remove them is our task. The symbol of the arrow is a sharp point directed toward something we want to acquire, achieve, or learn. The arrow can be the point on a compass, leading us to our true north. Arrows are often drawn on maps to guide us toward our desired destinations. The vehicle used for travel depends on the length of the distance, ranging from cars and boats to trains and airplanes. Sometimes the vehicle is imagination.

Sagittarius placements point out the areas where we refuse to be pinned down or limited in any way. They often reveal a religious orientation, philosophical leaning or a love of travel and culture. This sign loves freedom and exploration and indicates where or how we see ourselves in the grand scheme of things.

- **Sun** – Strong, creative, gregarious, eager to learn but sometimes reserved, proud and aloof.
- **Moon** – Playful, fun-loving, creative and bold. An outgoing and adventurous personality.
- **Mercury** – Opinionated but also good-humored. Sees the bigger picture.
- **Venus** – Affectionate and sensual. Loves everybody in a general way, often flirtatious.
- **Mars** – Dynamic and multi-talented. Can be unfaithful or affected by partner's unfaithfulness.
- **Jupiter** – Outgoing, energetic and optimistic. Truth-seeking. Welcomes challenges.
- **Saturn** – Tests and learning around freedom, seeing the bigger picture, taking risks to evolve.
- **North Node** – Growth occurs through knowledge, travel, and exposure to less-known truths.
- **South Node** – Needs to overcome restlessness and to ground one's energies in the present.
- **AC** – Fiery and intense personality, strong and resilient despite challenges.
- **IC** – May move a long way from the place of birth. The gypsy at heart.
- **DC** – Chooses a wise and philosophical type of mate, or one who is involved in healing.
- **MC** – The world traveler, teacher, missionary, or ambassador.

Capricorn Self-Defense Tools – Staffs, Rods, Rocks

Rocks, mountains, forests, fields, and islands are among the most stabilizing features of planet Earth. Their weight and land mass serve to prevent flooding, to support wildlife, and bring balance to the ecosystem. A structure that is built with bricks or rocks is longer-lasting and more protected from the elements and other intrusions than one made of wood. By honoring and protecting the earth, we are both humbled and inspired. We may find that our own personal needs are more easily provided. We learn how to become more durable and resistant to stresses that would wear us down.

We become better equipped to survive when under pressure and to utilize the earth's resources in sustainable ways.

Capricorn placements indicate the areas in which we exert power and leadership abilities and where we assume the greatest responsibilities. They show us where we are the most tough and can withstand life's blows in an unwavering way. Capricorn represents authority and does not back down from challenges.

- **Sun** – Work oriented, focused and entrepreneurial. Creative in a grounded or earthy way.
- **Moon** – Productive and hard-working at home and in domestic matters. Family oriented.
- **Mercury** – The methodical mindset, cautious, serious and thorough. Can suffer depression.
- **Venus** – Love and relationships are serious matters. Seeks for long-term commitments.
- **Mars** – Highly focused and effective in problem-solving and work.
- **Jupiter** – Strong business savvy. Can get locked into materialism. A natural leader.
- **Saturn** – Saturn is in its own sign, responsible and hard working. Tests around authority.
- **North Node** – Work for the public in some way, strong ambitions or business acumen.
- **South Node** – Release the need to control others, get more comfortable being low-key.
- **AC** – Tough and durable. The self fully projects into work projects in general.
- **IC** – Responsible for one's family and home life.
- **DC** – Responsible for spouse or partner, accountable in relationships.
- **MC** – Much importance is placed upon career and social standing.

Aquarius Self-Defense Tools– Technology, Telescopes, Venues

Modern technology has both provided us with great conveniences and has been weaponized against us. It can be used to our advantage to communicate, inform and store knowledge that is used for beneficial purposes. Technology is what enables us to educate ourselves online and communicate electronically over long distances through our computers and phones. It can be used in many ways to connect with like-minded others. Thanks to the internet we are able to network with those from all walks of life, in all parts of the world and to forge meaningful relationships with them even if we cannot connect physically. Technology has also been used to perform some amazing feats in medicine and has saved lives.

Aquarius placements reveal that which makes us unique and that therefore connects us with those we share much in common with. These placements may indicate our alliances, shared goals and innermost hopes, goals and wishes. Conversely, they may reveal where we go our own way, and prefer to be alone.

- **Sun** – Intellectual, group-oriented, original, and opinionated. Enjoys being on the go.
- **Moon** – Intuitive, technologically advanced, innovative. Has friends but often a loner.
- **Mercury** – Intellectual and interested in world events. May be prone to conceit.
- **Venus** – Friendship comes before deeper involvements. Highly independent.
- **Mars** – Ambitious, communicative, revolutionary. Wide circles of friends and associates.
- **Jupiter** – Progressive and humanitarian. Great social organizer. May be dogmatic.
- **Saturn** – Tests and learning come through isolation, and/or social groups and events.
- **North Node** – Encouraged to join or lead others in group endeavors. Inventive.
- **South Node** – Need to release excess judgments and to join the human family.
- **AC** – Positive and intuitive. Fashionable and unique. Very strong individuality.
- **IC** – The black sheep, family rebel. Wants and obtains freedom. Marches to own drum.
- **DC** – Prefers freedom over commitment. May attract an unusual mate.
- **MC** – Group leader or way-shower, pioneer in the field of science and technology.

Pisces Self-Defense Tools– Prayer, Sacred Herbs, Power Symbols

There is an invisible side to life that everyone experiences although not everyone believes or feels comfortable with it. It connects us with something that is much greater than ourselves, and greater than the physical reality that most of us associate with during the day. It is a realm where dreams, visions, and divine intervention become real. It is a passageway through which symbols, drawn or imprinted upon objects, or envisioned become actual things and experiences. Through prayers, mantras, or quiet reflections we consciously attune to our divine origins. Sometimes it is via plant medicine that the visionary meets with supernatural forces, recollects their divine origin or carves out a new destiny. It is often when and where we least expect it that we experience a miracle beyond our wildest dreams.

Pisces placements reveal our deepest sensitivities and spiritual goals and hints at what dwells at the innermost core of our being. Can also indicate escapist tendencies. Pisces is a passive sign and as a general rule does not engage in combat. In some cases, there is a passive aggressive streak.

- **Sun** – Sensitive and introspective. Dreamy and artistic. May have escapist tendencies.
- **Moon** – Receptive and romantic. Giving nature. Prone to emotional dissatisfaction.
- **Mercury** – Imaginative and poetic mind. Feelings rule over logic.
- **Venus** – Self-sacrificing, philanthropic, and nurturing.
- **Mars** – High sensitivity. Talent for music and the arts. Indecisive in love.
- **Jupiter** – Saintly and service-oriented. Does well in the healing field.
- **Saturn** – Emotional placement. Tests around overcoming fears and letting go.
- **North Node** – Surrender to the unknown, embrace the spiritual life, service-oriented.
- **South Node** – Overcome escapist tendencies, ground spiritual ideas into reality.
- **AC** – Soft personality, artistic flair. Goes with the flow rather than push for results.
- **IC** – Seeks refuge from daily stresses. Sacrifices made for family.
- **DC** – Takes care of loved ones. Hides inner pain. Partner may often be out of reach.
- **MC** – Spiritual teacher or having a spiritual occupation, a performing artist or musician.

Chapter 7

Planetary Influences on the Soul's Journey

Although we should never refer to the natal chart as fate written in stone, we can refer to it as a general guidepost that shows the areas where we are most intent on evolving during the course of our life. The positions of the planets at birth reveal many potential strengths and weaknesses in an individual. They can indicate some of the various types of tests, delays and struggles that the native is likely to experience, including areas of life they may receive the most opposition in and by whom. Many people may find that they are in practice their own worst enemy. What can also be gleaned from a study of the natal chart is the source of strength and inspiration which enables one to overcome personal obstacles.

The famous occultist Manly P. Hall summarized the seven stages of alchemical transformation in reference to the spiritual journey of evolution:

> *"Man must overcome the seven planets and transmute them into soul powers. Their negative forces are the seven deadly sins, which are overcome by a symbolic struggle with demons and dragons, and in turn, are transmuted into the seven cardinal virtues. This is the key to alchemy, for from the seven base metals, first spiritualized and then brought together as a secret compound, is produced the Philosophers' Stone, the purified soul."*[1]

In the treatise Poimandres from the collection of Greek writings called Corpus Hermeticum, the soul could only ascend from earthly imprisonment by shedding the vices associated with each of the seven spheres. The planets were said to bestow certain faculties upon the human soul that had descended into incarnation from the realm of the fixed stars of the zodiac. In Dante's Paradisio, there were Nine Heavenly spheres, those being the seven planets, the fixed stars, and the primum mobile, the outermost moving sphere of the geocentric universe until ultimately reaching the Empyrean (the highest heaven) to be united with God. It is said that the concept of the Ninth Sphere was introduced by Claudius Ptolemy. These Nine Spheres seem to correlate with the Nine Worlds on the Norse Tree of Life known as Yggdrasil. In Greek mythology, there were seven daughters of the Titan god Atlas who supported the pillars holding the earth and heavens apart from each other.

In Gnostic teachings, there are a class of beings referred to as the Archons who are the builders of the universe, and each of them is tied in with one of the seven traditional planets. They have been known to tempt and torment each soul to various degrees, in order to bind them to material existence set into place by the Demiurge, and to prevent their ultimate spiritual liberation. This passage in the Bible describes the nature of the non-physical dimension that we must battle during the course of our earthly life:

> *"For we wrestle not against flesh and blood, but against principalities, against powers, against the rulers of the darkness of this world, against spiritual wickedness in high places."*
>
> *Ephesians 6:12*

The Seven Seals of God referenced in the Book of Revelation have been linked with the rites of passage associated with the seven planets, as well as the seven energy centers of the human body. Association of these seals with the chakras are found in the book *The Apocalypse Unsealed*, by Theosophist James. M. Pryse.[2] As the Sanskrit meaning of chakra is wheel, which implies cir-

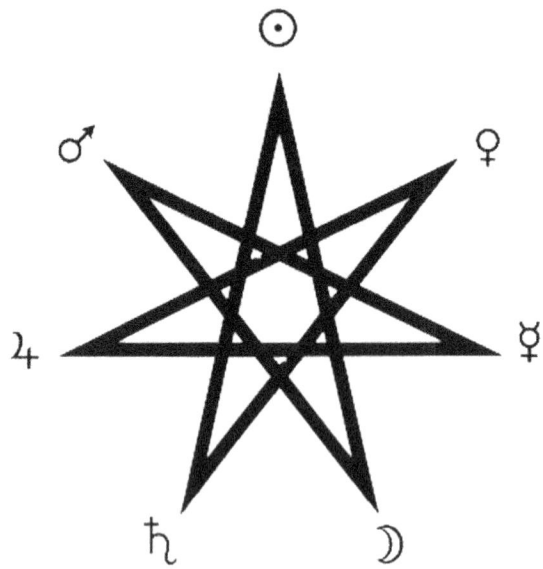

cular movement, what if the set of seven chakras truly are the microcosm of the macrocosm above us? As the Hermetic adage goes, "As above, so below". Vedic astrology has assigned planets to each one of these chakras. Physically, the human body is known to regenerate itself approximately every seven years.

The 7-point star holds significance in various religions and occult practices, including alchemy, representing the seven planets, the seven days of the week, and the seven alchemical substances: fire, water, air earth, sulphur ,mercury, and salt

In many religions the view is held that one of the greatest challenges we face is that of overcoming the bondage to our own astrological blueprint, to rise above pettiness, addiction and negativity that holds us back from complete enlightenment by the time we have exited our physical vehicle. Some attempt to do this by rejecting astrology altogether. In Buddhism this freedom from the cycles of death and rebirth, and of desire and aversion is called Moksha.

The symbol of the heptagram, or seven-pointed star has been connected with the seven major planets and their corresponding days of the week: Sun for Sunday, Moon for Monday, Mars for Tuesday, Mercury for Wednesday, Jupiter for Thursday, Venus for Friday, and Saturn for Saturday. The Chaldean order of the planets is traced in the lines of the star, starting from the Sun to Saturn, following the order of the days of the week. It has been used in Catholicism as a protective symbol, and as a reminder of the seven days that God created the world. In Islam, it represents the first seven verses of the Quran. Modern pagans refer to the 7-point star as the Elven or Faery Star. This star is considered sacred in many other cultures. Universally it is regarded as a symbol of celestial power and magic, and has been sewn, burnt and etched into talismans.

Many astrologers and magical practitioners refer to seven planetary hours that correspond to their work goals. Vivian Robson explained Planetary Hours in simple terms in his book *Electional Astrology*[3] Today there is free software online that allows one to look up the planetary hours for their specific location. However helpful this information may be, one should not rely on planetary hours alone for the best results. Other details need to be taken into consideration, such as the aspects between planets involved at any given time on a certain day.

In ancient scriptures, there were seven holy angels who stood around the throne of God in attendance. Benjamin Camfield in his work A Theological Discourse of Angels described the "7 spirits who stand in the presence of God" as the rulers of the seven planets.[4] In grimoires, there were Seven Olympic Spirits who governed the seven planets. In Matthew 12:43-45 of the New Testament, there is mention of seven evil spirits. The number seven actually appears 735 times in the Bible, or 860 counting variations of the word seven, such as "seventh". Seven spirits appear in many forms in folklore and religious beliefs throughout the Middle East. The Swiss astrologer, physician and alchemist known as Paracelsus (c. 1493) acknowledged the powers associated with the seven planets. He recorded Seven Rules pertaining to overall well-being and success.

In his book *Devils and Evil Spirits of Babylonia*, R. Campbell Thompson[5] made mention of an ancient "Invocation Against the Seven", which begins:

"Seven are they! Seven are they!
In the Ocean Deep seven are they!

Battening in Heaven seven are they,

Bred in the depths of Ocean.

Nor male nor female are they,

But are as the roaming windblast,

No wife have they, no son can they beget ;

Knowing neither mercy nor pity,

They hearken not to prayer or supplication.

They are as horses reared among the hills ..."

This number seven appears to us in so many ways, both positive and negative, but always spiritual in nature. No matter how many new planets or objects are discovered in the heavens, the primary seven have had and will always have the greatest significance to us. The number seven is referenced repeatedly throughout the Books of Enoch, in relation to the stars and the heavens.[7]

Planets can be favorably placed at birth but compromised by certain transits. The same general remedies listed for natal positions listed below can apply to transits as well. Those to whom spiritual traditions appeal may choose the recitation of Sanskrit mantras, the Orphic Hymns associated with the planets, or any other song or poem relative to the planet being emphasized. Great thinkers throughout history have linked the seven colors of the rainbow and the seven planets with the seven musical notes. The seven vowels of the Greek alphabet and heptachord (both the name of a musical scale and ancient 7-string lyre) corresponded with the seven planets. Pythagoreans gave much attention to geometry, color and sound in relation to the seven planets.

There are seven terms for various moods that people often use without even realizing the connection being made to the seven major planets. These are: sunny, loony, mercurial, venereal (not used much in this context anymore, but the word venerable also relates to Venus), martial, jovial and saturnine[6]. Everything that we do, feel and experience while incarnate in some way relates to the planets. Awareness of our relationship to the heavens can help us to better dial in to the areas of life we most need help with.

Sun

The Sun is the symbol of life force energy, self-expression and basic identity. The natal Sun sign indicates how a soul is growing and what they are working through in their lifetime. The entire chart should be taken into consideration for an accurate reading of its placement. The Sun rules the sign of Leo and its corresponding fifth house. It represents the father and husband, as well as the manner and areas where a person takes charge, asserting authority in their own life. It also has a profound influence on overall vitality.

Solar people are usually of robust health with strong determination and quick recoveries. They tend to enjoy being in the spotlight and are very creative. If the Sun's natal position is afflicted there may be health issues particularly in relation to the heart, brain, eyes, immune system and equilibrium. One might be prone to infection and low on energy. Sometimes the challenges relate more to life circumstances than to health. One may frequently be the target of others' attacks, or may frequently find themselves in situations that block their creativity. Burdens tend to come through marriage, children, the father or fatherhood.

The natal Sun may be especially challenged if it falls in two or more of these positions:

- In the Sixth, Eighth or Twelfth house
- In an intercepted sign
- In the sign of Libra or Aquarius
- In a conjunction with the South Node
- In a hard aspect to Mars
- In a conjunction or hard aspect to Saturn, Uranus, Neptune or Pluto

Remedies:

Solar based mantras, music and yoga positions can help to harmonize with the Sun. Wear or keep in one's environment orange, red and yellow stones such as Citrine, Hessonite Garnet, Ruby, Sunstone or Tangerine Quartz. Wear real gold jewelry and/or bright colored clothes often. Display bright colors or solar art in the home. Use solar motifs and symbols. Keep vibrant plants in the home or garden. The practice of sun gazing at sunrise and sundown is successfully used by many for overall well-being. There are definitely correct and incorrect ways of doing this, so it's wise to do research first.

Moon

The Moon by sign, house and aspects to other planets describes the nature of one's emotional makeup. The Moon rules the sign Cancer and the Fourth House. Its sign is especially telling of that person's childlike nature, early life influences, what they do out of habit, and for comfort. Moon placements reveal the quality of the relationships with children and key females in life, but especially the mother. An afflicted Moon can indicate various types of distress that come through illness, isolation, slander, psychic attack, or emotional upsets. There may be difficulties around childbirth.

The Moon ruled person may be extremely empathic, psychic, impressionable and vulnerable to the moods of others. They are often imaginative, having a talent for poetry, music or creating ambiance through domestic activities. The Moon reflects many rapidly shifting highs and lows that can make for mental and emotional instability. Physically, the Moon affects the bodily fluids, digestion, and in women the hormones, which can affect the entire endocrine system, cellular repair and organ functions.

The natal Moon may be especially challenged if it falls in two or more of these positions:

- In Scorpio or in Capricorn
- In the Sixth, Eighth or Twelfth house
- In a hard aspect to the Sun
- In hard aspect to any of the planets

Remedies:

Lunar-based mantras, sound frequencies and yoga positions harmonize with the Moon. Wear or carry stones such as Rainbow Moonstone, Labradorite, and Selenite. Wear the metal silver to help balance lunar energies. Listen to soft, relaxing music. Work closely with lunar cycles for manifestation, healing and detoxification. The time of the waxing New Moon to Full is for manifestation and increase. The Full Moon waning to New is for completion and release.

Mercury

Mercury represents mental orientation and communication styles. Mercury is dual-natured and often seen as androgynous, ruling the two signs of Gemini and Virgo. If this planet is pronounced in a natal chart the person is a strong thinker and communicator, possibly with a great deal of nervous energy, especially so in mutable signs. Their mental wheels are always turning. Mercury is neutral in many ways. Its placement may reveal the mental outlook, general energy levels, and relationships to family members but particularly siblings, aunts and uncles.

When Mercury is afflicted in a natal chart, the person has some sort of problem with their mood, thought patterns or both. They may have difficulty in expressing themselves and are frequently misunderstood. Some challenges related to Mercury can result in high strung, jerky movements and scattered thinking. Other Mercury afflictions can indicate duplicity, mental density or a sharp tongue.

Thoughts may be heavy and depressive with Mercury in any of the water signs and houses, especially when aspects are hard. Certain challenges with communication can be indicated by Mercury Retrograde but this alone is not a negative factor in a birth chart so look for supporting evidence.

Mercury may be especially challenged if it falls in two or more of these positions:

- In a separating conjunction to the Sun, using a tight orb (up to 2 degrees)
- In the sign Leo, Sagittarius or Pisces

- Third decan of Cancer, Capricorn, Virgo, or Pisces
- In a hard aspect to luminaries or any other planet
- Mercury is Retrograde

Remedies:

Meditation and relaxation techniques help quiet an out of balance Mercury placement or transit. Wear or keep nearby the stones Aquamarine, Blue Topaz, Emerald, Lepidolite, Lithium Quartz, and Sodalite. If a Mercury transit is adversely affecting finances, thoroughly check the environment to see where blockages might be occurring or where money is being spent carelessly. Sometimes by cleaning up and organizing there is renewed cash flow. A de-cluttered home or office helps to calm the mind, and the activity of de-cluttering is one thing Mercury Retrograde is well-suited toward.

Venus

Venus is the planet of love, beauty, money and the luxuries it may afford. It is the ruler for the earth sign Taurus and air sign Libra, but is expressed differently in each. In both it tends to increase artistic appreciation or talent. Venus is a benefic planet so when it is found in stressful positions in a natal chart the good things that Venus represents may be overshadowed by other influences or hard to obtain. For some people it's the love life that experiences the most challenges. Venus afflictions can also reveal challenges in relation to women. For married men, Venus represents the wife.

The Venus challenged person may feel unlucky, may struggle with finances, and may experience conflicts with females but especially those who are competitive or are a financial burden in some way. Other challenges can show up with the appearance, causing one to feel unattractive. For various reasons one may feel unlovable, suffer from low self esteem, or simply the neglect of proper hygiene. In women, an afflicted Venus may related to health problems, especially relating to the reproductive system. Conversely, in some cases the Venus challenged person could be a womanizer, misogynist, or suffer from the loss of a significant female in their life.

Sometimes a natal Venus or any planet for that matter appears to be challenged in multiple ways in people who are highly successful or happily involved in a relationship. Usually this is because the negative aspects are mitigated by positive ones.

Venus may be especially challenged if it falls in two or more of these positions:

- In the sign of Aries, Virgo or Scorpio
- In the Sixth, Eighth or Twelfth house
- Conjunct the South Node
- In a hard aspect with the Sun, Moon or other planets

- Venus is Retrograde

Remedies:

Massage and touch therapy. Balance Venus related issues with the stones Danburite, Diamond, Emerald, Kunzite, and Rose Quartz. Work with flowers in some way, which may involve gardening, floral arrangements, or aromatherapy. Interior design, a pleasant change of scenery and moderate comfort foods may help. Monitor monetary spending habits to direct them wisely.

Mars

Mars is a power planet that represents personal ambition and other masculine qualities. It rules the sign Aries and co-rules Scorpio along with Pluto, and the first and eighth houses. The placement of Mars in a birth chart can appear to either bestow strength or suffocate one's overall energy and drive. Mars can reveal challenges with general life force energy, libido, and with males and men. It also relates to worldly ambitions and the energy to carry through with plans and ideas.

Certain challenging patterns involving Mars may be the cause of hubris, excess anger and lust. An afflicted Mars could otherwise result in difficulties with expressing anger, inhibition and feelings of being stifled. Whether Mars is weak or overpowering, it makes one prone to accidents, inflammation and infections. One may frequently misuse their energy or be a victim of violence and cruelty. There may be difficulties with male competitors. If Mars is too strong there might be too much emphasis on physicality and not enough on inner development. If Mars is hampered there is a lack of energy, confidence and libido which tends to cause obstacles in work and career. There are health issues related to the sign, house and aspects being made to Mars. There could be problems with male romantic partners.

Mars may be especially challenged if it falls in two or more of these positions:

- It occupies the signs of Taurus, Cancer, or Libra
- Is in the Fourth, Seventh, Sixth or Twelfth house
- Makes hard aspects
- Mars is Retrograde

Remedies:

Weight resistance training, martial arts, walking, dancing, and Pilates are various activities that can help to harmonize with Mars. Wear or keep nearby stones such as Carnelian, Onyx, and Tiger's Eye. Wear or use the color red in decorations if the expressions of Mars are underactive or stifled. If Mars is overly active, wear or use the color blue for cooling and quieting one's energy.

Jupiter

Jupiter is the planet of luck, travel, belief systems including religion, higher education and abundance. It rules the signs of Sagittarius and Pisces and the ninth and twelfth houses. Jupiter is not typically viewed as a challenging planet because of its benevolent nature. It can however indicate an over-abundance of something which leads to imbalance. It rules the liver so when emphasized in some charts it indicates an overindulgence in alcohol and drugs leading to toxic overload and possibly a short life span. For heterosexual married women specifically, Jupiter represents the husband. For a married man, Jupiter could represent himself as a husband.

Problems can be brought to Jupiter by other planets, and thereby amplified, multiplied or intensified by Jupiter's expansive influence. The Jupiter challenged person may be egotistical and have an addictive personality. Conversely they may suffer from attacks by egotistical people, may be either overly optimistic or too trusting, giving others the benefit of the doubt too often. "Generous to a fault", they may need to learn the proper modes of giving their time, energy and money because they often pour them into the wrong avenues. They may need to examine why they are so quick to rid themselves of their own much-needed resources. Jupiter problems sometimes manifest in challenges with religion, religious leaders, spiritual or pseudo-spiritual people. For married women, Jupiter challenges may involve their husbands in some way.

Jupiter may be especially challenging if it falls in two or more of these positions:

- In the sign of Gemini, Virgo or Capricorn
- In the Sixth or Eighth house
- In hard aspects
- Jupiter is Retrograde

Remedies

Reading scriptures, philosophy, mythology or old writings of interest can help to harmonize with Jupiter. One may wish to wear or keep nearby stones in resonance with Jupiter such as Chrysocolla, Lapis Lazuli, and Turquoise. Honoring divinity in a way that resonates with can help to abate problems associated with Jupiter. One of the most traditional is having an image of a certain deity on an altar space and providing it with daily or weekly offerings. Effects may be amplified by including images of one's ancestry. Travel to sacred places physically or through reading, watch documentaries and visit museums. Prayer and meditation practices help attune to and strengthen the Jupiter energy.

Saturn

Saturn is the planet associated with limitations, work, delays, and death. Whereas Jupiter's influence is expansive, Saturn's causes contraction and narrows our focus. This is the planet that helps bring structure to endeavors and the world in general. It rules the sign of Capricorn and the tenth house as well as Aquarius and the eleventh house. Saturn placements can reveal the relationship to authority figures in general. It is usually linked specifically with the father and patriarchal figures, as well as with elders.

Those with an afflicted Saturn may either lack self-discipline or may, for reasons beyond their control, experience a huge amount of constraint, limitation, humiliation and responsibility, especially in their early life. This person may suffer from many setbacks or from chronic depression. Burdens tend to come through a parent, employers or legal institutions. Goals are not easily achieved and are only gained through hard work, usually over long stretches of time. Saturn not only brings old age but the wisdom that comes with it.

Although Saturn's influence is known to be difficult, the aspects it makes may turn it into more of a positive and constructive one. The effects of Saturn can weigh heavily on one's heart and weaken one's health, or can help them to become stronger. One determining factor in this may be whether Saturn is in a state of excess or deficiency in the natal chart. If it is deficient, then certain transits or locations highlighting Saturn may actually serve to boost the individual to greater levels of stability and success.

Saturn may be especially challenging if it falls in two or more of these positions:

- In the sign of Cancer or Leo
- In a conjunction to any of the four angles
- In a conjunction or hard aspect to the Sun, Moon, or Venus
- In a conjunction with the South Node
- Saturn is Retrograde

Remedies

Acupressure and Reflexology can help release the chronic tension and rigidity associated with Saturn. Stones such as Black Tourmaline, Blue Sapphire, and Jasper tend to strengthen the stabilizing or crystalizing qualities of Saturn. When Saturn is too strong of an influence, instead use the warmer stones such as Yellow or Orange Sapphire, Golden Topaz or Garnet. Keeping a water fountain, visiting natural bodies of water, or having imagery of water in one's home can be helpful ways to balance out the dry and rigid nature of Saturn.

Beyond the Seven Lights: The Transpersonal Planets

Saturn is the last of the visible planets in what is also known as our very ancient set of celestial lights. Of these seven planets, only five are considered to be "personal planets" due to their great significance in natal chart interpretation. They are the Sun, Moon, Mercury, Venus and Mars. They are also known as inner planets, while Saturn and Jupiter are known as outer planets, having greater effects upon the masses. Just beyond these two outer planets are the planets of more recent discovery that cannot be viewed with the naked eye. These are often referred to as the transpersonal planets and they include Uranus, Neptune, and Pluto. Chiron is currently classified as a comet or "minor planet" between the orbits of Saturn and Uranus. It is still being investigated as are the transpersonal planets for their precise attributes, although many astrologers have concurred on the basic correspondences that each of them seems to have. The rulerships of these planets over certain signs is also hypothetical since they have not been used nearly as long as the seven traditional planets.

Uranus

Uranus is the planet of invention, freedom and electricity. Along with Saturn it is believed to co-rule the sign Aquarius and the eleventh house. The influence of this planet is known to be unpredictable. It has been said to cause sudden reversals and unexpected events. Due to being a slow moving planet that takes about seven years to transit a sign, the house placement of Uranus in a natal chart is often a more significant indicator of how it plays out in one's life. Uranus's challenges can physically involve the nervous system and in other ways relate to socializing or unforeseen events.

The Uranus challenged person tends to be very strong willed, high strung and accident prone. One who is at the mercy of Uranus's unpredictable weather is impulsive and may run into many obstacles or mishaps in their personal and professional life. Distance is often chosen away from family. They may be unreliable, self-centered or too explosive in temperament as partners or parents. Conversely, they may not act this way but be victimized by such people. Uranian challenges can come through bizarre entanglements, sudden reversals of luck, extreme individuals or events, automobile breakdowns, and internet schemes.

Uranus may be especially challenging if it falls in two or more of these positions:

- In conjunction to any of the four angles
- In a conjunction or hard aspect with the two great luminaries or any of the planets
- Uranus is Retrograde

Remedies

Warm baths and nerve tonics help to release some of the nervous energy associated with Uranus. Wear or keep stones nearby such as Angelite and Celestite, and grounding stones such Hematite and Shungite. Innovative types of therapy and tools such as oxygen therapy may help to release some issues associated with Uranus. Even something as simple as a relaxing stroll in nature or a warming meal are some ideas to calm unsettling kinds of energy associated with this planet.

Neptune

Neptune's influence is not of this world but its impact upon world affairs can be great. It represents all that is unseen for good or ill. Under its influence one can get lost in illusions or grow in compassion. It co-rules the sign of Pisces with Jupiter and the twelfth house. Like Uranus, the house placement of Neptune in a natal chart is often more significant than the sign it occupies. Neptune challenges are difficult to trace, and they tend to cause an erosion in some area of life until properly addressed.

With Neptune afflicted, one seems more susceptible to illness and disease than the average person. Drugs are very dangerous and have immediate effects. Attacks through Neptune are often psychic in nature. There is much psychic disturbance in life, health and relationships, and illness if present, is difficult to diagnose because it does not stem from the expected causes. They are usually related to energy "leakages" of some sort. The planet or planets making aspects to Neptune indicate the areas involving the cause or effect of such leaks. Psychic abilities are usually heightened but not necessarily in positive ways. One may be susceptible to being deceived by others who wish to take advantage of them.

Spiritual interests or abilities need direct application because they serve as the person's primary route of deliverance from their earthly troubles.

Neptune may be especially challenging if it falls in two or more of these positions:

- In the Sixth, Eighth house, or Twelfth house
- In conjunction to any of the four angles
- In hard aspects with the Sun, Moon, Mercury, Venus or Mars

Remedies

Natural settings near large bodies of water, or in the forest can help attune to Neptune's energy. Stones such as Jade, Larimar, Super Seven, and White Sapphire may bring balance to Neptune placements or transits. Water based therapies may also help to clear certain Neptunian ailments. Tinctures, essences and homeopathics may be more effective than pills and unrefined herbs. Beware however that in some people with Neptune in hard aspects, vibrational medicine has unpredictable results and warrants some degree of caution.

Pluto

Pluto is the smallest planet, now considered to be a dwarf, that is farthest away from the Sun. It has so far been observed to be powerful in its effects overall. This planet has been given rulership over the masses, nuclear fission and deep irrevocable change. It co-rules the sign Scorpio with Mars and the eighth house. As with Uranus and Neptune, the house placement of Pluto in a natal chart is often more significant than the sign it occupies.

Some of the problems associated with Pluto include paranoia, obsession, trauma and rage. Those with Pluto emphasized in their chart are usually very perceptive but tend toward extremes in their mannerisms. Most of what has been written about Pluto people and their issues point toward egotism, guilt and jealousy. They are often seekers of truth and have a keen sense of what lies beneath the surface of things. They might be domineering or strong-willed. They may also be victimized by people who wield tremendous power and authority in general, or they may find themselves caught in many types of battles with dark forces. I have observed that many individuals who have Pluto prominently placed in their charts have at some point struggled with suicidal thoughts and urges, or other heavy emotions at their most extreme degrees, such as anger and grief. Some of them might be involved in underground crime, whether to fight against it or hide within it. In relation to health an afflicted Pluto can make one susceptible to pathological invasions or deep-set infections that are difficult to get rid of.

The more aspects being made whether harmonious or challenging, the more intense Pluto's presence is likely to be in a person's chart and life and that alone is a challenging factor to take into consideration.

Pluto may be especially challenging if it falls in two or more of these positions:

- In conjunction to any of the four angles
- In conjunction or hard aspect with either of the luminaries
- In conjunction to either of the Nodes
- In the Twelfth House
- Hard aspect to any of the personal planets
- Pluto is Retrograde

Remedies

Spiritual counseling, silent retreats, and artistic mediums for buried emotions may all appeal to the Plutonic person's inner depths. Stones such as Obsidian, Hematite, Onyx, and Smoky Quartz can help to balance the intensity of Pluto's energies. Nuumite can help to retrieve lost sense of power. You can often identify a Plutonian person by their gravitation toward either darker colors, music, or motifs in general. The same is true of Saturnian people but the difference in Plutonians is that they are more cryptic and harder for people to understand.

Chiron

So far in the modern astrological community, Chiron has widely come to represent a childhood wound in each of us, and appears to be a stress factor in any sign that it occupies. Many traditional astrologers do not include Chiron or any of the asteroids since they do not fit neatly into the tried and true system that forms the basis of astrology. It is added here as a curiosity, and as something to consider as secondary in importance to any of the planets. Whether or not incorporated into the chart Chiron's archetypal energy can be harnessed for healing and empowerment.

A less known meaning of Chiron is said to be that of true love, soul mate union and marriage. This description has been outlined in the book Magi Astrology: the Key to Success in Love and Money by the Magi Society. The famous singer Frank Sinatra had Chiron conjunct Jupiter in Pisces and married four times. The comedian actor Richard Pryor had Chiron conjunct Pluto in Leo and married seven times. Then again there are other details in their natal charts to account for all of their relationship changes, and Chiron adds to the testimony of this.

One problem with this love related definition of Chiron is that it does not always seem to apply in natal charts and transits that I have tracked. The more widely accepted view of Chiron being associated with pain, the inner child, and spiritual work has seemed more applicable in most cases. For example, transits from Chiron to the Sun seem more to highlight health issues in many people rather than periods of romance and prosperity. In some cases there are injuries, and in some a great focus on healing. Chiron transiting Mercury may highlight emotional or insightful conversations with others.

People have a Chiron Return between ages forty-six and fifty, not far after their fourth Jupiter Return which may bring great opportunities and windfalls. Due to Chiron's exceptionally long orbits everyone born between the years between 1950 and 1989 have Chiron opposite of Uranus in their natal charts. Because of how many people in different age groups have this aspect I don't think it is unique enough to indicate problems experienced on an individual level, and this is especially since Uranus is one of the slower-moving, generational planets that relates to the collective.

Chiron may be especially challenging when it falls in two or more of these positions:

- In conjunction to any of the four angles
- In the Sixth, Eighth or Twelfth house
- Makes a hard aspect with any of the personal planets
- Chiron is Retrograde
- Transiting the Sun or Moon

The Chiron challenged person may take a long time to heal from both emotional and physical wounds. They may have certain healing abilities that they have greater success using on others than themselves. It may take them a while to utilize or appreciate their greatest talents. Painful recurrences seem like pouring salt over their psychic wounds, which makes it difficult for the wound to close and heal. In order to heal, there must usually be some kind of reorientation to the themes relative to the planetary ruler of the sign that Chiron occupies. Check the position of that planet by sign, house and aspects to other planets for clues as to what may be causing the person pain and suffering.

Remedies

Art therapy can help to address challenges associated with Chiron placements and transits. Wear or keep stones such as Chiastolite, Chrysoprase and Healerite. Working with oracles for insights can be helpful. One might become especially drawn to trying certain types of holistic medicine or experience a breakthrough in their existing health practices relative to the sign, its element and house placement of Chiron.

References

1 *The Cabalistic Keys to the Lord's Prayer* by Manly P. Hall Philosophical Research Society (January 1, 1964) Los Angeles, California

2. *The Apocalypse Unsealed* by James M. Pryse. 1910, New York.

3. *Electional Astrology* by Vivian Robson. Samuel Weiser, New York, 1972.

4. *Theological Discourse of Angels* by Benjamin Camfield. 1678, London, England. R.E. for Hen. Brome (*Of Angels and Their Ministries*):

> "*For the seven Planets: To Saturn Zapkiel, to Iupiter Zadkiel, to Mars Camuel, to Sol Raphael, to Venus Haniel, to Mercurius Michael, to Luna Gabriel, which they affirm to be the seven Spirits, that always stand in the presence of God, and under whom the government of Heaven and Earth is disposed.*"

5. T*he Devils and Evil Spirits of Babylonia: Being Babylonian and Assyrian Incantations Against the Demons, Ghouls, Vampires, Hobgoblins, Ghosts, and Kindred Evil Spirits, which Attack Mankind,* Volume 1 by Reginald Campbell Thomspon, M.A. Luzac and Company, London 1903.

6. The Rainbow Book, 1975, Fine Arts Museums of San Francisco, page 128

7. The Books of Enoch, Complete Edition. Paul C. Schneiders. Translated by R.H. Charles, International Alliance Pro-Publishing 2012.

Chapter 8

Aspects of Power, Danger and Potential

Certain aspects in a natal chart can serve as important warnings and guideposts, even when the exact time of birth is unknown. That is because many aspects can last for several days, months or even years. There are a few major ones to look out for in shielding yourself both on the psychic and physical levels. One of these aspects alone is not necessarily the indication of any major problem, but if there are several of them present one should be especially alert to their potential dangers.

Basically, any challenging aspects involving Mars can be viewed as possible indicators of anger, violence or a disturbed psychology, relative to the planets, signs and houses involved. They can also mean that a person is very masculine and action-oriented in positive ways, so always check for surrounding factors. By the same token, hard transits involving planets such as Mars, Uranus and Pluto can trigger certain types of weather catastrophes, violent outbreaks, and radical world events.

Mars, Up Close and Personal

When the Moon of the subconscious or the Sun of individuality is in close contact with Mars, or when Mars connects with any of the planets for that matter, desires are increased. With either the Moon or Sun conjunct Mars, sexuality is also usually pronounced. Mars also gives physical strength and regenerative powers which are particularly helpful in overcoming injuries and illness.

Moon conjunct Mars

The expression of the Moon is already subjective and emotional in nature, but in conjunction with Mars it can become impulsive and snappy. The Moon conjunct Mars person tend rule their family or household. Mars brings much force to the personality, which can be useful for leadership positions. One may gain a large public following or become an influential member of their community.

Sun conjunct Mars

The Sun conjunct Mars produces an extroverted and energetic type of character, and denotes a competitive drive, especially in business and career settings. For example, in a fire sign it usually indicates a person who is highly active and a force to be reckoned with. They may be natural and enthusiastic leaders, or pushy and domineering individuals who aggressively pursue their desires no matter who gets hurt in the process. This is a great aspect for any type of athlete, for there is great courage and energy to tackle physical challenges. Depending on the tone of their chart, those with this conjunction may motivate and uplift others or exhaust those who must endure their company for prolonged periods of time.

Moon or Sun square Mars

There tends to be a lot of frustration and anger that needs to be dealt with. If the Moon is involved this stems from the conditions of their childhood. The person may be able to transmute their anger into healthy channels but if not, they can at times become their own worst enemies or make enemies needlessly. In either square, unless there are other kinds of aspects to warm their hearts, they can become self-centered and cruel. The person may be very accident prone.

Moon or Sun opposite of Mars

Oppositions are similar to the conjunctions but in some cases can cause even more aggression. The person can be antagonized by others or the one who antagonizes them. Many who have one of these aspects tend to be strong victims who seek revenge. They may compulsively rebel against the legal system or get into trouble with the law through their extreme reactions. With the Moon opposite Mars there is often anger toward the mother or other family members.

Lost in Luminous Haze

Aspects involving Neptune can be tricky to deal with, let alone understand. They can sometimes be highly fortunate, but when they are operating in a negative way, their effects can be demoralizing to say the least. Challenging themes involving Neptune may include addiction, deception, deterioration and loss. Any stressful aspects with Neptune can indicate that one is either dishonest or prone to deceit by others. It can also mean they are too soft, too open, and too porous, or that they tend to martyr themselves too often. The influence of Neptune can blur the lines in conversations and boundaries, leaving one vulnerable to any number of "pathological" invasions. When the root of any type of illness, crime, or other problem is exceedingly difficult to trace and remedy, Neptune is likely to be exerting its elusive and erosive influences.

Depression is a common struggle in any hard aspects to Neptune. With the Moon in any kind of stressful aspect to Neptune, there is often high sensitivity and difficulty dealing with everyday, mundane concerns. There is likely to be some sense of alienation or distance from one's family of origin. One may not feel as though they belong in a human body or even on this earth at all. There may be substance abuse or neglect of the health or personal hygiene. It has often been said that the Moon in stressful contact with Neptune produces delusion or poor intuition, but this is not always true. In many cases, psychic abilities or phenomena can present problems such as being overwhelming and out-of-control. One solution to this is to build a greater sense of order and discipline for psychic energy to be directed into, such as practicing one of the martial arts aimed at energy cultivation. The energy of planets such as Mars or Saturn actually become the antidote to Neptunian woes. Then one becomes a stronger channel for all of the psychic energy that was previously flooding them, causing so much confusion and distress.

Moon or Sun conjunct Neptune

Either one of these conjunctions can indicate a high level of compassion, and often spiritual awareness. In some it can indicate escapism, or the tendency to get lost with regard to one's purpose in life. There is a love of fantasy, and the creative works tend to have a whimsical element to them. The Moon highlights more of the person's psychic abilities and the Sun highlights their soul qualities.

Moon or Sun square Neptune

Such a square gives an imaginative and creative mind, but one that also experiences much disillusionment. There is a caring and compassionate nature that others may sometimes take advantage of. The person could be highly driven by subconscious fears that keep them locked into unproductive patterns and relationships.

Moon or Sun opposite Neptune

Other things, entities or people may hook into and drain the person's energy. Any type of drugs are potentially more harmful than helpful and should be handled with more caution than usual. With the Moon, many problems stem either from the mother or certain women in the person's life who have parasitic tendencies. In either opposition there may be obsession, or frequent and troublesome misunderstandings with others. There may be paranoia of being attacked but also the experience of real jabs and projections from others. There is a strong need for psychic protection.

With the Sun there may be a lack of will and self-confidence. One may frequently feel stifled, or have the sense that they are losing themselves to some situation, relationship or cause. They may experience an identity crisis, or feel disappointed by their circumstances and achievements.

The Heavy Duty Hitters: Saturn, Uranus and Pluto

Saturn is often pronounced in the chart of the classic "control freak" such as conjunct the Ascendant. This doesn't mean everyone with Saturn on their Ascendant is controlling, but they are at least likely to be conservative and hard-working. Another indication of a controlling nature are exaggerated placements in Leo, such as a stellium making hard aspects.

Mars is usually emphasized and in agitation with personal planets in the charts of lawless individuals or those who abhor the law. Hard aspects between Mars and Saturn are often present in rigid individuals. Mars square or opposite Uranus may spell out major disaster if the person is not of sound mind and spirit. Although this combination can make for creative genius in some people, in others the behavior is highly destructive. Any hard aspects involving Uranus can emphasize a strong will along with hugely iconoclastic and erratic tendencies.

A strong focus in the sign of Scorpio (ruled by Mars and Pluto) can sometimes indicate one who is especially selfish, mean, controlling, and manipulative. In their envy they may wish someone harm, because they cannot stand that others are so admired, successful, or happy. To the contrary, a predominance of Scorpio's influence can be the mark of a great and powerful healer, so check for aspects being made and other details. In surgeons, therapists, and holistic practitioners "manipulation" is rather aimed toward ending disease and restoring wellness.

Hard aspects to Pluto can be indicative of a violent nature, especially when involving Mars or Saturn, but sometimes also when involving a "benevolent planet" such as Jupiter. The Moon opposite Pluto can cause extreme mood swings and conflicts with loved ones.

Any of these planets in stressful contact with each other can lead to destructive behavior that alienates many people. In spiritually oriented or conscientious people, these types of aspects have very different effects, which can change over time. To the person who seeks personal growth, such challenging aspects indicate the type of internal pressure that is building within the psyche in order for growth to occur.

Mars and Pluto: Brushes with Death

There is tremendous power in any major aspect between Mars and Pluto, whether it is used for good or ill purposes. Even their harmonious aspects can bring intense power struggles. Mars and Pluto aspects can also increase psychic phenomena, but often tend to attract that which is dark or morbid in nature. Sexual perversion is a theme that may rear its ugly head up for any number of reasons. Some people with these aspects "play with fire" so to speak, being drawn into dangerous, life-threatening situations. They are fascinated with death and the afterlife. Others may find that they are frequently engaged in spiritual combat, discovering that they have become "spiritual warriors" over time.

Mars conjunct Pluto

The conjunction can drive a person to the pinnacle of honorable success or into acts of deviance and ruthless manipulation, where the end-goal is to have complete control over others. There is often an egotistical streak that is present, unless other aspects indicate otherwise. The sign, degree, and other aspects being made reveal more details of one's overall character.

Mars square Pluto

The person with this aspect must find outlets for the intense energy that builds up inside of them, lest they brew in the fires of fury and rage. This energy may be wisely directed toward mental, spiritual or physical pursuits. Those who lack personal reflection can become violently abusive. Even in those who are on their best behavior, others can sometimes feel threatened by such individuals and seek to oppose them in some way. This is due to their powerful aura of intensity which causes them to be feared, envied or misunderstood.

Mars opposite Pluto

There is a lot of personal ambition that can be directed toward high achievements. As with any combination between Mars and Pluto, this aspect can make someone either violent or victimized by violent behavior by others. Their anger may erupt at any moment, and they can be especially dangerous as alcoholics. This is the kind of aspect that can too easily cause one to become entangled with drug dealers, gang lords and mafiosi. In other situations, they may live in a shady neighborhood, or their work could be focused on crime scenes.

Chapter 9

Mars and Jupiter – The Inner Warrior and the Inner Protector

The astrological placements of Mars and Jupiter in the natal chart reflect personal strengths and self-protective measures. Each of these two planets represents big attitudes and have big effects, but in very different ways.

Mars – The Inner Warrior

If you ever wanted to find out what really gets someone fired up, turns them on, or what gets their blood boiling, look to the sign placement of Mars in their natal chart. Mars, named after the Roman god of war, is the fourth planet from the sun. Known as the "red planet" due to its glowing reddish hue, this planet is the symbol of our physical energy and drive overall.

Mars describes where our physical strengths lie and where psychic energy may be amplified and directed. This is the planet that describes how you fight and defend yourself against attacks of any kind. Do you accomplish this with physical force, mental prowess, emotional potency or spiritual will? Traditionally Mars has been considered a malefic planet, but it can be seen as operating in both constructive and destructive ways, for better or for worse. Mars's influence is hot and aggressive in nature which is why it is known to get us excited and worked up. Mars rules Aries and originally it was also the sole ruler of Scorpio before Pluto was discovered. The sign, house position and aspects made by it reveal the particular qualities of your life force energy, libido, and general immunity. It describes how you assert yourself in the world of business. Conversely, it can also indicate areas where you may suffer the most from conflicts, violence or illness.

Mars is the masculine principle within each person's consciousness that continues onward despite the rigors of earthly experience. It is the planet that represents the unique expression of the inner warrior, and all warriors get hurt occasionally. He is the one who picks you back up after getting knocked down in the boxing ring of life, and it is he, your inner Mars, who presses you to make a comeback after you've lost a game. Mars is not a loser and won't stop playing, or fighting, until he wins. Whatever happens, he thoroughly enjoys the competition.

Each warrior has a different superpower to draw upon to help avert danger and recover from life's blows. The placement of Mars in a natal chart offers clues as to what that superpower is and where one's source of courage lies. Mars is the recuperative power of healing, such as the scar tissue that forms around our physical wounds. Without the influence of Mars, none of us would be here today.

Mars in Aries

Positive – Courageous and resilient

Negative – Reckless and impatient

Being in its natural element and sign placement, Mars in Aries gives high energy and an ultra-masculine approach to life, sex and challenges in general. This placement of Mars bestows a notable courage and confidence, a sort of take-on-the-world attitude that brings much adventure and excitement into their lives. Sometimes those with this placement can be too rash and foolhardy in their actions, but also ambitious and destined to succeed in business and anything else they put their minds to. In haste, they may be prone to self-inflicted injuries.

Conflicts are typically experienced with male supervisors or competitors and in situations where they must take the lead. Others gladly welcome their leadership or vehemently oppose it, with seldom a reaction in between. Part of their challenge is to find a balance in self-expression, and to maintain a position of strength without alienating others or upsetting them unnecessarily. They tend to be exceptionally direct, which can work for or against them in relationships and social situations. They operate with dynamic energy and generally don't hold themselves back. After a misfortune they tend to recover quickly and keep going. On a psychic level, those with Mars in Aries are naturally resistant to any lasting impact by intrusions. They may temporarily feel angry or weary but ultimately they become stronger and more immune over time.

Mars in Aries people tend to express themselves in a direct, immediate way which may or may not seem like the socially acceptable thing to do at the time. They would rather come out with it than play it safe as they understand how toxic feelings can become when they are bottled up inside for too long. They also expect others to do the same, desiring truthfulness no matter how painful the repercussions may be.

Mars in Taurus

Positive – Focused and persistent

Negative – Stubborn and obsessed

The strength of Mars in Taurus is exhibited through physical tenacity and stamina. There is heightened sensuality. The life force energy of the native is calm, constant, and resilient but the mind can be very stubborn and unyielding at times. They can become very attached to romantic partners.

Mars in this sign indicates big money-making abilities and a fairly consistent attitude in the workplace or livelihood. Money may be a struggle at times but there is a drive to overcome any setbacks and obstacles. It can take time for them to build up momentum, but once they have it they maintain it.

Natives tend to pick a path and then stick to it. They want the good things that life has to offer and are willing to work for them, understanding that many things take time to achieve or manifest. They go that extra mile to obtain the showy sports car, high-end suit, or the sparkly diamond earrings that complement their eyes so well. The men like to take their dates to fancy restaurants. They can be skillful at self-marketing and others can learn a lot from the manner in which they promote their services. Due to their highly fixed views, they sometimes experience trouble with coworkers or employers. They may experience power struggles with others around finances or possessions. Eventually, with applied effort they will reach their goals and obtain their desired position, which in many cases leads to accumulated wealth.

On a psychic level, Mars in Taurus people can be sluggish or get into a funk now and then and may need some motivation to pick up the pace and develop a more positive outlook. They tend to fester with bitterness and resentment rather than anger and become fixated on a certain outcome. This can lead some of them to adopt a depressive attitude at times. Once they realize that they're sliding downhill in their mentality they generally decide to pick themselves up and get back into gear for optimal performance.

Mars in Gemini

Positive – Quick-witted and versatile

Negative – Unstable and argumentative

Mars in Gemini tends to promote seemingly random and unpredictable dispensations of energy. Those with this placement have the combination of sharp intellect and athletic capacity. One minute they may be at rock bottom and the next there is nothing in the world that can stop them. One minute they are with you and the next minute they are nowhere to be seen and you have no idea when you'll see or hear from them again. Quick- tongued and witty, they have brilliant minds filled with all kinds of wildly genius ideas. They can be stealthy, swift and unpredictable in their movements which are useful skills to have when it comes to combat. Most conflicts are experienced with siblings, relatives or housemates when Mars is in this sign or its corresponding third house.

When you need to know how to win a case or fight for some social cause in the form of a moving speech you would find an ally in one who has Mars in Gemini. There is a high degree of intelligence and an ability to appeal to those from all walks of life. There is a restlessness here that indicates these folks need plenty of variety in their daily activities. They can be prone to excess worry and obsessive thoughts. They should avoid stimulants such as caffeine which only amplifies their already high-strung nervous system.

Mars in Gemini talks their feelings through, sometimes to the point of exhaustion. These folks can be outspoken but often know exactly what to say to get things moving in a stagnant situation. Their tongues can be as sharp as their clever minds. As wordsmiths they can easily cut others to bits with their words. Humor is dark and often sarcastic.

Mars in Cancer

Positive – Nurturing and devoted

Negative – Emotionally overbearing and needy

The Mars in Cancer native is intensely emotional but resilient, with great reserves of inner strength that rise up when needed. Sensitivities are concealed, and you won't know what these people are going through unless you know them very well. They can appear completely well-adjusted and unaffected on the surface when they are experiencing a lot of stress. Conversely, they may have an understated courage, but the appearance of cowardice. Most of their conflicts are experienced at home or behind the scenes. They often erupt from the person's subconscious mind in the form of bizarre dreams, due to all of their unresolved issues.

Those with Mars in Cancer who were hurt or witnessed a lot of violence as children learned not to let others get too close until they were sure they could trust them. Self-defense is accomplished with storms of emotion or total avoidance. Typically, this person makes for a loyal friend, ally, and lover. There is a strong sense of devotion and protectiveness toward family, and they will take on the fight with anyone who threatens their loved ones. They may be advocates of children's rights or work in battered women's shelters. In some, Mars in Cancer can produce a state of hyper-vigilance, preparedness and keen alertness to potential dangers of any kind. They are not the type to lose their keys or misplace their wallets, but they'll be the first to arm up with shotguns and front porch surveillance cameras.

Some may feel there are no available routes of expression for their many pent-up feelings that have accumulated over time. If they have repeatedly been met with hostility, they may have been forced to swallow their anger which boils inside of their bellies, causing an internal implosion that wears them and others down. They need sports or other activities of a physical nature to be able to distribute their energy in safe and effective ways.

Mars in Leo

Positive: Creative and exuberant

Negative: Pushy and domineering

Mars in the sign of Leo is "on fire", figuratively speaking. That is to say, fire meets fire in a piping hot combination. The native of this placement tends to be full of dynamic energy with a huge drive for creative self-expression and success. They can be playful and outgoing, and others can learn from them how to extract greater joy out of life overall. There is a latent controlling streak which can be overbearing at times, especially when Mars in Leo's ego is bruised. Their pride can be their downfall if they go too far with it. They despise appearing weak in any way and will even lie sometimes about how they feel to avoid sympathy and maintain their powerful image.

Due to their confidence, colorful personalities and highly sophisticated natures, these people can attract very powerful and influential people into their orbit. Commonly, they take well to the spotlight with their regal bearing. They make passionate lovers and equally passionate enemies. As leaders of society, they are here to direct rather than to take orders, which can become a heavy burden of responsibility for them at times. Their views about certain issues and occurrences are often one-sided and when their temper is ignited in addition, this can be particularly unnerving for others. When operating at their highest potential, Mars-Leo is a strong defender of all those who are young and helpless, including animals.

These people often don't quite fit in with their family, in school or in most social settings. However, they make powerful allies to others in creative expression and business endeavors. It is amazing for others to behold how much confidence they can exude, which can be positive or negative depending on circumstances. They have something important to teach the rest of humanity about dignity and self-respect.

Mars in Virgo

Positive: Service-oriented and humble

Negative: Judgmental and intolerant

In Virgo, Mars is hard-working and determined to improve in a number of areas, both in themselves and the world around them. Service-oriented and ever ready to help another, they tend to hold high standards for themselves as well as for everyone else. Many with this placement are interested in natural foods and healing methods, and it is common to find them in the medical profession. Somewhat perfectionist in their outlook, those with Mars in this sign or in the sixth house may come across to others as being cool, detached or ascetic as they work steadily toward a goal. Their criticisms may seem harsh and abrupt at times.

It often appears that they deprive themselves of certain earthly pleasures but in truth they are simply prioritizing the things and activities listed on their very full calendars. They are able to put aside their emotions in favor of work and wait until they are alone and can process what they've kept inside all day. Behind closed doors they can be very sensual, indulging in foods, things or behaviors that most people will never know about.

As a warrior Mars in Virgo is the full-on "fix-it" hero or heroine. Being very interested in the welfare and progress of their fellow humans and sentient beings, they are here to solve problems that others either can't or won't, and to help heal those who have not been able to in other ways. Mars in Virgo is not angry by nature, but can express irritation in the form of micromanaging and seeking to control others. They are acute observers of other people's problems and weaknesses, often inwardly calculating in what large or subtle ways they could improve others' lives. Unfortunately, this behavior sometimes backfires on them.

Mars in Libra

Positive: Artistic and intelligent

Negative: Relationship crisis-prone and irritable

Both beauty and fair play are very important to those with Mars in Libra. They are passionate about justice and may become involved in some form of activism. Some of the areas that they most excel in are the literary arts, theater, and other creative pursuits. They can make effective lawyers and judges, and enjoy holding a position that oversees human affairs. They have many attractions to others and attract many to them. Divorce or other types of relationship endings tend to be common when Mars is in this sign due to major relationship imbalances. Marriage may occur a few times before one settles down with the right match.

The Mars-Libran can sometimes be the third-party agent who makes or breaks bonds. This of course can be good or very bad depending on the circumstances. Some relationships are so dysfunctional that the best solution is separation. In some cases, they may become stuck in the middle of a three-way relationship of some kind that is not necessarily romantic. They can find themselves taking on too many of the problems of their loved ones. Business ventures should always include solid legal contracts to avoid arguments and legal disputes later on.

Mars in Libra often processes many of their emotions first through their intellect and then through their conversations. They might not allow themselves to fully experience their own negative feelings. They sometimes prefer to talk in the third person as if those feelings don't even belong to them. They can become dynamic public figures.

Mars in Scorpio

Positive – Perceptive and determined

Negative – Vindictive and relentless

The survival instinct and capacity for self-discipline is incredibly strong with Mars in Scorpio. Mars was the original ruling planet of this sign. The native of this placement is high in vitality, often with a voracious libido. The Mars-Scorpio person has staying power and does not waver from their intentions. The emotional water element is warmed by Mars, and it flows as steadily as blood courses through the body. Here is the capacity to initiate deep healing or to inflict tremendous damage. In some cases, a person demonstrates both positive and negative polarities of Mars, depending on their spiritual orientation or personal levels of fulfillment.

The person with this placement of Mars may have special occult abilities, used for good or evil purposes. They also tend to attract powerful people with these same abilities. This can bring serious conflicts into their life if they are not careful. Death and danger are more thrilling than frightening to these people and they tend to toy around with both. They exude much energy, are skilled in what they do and determined to win any kind of battle they find themselves engaged in. They are often found in professions that require a great deal of concentration. They enter into a super focused mode of consciousness while they work.

Some Mars in Scorpio people can seethe with rage and jealousy if they do not keep these emotions in check. Many of them have powerful healing abilities and make excellent surgeons, body workers, and Reiki practitioners. They need appropriate outlets for their passions and creative expression.

Mars in Sagittarius

Positive – Enthusiastic and enterprising

Negative – Scattered and unfaithful

Mars thoroughly enjoys his freedom in the fire sign of Sagittarius. The native of this placement is an adventurer, and may be somewhat of a daredevil to boot. There is a great love of the outdoors and of all kinds of exciting activities. That's not a problem in and of itself but it can be too easy for temptations to steer these people off course and cause them to scatter their energies. It is often hard for them to settle down with just one person and that is one of the things that most often gets them into "psychic" trouble. Eventually they may, but it would probably take a long while.

Nonetheless, the Mars in Sagittarius person accomplishes many things in a short amount of time when they are really engaged in their work. These are the Renaissance men and women of the Zodiac, so well versed in several areas. They are naturally confident and can be socially outspoken, though rarely out of spite and malice. They often come across as dogmatic in their views, which is at times the cause for heated debates. Their wild sense of humor is one of their most endearing qualities. Some of them also take a strong interest in religious and philosophical subjects, which would become closely entwined with their careers in some way. As long as they don't spread themselves too thin, they tend to be loyal to their friends and family.

Although Mars occupies a fire sign in Sagittarius, the person with this placement is not angry by nature. They may stir resentment in others with their words or actions, often without realizing the impact they are having until and unless it becomes super obvious to them. It helps them to slow down a little bit sometimes to hear themselves think, to reflect on their lives and listen to the feedback of others.

Mars in Capricorn

Positive – Hard-working and responsible

Negative – Power-hungry and cold

Mars is powerfully placed in the sign of Capricorn. There is both ambition and endurance which enables those with Mars here to work longer hours and under more stressful circumstances than most others would be capable of handling. With tremendous dedication, they pour their passion into their work and careers. In some cases, their close relationships may suffer as a result of this, as loved ones may complain of neglect. Their greatest conflicts tend to revolve both around work and at home because they can become overly serious, too rigid and obsessed with rules and order. Whether or not their personal space is orderly may be an entirely different matter.

There is an inherent preference for taking on the role of leadership, and only those who are in an obvious position of authority above them will be respected in such a way. In this sign, Mars is a force for high levels of productivity. Mars-Capricorn natives make some of the most successful statesmen, executives, and business-owners. They approach their hobbies with the same amount of zeal and as their livelihood and work, but of course place them lower on the list of priorities. They live to work hard and play hard, and they may take others by surprise by being the life of the party.

Mars in Capricorn natives don't get mad, at least not in the same way that ordinary humans do. They simply get even, or else they set aside their irritation and, by choosing their battles wisely continue to go about their work in an efficient manner. Emotion does not dictate their major decisions, unless other factors in the natal chart indicate otherwise.

Mars in Aquarius

Positive – Innovative and friendly

Negative – Proud and condescending

Mars in Aquarius denotes original thinking, erratic spurts of energy and a highly innovative nature. It indicates a rather unorthodox approach to most things that are considered to be traditional in nature. This placement of Mars makes for leaders, visionaries and way-showers, here to guide or uplift humanity. Whether or not they become well-known, and they often do, they tend to feel energized within groups, friends and people outside of the family circle.

Paradoxically they are also somewhat detached from deep involvement. Their strength lies in their intellectual abilities and passionate dedication to learning. They may be considered eccentric in many social settings, and both their words and actions often take others by surprise. They are naturally contrary and do things differently than others in part due to their strong sense of independence, but in part because they are genuine truth seekers. Sometimes they can be domineering and egotistical in their approach to problem solving. Their conflicts generally lie in their unwillingness to compromise or their tendency to push their ideas onto others. They are hard workers.

Mars-Aquarians are often the defenders and champions of their friends, unafraid to speak up or stand up on their behalf. They are bold in their self-expression in general as they go against the grain of society, which can either inspire or invoke fear and discomfort in others. In whatever group they may belong to, they will always be the rebel who stands out among the rest.

Mars in Pisces

Positive – Spiritually oriented and forgiving

Negative – Sadomasochistic and evasive

The aggressive qualities of Mars are softened in the deeply sensitive sign of Pisces. That is, unless there are deeply buried tensions, in which case they may seek physically intense or therapeutic means of releasing their pent-up steam. The strength of this planet is expressed through giving and helping, whether through mundane or spiritual service. There is a high tolerance level for many types of settings and situations that would be too stressful or distasteful for others. Anger is so quickly diffused into different avenues that it rarely has the opportunity to dominate this person's actions.

In rare circumstances, accumulated frustrations may finally explode in a moment of completely irrational behavior. The Mars in Pisces person may quickly forgive others or else channel their intense feelings through art and music. Their weakness is a tendency to swim away from certain kinds of conflicts and problems rather than facing them directly. This means that unless there are strong down-to-earth factors in their chart as a whole, they may be easily deceived and prone to escapism or fantasy of some kind. They prefer to do work that is somehow charitable, emotionally based or spiritually fulfilling. They may have a tendency to sacrifice themselves in intimate relationships.

Mars in Pisces can be a challenging and unpredictable placement. In an unstable personality, projections would be extreme. In a conscientious person, there are heightened senses and creative abilities combined with a spiritual outlook.

Mars Retrograde

Every two years the planet Mars goes retrograde, but it takes seventy-nine years for it to pass retrograde through all twelve signs. The period when Mars stations Direct is particularly explosive, bringing with it the collected forces of all that went unexpressed while retrograde.

The person with Mars retrograde may experience a feeling that they are not able to fully express themselves until they have passed certain tests. Anger, and creative or sexual energy might be repressed for long periods of time, and they may hold themselves back a lot, particularly when it comes to relationships and career moves. Deep emotions are processed inwardly before being expressed. There will be triggers that must be handled carefully as many of the life lessons necessitate a pause before action or reaction. In a spiritual sense, those with Mars Retrograde can become very much in tune with the life pulse in nature and the environment, and therefore capable of addressing any imbalances that arise with tremendous precision. If they choose to meditate, their personal insights will be profound.

Jupiter – The Inner Protector

The planet Jupiter is traditionally known as the Great Benefic, and is associated with good fortune and abundance. Having governance over the signs of Sagittarius and Pisces, its sign and house placement in your chart reveals the nature of your moral character, belief system, and the kind of metaphorical cushioning at your disposal when you find yourself in danger.

In Eastern mysticism, Jupiter is literally seen as the guru, teacher or planet of wisdom. It would not be far off to say that Jupiter is the planet that reflects one's dharma, a Sanskrit word that relates to one's true calling in a spiritual, but not necessarily in a worldly sense. The Sun is what represents one's cosmic purpose and creative spark, whereas Jupiter expands the nature of one's soul qualities. The more awareness you have of these divine gifts the more likely you are to utilize their benefits. The symbol for Jupiter is the crescent of spirit rising above gross matter.

Before the discovery of Neptune, Jupiter was the planet believed to preside over spiritual benefactors, angels and guides. It still has an influence relative to our awareness and connection to such beings. Jupiter's sign can reveal where and how our guardian angels are most actively involved in our lives. It shows the kind of buffering influences at our disposal and how they may be of benefit to ourselves and others. The traditional qualities of Jupiter are moist and hot, and like Neptune, this planet has some astrological connection with the water element overall.

Part of Jupiter's protective qualities on a metaphysical level may stem from its enormous size. The Great Red Spot seen with Jupiter is said to be a high-pressure storm that rotates in a counter-clockwise direction. It may be viewed as a symbolic representation of Jupiter's capacity to erase, vacuum and purify so-called negative karma that might be reflected in the placements of the malefic planets Mars and Saturn. While Mars is seen to bring conflict, Saturn is associated with limitations and hardships. Jupiter is known to expand our horizons, options and luck overall. That the Great Red Spot could be some kind of metaphorical healing vortex is an interesting idea to consider.

Since Jupiter's influence increases whatever he touches it can be easy to overdo a good thing, or to create excess. In any case, Jupiter's sign, house placement and aspects made to other planets point toward where and how we are most likely to become educated by experience versus memorizing the ideas that have been presented to us by others. It is life itself that enables us to grow spiritually, and thus Jupiter represents true wisdom rather than mere knowledge collected from books or by scholars. It also shows what forms of protection we automatically draw to us in life, as a result of being wise in some area. There is a close link between ignorance and suffering, and Jupiter plays an important role that leads to salvation. He highlights the tools and resources at our disposal in order to overcome the challenges that we are faced with.

Jupiter in Aries

Positive: Confidence and exuberance

Negative: Burnout from overexertion

Jupiter in Aries brings protection as a result of being assertive and taking the lead. This position of Jupiter stimulates both energy and optimism, two qualities that contribute to overall immunity. It is one indication of having been born under favorable circumstances where the person had good opportunities to develop themselves physically, intellectually, spiritually, and financially. They come into this life with a strong sense of identity and self-esteem, unless other factors in the natal chart interfere. It is therefore generally easy to attract benefits into life and to stand up for themselves when necessary. Jupiter-Aries people tend to inspire, uplift and encourage others with their natural confidence and enthusiasm.

Jupiter in Taurus

Positive: Easy-going nature, love of beauty

Negative: Stubborn, addicted to pleasure

Jupiter in Taurus brings beauty and luxuries in such forms as financial abundance, an attractive mate or a beautiful home. Many people with Jupiter in Taurus are highly sexed. This placement also indicates creative abilities, a love of nature and in many natives, a green thumb. Jupiter in Taurus people prefer to plan ahead which gives them the security that there will always be something to fall back on if a certain plan fails. There is a skill for salesmanship if the person chooses to develop it. Overspending can sometimes be a problem but new methods of making money will also be devised. Their nature is conservative in many areas and decisions are made carefully after thorough consideration. The tendency to make major investments is strong.

Jupiter in Gemini

Positive: Skilled communicators, curious, open-minded

Negative: Scattered, argumentative

Jupiter in Gemini brings protection through mental fields and communications. There are many talents and many interests that lead in different directions. The mind is sharp and able to quickly sift through and process vast quantities of information at high speed. This position of Jupiter can sometimes cause one to become scattered and restless but there is often a love of and good fortune around traveling. They may not settle for long at one job or line of work. Their careers are diverse, and they may have multiple streams of income. Jupiter in Gemini natives may offer guidance and protection to others through both the spoken and written word. They tend to receive benefits through friends and in-laws, even when Jupiter's position is afflicted.

Jupiter in Cancer

Positive: Nurturing and protective

Negative: Prone to indulgence and emotionalism

Jupiter in Cancer provides emotional protection and actual physical refuge whenever the world outside gets too overwhelming. Due to the nurturing capacities of those with this placement there will usually also be some degree of reciprocal assistance that they receive from friends, family or allies that supports them in times of need. This helps to ensure that they always have enough food and a place to sleep, whether luxurious or humble. The Jupiter in Cancer person naturally makes others feel comfortable and cared for. They may especially benefit through inheritance or real estate, but usually not until they have reached middle age. This is when their lives really begin to improve overall.

Jupiter in Leo

Positive: Creative and dynamic

Negative: Egotistical and overbearing

Jupiter in Leo brings protection in creative endeavors and self-expression. The drive for significance or a position of leadership is very pronounced and often aimed at large causes. Those with Jupiter in this sign take great pride in their children and should be careful not to spoil them. For some, the pride revolves around creative projects which tend to stand out in some way, so they are great at self-marketing. These people are inherently artistic and prefer to put their own stamp on things rather than using generic models. Lively and outgoing, they make great entertainers and entrepreneurs. Generosity with others is what keeps their good fortune coming.

Jupiter in Virgo

Positive: Hard-working

Negative: Excessively critical

Jupiter in Virgo indicates that protection may be found in the workplace, the healing profession, and in service to others. This is not an especially ambitious placement for Jupiter, unless the ambitions are aimed toward helping others. There may be a strong interest in the field of nutrition or in performing random acts of charity. They find both comfort and benefits in their work. It is possible that work entails travel or they find themselves doing a lot of different things on different days. The Jupiter in Virgo person seeks solutions to problems both large and small in order to make others' lives easier. Jupiter's biggest blessings are found in working and in matters and items that require much attention to detail.

Jupiter in Libra

Positive: Cooperative, fair, justice-oriented

Negative: Overly empathic, lost in others' problems

Jupiter in Libra brings protection through the practice of fairness and mediation with others. Although their task in helping to resolve disputes may be great, those with this placement tend to receive benefits through marriage or other committed relationships, including those focused on business ventures. Even if Jupiter is challenged in the natal chart, relationships will eventually work in their favor, and those that don't will be released amicably. Those with Jupiter in this sign may do well in politics and the literary arts. They prefer mental rather than physical work overall. They tend to be scholarly, possessing a certain kind of charm and diplomacy that wins the favor of many people.

Jupiter in Scorpio

Positive: Intuitive and passionate

Negative: Cunning and obsessive

Jupiter in Scorpio brings protection in deeply complex situations that require a great deal of focus and stamina. Magnetism, libido and life force energy are strong and consistent. Others are drawn to these people like moths to a flame. There may be both interest and abilities involving psychic healing, psychology or research. Nothing is too scary, deep or unfathomable for those with this influence. Even if Jupiter is negatively impacted, there is a strong drive to overcome challenges and great knowledge gained from experience. Jupiter in Scorpio shows the way through emotional entanglements or intrigues and reveals hidden gems of truth in the process.

Jupiter in Sagittarius

Positive: Outgoing and upbeat

Negative: Overly confident or reckless, big spenders

Jupiter is in its home in Sagittarius, highlighting both an interest and protection in travel, education, foreign cultures and daring enterprises. Adventure, education and new opportunities are all big priorities with Jupiter in this sign. An outgoing nature and love of the outdoors attracts all kinds of interesting people and experiences. Freedom-loving, good-humored and philosophical,

Jupiter in Sagittarius native brings inspiration to others. A strong sense of ethics is also what helps steer these people and those they care about out of danger. They can get along with most anyone and are great fun to be around, getting others laughing until it hurts.

Jupiter in Capricorn

Positive: Resourceful, mature, disciplined

Negative: Can be prone to power trips

Jupiter in Capricorn brings protection through organization and resourcefulness. Jupiter here encourages one to make quilts out of scraps, and lemonade out of lemons, figuratively speaking. Those with Jupiter in this sign have a strong aptitude for business pursuits and environmentally focused work. When they have made up their mind about doing something, they put all of their efforts into achieving it. They are very skilled in woodwork, gardening and mundane projects that can take a large amount of time and dedication to build. They have the patience to work their way to the top in any area and to obtain a position of leadership in their chosen field.

Jupiter in Aquarius

Positive: Unique, innovative

Negative: Willful and overly intellectual

Jupiter in Aquarius brings protection through open-mindedness and intellectual pursuits. Those with Jupiter in this sign have a unique perspective on life and are always sifting through vast quantities of information and considering the overview of all things. They may greatly benefit through friends and groups that they closely associate with, and often have a wide circle of friends and associates on the internet. There is a strong interest in scientific advancement, sociopolitical matters, philosophy, and justice. Being adept at keeping up with the latest trends and developments in technology, they are naturally suited toward teaching others what they have learned.

Jupiter in Pisces

Positive: Intuitive and divinely inspired

Negative: Isolated or unmotivated in worldly matters

Jupiter, in its home sign Pisces, brings spiritual protection. They may work or offer charity behind the scenes. Emotions and spiritual leanings are usually much stronger than personal ambitions, and psychic abilities are strong. Those with these placements make ideal healers and caregivers. No matter how much danger they brush up against, there always seems to be something or somebody who is ready to come to their aid, even if just in the nick of time. They may often seem to be confined to solitude, but they make great use of their alone time and gain strength and inspiration from the silence.

Jupiter Retrograde

Every year, Jupiter goes retrograde for about four months. It makes a retrograde cycle through each of the signs in approximately thirteen years. A period with Jupiter in a trine with the Sun ends with the Sun entering a square with Jupiter. Even then retrograde Jupiter has a benign influence, but is turned inward and has some different effects than it would when direct. There is a pronounced Jupiterian quality in those who were born with Jupiter Retrograde, in that they tend to be innately philosophical, generous and kind. They are more likely to tune inward for guidance than to seek it outside of themselves. They are humble and hate asking others for help, mostly because they do not wish to trouble anyone. The usual daring and enterprising nature of Jupiter may be subdued, and they could have difficulty in trusting their own decisions. There may be a need to develop stronger faith and a positive outlook, or to take some bigger risks in order to grow and prosper.

Major Aspects between Mars and Jupiter

Major aspects made between these two planets greatly heighten their effects. Traditionally these planets are not known to be on friendly terms with one another. Whether harmonious or challenging, there is a strong sense of ego present when they are connected. The union of two very potent planetary energies greatly amplifies one's overall personality and livelihood. There is a tendency to tackle challenges in a macho sort of way, and often it may be easier for the person to relate to men on an intellectual level than it is to women, or it could mean that they are very masculine and driven in a career or physical sense. There may be important male figures in the person's life who share a similar philosophical outlook. Whatever their occupation may be, they are highly productive.

Conjunction

With Mars conjunct Jupiter there is good health and tremendous powers of recovery, even if other aspects of the other indicate poor health or misfortune. There is an ability to overcome life's challenges and to achieve worldly success, comfort and prosperity. The tone of the chart will indicate whether this comes naturally, at a young age or will be worked toward and achieved later in life. The person with this aspect is a fighter and will always stand up for what they believe in, and most often they do take a strong stance in the areas of their personal value system. This may win them the favors of admirers but may also create enemies who are threatened by their powerful magnetism and audacity. Excessive pride may be the cause of self-undoing. There also tend to be strong religious, spiritual or philosophical leanings that influence their major decisions.

One with Mars conjunct Jupiter would do well in teaching, publishing and general work with the public. There exists a certain kind of determination and willpower that others only wish they had. When they set out to do something they thrust themselves into it wholeheartedly. At some point their work may involve long-distance travel. They should take caution against outrageous risks, as willpower can be stronger than logic. The desire to overcome fears and limitations can sometimes override reasoning abilities. They may sometimes push themselves too hard and need to learn moderation when it comes to both work and play.

Sextile or Trine

When Mars forms either a sextile or trine to Jupiter there is a healthy balance between the warrior aspect of one's personality and the protector. With either a sextile or trine there is general harmony between your body and mind. There is usually good health along with a love of adventure, sports and the outdoors. With either a sextile or a trine between Mars and Jupiter, the individual tends to be friendly and outgoing, and a champion to loved ones. Judgment is fair and gains the respect of others. There is a strong sex drive, but sex alone does not satisfy. A deep and meaningful relationship is desired and with this aspect one is willing to work to achieve that. Their nature is outgoing and nothing is considered to be oppressive for too long. Because of this, the person can be very successful in business, especially as an entrepreneur.

Square

Many of the qualities of the conjunction also apply to the square. In both there is often overconfidence and an extraordinarily high libido, but possibly more so in the square. The difficulty here is that there can sometimes be too much force and recklessness behind many actions. Desires are amplified and can disturb the peace in relationships. Sometimes the choices being made lead to self-sabotage, but a high degree of intelligence often acts as a saving grace. These people are powerhouses of energy that can be used in any number of areas with skill and precision.

One with a square between Mars and Jupiter cannot tolerate being fenced in and wants freedom more than anything. Whether male or female there is a strong masculine presence, but in a female chart this can be challenging to deal with when it comes to certain mundane affairs and romantic involvement. In the heat of any battle, this person can be a formidable foe, but usually will walk away from a fight rather than waste energy and time on someone found to be unworthy of the expenditure. When spiritually inclined, energy is directed toward evolving and growing in profound ways.

Opposition

The opposition between Mars and Jupiter can be very good or very bad, depending on how the person chooses to direct this energy. They may experience much resistance from others due to their strong personalities which can often invoke fear or anger. There is a pronounced competitive attitude, which is not necessarily exhibited in an unfriendly way but in a way that provokes others nonetheless. Sometimes one is unaware of this effect that they have on people. Personal convictions may be too strong, and if there is a religious orientation this could easily increase one's bias overall.

There is a tendency toward pushiness and domination.

Positive expressions of the opposition include strong recuperative powers, athletic abilities and physical strength. Some kind of physical outlets are necessary for the consistent libido and energy levels implied. A work position where one maintains some degree of authority is preferable because a lot can be both accomplished and directed by them.

Chapter 10

Coping with Eclipse Season

In ancient times eclipses were ominous occurrences that warned of impending doom. Certain cultures thought that when the moon was eclipsed it resembled a demon, and that when the sun was eclipsed it had been devoured by supernatural beasts. Solar eclipses, also referred to as rings of fire, are such mysterious phenomena, as the sun appears to be suddenly devoured by darkness. They have been known as the Alchemical Wedding between Sol and Luna, and were widely depicted in Medieval artwork. During a lunar eclipse the luminosity of the moon increases dramatically while also being obscured from our earthly perspective. From an astrological standpoint, eclipses tend to test us and obscure certain things from view in our lives. It is only after the eclipse that the true nature of what was hidden from us becomes revealed.

The Lunar Nodes spend about 1.5 years (just over 18 months) in their signs, and eclipses revolve through the Zodiac approximately once every 18 years. Each eclipse belongs to family of approximately 70 eclipses that cover a span close to 1,300 years. These eclipses form what is known as a Saros cycle. Bernadette Brady shared interesting information about Saros cycles in her book on Predictive Astrology, The Eagle and the Lark.

Most modern day astrologers refer to the eclipses in relation to the model of the globe, with the family of eclipses spiraling either up or down, toward one pole or another. I take the geocentric view as it appears to us that the eclipses, planetary bodies and fixed stars above us are moving in concentric courses, at various distances from a northern center and southern/outer circumference. An ancient bronze device known as the world's oldest computer, the Antikythera mechanism, was discovered on a shipwreck in Greece in 1901. The device, estimated to be thousands of years old, was designed to accurately track celestial phenomena including the Saros cycle using dials. It shows accuracy to this day.

Eclipses are most notable when it comes to world events but can also bring irrevocable change to our personal lives, especially when they transit a natal planet. Unpredictable in many ways, the changes that take place can be positive or negative depending on where we are at the time and what has been built up in our lives beforehand. When the eclipse is conjunct the North node, something is being brought into our lives. It is known as the Dragon's Head and it acts as a point of entry. When conjunct the South node, known as the Dragon's Tail, something is exiting relevant to the sign and any planets affected. There is often a jolt of energy shot into our electrical systems that may either weaken or strengthen us. A person could be struck with sudden illness or instead they could finally overcome it. A certain body part associated with the planet being eclipsed could begin to malfunction.

One can gain insight into what will be happening throughout the year by studying the areas where eclipses will be transiting in the natal chart. There are approximately four eclipses per year, occurring in two sets. On the day prior to, the day of and the day just after an eclipse, what we see is not necessarily what we get. It is wise to wait on major decisions and investments or signing important contracts. Many people find they are more vulnerable to astral influences and negativity within their environment.

When an eclipse falls on any of the four angles of the natal chart, important changes are indicated by the nature of the angle. On the Ascendant, the eclipse signifies a new cycle, and possibly a renewed self-image, especially if the North Node is there. The eclipse will simultaneously draw energy into the area of one angle and clear some energy out of the opposite one. If an eclipse is impacting the Ascendant it will also be impacting the Descendant but in a different way. On the Descendant the eclipse highlights relationships, which may be coming in with the North Node or possibly ending with the South Node. On the Nadir, the eclipse is bringing domestic and emotional changes. On the Midheaven, the eclipse brings attention to one's career or life purpose. The tighter the orb involving an eclipse, whether to a planet or an angle, the stronger the influence. Whether or not a transiting eclipse makes any conjunctions or major aspects in the natal chart, the house it falls in will reveal the area of life undergoing dramatic changes.

Sun

When an eclipse contacts one's Sun, it can become important for a person to redefine or clarify some aspect of their character, social image or their life path. It can highlight fatherhood, relationships to paternal figures, the role as a husband, or in serving as a protective influence over others. This is a highly significant transit. The solar eclipse conjunction to one's Sun coincides with one's solar return and represents a new beginning for the year to come. When the Moon in a Lunar Eclipse forms a conjunction to one's Sun, it can help to recall or clear something from the past. Egotism or insecurity can undermine success, but true confidence can also emerge where it was lacking. With the North Node, positive energy is incoming and with the South Node there may be less energy to draw upon, or perhaps there is simply a greater focus on the spiritual rather than physical life. Psychic protection methods that assist one during this transit may include herbs, gems, flower essences and exercises that bring strength to the heart and eyes. You may wish to visualize and surround yourself with solar symbols. Color therapy using yellow and gold, and wearing genuine gold jewelry can be helpful. Wearing white, light or bright colors are generally better than wearing black or dark ones during the year when an eclipse to one's Sun occurs. More importantly, though, are the colors received by the body's electrical system through light and health-giving foods.

Moon

An eclipse in conjunction to the Moon can trigger emotionally charged events. It can highlight fertility, maternity and maternal figures in the native's life. Changes may revolve around home life or security. There may be visitors in the home or a relocation to another place of residence. Overall sensitivity is increased. A pearl, worn or carried can help to bring balance in some cases. Selenite is also a lunar stone with clearing and protective qualities, more affordable than pearls. Wearing the color white, burning white candles or taking soothing baths may be helpful during this time. It may be the perfect time to get a massage or head to a spa for some much-needed self-care. Medicine and any major medical procedures should be chosen carefully, as effects are stronger now for better or worse. It may be best to lay low and not do too much socializing when the South Node of the eclipse is transiting one's Moon. The aura is too permeable and open to outside influences. Popularity may soar or plummet depending on the condition and other aspects made to the Moon.

Mercury

Eclipses to Mercury can affect mental states and the nervous system. Social interactions are heightened now in general. There may be new job opportunities or lots of small trips being made. Negative associated issues may involve mental breakdowns, communication glitches, double-dealing, and theft. They may be a focus on pets and small animals, or on siblings, relatives and neighbors. When the South Node eclipse transits Mercury be very careful about signing contracts and keep an eye on valuable possessions. It is possible that one will become misunderstood or misunderstand what others are trying to convey during this time. When the North node transits Mercury, things can get very busy and hectic and there is a high possibility of becoming scattered, spreading oneself too thin. Any writing or speaking endeavors may be enhanced. It is possible that for some people the opposite would be true, in that things come more into focus. Either way, avoid falling into the wrong kind of trance during this general time period. The mind can more easily fall under outside influences, but this is particularly so if self-awareness or self-discipline is lacking. In short, avoid anything that could make one vulnerable to mind control. Taking time-outs to stretch or meditate can help immensely. Simplification is key. Slow, relaxing music can help to quiet one's thoughts and reverse shallow breathing. Herbs that calm and support the nervous system can be helpful. Examples of these include Chamomile, Lavender and Valerian.

Venus

An eclipse to Venus can bring in radical change associated with love, beauty, self-esteem or money that is welcome or not depending on various factors, with the North Node eclipsing Venus usually being more of a favorable influence than the South Node. This does depend on the sign and other details either way. Relationships to females are going to be highlighted. New relationships have an electric, fated quality to them. Their durability and longevity are another matter and could depend on the sign it's in among other things. In some cases, a relationship ends under this influence or a couple is focused on their combined finances. Social activities may increase. People may need to watch for overindulgence in sex or food which could lead to problems later on. Sugar could be especially tempting but not good for health. Artistic and musical endeavors are favored. To protect oneself in a romantic sense, don't jump into a new relationship without thorough consideration. The same goes for financial investments. Attraction is at an all-time peak but all that glitters isn't gold. Keeping fresh or live roses in one's environment can be helpful. To harmonize with Venus through color, wear or use colors in one's environment in the white, pink and red spectrum. Green is also Venusian. Copper jewelry or amulets can be especially protective during this time.

Mars

Eclipses to natal Mars can be explosive in nature but especially in fire signs. In water signs they can be implosive, in air signs stress-generating, and in earth signs volcanic. Masculine energy and relationships to men are emphasized. If there are no appropriate outlets for physical expression, the energy of this contact can cause implosions of some kind on physical or psychic levels. Positively, there may be an increase of healthy vitality or negatively a surge of rage and destruction. When activated by the North Node, the person's energy is amplified overall. Activated by the South Node, life-force energy may be depleted or one may be the victim of some accident. Such an eclipse can stir up arguments, agitation and eruptions of a physical or psychic nature. Infection is a high risk. Someone might attack or be attacked by others. This can be determined in a person's lifestyle. If overactive they need to wind down and cool off. If they have been underactive, they may receive the nudge to get moving again. Weight lifting and calisthenics can be helpful in this regard. Anti-inflammatory herbs, naturally blue oils and stones are recommended for this transit except in rare cases when Mars does well with even more heat.

Jupiter

Eclipses to Jupiter bring big waves of energy and optimism that encourage one to reach for new heights and to take worthy and honorable risks. With the South Node transiting, impulsive behavior and gambling is tempting but should actually be avoided because more money is going out than coming in. There could be trouble around publication. With the North Node transiting good fortune may increase but is also easy to indulge oneself or overdo certain activities. There may be a focus on growing awareness in a spiritual sense or education involving culture, archaeology, or history. Travel may be highlighted whether for pleasure, education or business purposes. Legal activities may intensify or gain resolution. A significant teacher may appear or disappear from one's life. One may become an initiate of a spiritual discipline, but it is also possible that a person breaks away from some kind of religious tradition, cult or belief system that no longer serves them. Jupiter is a naturally protective influence but can produce excess which can lead to illness or other issues. Jupiter can help one to grow a "thicker skin" so that one is not so affected by outer negative energies. Jupiter energy remedies include bright yellow flowers, protective stones such as Turquoise, Azurite and Malachite. Herbs such as Dandelion and Milk Thistle have been used to support the liver which is ruled by Jupiter.

Saturn

An eclipse to Saturn can bring on extra workloads, responsibilities or limitations. It may bring one into contact with wise elders, authority figures or older people in general. One may experience the loss of an important elder in their life. Positively, challenging situations of importance begin to show signs of improvement. Negatively, one may feel hemmed in by Saturn's stern influence, unable to act or escape until the effects of this eclipse are over, which can last for a long time. A South Node eclipse over Saturn can be a trying and triggering influence that exacerbates bodily aches, pains and sickness, but in reverse (Saturn over one's South Node) this could be even more pronounced and long lasting if Saturn goes Retrograde over the planet. It could especially bring a period of loneliness. A North Node eclipse over Saturn can also solidify plans, particularly if a person has long been working toward a goal. The most effective forms of protection against the influence of the Nodes combined with Saturn is to put forth effort toward bringing order, strength, structure where it has been lacking. You can also appeal to Saturn's sense of duty and structure by committing to a discipline of some kind, or by utilizing its themes and colors. Chiropractic adjustments or stretching may be helpful for the spine for some people. Earth tones, black stones, salts, and square shapes can be applied in the home and work environment to strengthen psychic integrity. Herbs such as Horsetail and Mullein help support the connective tissues ruled by Saturn. Water-based types of therapy may be helpful. Getting and staying hydrated may become very important.

Uranus

Uranus's energy is akin to that of an actual eclipse in that its influence is erratic, unpredictable and often disruptive to one's sense of order and stability. One who is seeking to break free from some rut or limitation will probably appreciate this transit. Uranus unbinds individuals from that which no longer serves them. For the person clinging too tightly to something or someone, an eclipse to this planet may bring shock and disturbance. In other cases, the upsets are minor, and the benefits outweigh them. The South Node can cause jerky electrical discharges from the body and various types of unexpected occurrences. The North Node can bring excess stimulation. Either way, for those who work with electronics or computer technology there could be a heightened focus or big upgrades in these areas. Uranus can stimulate the creative spark, so allow yourself to channel this energy positively. It can also bring allies, friends and exciting new contacts. It is connected with recorded music or music which uses electrical equipment, such as rock n roll and "techno". Being associated with astrology itself, the practice of astrology, or astrologers may become a highlight. Protection against the negative impacts of Uranus may include calming oils, herbs and stones. Uranus has an influence over the third eye and intuition, and when it is eclipsed, it is possible that intuition is either blocked or enhanced. Since its influence is unpredictable it can help to meditate daily to develop greater mental equilibrium which increases the capacity to cope with stress. Keeping stress levels low also helps to support the optimal functionality of the bio-electrical system.

Neptune

Since Neptune rules illusions, delusions, visions and dreams, an eclipse to it can either cast a veil over one's conscious mind or bring deep yearnings, spiritual experiences and inspiration. It can be a very romantic influence but usually with a hidden twist. We tend to wear rose colored glasses when Neptune is involved. A South Node eclipse to Neptune might be the cause of confusion and misunderstandings. A sense of disenchantment or deception affecting others or oneself is possible. Getting involved in hypnosis is ill-advised. Spiritual possession is a possibility in extreme situations. Yet another possibility is that one becomes creatively inspired. Astral experiences may become very vivid. Drug use, especially of the mind-altering kind, tends to be extremely dangerous. There is great musical potential when either North or South Node transits Neptune. A North Node eclipse to Neptune can sometimes bring a wave of good fortune, depending on other factors. The best type of protection from psychic harm is spiritual in nature which may be gained through prayers, mantras, and meditations to reach higher, more expanded states of awareness than those of the mundane level. Having stones like Auralite and Cacoxenite around or worn can be helpful in supporting this awareness. Experiences in, on or above water could become pronounced at this time. Enter into them with caution.

Pluto

An eclipse to one's Pluto tends to elicit an extreme reaction of some kind. Buttons are being pushed. There may initially be resistance. A radical change is occurring in the person's life that could ultimately be empowering if they are willing to take on the task being presented to them. There is tremendous strength in Pluto and nothing that he touches or is touched by is left unchanged. Huge breakdowns or breakthroughs can occur at this time. Big secrets could be withheld or spilled. A death, whether literal or metaphorical, could occur in that some aspect of a person may die and be reborn. Someone close may die or disappear or a relationship might come to an end. The transformation of a previous way of life is occurring on a deep level that alters the way one behaves and moves forward from this point on. This transformation could eventually bring greater wealth, success and recognition in life, but it will initially involve a confrontation with that which stands in the way of progress. Only if the person is incapable or unwilling to rise to the occasion would the results likely be opposite in that they bring grave loss. When the South Node eclipses Pluto, radiation can be especially hazardous. One would do well to boost the physical immune system overall. General psychic protection methods, psychic readings for supportive insight, and vibrational healing methods can be helpful any time an eclipse involves Pluto.

Part Two

Chapter 11

The Astrology of the Spirit World and Psychic Phenomena

Astrology is not typically a tool that people reach for when they are plagued with problems of a paranormal nature; however, when applied appropriately, it could serve to shed a lot of light in the dark. William Lilly, author of Christian Astrology in the seventeenth century used the horary branch of astrology to help solve certain spiritual issues in addition to physical ones. He made some interesting contributions to this fascinating field of study. Astrologers of the Medieval and Renaissance periods made use of the 28 Arabic Mansions of the Moon for making remedies and talismans. The practices associated with the mansions and fixed stars are still very much alive and in use today, by practitioners of both White and Black Magic. Talismanic magic is not recommended for beginner astrologers until they have gained a clear understanding of the influences and archetypal energies that they are working with, and they know how to direct their focus accordingly. The medieval grimoire Picatrix is a compilation of Hermetic philosophy, astrology, magical spells and recipes, sometimes calling for bizarre and gruesome ingredients that would be illegal to use today, not to mention unethical. It nonetheless provides an interesting glimpse into some of the beliefs and supposed practices of its day along with timeless alchemical principles. One may refer to the works of astrologer Christopher Warnock for guidance on these matters.

Whether or not we pay attention to the influence of the luminaries, to speak of psychic self-defense without the acknowledgment of spiritual energies would be to ignore the elephant in the room. This would become a subject of mere psychology, and we would primarily use Freudian terms to describe the causes of our malaise. While there are obvious causes of several types of illness, there are also supernatural ones that have not yet been validated by many modern health practitioners. Others have come to know beyond a shadow of a doubt, as the ancients did, that the world we live in is rife with all kinds of spiritual beings whose natures range from benevolent to malevolent or neutral. Spirits may be invisible to many people, but their influence can be tremendous, even upon those with no awareness of their existence. There are also psychic influences that emerge from the depths of the earth and heavens above.

Many people are not only deeply injured psychologically but accumulate a lot of negativity that they trail behind them. For myriad reasons they have become the living warehouses for any number of the vast variety of malignant entities that roam upon the earth. This has nothing to do with their Sun sign, for in truth there are people of all zodiac signs who exhibit toxic behavior. We can all aspire to greater wisdom and compassion and that is one reason to utilize astrology.

From a metaphysical standpoint, all forms of physical attacks first begin in the mind and within the astral plane of existence, which is a more subtle reality than that of the dense one that we associate with by day. Curiously, the etymology of the word astral is "pertaining to or coming from the stars". This begs the question as to just how much of an unseen influence the stars exert in our everyday lives. This other plane is invisible to most people until they drift off to sleep or catch the silhouette of a moving figure from the corner of their eye. Just as the roots of many forms of disease can be traced back to mental and emotional scars and patterns, the impetus for outward forms of attack originates in the psyche rather than in outward events.

My conclusion is that to some extent, if even based on our own reactions to them, certain types of spirits may be influenced by planetary configurations, although obviously not in the same ways that we are. The closer the spirit is to material existence, the more likely it is going to be influenced, indirectly by astrological phenomena, because astrology can affect the earth and all things in it. It seems more plausible however that our observances of such beings and their activities are often due to planetary influences. Sometimes the planets align in such a way as to stimulate more psychic awareness upon the earth for embodied beings, so that it seems as though suddenly we are surrounded by spiritual influences that have actually always been present.

One example of the influence of the outer planets on psychic events relates to the creation of a federal prison on the island of Alcatraz in California. Inmates first arrived on the island on August 11th of 1934. Both Mars and Venus were in conjunction with Pluto in Cancer, indicating much psychic activity was brewing beneath the surface of things. This island became infamous for its ghost hauntings, which were said to drive many of its prisoners to insanity. These results are probably also due to the coarseness and brutality of the prison itself. Saturn was in Aquarius when it first opened, which seemed to reinforce the isolation and non-human feel of this place.

Just as with the mental development of humans and other animals, there are many grades of intelligence within the spirit world. Some beings are dull and incapable of interaction with humans, some are only slightly interested in us, and some are extremely advanced. There are spirits, referred to as angels, whose very livelihood involves assisting humans and beings who are in need. The polar opposite of what we call angels are demons, and those are the spirits who wish us harm. These spirits also range widely in their levels of capacity for interaction with humans. Just as there are angels of healing and goodwill, there exist their malevolent counter agents who spread calamity and sickness. Full-on demonic attacks on individuals are relatively rare, depending on who you talk to, but what is far more common is for humans to be negatively impacted by what are called elementals (vaguely conscious entities that take on the characteristics of the elements, especially those prominent in their location), harmful energy imprints from various people and things, and unhappy discarnates who latch onto those who seem receptive to their presence in some way.

It is important to recognize what makes people vulnerable to attack by malevolent spirits in the first place, because each case is entirely different from the other. One frequent reason is that there is damage to someone's aura, which draws unwanted spiritual attention and exacerbates illness. The aura is the field of energy surrounding someone's physical body that is invisible to most people. Due to its ethereal nature, the aura may seem easy to injure, and although astral level injuries are a common occurrence, they are actually owed to specific radical events that can either be recent or traced back to early childhood.

A child's aura is naturally strong and resilient, and it takes much in the way of trauma to throw off the equilibrium in such a way as to draw in harmful energy. The cause of a rip or hole in a child's aura would be the result of a single terrible event, repetitive abuse, or toxic exposure that is painful and shocking to extreme degrees. The aura of an adult could also be heavily impacted from trauma, environmental disasters, violence or psychic attacks by others. Such rips could also be the result of drug abuse and alcoholism. In some cases, they could be due to entering or spending too much time in a particularly haunted area, in the same way that poking around a bad neighborhood could invite trouble. It is often the result of dabbling in the occult.

For example, the use of a Ouija board without any spiritual protection can open the flood gates for mischievous entities. It is not an appropriate toy for children, nor is it to be taken lightly. Some people think they are receiving messages from loved ones through the board while they are being deceived by tricksters. By using this object, the message is being conveyed that one relinquishes partial control of their body movements, leading to a form of mediumship. For untrained people this is a recipe for disaster, and one should consider themselves lucky if nothing at all happens when they engage in it.

Day after day, year after year no matter how rich or poor, no matter what age, race, sex, or creed, people everywhere experience various challenges, some due to their own actions and others brought upon by the actions of others. Much of the time, they are unaware of the underlying causes of their discomforts. This is not to say that all problems are spiritual in nature, but many of them are. Some psychics refer to an entire glossary of terms for different types of spiritual conflicts, causes and their possible remedies. A combination of symbols is used to indicate how people are affected by negative energy and how they may free themselves from spiritual impositions.

Words like darts, snakes, arrows, and black clouds may relate to psychic attack, because to a clairvoyant person the attacks can be perceived as such. They often appear as objects that have been thrust into the aura and energy vortices of the victim, known as chakras. Energy cords are usually the result of subconscious attachments to people and naturally occur between mothers and their young, and between monogamous couples. When cords persist in codependent or abusive relationships, they can lead to serious problems both ways, but more immediately for the person who is being corded into. Whatever the type or style of spiritual attack involved, astrology can be a helpful tool in figuring out how to dismantle these menacing influences from our spiritual bodies and our lives.

Grimm's Fairy Tales are full of metaphors for both psychic attack and spiritual redemption. The story of Snow White and the Seven Dwarves is one of many that illustrate how a young girl who is coming of age is cursed by an evil spirit or sorceress. It just so happens that when a girl reaches adolescence during her first Jupiter return, she may become more susceptible to psychic influences than at any other time in her life. She is close to her first menstrual cycle. In the profection chart, she is just coming out of her twelfth house influence. Her energy reaches one of its ultimate peaks, as her aura is greatly expanding. Poltergeist activity is one possible manifestation of this. Yet another trial appears around the age of eighteen when the North Node returns to its natal position in her chart. She is at a critical phase of renewal in her human development and, depending upon circumstances, there may be entities that seek to steal her energy or impede her progress. There are so many other symbolic layers to the story of Snow White to explore that can be applied to our own lives. The poisoned apple that put her to sleep could be yet another version of the Biblical Eve who was presented with the tree of knowledge and was "corrupted" by what she consumed. The Seven Dwarves may be seen as the seven major lights and planets that guided Snow White through the darkness of ignorance.

Boys and young men tend to go through a different yet equally intense sort of process that is rather about self-assertion and courage. There are many myths, fables and fairy tales that describe their rites of passage into manhood. *Iron John* by Robert Bly, offers a profound metaphor for this passage.[1]

Signs, Planets and the Spirit World

There are three signs in particular that represent the spirit realm and its features. Those are the three water signs: Cancer, Scorpio, and Pisces. These signs and their corresponding Fourth, Eighth and Twelfth houses are known to relate to the psyche, the imagination, spirits both good and bad, the occult, and the afterlife. All of the planetary rulers of these three water signs also relate to the spirit world in some way. The Moon, ruling Cancer, relates to the subconscious, the astral plane, reincarnation, and female influences including non-physical ones. Jupiter, the original ruler of Pisces before Neptune's discovery, is a planet that relates to spiritual aspirations, higher spiritual realms and traits. Rather than the dense astral plane, it has influence over the more refined aspects of the soul. The planet that seems to have dominion over the spiritual world in general is Neptune because it rules that which is both hidden and impossible to pin down. Neptune makes boundaries thinner or disintegrates them altogether. Originally it was the Moon that was known to rule over many things that Neptune has come to be associated with. Pluto, the co-ruler of Scorpio in addition to Mars represents the influence of the Underworld, and of the worlds between worlds. It can indicate both spiritual heights and depths, angels and demons, heaven or hell. This planet may relate to ghosts, although this has not yet been explored to my knowledge. It would make sense since Pluto is the planet suggestive of both death and the afterlife.

When dealing with psychic phenomena or trying to figure out why you are experiencing a certain kind of psychic challenge or turbulence, it can help to gain an understanding of astrological symbols and transits as they are occurring, in addition to your natal chart. With certain illnesses which are very difficult to diagnose, or when someone seems to be frequently antagonized by invisible forces, the Moon or Neptune is usually a prominent influence that is being challenged by another planet. The source of the trouble coming from the astral and invisible planes is indicated by the nature of the planet that is making a stress aspect to the Moon or Neptune. With lunar aspects, the mother or certain females might be a draining influence, and other humans or entities that latch themselves onto and attack this person tend to be feminine in nature.

When a person does not know their time of birth and has an acute situation that they would like to look into by way of transits, they can use what is referred to as the Sun-over-Ascendant method of casting a chart. This makes the sign and degree of the Ascendant the same as the Sun on the day of birth, containing the Sun right beneath it. This becomes most tricky for those born close to a cusp. Even a minute can make a difference in making a person one sign or the other, but a thorough examination of the personality and life patterns can help to clarify this.

Horary astrology can offer some insight into the cause and solution of a problem with an occult origin. It does not by any means replace the natal chart, but it can provide helpful clues. This branch of astrology entails looking up the chart for the exact time and place in which a certain question is being asked. The chart is then used to decode a situation based on the planetary aspects within the chart. Whether one is looking at a horary chart, or a natal chart that includes transits, there are some key aspects to look out for when it comes to psychic attack or a spiritual crisis. A few examples are listed below.

Attacks and Attachments viewed with Astrological Transits

Hidden attacks by others, including those by entities, tend to occur through the water signs and by transit through the natal chart, in the Fourth, Eighth and Twelfth houses The

Fourth house, ruled by the Moon and Cancer deals with ancestral energies and unresolved issues that have been passed down through one's bloodline. The Eighth house ruled by Mars, Pluto and Scorpio deals with death and the afterlife. The Twelfth house corresponds to the sign Pisces and the planets Jupiter and Neptune, and this house deals with unseen enemies. This doesn't mean that everyone with planets in these signs or houses will experience being attacked, but it means that if someone does experience such things, there is information to be found regarding the nature of the attack by examining these houses in their natal chart, or planets that are passing through. Questions to ask include: What, if any, planets occupy the houses and what aspects do they make to other planets? What is the planetary ruler of the house being highlighted? The answers to these questions will more often than not reveal who is attacking and how.

Unexplained bodily scratches are typically known to be caused by entities or black magic. If you or someone you know experiences these things, check for the sign the Moon is transiting. Chances are the Moon will either be in water sign or in a major aspect to Neptune. These types of scratches tend to disappear within a few hours; by contrast, it can take at least a day if not several for physical bodily scratches to fully disappear. Suddenly appearing and disappearing scratches from non-physical sources may be a cause for an exorcism, but by succumbing to fear, the entities involved only gain in their momentum. The Austrian spiritualist and author Rudolph Steiner described how entities often use humans as an energy source:

"There are beings in the spiritual realms for whom anxiety and fear emanating from human beings offer welcome food. When humans have no anxiety and fear, then these creatures starve." [2]

There are some people who believe they are completely immune to bad spirits, but their mental and emotional states are so unstable they do not even realize the ways in which they are being manipulated spiritually. They may be delusional at best or hosting ravenous parasites at worst. Those who are the most immune to psychic attacks by entities tend to be grounded, earthy, and physically fit. They do not take recreational drugs or drink alcohol except on special occasions. They are very physical beings, and this makes it difficult for spirits to engage and impossible to steal energy from them. That is because they are in total habitation of their own bodies, leaving little to zero room for anything else to enter their psychic or physical domain.

Planetary alignments that indicate psychic interference often involve conjunctions, squares and oppositions of personal planets with the planets Uranus, Neptune and Pluto. For example, a square from Mars to Neptune could potentially bring a great deal of frustration into a person's life that would cause them to feel very unusual, unlike themselves, or to behave in an erratic way. Under the influence of a transit, they might be subjected to psychic projections or attacks from unseen realms.

The Moon opposite Uranus is a very fleeting transit that we each experience once every month, but in reverse, the planet Uranus making an opposition to one's Moon would be much more dramatic in that person's life, with its effects rippling out over the course of at least a year. It could be a very disruptive influence. If Neptune is transiting the Sun or any personal planets by conjunction or opposition this is usually an indication of peak psychic experiences in that person's life that may be positive or negative depending on several factors. The person may be easily deceived or victimized by hidden forces. Drugs are not advised and should be handled with caution as they may have severe health repercussions.

Here is a description of an imaginary person and story to help paint a picture of how transits might work when it comes to death and the afterlife. Pluto is beginning to transit a man's eighth house in Capricorn, making a conjunction to Venus while also a square to Saturn in Libra in the fifth house. Due to the planets involved and the strength of the aspects, the effects of this transit may be far-reaching and long-lasting, over the course of about three years but making their mark for the rest of that man's life. This man has been happily married for many years but suddenly his wife dies in a car accident. In addition to grieving his loss, he is haunted by her every night in his dreams, and he needs help in letting her go so she can peacefully cross over to the other side. It is a lonely and sad time for him, and he is challenged to find deeper meaning in his life as a whole and to connect with the divine. After some time, through his deceased muse, he comes to the realization that he never fully developed his talent for painting. He finds new, unexpected meaning in this expression of himself with Pluto squaring Saturn in his fifth house of creativity.

Hauntings, Dreams and Psychic Impositions

A place is known to become haunted by deceased humans in most situations. A person can remain stuck on the earth plane by remaining connected to a familiar location after their body, that served as a temporary host for their existence, has died. Those who remain on the earth as ghosts often do so in an unconscious manner rather than out of choice. Their attachment may be to a specific place, person, or a way of life. The reasons for this are many and unique to the individual. If someone was extremely materialistic, they may continue to identify with their previous personal belongings after death, becoming upset by those who have assumed new ownership. Some ghosts are both lustful and powerful, and they continue to haunt locations where they had indulged in their senses. They prey upon those who enter their territory. This accounts for the tales of the incubus and succubus, beings who sexually violate the living during their sleep.

Another reason for beings to continue their association with the earth plane may be due to a traumatic and untimely death in which the consciousness has not come to terms with the end of that particular life and body. They may be stuck in a time-loop where the scenario of their death keeps replaying itself like a broken record. These spirits are generally more open to assistance than those who cling to their previous identities due to greed. Some beings can get stuck when their soul is not at rest due to the decision that they made to commit suicide. Their mere presence can have a very negative impact on the living.

Many people don't think of animals when they think of ghosts. Those creatures who live in the wild usually make quick transitions from death into the great beyond, and their presence does not tend to remain. The animals who remain earth-bound were usually either pets that had particularly codependent owners or had been ritually abused. There is usually a human or several humans associated with animal hauntings. In rare cases an animal spirit that attacks humans might have been conjured, taking on more of the attributes of a demon. It could also be an unexplained spiritual beast that has never even had an embodied life as an earthly animal.

Residual hauntings are often mistaken for hauntings by actual ghosts. Common causes for this are due to either repetitious or extremely traumatic events. These types of occurrences can leave certain types of imprints that are difficult to get rid of even when the spirits of those involved have already passed on from the scene of a crime or tragedy. It is the emotions of those who were the most closely involved in the death that linger indefinitely, in turn influencing the thoughts, emotions and even the health conditions of the living.

Certain areas are constant sources referred to as portals for paranormal activity and attacks. Many references have been made to evil spirits being driven into remote places, such as "the desert and inaccessible mountains" as described by R. Campbell, in his book *Devils and Evil Spirits of Babylonia* [3] They have also been known to dwell in abandoned ruins, filthy homes, and places where sewage collects.

Sometimes, a high amount of spiritual activity may be due to the presence of what have commonly been termed ley lines, which are lines of energy that run through the land in association with ancient monuments and historical structures. Dion Fortune, the occultist and author of the book *Psychic Self-Defense* acknowledged their significance in her novel called *The Goat-foot God* in 1936.[4] These exist in many parts of the world in different measures. Fault line areas where earthquakes are frequent tend to generate a lot of psychic activity as the friction of minerals beneath the earth triggers many types of beings and energies.

The Eyes Have It

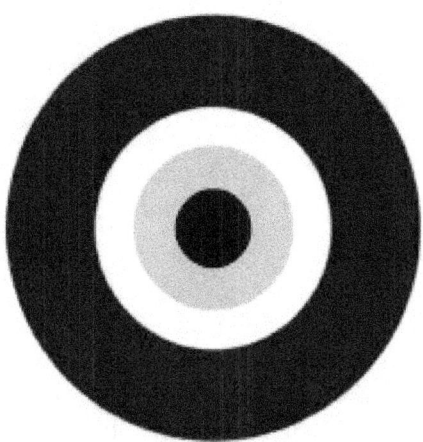

Nazar Evil Eye

A popular and ancient amulet used in many Middle Eastern cultures for protection against the "evil eye", It's color is usually blue, in the shape of an eye. The meaning of the term "evil eye" includes any ill wishes, curses or negativity that is aimed toward another or others.

Clairvoyants throughout history have observed that the psychic atmosphere that each of us lives in is constantly impressing itself upon us, both while we are awake and asleep. The more unconscious we are, the more we are influenced by factors that go unseen by us when we are fully awake. One of the reasons we tend to see spirits more easily during the night is that we drop our defenses as we relax, and for many of us that guard is still down while we are just waking. The darkness also makes it easier to focus on what is seen with a different eye, referred to as the third eye. This third eye is naturally more active in children than most adults.

My own encounters with spirits, both good and bad, began at a very young age. This could be explained by the Moon, Neptune, and Pluto all being particularly pronounced influences in my natal chart. My parents were Christian churchgoers so when I relayed my experiences and concerns to them their response typically involved prayer. This didn't stop the experiences I continued to have, but eventually I became quiet about them. Many children automatically connect with the spiritual world, including those beings called fairies and elves when their contact with nature is not heavily interfered with, as it tends to be in big cities. Some of these beings are helpful, and as folklore suggests, some are quite mischievous or even mean. Children who are happy and healthy tend to attract benevolent spirits as companions.

Dreams and nightmares are common ways that people become affected by the spirit world. Interactions with ghosts and other spirits very often occur on the astral plane during sleep. Usually, these interactions are harmless, but on rare occasions one may run into some very sinister entities while the body is in one of its most vulnerable states. Unlike nightmares, nighttime energy disturbances do not necessarily involve REM. Such disturbances may include pressure on the chest, sudden panic, or other dreadful sensations. Many people have had the experience of waking up in a state of paralysis, face to face with an entity but unable to move our bodies. A Cambridge neuroscience study[5] revealed that in Egypt, sleep paralysis is often regarded as an attack by the "jinn" spirits. Many who believe they have been attacked by jinn in their sleep recite verses from the Quran to prevent further attacks.

For some, the physical reaction to spiritual attack during sleep is body tremors. If this is a recurring problem, it may just be an indication of stress. There are so many possible causes that should be looked into before taking action. In some cases, an exorcism or space clearing may be in order. Spirits may be trying to drain a person of their vital energy to use for themselves. They are attracted to some people and not others, which is why some people cannot sense their presence or feel the least bit affected. It's similar to some people getting bitten from head to toe by fleas and mosquitoes while others are ignored by such hungry flying pests. For mild or infrequent cases, or simply to add a sense of peace and protection in one's sleeping quarters, there are many kinds of herbs, stones and amulets that can be of assistance. Certain visualizations before sleep also help to build up psychic immunity. A salt lamp left on at least one hour prior to bedtime can help clear the psychic atmosphere. Lamps in the bedroom should generally be turned off before going to sleep so as not to interfere with melatonin production.

The night makes people more vulnerable for many reasons, not only because of the darkness. The wee hours of the morning before dawn are very quiet on the material plane but seem to be highly active in the astral, probably because many people are still asleep and open to impressions from the psychic atmosphere. These hours seem more common than nighttime hours for attacks to occur during sleep. The key to avoiding this is preparation in advance. Some kind of nightly ritual for leaving behind the worries of the day and visualizing a golden light around oneself can be helpful.

Attacks through black magic are not considered to be common in modern times but are known to be most prevalent in specific regions and cultures such as in the Voodoo religion of Haiti and in the jungles of South America. It cannot be easily proven that black magic is also utilized by certain people in elevated positions of government. Those who practice it are not necessarily open about it like some of the Satanists dressed in Gothic clothing that people typically associate with "the dark arts". It just so happens that some of the most dangerous practitioners of black magic are quite casual or even businesslike in their personal appearance.

That being said, in addition to those occupying the world's high echelons of power, there are definitely some seemingly harmless, "less significant" people walking among us who practice both Red and Black Magic, in contrast to White Magic which is usually performed for the benefit of others and never performed for the sake of revenge. Red Magic is differentiated in that it may be sexual in nature and not necessarily meant to harm others. Practitioners of Black Magic adhere to their own code of ethics that do not include any of the qualities or beliefs associated with kindness or cosmic justice. Some might even appear to be quite shy or friendly in their demeanor. Their philosophy is not one of good vs evil, but of tapping into life force energy and directing their will for any purpose that they choose. In today's popular culture infused with New Age jargon, that sounds innocent enough, but their motives seldom are. They may attend the common church or easily lie about their orientations as long as doing so suits their own desires. Just as any well-meaning spiritual adept meditates to cultivate compassion, increase awareness or hone their abilities, these Black Magicians employ psionics as a tool for manipulating unsuspecting victims, typically as a form of entertainment, from which they sometimes derive a perverse kind of sexual satisfaction. They take pleasure in exerting dominance over others, regardless of the distance of their targets. One thing to bear in mind is the level of both emotional and spiritual immaturity that is usually present in such mentally disturbed and lustful individuals. Also, if they were truly happy in life, they would have no need for using subversive techniques to get their thrills.

Fear of such people is a form of submission, for one cannot spiritually dominate another who does not allow it on some level. The spiritual antagonist believes it is within their power to do whatever they want without consequences, and without fail, having gained confidence through the magical spells of self-hypnosis. In truth, no one can force their will onto another person through magic unless the target has the type of weakness that allows entryway. These antagonists and "terrorists" of the astral plane believe themselves to be above Universal Law, and thus they attempt what may be described as a sort of competition with Creator, actually viewing themselves as gods, in that they are literally "playing God." Many of them recite ancient invocations to specific demons for assistance in various endeavors.

Many people are superficial in that they don't pay any attention to subtle nuances, and only listen to the words being said by clever speakers, as if they are caught under a spell...and they are. You can tell what someone is about by looking (but not for too long, so as not to absorb their qualities!) at their eyes. Whatever comprises one's attire or speech, the eyes never lie. Iridology recognizes that the eyes are a reflection of one's entire health history and current health status. That is probably one reason why digital eye scanning technology is becoming more popular at airports. We are told this is a matter of convenience, but many consider it to be another way of robbing people of their privacy.

Spiritually, there is much truth to the saying that the eyes are the gateway to the soul. In Vedic astrology the right eye of a man and left eye of a woman signifies the Sun while the right eye of a woman or left eye of a man is ruled by the Moon. The eyes can also be represented by the planet Neptune, as they reveal that which is not obvious on the surface of one's being. They are points of entry for light, spiritual energies and sometimes, even beings. There are numerous examples of psychic attack through the eyes throughout history and this is something that almost everyone has witnessed at least once in their life. Have you ever met a person who stared into your eyes in a creepy way that made you feel uncomfortable? They could have been attacking you on a subconscious level, or even consciously, and that is why you had the sudden urge to get away from them. If you can catch this before the four second mark and look away from their direct gaze, you will be better able to avoid your energy field getting tapped into. If the stare persists with your cooperation for longer than five seconds, they have already successfully tagged you in some way and then you will need to find some way to rid yourself of their psychic imprint, and to regain the energy that they stole from you.

One of the most commonly used psychic attack methods employed by occultists is hypnosis. There is nothing mystical about this technique. They use anything and everything at their disposal, including the expressions of their eyes, the tones of their voice, their body language, and sometimes technology. Attack through hypnosis occurs in a way that is not consensual. This means that the other person has not agreed to it in advance and that the hypnotizer has an agenda with regard to the person or people who are being hypnotized. They can be hypnotized in ways that are sexually arousing, fear-inducing, or in ways that encourage them to part with their money. The next time you turn on the television set or see another person watching it, you may wish to try this little experiment: an hour or so after you have watched something such as the evening news, a slew of commercials, or some major interview, try to recall not only who was on the screen but whether you were watching casually, in a receptive way, or with a hawk's eye, taking note of every movement and nuance taking place.

Are you, or another person close to you, watching, just taking it all in without question? If so, you or they are being hypnotized. If you are analyzing what is being said by whom, then you realize that something is going on that does not meet the eye. You realize that the program could be meant to dupe viewers when they are receptive, through their own eyes. CGI technology has proven that many people can easily be fooled by what they casually view on a screen. What this leads to over time and through repetition is spiritual enslavement on a massive scale.

Symbols, Songs and Divine Interventions

Some people will never experience a spiritual attack in their entire life and others are besieged by ongoing spiritual afflictions; others experience a combination of oppression and divine interventions at different periods of their life. It is said that the brighter the light a person has, the more they will attract forces that try to keep them down, to prevent them from doing good in the world. Guardian Angels do not usually step in automatically, because of our free will and the lessons that we have chosen to learn in human form. When benefactors intervene for spiritual purposes, it is often in the form of the archetypal Messenger, offering a guidepost rather than doing the work for us.

Symbols, statues, and other tools have been used throughout history for magickal and religious purposes including the deflection of negativity and psychic attacks. Western cultures are rich in their own spiritual traditions and don't necessarily need to borrow from the East in order to experience spiritual breakthroughs. Christians refer to the oppressive forces that surround us as the works of the adversary, also known as the devil. They are right in that there are adversarial beings and energies that feed on pain and suffering. Some people are not even aware of how they are being affected by these influences until it is too late, and the worst damage has been done. However, we need not succumb to spiritual defeat.

A crucifix is a popular item used for spiritual protection but in many cases, it is ineffective, especially when used by a novice. For one thing, it depicts Jesus Christ being tortured to his death. This symbol, although not evil, can sometimes offer fuel rather than serving to counteract demonic forces. Within an actual church setting this is offset by many other benign influences, and the fact that this is a place where people go to sit in silence and pray. The crucifix is also a Gnostic symbol, representing one who has been crucified through the trials and torture of human existence, and reborn to their divine nature. Outside of a traditional Catholic church, I find a regular cross to be more effective, and better yet, a Sun cross which reflects the true pagan origin of this symbol that has been found in ancient carvings, from the Celtic wheel of the year to the Native American medicine wheel. The symbol of an equilateral cross within a circle is used in astrology to represent the Earth, as well as the Arabic Part of Fortune, which is a calculation involving the placements of the Sun, Moon and Ascendant. The cross has long served as a representation of the vastness of space, the four directions, the division of the year into four seasons, and the four elements of Earth, Air, Fire and Water. It is the cross of the zodiac, held in place by the four cardinal signs. It is also seen as the cross of spirit and matter. Out of the cross, the geometry of many other sacred symbols has been born. There are many variations of it found in different cultures, including the Swastika, which is linked with the stars of the Big Dipper as they revolve around Polaris, their shape and rotation throughout the year highlighting the four seasons. The cross also gave form to the Old Norse shields known as the Vegvisir and the Helm of Awe.

Many have wondered how the villains in this world sleep so peacefully at night, knowing full well that they are causing so much harm to others. How can they get away with so much, be so happy and fulfilled, for so long? It could be that whatever remaining conscience they do have has been shoved so far down into the gutters of their perverse, Plutonian existence that whatever is down there will simply have to catch up with them at a later time, perhaps not even until death. Many people refer to this phenomenon of energy returning back to us at some point as karma, but that is only one of many interpretations of the law of returns in our earthly reality. There are many metaphors to explain how the mind functions and how life flows accordingly. There comes a day when they cannot fit another thing into their already full container, basement, closet or dark corner where so many useless things accumulate and cause a stench. Under such conditions, a space not only becomes dysfunctional but tends to attract foul spirits. In psychic trash overflow mode, so long as we don't lose ourselves in it, we are jolted awake, and we finally realize what needs to change. We begin to liberate ourselves from self-imposed bondage.

Stages of Spiritual and Demonic Possession

People can become spiritually possessed by spirits, but not necessarily in the ways that are commonly imagined, with red eyes, projectile vomit and walking backward on all four limbs. One of the most common forms of spiritual possession is actually by discarnates who latch on to a person who is vulnerable due to some type of weakening factor such as excess drug and alcohol consumption. It is common for people to experience mild or brief states of possession at bars, where people regularly leave themselves open to one spirit or several spirits who "hop" from head to head for the fuel that is gained from the human vessel. The psychologist Dr. Edith Fiore wrote about this phenomenon in her book called *The Unquiet Dead*.[5] In it she described her clinical experiences helping to relieve many people from their discomforts and addictions with her own technique for removing earth-bound spirits.

The first stage of any type of possession is the introduction to the spirit. This can occur under a wide range of circumstances, such as at a public event, out in pristine nature, in an old building, or through the invocation of magical spells. The person may or may not be aware of what they have come into contact with at the time. The greatest danger lies in ignorance, when one is unaware of what they have either drawn into their space or come into contact with through no fault of their own.

The second stage of possession is that of a combination of emotional and bodily changes that begin to take place once an entity finds its way into a person's psychic space. One tell-tale sign that a person has become possessed is that they no longer act like themselves but more and more like a person that others do not recognize. The change is typically not a good one and tends to be very unusual. There may be changes in the person's usual tone of voice, and in their daily habits. They may become extremely depressed, sick, or given to unhealthy patterns of addiction. Their life force energy has become heavily oppressed, and there is less of the person's soul in animation and more of the entity who is possessing them taking hold. It is at this point that a person may become more aware of the true nature of their situation and forced to make a choice of either surrendering or reaching out for help. A person who is spiritually strong can shake off an entity more readily than one who is either weak or lacks experience in this regard.

The third stage of possession is the final stage, and the hardest one to remove from oneself or another person, because it has gone to the level of consumption and complete absorption, meaning that one has merged with the entity who has seized control of every aspect of their life. It is an important thing to recognize in such a situation that in most of these cases, the person has given up their will to an entity, for some reason that might not be apparent on the surface. This sort of thing does not just happen to anyone; it does, however, happen very frequently to addicts. It may be hard to comprehend why a person would give up their physical body for another entity to control, but the underlying reason is often that they have committed spiritual suicide. Some of them can be saved, but many of them cannot. They stir much chaos wherever they go and cause much harm to others, unconsciously. Deep down inside they do not enjoy this. They gave up their will, which enables them to distance themselves from their emotions and actions much of the time.

Some people are psychopathic and there is something seriously imbalanced within their brain chemistry. They may or may not be possessed by entities. It is believed that the most effective treatment for demonic possession is an exorcism by a Catholic priest. This may work for some, but others may find an exorcism by a person of their own lineage and its religious pantheon more effective. Much will depend on the person, as well as who or what they are being possessed by.

Take Charge of Your Personal Space

Many types of attacks by entities occur through dreams or during sleep, when resistance levels are down. These and many other unsettling paranormal occurrences seem to be more frequent or noticeable when the water signs are in prominence, and when there are strong aspects being made with Neptune or Pluto. This includes the Moon being in any of the three water signs.

Just because one senses that a ghost is present, it doesn't mean that it is attacking them. A vast quantity of ghosts actually do not actively engage with the living. If, however, you believe you are being targeted by advanced malevolent spirits, there are a few things that can help to neutralize their effects. The first is to show outward courage despite how scared you may actually feel. This is also assuming that you are not foolishly entering into territory that you have been previously warned about. If this occurs at random or in your own home, make loud and clear declarations to rebuke this evil and protect your psychic integrity. Roaming spirits of any kind obviously do not respond to doors and walls which serve as our physical boundaries, and they sometimes catch us off guard, without any ill will.

The intelligent ones do respond to strong convictions, especially when combined with spiritual faith in a Divine Providence. They tend to cower in the face of it.[7] While the physical body is fragile and can be easily destroyed, the soul cannot be. Some demons may cause bruises, but they have no authority over humans unless it is granted to them by the individual. Too many people in today's world have become spiritually weak, and they do not know how to fend off such negative influences. This is largely because they lack trust in themselves and in God, by any name.

The iconic historical figure Joan of Arc in France was said to show tremendous courage in battle and faith in divine power, despite the attempts to halt her influences over pagan soldiers. She was born under the leadership-oriented sign of Capricorn on Jamuary 6, 1412. Her final punishment was being burnt at stake by the Church as a witch in 1431. It is recorded that she had received her mission at a "Fairies' tree" growing near her village. She refused to sell herself, succumb to rape or give in, and for this her legend lives on and continues to inspire humanity to this day. In modern times, the most prevalent types of persecutions for steadily resisting the snares of evil are generally less severe. If anything, relative to our physical existence, they are more likely to take the form of censorship, misrepresentation through slander and possible exile.

Here are some suggestions for what to do if you find yourself being plagued by spirits when you are just trying to live your life in peace.

- 1. **Stand Up for Yourself!** State what you refuse to allow near your body and in your living space. Do not ever cave in to an entity's attempts to dominate you, which is exactly what they desire. You don't necessarily need a paranormal swat team although that may be helpful and reassuring in many ways. That should be your last resort if things have gotten out of control. What you might need more than anything is to learn how to stand up for yourself, or to identify your own emotions from those of others. Figure out if what you feel is your own negativity or a form of spiritual oppression, which can be a very sneaky thing for many people who are victimized by it. It can manifest itself as confounding depression or unexplained illness. When you put your foot down and state that enough is enough, the spirits who are tormenting you, moving objects around or causing so much strife have no choice but to back off. You are in charge, not these bullies of the spirit realm. Issues with entities are actually not terribly different from issues with people in the third dimensional world that we inhabit. They are just more unnerving because the spirits are difficult for most of us to see, and they gain increased leverage when they sense either our fear or our submission.

- 2. **Clean Your Space:** There is something to the saying that "Cleanliness is Godliness". You have to be willing to back up your statements above by keeping your living space clean and as free from clutter as possible. Just because your home might become messy from time to time doesn't mean it will attract evil spirits. However, many homes that are heavily affected by entities are usually old, dirty and unkempt for long periods of time. Negative spirits thrive in the states of tension and disorder, and they abhor a sparkling clean environment. Maybe the answer to your haunting is to get to work and scrub those floors, clear the cobwebs, take out the trash, and give your home a complete makeover inside and out. Get rid of any objects that trigger bad memories or carry the residue of exes, previous owners, or ugly events. Make donations if you have too many things that you don't love or utilize. Try to avoid harsh chemicals because they have detrimental effects on health as well as the earth when they are spread. You probably already have some of the simplest and most effective cleaning supplies in your kitchen, which include baking soda, white vinegar and scrubbers.

- **3. Check For Blind Spots:** Bullies sometimes come back in aggressive ways after they have been temporarily put in check. Fighting back can mean taking the time to develop a stronger spiritual practice and to overcome personal ignorance. Ask a loved one that you trust what your apparent blind spots are and ask them to be completely honest with you. This is also something you might gain insight into from a psychic reader or astrologer. Your blind spots can become the spots targeted by malevolent beings. Be it through physical, verbal or non-physical means, do something that works for you to increase both your awareness and your resistance to stress. This requires willpower, which is harder for some people than others to muster within themselves. The propensity to attract, empathize with and communicate with spirits is feminine in nature. There is nothing inherently wrong with that unless it becomes a problem. Although there are many goddesses associated with war, the ability to intimidate, rule and dispel spirits is in a general sense, masculine in nature. In order to gain spiritual immunity and strength, the masculine principle must be integrated with the feminine. Summon the power of Mars!

- **4. Prayers and Mantras:** Prayer is and has always been a powerful means of bringing in desired changes. If the prayer is sincere with full trust, you may be amazed at its effects. Chanting in one of the sacred languages (such as Greek, Hebrew, or Sanskrit) can also help to create a stronger energy field, but their proper pronunciations should be used for optimal effects. Those with a Scandinavian background may find strength in the long chanting of certain Runes. Natives in every continent have their own chants for banishing evil and connecting with the divine. The reason why these other languages tend to be more effective than chanting in today's widely used English language is that they are often closer to the languages of the spirit world, and they elicit more powerful responses. That being said, many people find there is great power in reciting Psalm 91 in the Bible, in any language, for the purpose of gaining spiritual protection. Another Bible verse also recited for protection is Isaiah 54:14-17.

Ultimately, the most powerful spiritual armor is a combination of faith, a higher, benevolent and divine presence, along with strong intentions and the appropriate actions to back them up. This can mean tuning in to our own Jupiter energy. There is nothing that can substitute for a personal sense of integrity to bring life to what it is that one is praying, visualizing or reciting mantras for. We do not always know exactly what to do in a given situation, but it becomes laborious and non-fulfilling to act in counter-intuitive ways. It takes far more strenuous effort to shoot oneself in the foot spiritually than does seeking and acting upon one's inner guidance, and regardless of life circumstances, there is a subtle yet identifiable sense of inner knowing that everyone has access to. Thus, when you are on the right path, you know on some level that you are, just the same as knowing if you are on the one that will lead to grave loss and despair. You also know that despite your adversaries and hardships, both seen and unseen, you will in some way, eventually, be the victor. This is not attained by seeking revenge but by growing in character and spiritual strength.

- **5. Herbal Amulets**: There are several tools that can assist with psychic protection, including the use of certain herbs, oils, and stones. Special herbs and stones can be combined and worn in a small drawstring bag hung around the neck or carried in the pocket. One of the most potent herbs for this purpose is that of Galangal root. It has a long history of use for reversing hexes, psychic attack and attachments. You may take a single drop of the essential oil, rub it into your hands and pass them lightly over your body making physical contact from the top of your head to the tip of your toes. It is not the quantity of the oil or herb that you use but the intention that you have when using it that makes it work. For me this has been a very effective method for deterring spiritual attacks by entities when situations have called for it. They hate the smell and energy of Galangal, which is a close relative of Ginger. You can do this with any oil of your choice that has similar properties and that you are not allergic to. You could sprinkle dried Nettles around on your property while invoking the Norse god Thor to protect your home and family. Do this when the Moon is in Aries or Sagittarius to add to its effectiveness. If you have the space, you could grow Geraniums in the garden to deter psychic pests. Other highly protective herbs and essential oils include those of Bay Laurel, Eucalyptus, Pine and common Sage. You can make a wreath of dried Bay leaves and twigs and hang it at your front door to halt evil from the entryway. Many other suggestions are found in Chapter Thirteen, "Protective Remedies for Signs and Transits". Take this hint that many of the herbs associated with the planet Mars are extremely protective and powerful allies against evil forces.

- **6. Adjust or Relocate:** Too many mirrors open portals to the spirit world. Make sure that no mirrors face the bed in particular. If you have done all of the above and nothing has worked, consider that you might be living on property that will not change no matter what you do. The negative imprints and the entities who dwell within are too fixed. Relocate as soon as possible. The longer you stay, the worse your life circumstances can become under these influences, and it can drain too much out of you to try to fend them off constantly. Some people often find themselves in these types of places because it is their task to clear the space and help the earthbound spirits to move on, but you will already know if that is true for you. In the future, when you are considering a place to live, do some Astrocartography (the astrology of location) to see how a certain city may influence you. Saturn on any of the angles means that area will present you with many challenges. Pay close attention to the way you are feeling and see if you can envision a pleasant lifestyle there. Do not settle for something that makes you very uneasy because it will always cost you more energy than you can afford to lose. One of the main reasons that people wind up trapped in situations like these is due to pressure from family members. Sometimes it is due to a lack of adequate funds. Winding up in a haunted home or homes is typically a Twelfth house issue, and you might have natal planets there that have caused you to feel stuck. Whatever your reason is, just do whatever you can to find your escape from the place of discord, and chances are, life will open up for you in ways you previously could not imagine.

- **7. Protective Pets:** Many types of pets, but especially cats can be powerful allies and provide much spiritual protection in the home environment. This is why the classical "Witch's Familiar" has often taken the form of a cat. Cats are highly sensitive to subtle nuances and energies that people and many animals often don't notice. They know where evil entities are lurking, and they are fearless in asserting their own dominance in any given territory. Just as they are stealthy and adept at chasing prey, they can be extremely protective of their owners, especially at nighttime when their humans are sleeping. If you don't have one already and are not allergic, consider taking a cat into your home that you will cherish and take good care of. In return, their protective aura will help to clear the energy of your living space. Sometimes when your pet is behaving very strangely it is because they are reacting to entities or changing influences in the environment that are not visible to their owners. Check to make sure there are not physical reasons, of course, but be alert to what they might be trying to convey to you.

Ancestral Burdens

In some cases, the root of one's suffering stems from burdens that have been passed down to them over several generations. The likelihood of this phenomenon can also be spotted in the natal chart, usually indicated by any number of heavy aspects of the Moon, as well as an ill-placed Saturn. This may also be indicated by planets in hard aspect in the fourth or twelfth houses. Those who bear the brunt of their family's dysfunction seem to carry the weight of the sorrows and transgressions made by those who came before them, for them alone to correct and atone for even when they apparently did nothing wrong.

It may take considerable determination and courage to extricate oneself from negative family patterns. Usually, an individual is aware if and when this is their underlying issue, and they tend to have a personal choice in whether to continue the negative familial patterns or to set forth in creating new ones. This burden may be viewed as a gift rather than a hindrance. It is the opportunity to heal and empower not only oneself but the energy that runs throughout one's family tree, including those who are yet to be born within it.

The Influence of Uranus and Effects of Radiation on the Aura

Another less discussed but highly insidious cause for fractures and weakening of the aura is radiation, which has increased exponentially on this planet over the past three decades. Whether the exposure to radiation occurs in one huge overdose or accumulates over time, once the damage has been done, it becomes easier for hungry spirits to prey on one's energy or attach themselves to it like leeches. This is one of many reasons to limit time spent on wireless electronic devices such as smart phones and other smart devices, or to at least wear protective devices while doing so. These days there are many varieties of EMF protection products from jewelry to bedding materials that can be purchased in specialty stores or ordered through the Internet. They are not all equally effective, so it can take time to determine what works best for one's personal needs.

Uranus, in addition to Mercury, is a planet that rules electricity, so it would be wise to be particularly careful with electronics during hard transits to or from either of them, especially regarding the natal chart. Uranus also has some relation to spiritual phenomena whenever electricity is involved, including through natural disasters such as earthquakes and through thunderstorms. This is the planetary co-ruler of Aquarius, and this sign relates to the sciences, advancements in technology and the collective mind. One of the interesting aspects of the Aquarian Age that we are said to be entering is the growing use of electronic devices and smart phone apps designed for certain types of contact with the spirit world. The high amounts of EMF shown on some EMF detection objects such as the TriField Meter is being used indicate the presence of discarnates and other non-physical energies. Devices include the Kinect SLS (cameras to "map" human-looking figures, even those invisible to the naked eye) and thermal imaging cameras frequently used on television programs such as *Ghost Adventures* which is one of the first paranormal television series that made these objects popular, in addition to the occupation of paranormal research itself. These devices open up many exciting yet also dangerous possibilities for the human psyche. With the proper protective measures taken, this bridging between science and the spirit world may lead to many helpful and amazing discoveries for humankind.

Not surprisingly, many of the crystals, stones and gems worn for protection against spiritual intrusions also help to protect against the harmful effects of radiation. These stones can also be helpful when carried and strategically placed in the environment, such as in the car, near the bedside, and next to the computer. They include Black Tourmaline, Fluorite, Hematite, Lepidolite, Malachite, Turquoise and Shungite among many others. Anyone who uses a smart phone might do well to attach either a piece of Shungite or Organite to the backside of it. There are many types of flat stone stickers available for this purpose. The main downside of this, as explained by Arthur Firstenberg, author of *The Invisible Rainbow*,[8] is that the cell phone sticker would cease to be of any health benefit when the phone is actually in use on your person. Your hand would still be holding the device, with electrical currents running up your arm. The only way to get away from that is to limit exposure as much as possible. To help protect you from both radiation and an invasion of your privacy while traveling, a Faraday bag would probably be more effective.

Radionics, also referred to as EMT (electromagnetic therapy) is a form of "metaphysical science" based on quantum physics for the purpose of picking up hidden information and balancing the energy levels of any living organisms, from any distance. This therapy was developed by the American physician Albert Adams in 1909. Raymond Rife (May 16, 1888 – August 5, 1971) is also credited with developing similar devices that were used in the treatment of cancer. Many types of radionics devices used by some modern holistic practitioners are not generally known by the public. Today the work associated with such devices is tossed into the category of pseudoscience by the medical establishment. As crazy as it might seem to some people, radionics can serve a valuable function in the field of alternative medicine. I have personally experienced and witnessed the easing of a wide variety of mental and bodily discomforts, on countless occasions. It should not come as a surprise in our present-day influence of medical dictatorship that any such tool would be deemed as quackery. These types of tools are known to be so effective in altering emotional, mental and physical states that there are some people who use them for nefarious ends, often at a long physical distance from their intended victims. What they don't realize is that they are also subjecting themselves to the same type of energy that they are sending out to others.

Astrology, Psychic Abilities, and Spiritual Prowess

Since the dawn of time there have been seers, oracles and those whose work has been focused on the invisible workings of this world and beyond. Although each of us possess psychic abilities to some extent, those whose life's work revolves around them tend to have certain astrological configurations in common. It has been my observation that emphasized placements in the signs of Cancer, Scorpio and Sagittarius are very common among professional psychics.

A strong spiritual immune system enables both readers and healing practitioners to continue to do the work they are doing, for without that they would simply not be able to function optimally in their daily lives. As for the astrological factors that tend to give them so much psychic resilience, I would venture to say it most often comes down to the influence of Scorpio, the eighth house and both of Scorpio's ruling planets Mars and Pluto. Look toward these areas when studying the chart of a psychic that you know or of your own. Even if there is no planet inhabiting Scorpio, therein lies much endurance for levels of intensity that other signs might shy away from or even be destroyed by. Both Scorpio and Pluto rule regeneration - the capacity for something to spring back to life after it has run out of fuel or has died. These are the archetypal energies that deal with death and the afterlife itself, and many whose charts contain strong patterns involving them often wind up becoming healers, mediums, psychopomps and interpreters of the signs and symbols of life's greatest mysteries.

Mysteries of The Sleeping Prophet – Edgar Cayce

Edgar Cayce was a beloved American mystic and clairvoyant who was known as "The Sleeping Prophet". He was aptly named, for his Sun sign Pisces is associated with both sleep and mysticism. He was a highly altruistic man, interested in helping others to achieve wellness, also true to his Sun sign. He had a simple background, born to farmers but went on to do great things in his life. He founded a hospital, a university and the A.R.E. (Association for Research and Enlightenment). He was one of those rare and gifted psychics who gained in popularity due to word of

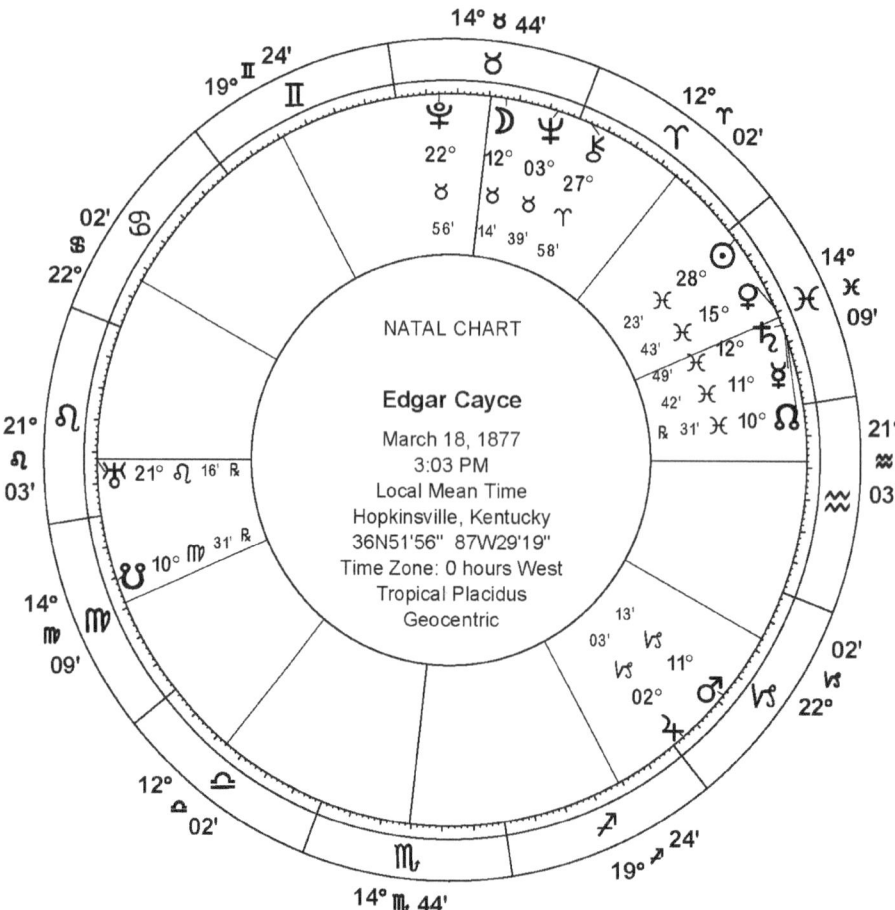

mouth rather than by making any claims. He spent his days seeking ways to help people with his abilities without collecting money for doing so. After he married and had a family, he was known to continuously work extremely hard, going against his own advice in limiting the number of readings given in a day. Eventually he died of a stroke on January 3, 1945, in Virginia Beach.

According to A.R.E. records, Edgar was born at 3:03pm, LMT. This time would place Uranus in exact conjunction to his Leo Ascendant, in the first house, accentuating his unique personality. It is clear that Pisces was a very strong influence for him, including a stellium of Venus, Saturn, Mercury and the North Node within it. It appears that his Moon in Taurus was in a conjunction with Neptune, which also explains his giving nature and strong psychic abilities. This pair of planets form an earth trine to his Mars and Jupiter in Capricorn, highlighting his powerful drive and work ethic. Edgar Cayce considered himself to be a Christian although he also valued the

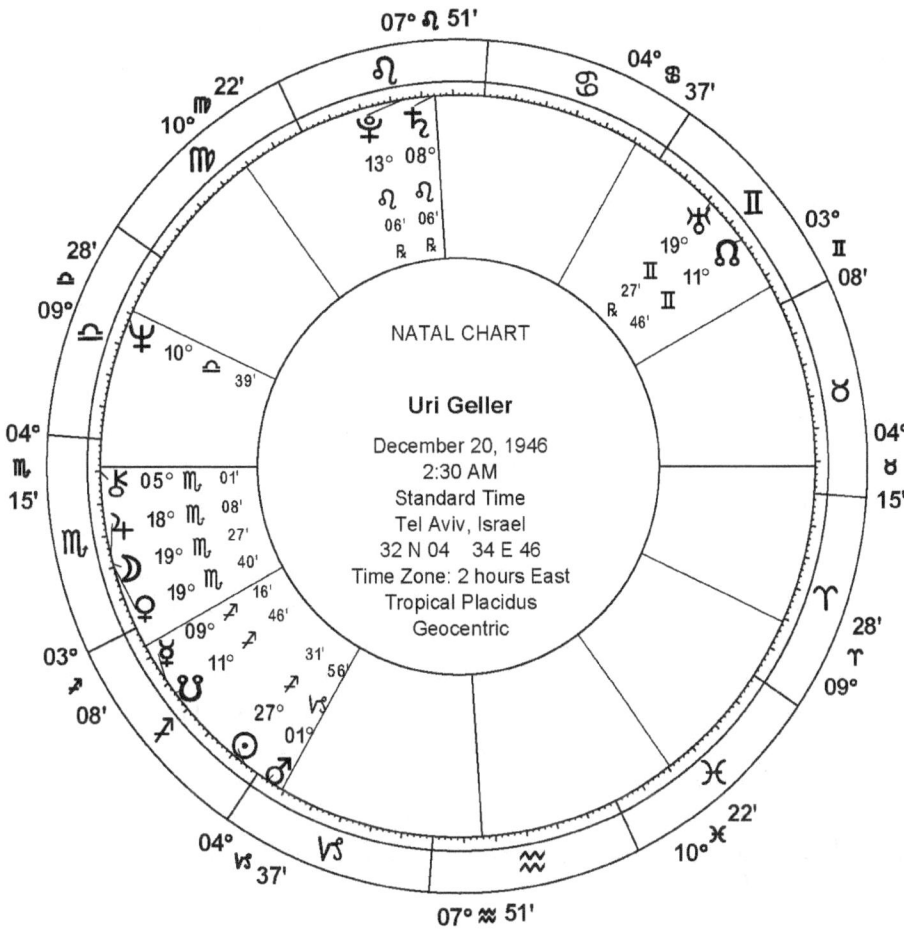

input of comparative religions. He taught that one of the best ways to protect oneself in a psychic sense was to monitor one's own negative thoughts, and to think and speak in positive ways as much as possible. This seems so simple, yet so difficult for so many of us to sustain on a daily basis. In essence, he believed that compassion was the key to living harmoniously. How different life on earth would be if we adhered to this simple principle even ten percent more than we do.

Psychic Powers and Sleight of Hand — Uri Geller

Uri Geller was a famous psychic and illusionist who was known to read minds, bend spoons from a distance and see through objects with a sort of x-ray vision. His talents were proven so great that he became an asset to the CIA. December 20, 1946, 2:30 am Tel Aviv, Israel. He was born with the Sun in Sagittarius in a highly charged conjunction with Mars in

Capricorn. Sagittarius is by nature a highly intuitive sign, and many with the Sun here are psychic in a general sense, without taking on a lot of the empathic suffering that sensitive water signs tend to experience. His Rising sign is Scorpio with the Moon, Venus and Jupiter all in conjunction in Scorpio in his first house. This combination indicates highly developed, laser sharp psychic powers along with an ability to charm and mesmerize an audience. Neptune, the planet of psychic visions and phenomena is in the sign of Libra in his twelfth house, where mysteries abound. The Sun opposite of Uranus is one of many other indications of a strong sixth sense.

Astrology and World Predictions — Michel de Nostradame

There was a fascinating alignment of planets on the day that the French astrologer and seer Nostradamus was said to be born. The controversial historical figure was best known for his book Les Prophéties, containing both poetic and prophetic visions of the catastrophic events regarding the end of the world. In the Julian calendar he was born on December 14th of 1503, which in today's Gregorian calendar would equate with having been born on December 21st of 1503. This would mean he was born near the Solstice, with his Sun in either Sagittarius or Capricorn. Although the time of his birth is unknown and therefore his Ascendant is unknown, one of the most notable features of his guesstimated natal chart is the grand water trine between his Moon in Scorpio, the cluster of Jupiter, Saturn and Mars all Retrograde in Cancer, and Uranus (not yet discovered) in Pisces. Such a trine would indicate that Nostradamus was sensitive to invisible currents of energy while being exceptionally gifted in the expression of his psychic impressions. Water signs are naturally more emotional than the other signs, so there is a tendency to exaggerate on certain issues. There was an artistic streak to Nostradamus's method of communicating his visions, which is also very characteristic of water signs. The strong emphasis in the sign of Cancer, opposite of his Sun and Mercury, indicates a great deal of tension between his inner and outer life.

The opposition between Mars and Neptune speaks of challenges and trouble on the psychic planes and sometimes eccentric occult abilities. In relation to the water element, it is interesting that he was said to use a bowl of water for gazing into the future

Legal Investigations with the Aid of a Psychic - June Ahern

A well-known psychic and author from the San Francisco Bay Area of California named June Ahern allowed me to use her birth data in this book. She was born during a Balsamic Moon with both Sun and Moon in sign of Gemini on June 14th, 1950, in Glasgow Scotland at 6:05 pm. With Scorpio on her ascendant, the Moon, Sun and Uranus all fall in her eighth house of the afterlife. Due to a car accident in her late teens, June had a near-death experience which opened the door to the spirit world and formed the genesis of her future career as a

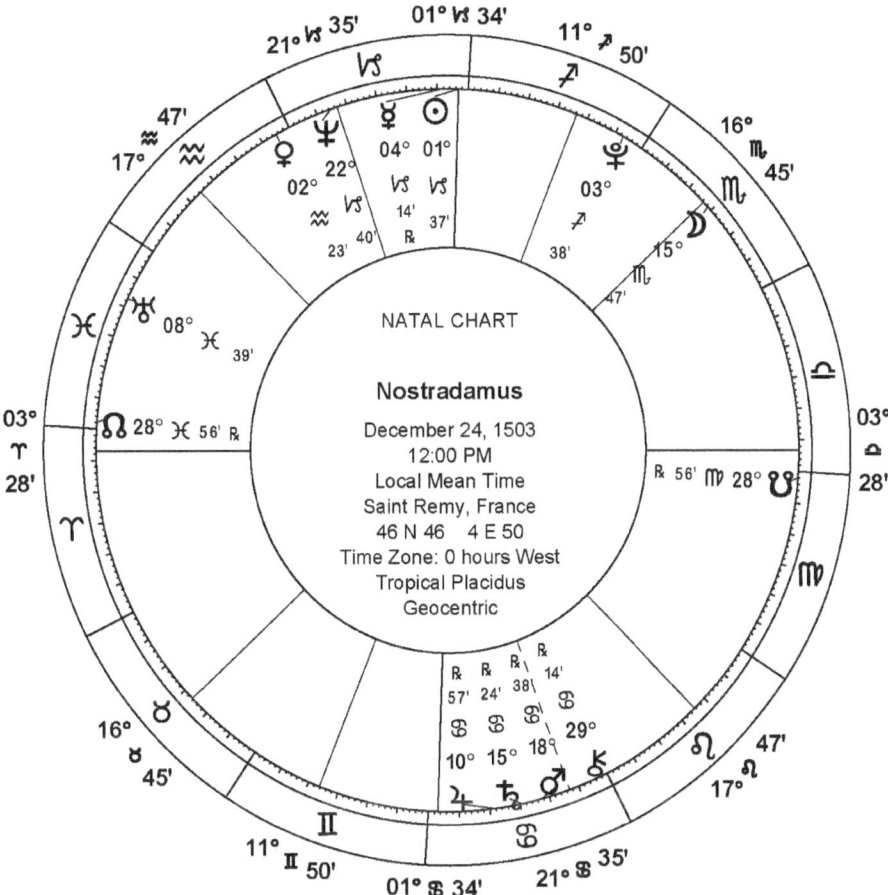

medium. After this traumatic event she was able to see and hear spirits on a regular basis. The ability to converse with ghosts is a gift that has continued for the rest of her life.

In the early 1980s June was asked by a local police department to assist them in locating the whereabouts of criminals. Her first case revolved around the murder of a young mother in Oakland in 1982. Her first success took place in 1984, ending with the conviction of a killer The insights that June provided matched the family of the woman, although it took 20 years for them to verify what she saw. The case was finally solved by tracing the DNA of a serial killer.

On another occasion, June provided proof, with a policeman during a car ride to court, to convict those responsible for the theft of her car in 1990. The police officer was amazed by her knowledge. One time she helped to find a child, missing due to parental abduction, by coming up with the street name of their location, with local areas being a subject that Gemini would

The Astrology of the Spirit World and Psychic Phenomena

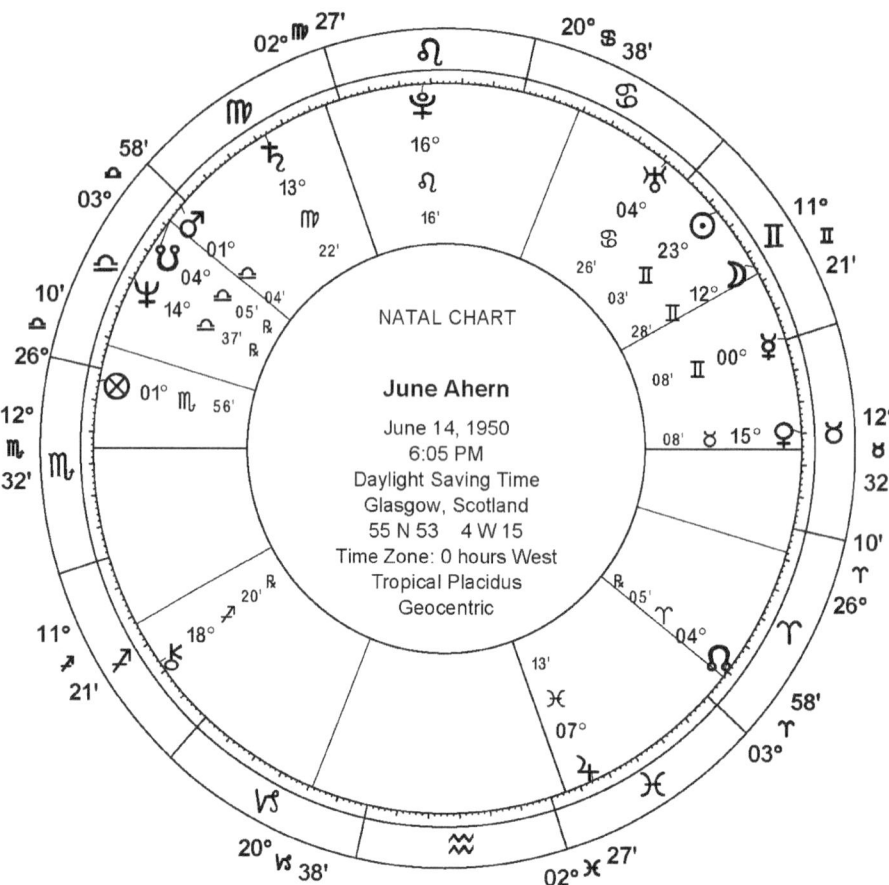

excel in. Another time with the police, she identified the theft of a parrot and jewelry through clear and exact descriptions of both the house cleaner and her husband who had snatched them up. June's double Gemini influence in the eighth house was apparently at work on this one. There is just a little bit of humor in that situation, so fitting for the sign of the Twins.

Her last case was being asked to give insights into the murder of a little girl in 1999. Her involvement lasted from about 2002-03. The detective contacted her because his wife knew her, and about the 1984 case. Although details about the exact location were off, the images of the site, wraps and more were exact

The Power of Water — Bruce Lee

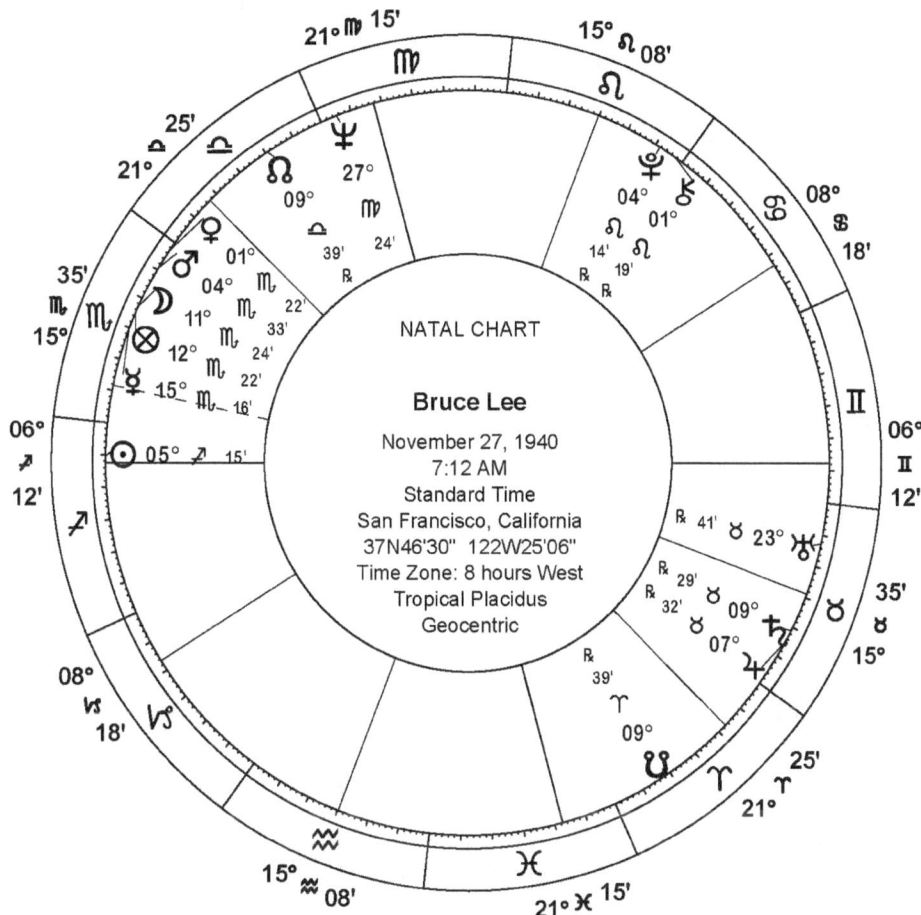

Bruce Lee was one of the most famous martial artists of all time. He was featured in action movies and interviewed on talk shows. He authored a book called the Tao of Jeet Kun Do, [9] sharing various techniques for self-defense. In order to perform the way that he did so expertly, some degree of intuition in addition to discipline would have been crucial. Most masters of the martial arts will agree with this, and they include meditation and inner self-development as a part of their daily regimen. Bruce Lee was as much a philosopher as he was a fighter, which is evident in his widely used quote about the power of water:

> "Empty your mind, be formless, shapeless, like water. If you put water into a cup, it becomes the cup. You put water into a bottle and it becomes the bottle. You put it in a teapot and it becomes the teapot. Now, water can flow or it can crash. Be water, my friend."

He did have a huge emphasis in the water sign of Scorpio, spilling into the watery twelfth house of sorrows, sickness and unsolved mysteries. He died at the young age of thirty-two from a brain injury that was said to be linked to painkillers. His vulnerability was never visible to the public. His Sagittarius Sun and Ascendant account for both his athleticism and strongly academic nature. Bruce Lee has become a worldwide pop icon who has had a deep impact on people, including spiritual seekers from all walks of life.

References

1. Robert Bly, *Iron John: A Book About Men* 3rd edition (Philadelphia: Da Capo Press, 2015)

2. Rudolph Steiner quote translated from German, translator unknown *Die Erkenntnis der Seele und des Geistes (Knowledge of Soul and Spirit: The So-called Dangers of Initiation)* (Berlin: December 12, 1907)

3. Reginald Campbell Thompson, *Devils and Evil Spirits of Babylonia: Being Babylonian and Assyrian Incantations Against the Demons, Ghouls, Vampires, Hobgoblins, Ghosts and Kindred evil Spirits which Attack Mankind,* vol 1 (London: M.A. Luzac and Company,1903)

4. Dion Fortune, *The Goat-Foot God* (a novel) (Wellingborough: Aquarian Press, 1936)

5. Jalal, Baland; Simons-Rudolph, Joseph; Jalal, Bamo; Hinton, Devon E. (1 October 2013). "Explanations of sleep paralysis among Egyptian college students and the general population in Egypt and Denmark". Transcultural Psychiatry. 51 (2): 158–175

6. Edith Fiore, *The Unquiet Dead: A Psychologist Treats Spirit Possession- Detecting and Removing Earthbound Spirits* (Garden City: Doubleday & Company, 1987)

7. James 2:19: "even demons believe in one God- the thought of this causes them to shudder with fear."

8. Arthur Firstenberg, *The Invisible Rainbow* (White River Junction: Chelsea Green Publishing, 2020)

9. Bruce Lee, *The Tao of Jeet Kun Do* (Black Belt Communications, Expanded edition, 2011)

Chapter 12

The Ascendant and Descendant

It is from the vantage point of the Ascendant that one is able to determine where the planets reside in a personal horoscope. This chart reveals how we carry the characteristics of each and every sign of the zodiac but in different areas. For example, although one may not be born under the sign of Virgo or have any planets occupying it, somewhere in their chart its influence is being exerted. In the third house of communications, it could make for a very detail oriented but worrisome mindset. In the eleventh house of group aims and humanitarian service Virgo may play itself out through volunteer work for the community, or in assisting animals. Within each of us there is an Aries warrior who shows up, maybe in the workplace of the sixth house or the first house of self-identification. Having the Sun, Moon or a planet conjunct the Ascendant amplifies its energy in a certain way, bringing it more to the forefront of a person's life.

In particular, the Ascendant influences the general livelihood, health and appearance of the native. It is one of the top three signs that astrologers tend to refer to succinctly. It can often give even greater insights into life's daily rhythms and challenges than the Sun sign, which is a symbolic representation of the soul's essence. The Moon points toward an area of combined ease and vulnerability, as it represents our most deeply ingrained habits. The sign and house it falls in reflect many bodily conditions in relation to the subconscious. Out of these three influences it is the Ascendant that serves as a representation of the helm of the wheel by which we navigate ourselves through life.

It is most often the Ascendant and any planets near it that make the first social impression, indicating how one is received by others regardless of what lies at the core of one's being. Venus would attract many with her charm and grace but with Mars, a competitive or defensive response from others is more likely. That is because others sense the potency or competitiveness of the Mars person, even when it is being masked by other factors. The energetic output of this planet can be highly appealing, but unlike Venus it stands an equal chance of registering as intimidating, off-putting, or repulsive to certain people. The same goes for all of the "sweet" or "tough" planets. People seem to be more comfortable around those with the Moon, Venus, Jupiter, or Neptune on or ruling the Ascendant, and uncomfortable around those with Mars, Saturn, Uranus and Pluto there. In some cases, challenging planets on the Ascendant also indicate issues such as self-sabotage or conflicts with one's own identity or appearance. Responses to a rising Sun or Mercury more heavily depend on the signs that they occupy, and the aspects being made.

What happens when there are placements such as Saturn in Libra on the Ascendant is that other people respond to both the influences of Saturn and Venus. If this describes your chart, others may sense that you are responsible and fair, so they are willing to place their trust in you. Conversely, they may be attracted to you but at the same time the contradiction of feeling repelled, constricted, or on some level judged and put to the test by you. Jupiter denotes confidence or magnanimity so with this on your Ascendant others might feel uplifted in your presence, more or less depending on the sign it's in. Mars makes you passionate about a certain cause and you therefore excite others in some way. As with all other planets the type of response you get varies according to various details including the method in which you choose to channel them. Pluto on the Ascendant is one that often seems to make others uneasy, no matter how soft and kind-hearted the Pluto person is.

The Descendant, directly opposite of the Ascendant, describes more of the long-term or impactful results of others' responses and reactions. In relationship focused astrology it represents the spouse or romantic partner. It can also indicate the nature of one's open enemies and whatever tools and methods they happen to use against the person. These enemies are not necessarily always physical beings but can be spiritual in nature, although traditionally it is the Twelfth house that represents unseen enemies. When there is a mutual sense of karma, fate, unfinished business, or urgency, the synastry charts between two people tend to show many important planetary conjunctions, whether or not they seem positive or negative in nature. Some people in healthy relationships have challenging aspects and corresponding issues that they work through together equally and consciously, while other couples have particular aspects and undercurrents between them that they are very unconscious of. One example of a relationship that has a fated quality is one in which the Sun signs are not only the same but in the same exact degree. This can either be a very good or a very bad thing, depending on several other factors. If Saturn or Pluto is involved there may be something very destructive taking place within the connection. In another scenario, if one person's Venus is in a square with another person's Saturn, the Venus person might feel belittled or even betrayed by the Saturn person in some way. The touch of Neptune in synastry seems to either elevate a relationship to spiritual dimensions or erode its very foundations.

The Descendant is sometimes referred to as the shadow that a person is unable to accept as their own, so it is easier to project its qualities onto either a loving partner or an antagonist.

In this vein, I think of so-called enemies not only as being outward manifestations or people but as emotional and spiritual challenges that can make us stronger when we are willing to acknowledge and integrate them into our lives in a healthy way. Some people don't seem to have any external enemies and the worst enemy that they must come to terms with is internal. For instance, they might frequently speak negatively about themselves which prevents them from achieving happiness or success.

The Descendant and its seventh house represent open enemies while the twelfth house indicates the nature of one's hidden enemies.

Aries Ascendant, ruled by Mars:

With Aries on the Ascendant the outward personality is fiery, passionate and direct with much creativity and inspiration to share. All the following signs fall on or close to their natural placements. There is a vibrant, youthful countenance that stands out as unique. Intuition is strong and action tends to come before analysis. This is a person who begins and introduces many things to people that he or she does not necessarily bring to completion. What they do is point the way for others by planting seeds and igniting flames of interest. The house placement of Mars and its aspects to other planets reveals where personal drive is directed.

In some, a competitive or non-committal streak causes distrust in relationships. A love of romance and the desire for a life partner, or in some cases for several partners, is very strong. They may frequently find themselves engaged in a personal challenge of their own personal choice because they like to keep themselves sharp. They are self-starters with much ambition, and high adventure gives great meaning to their life. The extreme type might throw themselves into some dangerous situation that must be overcome through stealth and agility as a form of sport.

Fortunately, they have the energy to accomplish this, although unfortunately they may be accident prone. There can be a tendency toward narcissism in some Aries Ascendants, which winds up in a bit of drama. What these types are usually seeing in others held close is a reflection of themselves in the mirror, so unless or until something that they perceive as ugly shows up, all is well.

Libra Descendant, ruled by Venus: Aries Ascendant may feel let down by those who don't live up to their expectations, who don't stand by their word or who are otherwise superficial. They could feel used for their money or their appearance. Their partner can either be their best friend or their nemesis. They might often be working hard to support their partner in some way, or often have to take the lead.

Problematic people or enemies in their lives can be very flighty and unstable. They are often attracted to Aries who seem to have all the answers to allay their troubled minds. It is also possible that Aries Ascendant finds themselves having to deal with complications pertaining to the law, since their Libra Descendant rules the justice system.   With the influence of Pisces in their twelfth house, Aries tends to experience much of their greatest suffering in silence. There may be addictive patterns that must be dealt with.

Taurus Ascendant, ruled by Venus.

Taurus on the Ascendant bestows a durable yet very comely appearance. With Venus as their planetary ruler, they may also have a highly sensual nature. These are the kinds of lively people who do things like burst into a room with bells, glitter, and giggles. In whatever fashion, they tend to make lasting impressions wherever they go. They may give everyone hugs and compliments or pass around a tray of sweet treats. They are willing to work hard to gain a position that earns them both respect and monetary security. Many of them are particularly successful in the culinary arts.

There is an innate talent for speaking, acting or singing, as the voice tends to be strong, deep and resonant, with something interesting to say. They may be teachers of some kind due to their gift of communicating with ease. They may attract a mate who is controlling, but positively a mate who supports them in being the best version of themselves.

Due to the influence of Aries in their twelfth house, their worst problems exist behind closed doors and frustrations are difficult to express. Occasionally you might catch a little glimpse of their aggressive tendencies but only the unconscious types would tread on others to climb the ladder of success. The evolved Taurean is so gentle and kind they would not so much as hurt a fly. They are great lovers of nature.

Scorpio Descendant, ruled by Mars and Pluto: The partner, or the enemy of Taurus Ascendant is powerful or influential in some way. They commonly come from wealth or are otherwise successful in business. A true enemy, if they exist for this person is particularly cruel and possibly sadistic. A nuisance of minor consequence is simply a selfish type of person who betrays their trust but does not necessarily engage with them a great deal.

If they happen to be a romantic partner gone wrong ('off the deep' end kind of wrong), they are likely to leave a deep psychic scar that can take many years to recover from. Taurus's antagonist is like a hidden parasite who drains their energy for as long as they can, and with the influence of twelfth house Aries there is a lot of aggression being used. In the most terrible situations, they may use devious tactics in order to achieve this such as through hypnosis, drugging, or sexual abuse.

Gemini Ascendant, ruled by Mercury.

Gemini on the Ascendant indicates one who seeks to understand the nature of things and how they function, and ultimately a deeper understanding of life itself. This person is agile, multi-talented, and often on the go. They hate to feel weighed down in any way, and they prefer to take many things with a grain of salt. Their bodies may be very coordinated and flexible, which becomes evident if they are engaged in any sport activities. They may become popular and loved by many, including those whom they greatly admire. They are often particularly gifted with the use of their hands, and they exhibit this in a multitude of ways such as through crafting, needlework, construction, or playing musical instruments.

Mercury is their ruling planet, keeping their minds constantly occupied and eager to both communicate and take in new information. These people love variety, and their Mercury placement indicates the general area where variety is being sought after. They prefer relationships that allow them much freedom to express themselves. At times they may seem like walking contradictions in that they say something one day and do something going against their word and supposed values the next. They may say two very different things in a single sentence to reveal their own double standards. It is also possible they have completely changed their mind about something that they used to believe in, or didn't believe in. They tend to remain youthful in both appearance and mental outlook even into their old age.

Sagittarius Descendant, ruled by Jupiter: Partners can be as fun and outgoing as they are, but also as difficult to gain solid commitments from. Enemies are more likely to appear while traveling than in the neighborhood, since Jupiter rules the Descendant. With a planet on any of the angles they may be just as likely to experience problems on home turf. Gemini Ascendant should be careful, especially in a foreign country, to make sure that they are not being followed or the subject of pickpocketing. Attacks can also occur in areas like bars and pubs, so these are areas in which to be particularly cautious in as the over-consumption of alcohol lowers one's resistance.

Taurus tends to be the ruler of Gemini's twelfth house, and with this influence there can be buried fears around survival. Certain people of unkind motivations who may notice this fear can take advantage of them or seek to control them in some way. There is protection for them in developing their own sense of security rather than depending on others.

Yet other types of enemies could turn out to be those who represent themselves falsely under a religious or spiritual pretext. They may the cause of draining one's bank account if gullibility permits. As a seeker of truth Gemini may be drawn to many types of spiritual leaders or people of high status in general. They may need to scope out their work thoroughly in order to avoid becoming duped by charlatans, licentious gurus and imposters.

Cancer Ascendant, ruled by the Moon.

Cancer Ascendant is highly receptive to the moods of others and to the subtle nuances of the environment. There are generally two different Cancerian types. The first one is physically large or voluptuous with a sociable and merry countenance. The second tends to be delicate or slender, with a rather introverted disposition. The conditions of the Moon reveal more details on either type (waxing or waning). In the first type worldly skills are accentuated and in the second type psychic abilities or mediumship are pronounced but not easy to live with, as they tend to have visceral effects. It is possible that the characteristics of both types can merge into one, and this would be the result of greater balance overall. *{The Astrological Body Types by Judith Hill, Stellium Press 1993.}*

Cancer seeks to establish themselves in relationships, places, and in hobbies that give them a feeling of comfort and familiarity. Their personality may fluctuate between being closed off to soft and sentimental. Depression is common and the Moon's influence can cause them to behave in an emotionally reactive way. Surroundings have strong positive or negative effects on the health, which is particularly sensitive to unhealthy foods, causing issues with weight or digestion.

They may be sought after by many but often prefer to keep a low profile. They are nurturing by nature but must learn proper discrimination regarding people, as they are too emotionally swayed by them. This is due to their tendency to over-empathize and be siphoned of precious energy as a result. They may need to stop living in the past and to get on with their own lives.

Descendant Capricorn, ruled by Saturn: If Cancer Ascendant is being attacked it is probably by someone who is older, more influential, more wealthy, or perceived as more powerful than they are. With both Cancer and Capricorn Ascendants, the problems often involve family. I heard of a case in which a woman with Cancer Ascendant experienced a brutal physical assault by her own adult son that almost ended her life. She had actually foreseen that something bad would happen to her a month prior to this event, but she didn't know what it would be. She did survive the attack, but with permanent, debilitating injuries. They had some very hard aspects in synastry, and his chart indicated his violent nature. Usually, The status of the enemy represented by the Descendant somehow overshadows Cancer and is used against them. Cancer may use their intuition to regain whatever they have lost or to find a solution to the problems presented to them by their opponents. Their father may either be highly supportive or a source of grief and hardship.

Gemini is the generic ruler of the twelfth house for those with a Cancer Ascendant, so they may at some point in their life be susceptible to slander or betrayal by friends or family members. In the case of spiritual attack, the entities involved may have the sense of being ancient, wicked and relentless. Cancer discovers that when they shine their own inner light in the world, they no longer need to resign themselves to the idea of ongoing suffering.

Leo Ascendant, ruled by the Sun

Leo on the Ascendant confers a bright solar appearance, charisma and a commanding presence that draws a lot of attention. These people are highly attractive to others in numerous ways. Some are more shy or reserved than they appear to be on the surface while others are completely at ease in self-promotion and taking center stage. Their natural sense of leadership can be directed toward their career, family life or creative endeavors. There is seldom a dull moment with them, and they can be a lot of fun to be around. When energy is low or they're not in a good mood, they are likely to seek invisibility and go unnoticed until they are ready to face the world again.

Leo Ascendant is at ease in seizing control of a situation and won't take a back seat to anyone, although they will sometimes share the spotlight. The position of the Sun, if not afflicted, shows where they excel. Some of them need to watch for a tendency to be condescending toward others. They may not intend to do this but their confidence in certain areas can be expressed in ways that make others look or feel subordinate. When they are in their element they really know how to put on a show, perform at optimum levels and leave everyone impressed and inspired. The love life can range from the carefree, happy and adventurous to the extremely rocky and unstable, but in any case, there is a strong desire for both love and freedom. Commitments are best shared with those who share similar values.

Aquarius Descendant, ruled by Saturn and Uranus: The Leo Ascendant person may be attacked by strange people and false friends, or by jealous ex-lovers who want nothing more than to see Leo suffer. These attacks tend to be rather dramatic in nature, and sometimes the stuff of horror movies or the Twilight Zone. They could also be the types of scenarios that would be featured on tabloid talk shows like Dr. Phil's. Leo may consider themselves lucky if the attack is only a verbal one, which is still likely to be a bit weird. Spiritually, they are learning about the nature of unconditional love, despite all of the crazy things that they experience and struggle with. When Cancer rules their twelfth house, they may be coming to terms with a deeply buried feeling of insecurity that stems from their early upbringing. In some cases, it is their mother who is responsible for the emotional pain that they carry with them into adulthood.

Virgo Ascendant, ruled by Mercury

Mercury is the ruling planet of this earth sign, but the mental focus becomes very fine-tuned. This person is often a natural teacher who makes for an intelligent companion that one will learn many things from. Their appearance is generally youthful, vibrant, fit and well put together overall. They tend to be clean cut, whether or not they dress in a conventional way. There is typically something that others find quite adorable about them, but in some cases, something that is simultaneously annoying. This person is always busy but down-to-earth, and can sometimes border on being obsessive in their chosen line of work. Virgo does not miss a single detail in a place or situation, and they can be very devoted to causes that bring benefit to society.

An inborn helpful nature causes may cause them to go the extra mile for others and they are frequently found filling in the gaps. Any of their own plans laid out are very thorough. Their aim is to bring a greater sense of functionality and order wherever it is lacking, even if that means taking time out of their day to wash a friend's car or remodel their kitchen sink. He or she is a walking dictionary that breaks down information in segments, engaging others in enlivening conversations of all sorts. Each conversation had adds to the store of information that the dictionary contains.

Perfectionism and criticism can undermine them in relationships and career can be a source of stress until they are doing what they truly love to do. They need freedom to work on their own terms.

Pisces Descendant, ruled by Jupiter and Neptune; Virgo Ascendant sometimes does not recognize an opponent soon enough to do anything about it, due to a preoccupation with their internal dialogue. They may project their goodness onto others or in some cases they instead project their own personal naivety and weakness onto the other, and then become shocked at the results. They often need to learn how to see both others and themselves more objectively. Something is often amiss in the perception about the nature of their involvements.

Virgo can also be their own worst enemy when they pick apart all of the difficulties in their lives instead of highlighting the positive. With Leo ruling their twelfth house, they have a strong desire to be known as important. The person who attacks them is someone who takes them for granted or tries to take advantage of them. They do not usually remain a long-term problem in Virgo's life. To the contrary, they are likely to disappear, leaving a trail of dust behind them.

Libra Ascendant, ruled by Venus

Libra is the sign that represents the setting of the sun. Much is being reflected upon in life, and they feel they are at the threshold of a new one. The aim is harmonization with others and the world around them. This person is often physically attractive and has a great sense of style. A natural sense of leadership is often present. Libra is a charming sign and often knows exactly what to say to put people at ease. What you see and hear with Libra on the Ascendant is not necessarily what you get though. To assess who you are dealing with, look to the ruling planet Venus to see if they are the self-indulgent type or the selfless giver, or something in between in their search for balance.

One of the greatest struggles often experienced in this person is an identity crisis. From an early age they may have felt they had to bend their needs to please other people, and as time went on their entire life became one big costume party, as they lost sight of who they were underneath it all. Love could be mistaken for submissiveness and downplaying themselves in order to avoid upsetting others and they may even go above and beyond in serving them.

They may desperately want peace, but their radar is constantly picking up on all the troubles around them which can cause them to live in a rigid manner. They want to make a difference in the world, but they can only do this when they take care of their own backyard. They are lovers of nature and need to recharge in it often.

Aries Descendant, ruled by Mars: The Libra Ascendant native hates having enemies and does everything possible in order to avoid making them. When big, irreparable conflicts arise their preferred action is to just go the opposite direction, but not before having the last word. Even then, Libra leaves the "cage door open" as the rather crude saying goes. Libra is so suave that they make it difficult for others to hold grudges against them. Conversely, they may in extreme situations be the subject of random acts of violence. According to online records (astro.com) John F. Kennedy had Libra on the Ascendant. He was one of the most beloved U.S presidents of all time and he died by assassination. His antagonist, assassin Lee H. Oswald, can be represented by JFK's Aries Descendant. Gunshots are ruled by Mars. Lee was himself a Libra, born October 18, 1939.

Spiritually, Libra Ascendant's battles exist more within their own psyche than with goblins and ghosts. Virgo generally rules their Twelfth house, indicating that despite their friendly mannerisms they may harbor much criticism of themselves and others, which is something that others respond to instinctively.

Scorpio Ascendant, ruled by Mars and Pluto

Scorpio carries great mystique, and it is often said, one of most difficult tasks of the Ascendants. Their path is like razor's edge between morality and iniquity. They are often engaged in inwardly processing all that they perceive goes far beyond the surface of things. They may wrestle much with their inner demons before they finally achieve any sort of lasting harmony in their life. Some with this Ascendant are by nature very humble and kind, and others tend to be controlling as they seek to mold others into what they want them to be. They gravitate toward positions in society that grant them leverage and authority and they function well as entrepreneurs. With Libra often on their twelfth house cusp, many of their greatest tests come through relationships.

Both healing and psychic abilities are particularly strong if the native chooses to use them. They tend to need a lot of time alone to decompress and filter out all the external noise and things they have identified themselves with in the world. As a highly skilled manifester, there is nothing of significance that Scorpio Ascendant can do without experiencing quick returns from in some form or another, whether good or bad. They tend to elicit strong reactions from others that range from fear to wonder, to lust to fury. There is a sharp determination in everything they set out to do, and they are especially keen on gaining answers to life's riddles. They usually discover some type of talent, tool or information that is hidden from ordinary view, and whatever that thing is centered around will become their guiding compass in life.

Taurus Descendant, ruled by Venus: The loving partner of Scorpio Ascendant is both charming and easygoing. The spiteful enemy uses money, sexuality or persuasiveness in an attempt to undermine them in some way. Sometimes they discover a secret of Scorpio's and may threaten them with blackmail. An attack may revolve around property, legacies, and personal belongings. Spiritual adversaries can appear in the form of the classical or metaphorical succubus, incubus, or temptress. They try to lead Scorpio astray and lure them into traps by appealing to their desires, especially when addiction is present. Not all of them fall, but many will face at least one or two major temptations to do something morally wrong, for various reasons. This can be seen as a spiritual test that is faced in the wilderness of life. If they refuse to give in to their lower nature, the forces of evil will have no power over them whatsoever.

Sagittarius Ascendant, ruled by Jupiter

With Sagittarius on the Ascendant, there is a certain tireless quality in the persona. Jupiter lends tremendous drive, which is reflected in something slightly rugged, fierce or wild in the overall appearance. These people are natural warriors of a sort because no matter what life throws their way, even if they fall and cry momentarily, they just pick themselves up and keep moving. Because of their endurance they make excellent athletes, politicians, and public leaders. When they are not keeping themselves active in some way, they tend to suffer for it. These are people who aim high and often reach their goals, becoming successful in numerous areas. They can be generous toward those that they trust. They may carry dark secrets that occasionally cause them discomfort. They are great teachers who care about truth and speak their mind, but some of them can come across as blunt and rude. Others are just candid in a friendly sort of way. They tend to be open about what they are feeling and going through.

Many find that at some point, something stuffed in the back of their psyche they have been avoiding catches up to them and they are faced with an important, life-altering choice regarding whatever that thing is. If revenge takes over their subconscious, their actions can be the cause of their own undoing. Above all they crave freedom and will create a lifestyle that grants them that. They are fond of animals and nature, and may have many pets.

Gemini Descendant, ruled by MercurySagittarius: Ascendant may fluctuate between feeling invincible in the world and like a strong victim. Enemies often turn out to be either one's own blood relatives or neighbors. Scenarios range in severity from the serious to the downright silly. A concerning example could be one who is mugged in her own neighborhood. A rather humorous yet still intrusive example would be one whose vehicle that is parked in their own driveway is egged, possibly by teenagers with too much time on their hands. Many people with this Descendant have at some point in their life had an annoying neighbor or sibling that did something to make their life harder. Yet many others have been the victims of silent theft. They might have even felt robbed of their childhood in some way.

Attacks are performed with stealth so it's not always easy to pin down the perpetrator.

Mercury is a trickster planet and reflects the person who causes difficulties for Sagittarius Ascendant. Spiritual attacks may come from mischievous types of entities such as sprites who enjoy playing pranks on humans.

Capricorn Ascendant, ruled by Saturn

The Capricorn Ascendant personality is tenacious and capable of achieving great works over time. They have the patience to see things through that many people would give up on. This person can be both serious and quite humorous at the same time, although normally, not given to huge displays of emotion. Deep down inside there is a very caring individual who has either experienced some early hardship in life or for some reason has chosen to go at many things alone even when they have friends. In childhood, theirs was an old head on young shoulders. They have a strong sense of responsibility toward their loved ones, and they tend to sacrifice themselves in order to take care of them. They have much creative talent that must find outlets for expression, otherwise they may sink into a slump of depression without knowing why.

Workaholism and boredom are the results of one who has lost sight of their inner hopes and dreams and just gives their life away to duty without deriving much enjoyment from it. They make great custodians of the land and care for places of significance. When alone, it is easier for Capricorn Ascendant to relax and see the silver lining in the clouds,to laugh and make light of things. Many of them are old souls with a lot of innate wisdom that becomes more valuable to them the older they get.

Cancer Descendant, ruled by the Moon: Those with Capricorn Ascendant tend to be most mistreated by those of lower status and ability than their own. They may be harassed by people who are immature and needy and yet who manage to bring tremendous chaos into their life. When Capricorn is trying too hard to avoid acknowledging their own weakness, they become victimized. It is precisely when they are not paying attention that they tend to be taken advantage of. Displays of pride are often a cover for deep set fears. The other person is too self-absorbed to care about Capricorn's welfare or needs. This brings up the issue of abandonment for them, as their mother is either a source of great support or turmoil. In some cases, it is the father whose role is pronounced or absent.

In order to slay their personal demons, Capricorn Ascendant must confront their own fears, lest they become crippled by phobias that prevent them from living their lives as fully as they were meant to be lived. They should dream bigger and play again, as joyfully as children do. With Sagittarius usually ruling their twelfth house, they have a wellspring of hidden optimism and inspiration to tap into.

Aquarius Ascendant, ruled by Saturn and Uranus

There is something unusual about this person's appearance, habits or way of life. Two planets rule this sign and if Uranus is the stronger influence in their natal chart, they may have striking features and an avant-garde sense of fashion. They may be or appear to be non-binary, or just airy and light while also strong. If Saturn is the pronounced influence, they are often conservative, tall, of a slender build and with chiseled features. Keen observers of humankind and nature, they like to live their lives according to cutting-edge discoveries and may be autodidacts. They may offer their own inventions to help others, or they may sit quietly gathering data and results over long stretches of time before sharing their findings.

Aquarius is very open-minded and friendly toward others. Helpful and kind, they enjoy chatting and getting to know people, but simultaneously they are at "arm's length" away, metaphorically living in their own little galaxy. They may have many artistic gifts including musical ones. Acting and public speaking abilities are also accentuated. Their intelligence combined with their own particular set of values always seems to set them apart from others in some way. Although they are open, they appear as walking enigmas, difficult for many people to understand.

The immortalized rock icon David Bowie had Aquarius on the Ascendant. He was a Capricorn born on January 8, 1947, at approximately 9:00 am in London according to the Astro Databank website.

Leo Descendant, ruled by the Sun: Aquarius Ascendant stands out as unique, and draws a partner who is equally as special. The conflicts begin if the other person believes themselves to be more important and becomes not only high maintenance but obnoxious, overbearing or bossy. Power struggles are sure to arise if that other becomes a "drama queen" or "drama king". Aquarius's rival appears to cause some form of interference, whether to their plans and projects, or their peace of mind.

With Capricorn ruling their twelfth house hidden enemies may be people who are older, or who have at some point served as authority figures in their life. It might even be one of their parents. They may be confronted by those who wish to challenge their position in some way. Only to the degree that they are identified with their worldly status can they be negatively impacted. When they are spiritually oriented, they can remain unaffected by those who seek to undermine them.

Pisces, ruled by Jupiter and Neptune

Although this person does not neatly fit into society's norms, they are somehow able to blend in and camouflage themselves as if they do. They may have talents for symmetry, organization and design that are often put to use in their chosen profession. There is a faraway, otherworldly dreaminess and other soft, watery features in the overall appearance. They possess a combination of sensitivity and strong artistic flair, with a dash of genius. In many situations this person chooses to view the world through rose-colored glasses, or to escape into the realm of fantasy when the going gets to be too tough. They love traveling, both physically and mentally. To some people they may seem lethargic or spacey, but they are simply running on different frequencies than others do.

With Neptune as their co-ruling planet they can, like those with Cancer rising seem especially vulnerable to toxins and psychic invasions. For this reason, they should be very cautious with drugs and alcohol which are unfortunately tempting for many of them. In general, they are not particularly ambitious, but they know how to make good money doing what they enjoy, and enjoying life is one of their top priorities. As professional entertainers they can be very enchanting. Due to their deep insights and gentle nature they make great therapists. They can be very caring and philanthropic, choosing occupations that focus on helping to uplift, inspire and bring people together. Sometimes they have difficulty in making up their minds.

Virgo Descendant, ruled by Mercury: If Pisces Ascendant has any enemies, it is probably because they are envied for something that they possess, but not necessarily something material. It is that no matter what they do for living, they are somehow able to remove themselves from the hustle and bustle of daily life - the rat race that everyone else seems chained down to. Pisces just goes with the flow and allows things to come to them in their own timing. Sometimes they are disappointed in relationships because they gave their affection to someone who was unworthy of all they had to offer.

Although Pisces may appear to always be living the good life, they may be suffering in silence, feeling alone inside. When Aquarius rules their twelfth house it indicates that problems with others may arise with those who say they are friends but are mere associates or rivals. Their real friends are obvious. The others are always lurking, and only make an appearance when they want something.

Chapter 13

Tips, Tools and Timing for Empaths, Psychics, and Healers

Psychics and highly sensitive people are born under every sign of the zodiac but there seem to be certain astrological traits that many of them have in common. These are explained in the chapter: The Astrology of the Spirit World and Psychic Phenomena. Those who are empathic by nature or who do healing work for a living tend to be more susceptible to becoming overwhelmed on psychic levels than those with their focus on material pursuits.

One of the problems that some intuitive people face is the humiliation of falling into repeated situations with abusers that they later shame themselves for not having perceived early enough. It was often their kindness that was taken advantage of in some way. It seems logical to assume that if an attack was not perceived quickly enough, the victim's psychic radar must be malfunctioning. The mechanisms involved are not that simple. The subconscious dictates most of human behavior due to previous associations, both positive and negative. Abuse that began in childhood can cause a lack of proper boundaries and discrimination in certain areas as an adult. The child who was abused or whose boundaries were repeatedly trespassed may become overly tolerant of untrustworthy people because they have learned adaptation from a very early age. They were actually forced to adapt to toxic situations in order to survive. Situations like these can dampen intuition over time because they erode a person's self-confidence.

When either the planet Saturn or the fire element is particularly strong in a natal chart, there is often a boost in psychic immunity, because there is an innate sense of personal drive to overcome challenges. The inner fire within each of us can be likened to the spark of divinity that we have come to call the soul. The inner fire of humankind has been dimmed by many things including genetically altered foods and an increased dependency on technology. Therefore, in the modern world, the inability to recognize psychic attack is a relatively widespread phenomenon. Violent imagery is flashed repeatedly on television screens, through internet media, and in video games in ways that initially traumatize but eventually desensitize the viewers. Fear is what sells more so than wonderful new discoveries, acts of charity and kindness. Over time, the imagery and information solely centered around negative events creates constant stress which in turn wreaks havoc on mental equilibrium and lowers resistance to outside attacks.

Out of necessity, we attend to many types of cleaning rituals for our bodies and homes. We do laundry, wash dishes, dust and sweep. Those who practice yoga and meditation find ways to clear and freshen up their auras on a daily basis as well. If you are engaged in any type of work relating to the psyche, spirituality, or healing then keeping up your energy hygiene is absolutely imperative to your own well-being. If you are not a healer, astrologer or psychic reader but are sensitive and work with the public in some way, then daily energy hygiene is as equally important for you as washing your hands. Empaths can be found not only in healing centers but in many occupations, working as cashiers at a grocery store or bank. If you are one of them and constantly exposed to other people, your body probably alerts you in many ways to the need for space clearing and shaking off negativity that has accumulated throughout the day. It is important to pay attention to these bodily signals instead of only seeking to quell them with stimulants and sedatives. Doing regular cleansing rituals for the spaces that focus on healing and spiritual work is not only helpful but important for maintaining positive energy unless that space is exposed to lots of natural light. A ritual need not be elaborate, but should be clear enough for your mind to register. A rather troubling issue for the empath is being forced to deal with next door neighbors whose presence is somehow intrusive, directly or indirectly. Each case is different and there is not one solution for this type of situation. If negativity seems to "seep through the walls", without any physical interaction, try keeping a protective plant such as a cactus or stone such as Black Tourmaline at every window, entrance, or the wall or ceiling most affected. In Feng Shui, Snake Plant is considered to be highly protective when properly placed.

There is another cause of psychic disturbance that is hard for most people to identify. Geopathic stress, a term used to describe excess radiation and negative energy from within the earth, has been linked with many types of illness. Some areas are especially active on a paranormal level due to geopathic stress, but that is not always necessarily the reason. You can typically identify such areas by the way that you feel overall when you are in them, for no particular reason. There might be a certain room of the house that you always feel uncomfortable in, so you automatically avoid it for the most part. If your bed is placed over an area of geopathic stress you will likely have frequent nightmares and wake up feeling tired. The nineteenth century German geomancer Baron Gustav von Pohl discovered that domestic pets, insects and many other animals are naturally attracted to these areas of the earth's resonance. In 1929 he mapped out areas of disturbance in many houses in the small town of Vilshiburg which were afterward investigated by the German Central Committee for Cancer Research in Berlin. His research on several geopathic danger zones was confirmed as being linked with cancer and many other types of disease. If your cat or dog gravitates to particular areas or you find that infestations of insects tend to happen in one area of the garden, it is often a sign of geopathic stress. Often the best thing to do for well-being is to move furniture around accordingly. One who is highly skilled in the Chinese art of placement known as Feng Shui will be able to help locate geopathic stress and devise solutions for a specific home or building. If you must enter such areas for work purposes it can be helpful to wear a shield or clothing that neutralizes EMF.

You may wish to further investigate the energy of a place further by way of way of Astro-locality, specifically that branch of astrology referred to as Local Space which can be narrowed down to a single structure, in order to figure out the best areas for certain objects and activities. Through this method you can visually lay a whole chart map over your home, dividing it into different "houses" to decipher which areas are the most favorable for your needs and routines. If for instance your line of Mars cuts through your living room and especially if Mars is already problematic in your natal chart, you might find yourself very agitated and accident prone in this area.

Special care should be taken in the following types of settings:

The Healing Room

In many types of therapy sessions there is usually a considerable amount of energetic dumping that occurs, which is a natural part of the healing process. It is not ideal to practice healing in a room without windows, but if there is no other choice then certain adjustments can be made to the room to help circulate the energy. One is to keep a high-quality air purifier on in the room. Another is to keep an essential oil diffuser in the room, being courteous regarding the possible allergies and sensitivities of clients. The table that people lie upon undergoes a change of tissue paper, but the energy should also be "reset" between clients. There are many ways to do this, and they each have slightly different effects. There is not much time to perform anything elaborate on busy days, but in addition to disinfecting material surfaces adding the intention to release accumulated energy helps the practitioner to make sure they are ready for the next client.

There is a method of spiritual cleansing for every personality and the key to success is to discover what works for you. If you are a person who loves crystals, choose the sizes, hues, shapes and placements that will most enhance your work. Apophyllite is often used to defuse negativity and instill a sense of peace in the environment. Amethyst is another great stone for the healing room and more accessible, but it does need to be cleared regularly. This can be done by setting or running it under cool water or passing the smoke from incense over it. Bells or chimes or a Tibetan singing bowl used between sessions in the area where the healing took place also helps to clear residual energy. While washing hands, a strong visualization of releasing an accumulation of the negative energy released by the client or patient can provide an effective release. Some practitioners already do this during the session and have no need to do it afterward.

The Psychic Reading Room

Many psychic readers are already aware of the need to keep their space clear from the negativity of others but some who are new to this either were not trained properly or perhaps their busy schedules have not allowed them enough time to prepare and recover between readings. The same rules apply to astrologers who do not consider themselves to be psychic. To begin, make sure that the doorway and any other important areas such as where you and the client sit are not cluttered or blocked in any way. When you are gazing into another person's natal chart you are opening yourself up, temporarily, to their energy field. The importance of clearing space between readings cannot be over-emphasized. To neglect this aspect of doing readings and psychic work is like using a vacuum cleaner that begins to spit out all the dirt it collects because it has become long overdue to be emptied. This can lead to frustrating or embarrassing situations with clients. A strong visualization of a white, gold or blue-violet light throughout the room that purifies any stuck energy can be helpful. Keeping a salt lamp on or a candle lit during the reading can help to prevent psychic residue. As with the healing room, bells, gongs or some device that produces a clearing tone may be used between sessions in the area where the reading took place helps to clear residual energy. Using a mist bottle that contains essential oils and flower essences of a cleansing nature can clear the space between readings. A great ingredient for a space clearing mist includes the essential oil or hydrosol of Bay Laurel, which is both purifying and provides great psychic protection.

The Metaphysical Gift Shop

In any kind of metaphysical gift shop but especially one that contains crystals, the energy of both things and people is constantly being amplified for better or worse. For those who own or work within such an environment, daily and sometimes even hourly space clearing becomes critical when there is a lot of foot traffic and people handling the objects. The greatest responsibility lies in the hands of the owner, and this includes training employees to cleanse and protect themselves if they are not already learned in these areas. Unfortunately, this type of education rarely occurs. This accounts for the type of crystal shop that is dark, dirty, or otherwise heavy, becoming host to a dense layer of energy fog where business is either slow or just being there becomes a sticky situation for all involved. All types of hygiene are extremely important in these shops because allowing healing tools to get too dusty or collect too many fingerprints is not good for business and not good for the spirit. Clutter should also be avoided for success in sales, in addition to supporting the well-being of workers and customers. Living plants are helpful to keep in a metaphysical shop because they help to clean the air, but this is only when their own vitality is maintained with proper light and watering.

Energy Cleansing with Sacred Herbs

Smudging is a ceremonial practice common to Native tribes in Canada and the USA, in which certain herbs are burnt to purify an area of negative energy, sickness, and evil spirits and to bestow blessings. In modern times smudging is still performed on many occasions by people of all ethnic backgrounds, but this sometimes does not yield positive results. This is due to the combination of cultural appropriation and careless harvesting of endangered plants such as White Sage in the United States. This herb has been widely harvested illegally in order to sell at New Age stores. Unless White Sage herb bundles are purchased or received from Natives directly, or instruction gained from an elder to engage in their cultural practices, in many cases the results may be futile or in the worst-case scenario the opposite of what one had hoped for.

Long ago I learned from a Native American medicine man his cultural method for burning White Sage and other sacred herbs. This is to say a prayer for what one would like to accomplish, and to give thanks to the plant spirit for its help, with a heart of genuine humility and gratitude. The directions are acknowledged along with their corresponding elements, spiritual guardians and one's personal ancestors. The intention that goes into lighting the herb is of equal importance to its innate qualities. Commercially grown or mass harvested sacred herbs sometimes carry undesirable signals into the environment when burnt unless they have been grown and handled with respect and love. I have lost count of how many people I have both known and heard about who experienced negative effects from using White Sage in an ignorant manner.

This brings me to the sad topic of how many people of European descent (as well as others) have forgotten and neglected their own cultural roots. They think it's more exotic to pretend to be something they are not, or that their own heritage is boring. Every culture has its own unique spiritual practices and holds certain herbs in high regard for both their medicinal and spiritual properties. An individual actually tends to gain some of the most powerful results from honoring the traditions that are associated with their own lineage, rather than trying to adopt those from another that is radically different. The exception to this is that the spirit of the herb or a traditional practice is calling one on a deep level. Someone may strongly gravitate to a certain culture for various reasons that may be tied in with their ancestry, their significant other, or some feel it to be a past life. In many cases people are just seeking a sense of purpose and looking in random places.

The Scottish have an ancient practice called Saining that is similar to Smudging, only water is often used in addition to smoke along with certain songs and prayers. Herbs are burned such as Heather, Juniper, Lemon Balm, Rosemary and Thyme. These herbs are connected with the Faerie faith of the British Isles. There are many other herbs in addition to these that can be used for smoke cleansing. You may wish to check the area that you live in to discover those that are most abundant if they do not grow around your property. A common herb for this purpose includes Lavender which carries a gentle and calming aroma. When in doubt, do your research first to make sure that you are purchasing or harvesting legally and respectfully toward the land and its spirits. Many of the American tree herbs such as Cedar, Juniper and Pine are also sacred to Native Americans.

One of the most powerful cleansing herbs for spiritual cleansing that grows in many parts of the world is Mugwort. Traditionally this herb is associated with the planet Venus, perhaps due to its affinity for women and its ability to stimulate fertility. It has been extensively used in Traditional Chinese Medicine, Native American healing, and in European culture for feminine complaints and also for the purpose of assisting in dream recall and psychic work. In Korea, Mugwort is highly regarded by many as a healing food with anti-parasitic and anti-carcinogenic properties. This is one example of a very powerful and versatile herb that is not exclusive to one culture. Most important is that it is being used appropriately and safely for the issues at hand. This is one herb that can be especially helpful for psychic readers and astrologers to burn between sessions, to both help clear negativity and hone their abilities.

Fragrant resins placed on burning charcoal are also very powerful and effective in space clearing. Resins have been used in many cultures and are mentioned in the Bible. Types of resins include Frankincense, Myrrh, Dragon's Blood, and Benzoin to name a few. To burn them a charcoal incense burner or a small bowl filled with sand is needed to light the resin in. You can read more about these resins in the chapter "Protective Remedies for Signs and Transits."

The World's Most Ancient Tool for Psychic Protection: Salt

Salt has been one of the most revered earthly substances since the dawn of time. Ancient cultures used it not only as a spice but occasionally in areas such as Rome, as a form of currency. Today we take for granted its easy access, but long ago its production and trade became cause for competition between merchants. This speaks volumes of just how precious salt is to the human race. Due to its ability to absorb negativity it has always been one of the top substances used for both magickal and healing purposes.

In the Nordic myth of creation, the great void Ginnungagap gave birth to a cow named Audhumla who instantly licked a rock of salt from which the body of the deity Bure emerged. He became known as the grandfather of Odin. The human body contains many different types of salt which are necessary to carry out various processes. Because salt comes from the sea, it is naturally linked with oceanic archetypes such as Venus Aphrodite and with the Moon. Some people however rather link salt with the planet Saturn.

Salt can be used in many creative ways but keep in mind that it serves as a psychic vacuum.

Table salt often contains traces of crude oil waste which diminishes both nutritional value and metaphysical effects. The best types to use do not contain additives such as flouride or aluminum silicate which not only have negative health side effects but energetically changes the properties of the salt. After using any significant amount of salt for a space clearing it is important to replenish the atmosphere with sweet spice or aroma that supports the qualities that you wish to enhance. You can burn a favorite incense or diffuse some essential oils for this.

Here are a few ways to use salt for psychic protection:

- Sprinkle salt around the bed if psychic disturbances are frequent during sleep. This helps to discourage ghostly visitors and other unwanted experiences.

- Add a bit of salt to mop water to clean the floors of a home, office or other enclosed environment. This helps to clear and to prevent the establishment of negative and stubborn psychic imprints.

- Sprinkle it across every threshold including doors and windows to prevent psychic intrusions from entering. If the situation is extreme leave a trail of sprinkled salt around the entire building.

- Prepare a bath and toss a large pinch or small handful of sea salt into it. You may like to add essential oils along with a carrier that helps to create a more therapeutic soaking experience.

- Carry salt in a pouch for awhile during times of acute stress or when you feel that you are under psychic attack. It should be small enough to fit into a pocket or worn around your neck but concealed under your clothing. When it has served its purpose dispose of it some place in nature, such as into a running stream or bury it in the soil.

- Place salt around a white candle with the intention to dissolve psychic distress and clear the space from lingering negativity. Another option is to rub olive oil onto a candle and then roll it over salt.

Remote Viewing

Intelligence agenices associated with the U.S. Pentagon as well as leaders in all parts of the world have long sought out a combination of astrologers and psychics for help aid in determining the strategy and timing of their enemies' attacks. Specifically, they have utilized what has been termed remote viewing to gather information on the location of objects, people and events at a distance, including those in the past present and future.

Today many people are also being viewed remotely unbeknownst to them, through sateloons, radio towers, surveillance cameras, smart phones, and other remote viewing mechanisms. Now with the aid of modern technology and artificial intelligence, traditional methods of remote viewing are no longer may no longer be among the favored methods of successful spying from a distance. The "Age of Aquarius" that we are said to be entering is challenging our human rights to live peacefully in the privacy of our homes. Researchers at Carnegie Mellon University have tested a system using Wi-Fi signals to determine human poses and movements within a room, regardless of lighting. A few things that have been shown to help to block Wi-Fi signals are large sheets of metal, bodies of water, and dense materials such as rock, bricks and concrete.

Counterintelligence and espionage has occurred since ancient times but became growing concerns in the early 1930s, when Neptune was in the early stage of its transit through Virgo. Now about a century later with Neptune in its opposite sign of Pisces, we see that it has become impossible to truly live in privacy without living off grid entirely. With social media and online data brokers, there are no more boundaries that separate people's personal lives from the collective. People who value their privacy either have to pay exorbitant fees to conceal and protect their identities or they spend a great deal of time in learning legalese in order to take control of both their own legal rights and privacy as sovereign beings.

The first research institution to scientifically study remote viewing was Stanford Research Institute in California. Hundreds of experiments were carried out between 1972 and 1986. Studies suggest that the Soviet Union had already been engaged in the investigation of ESP long before this period, and the CIA wanted to catch up and figure out how this was being done. They took part in establishing Stargate Project in 1978, which was a secret U.S. Army unit focused on controlled remote viewing.

Over the years, many experiments concluded that the accuracy of remote viewing was not in any way affected by distance, size or electromagnetism. In one experiment called Deep Quest in the summer of 1977, remote viewers were placed in a submarine called the "Taurus". This was facilitated by Stephan Schwartz of the Moebius Group. Despite the fact that they were shielded in a submersed chamber under water, they were able to accurately describe distant targets on land, as well as previously unknown areas underwater. They discovered a shipwreck and in subsequent experiments, a buried city. This first experiment was carried out from the Santa Catalina islands in Southern California. Coincidentally, in that very same year and summer, a movie called The Deep was released by Columbia pictures. In this movie, scuba divers discovered ancient artifacts, and stumbled upon the secret cargo of a World War II shipwreck. Venus and Mars were both in the sign of Taurus when it came out, on June 17th.

Remote viewing can and has been used both to harm or help others. One may extend their remote viewing to the operation of remote influencing, and this is where this subject becomes even more dangerous. Astrologers often engage in remote viewing whether or not they label it as such. The map of the heavens is their tool for doing so. Looking into the past, future or specific details in the present that are far away or hidden is something nearly anyone can do successfully, with enough practice. With this in mind, you can choose the most auspicious times for your viewing, as well as the most effective times for shielding yourself against invasions. Generally speaking, Jupiter is the go-to planetary influence for remote viewing as well as astral traveling, so you may seek heightened or beneficial aspects involving it when you are training. Neptune is a hit-or-miss type of influence that often seems to lead one astray or bring mixed results. You can view remotely at any time, but you may benefit from taking note of the moon phases that enhance or dampen your results.

Astrological Timing for Purification and Protection

There are certain times and occasions that are both more conducive than others for removing obstacles and putting up energetic boundaries of protection, but in an emergency situation one must act immediately. This applies whenever one is being attacked on a psychic level or going through a difficult life challenge such as battling with an illness, going through a divorce or some other kind of hardship. Relocating from one home or business location to another is also an important time to be especially mindful of environmental energy hygiene, both of the space being left behind and the space being entered into.

There are also certain times when misfortunes and attacks of all kinds become more widespread or noticeable such as during full moons and eclipses. Mercury Retrograde is a regular occurrence three times a year for a month at a time. People who are not even astrologers complain that everything goes haywire under its influence, yet life goes on. There are positive possibilities for challenging transits if we but look for them. We can look to the zodiac signs being highlighted by such events for clues as to the areas being targeted and affected. The choices we make during these sensitive times can greatly improve or worsen our conditions.

As a routine, two of the most effective times to light herbs are night when clients and customers are gone or in the morning before they have arrived.

Optimal Times to Purge Negativity from our Lives and Environment:

The "In Between" times: Dawn, Dusk, and Midnight

During these times there is less interference from the ordinary human realm. Many people are asleep, just waking, just retiring or otherwise taking a break from daily routines. Because of this the energy clearing tends to be much more thorough and effective than during the middle of a busy day when most people are hustling and bustling about.

The Dark Moon

This is the phase just prior to the New Moon. About two or three days prior to the New Moon is a powerful time for clearing stagnant energies or doing a final purge of something. The hours just before the New Moon is also useful for camouflaging yourself or disappearing if necessary. If you need to hide something from the prying eyes of another, the Dark Moon may assist you.

Waning Moon

When the moon is waning, many projects that were initiated during the waxing moons are coming to fruition or ending. The time of the waning moon is best suited toward releasing, clearing, and finishing what has been previously started. It is suitable for ridding oneself of undesirable things, problems and ties. There are many methods and rituals centered around doing this that do not bring harm to anyone. The waning Moon is also well-suited toward the closing of spirit portals when they are a source of trouble (the places where spirits tend to enter into and exit from the physical dimension).

Moon in Scorpio

When the Moon transits through Scorpio each month, we are encouraged to clear, detoxify or transform something, no matter how seemingly insignificant in our lives. Emotions tend to run high during this brief transit, but the Scorpio energy can be directed toward changing certain things or habits that we don't like.

Pluto Stationing Retrograde or Direct

When Pluto is switching gears there is intensity in the air. This small planet goes retrograde for six months out of every year. The time period when it is getting ready to switch direction is particularly potent for any kind of ritual involving purification and a release of energy. The days before, during and after Pluto goes Retrograde are well suited toward banishing energy. The days before, during and after Pluto goes Direct are suited toward rituals for heavy duty protection and for deflecting psychic attacks.

Optimal times to Build or Enhance a Protective Shield of Energy:

Solar Returns

The Solar return is the astrologically precise birthday, when the Sun returns to the exact same position that it was at the time of one's birth. This could occur a day before or even after the actual date of one's birth. Around this time, one's vital energy is often either at its peak or slack, depending on the condition of the Sun's position and other aspects. In some cases, the need for special care becomes obvious. This is a very powerful time for strengthening an individual's psychic shield.

Moon to Sun, Sun to Moon

Every month the Moon transits the natal Sun sign and when it does, a little burst of energy can be effectively directed toward many things including spiritual expansion and psychic protection.

Every year the Sun transits the position of one's Moon, and this too tends to be a highly charged and energetic time, great for increasing awareness and psychic resilience.

Jupiter transits

Create more space around yourself or strengthen your psychic shield when Jupiter is making favorable transits in your chart. The Moon makes a conjunction to your natal Jupiter every month, providing an ideal time for strengthening your protective shield.

New Moon

Within ten hours after the New Moon, there is fresh new energy available to gather together for various purposes, including self-preservation. This is not necessarily a protective time of month but it can help support you in clearing the slates and in gaining a fresh new perspective on your situation.

Full Moon

The Full Moon amplifies energy and brings many things to completion. There is often an intensity during this time that can cause the need for psychic protection to suddenly become more urgent. Many people become unstable and vulnerable to various misfortunes. Within twenty-four hours before and after the Full Moon any intentions and efforts made to build a psychic shield may be enhanced. Energy can be erratic before the Full Moon and begins to calm down afterward.

The Moon through the Signs and Their Use for Psychic Work and Welfare

Moon in Fire Signs:

With the Moon in Aries and the other fire signs the most effective forms of psychic work are either executed or experienced in spontaneity. These Moon transits are generally better suited toward the output of energy rather than internal work. Aries helps us to get motivated on a physical level so that we take whatever actions are necessary for our well-being rather than waiting around for things to change.

With the Moon in Leo we want to enjoy life more so we are not as focused on our problems as we are at other times. This is a good time to experiment and try a new space clearing method. You might create your own meditation technique or formula for psychic integration and empowerment. Be aware of personal triggers and choose your battles or you could find yourself reacting needlessly to things and wasting energy.

In Sagittarius the Moon gives us more breathing room and encourages us to think and act with greater courage. Peak spiritual experiences may take us out of our ordinary routines. We may be more prone toward becoming scattered than at other times, and more stressed out as a result. This is an ideal Moon to meditate, to tap into one's own psyche or psychic abilities.

Moon in Earth Signs:

In earth signs we are typically less vulnerable to psychic influences as we are when the Moon is in signs of the other elements. Taurus is a sign that Luna favors, when we are more calm and grounded, making it a very good time to either establish and strengthen our psychic boundaries, in addition to physical ones. We may become more capable of decompressing on a mental level during this transit. It is also great for tidying up and beautifying the environment.

In Virgo the Moon assists us in getting organized, defining our priorities and taking the appropriate measures for our health and well-being overall. We tend to become creative about the ways that we go about doing our work and better at problem solving. This is a particularly favorable period for doing research or discovering the underlying cause of certain issues whether they are physical or spiritual in nature.

In Capricorn the Moon can be very productive and suited toward getting things squared away. With the Moon in this earth sign, the influence of Saturn comes to bear and can help to create a stronger shield. Emotions might be heavier than usual. We may have to work hard for our desired results but by staying focused and avoiding distractions we become more successful and resistant to intrusions of all kinds.

Moon in Air Signs:

When the Moon is in Air signs, we are very stimulated mentally and can more easily become anxious as a result. There is a lot of external activity overall and many obvious kinds of psychic problems can occur. In Gemini we are able to communicate more easily and gain answers to some questions that we have. Stimulants, excess alcohol and any experimental drugs should be avoided because they may compromise boundaries and draw entities into the energy field.

In Libra the Moon enables us to calm down and become more objective. It can, however, cause us to worry too much about how other people are feeling, what they are thinking, or draw us into heated conversations and debates with others. We may be aided in the attainment of greater understanding and wisdom than we had before about issues that have previously troubled us. This is a great time for reflection and planning future actions.

With the Moon in Aquarius, we may have surprise visitors, news or upsets. We may be drawn into group dynamics or conversely feel like hiding away from the world. Problems of a psychic nature are likely to be unusual or difficult to trace. They may be related to technology in some way. This is a good time to "clear cookies", update internet firewalls, and unsubscribe from spam.

Moon in Water Signs:

When the Moon transits through Cancer each month, we are more inclined than at other times to lay low, nurture our loved ones, to seek out comfort and avoid areas of danger. This is a good transit to use for the enhancement of self-protection methods, especially during a New or Full Moon in Cancer. This transit is well suited toward healing diets to support the body, mind and spirit.

The Moon in Scorpio provides us with the opportunity to process our recent emotional experiences and supports us in clearing our energy fields of toxicity. It is a good time to rid oneself of unwanted influences, energy cords and parasites. It can be effective for trauma release, emotional healing and for all types of purging. One should not go overboard with the detoxing but be gentle with themselves and others. This is an ideal time to guard one's privacy.

The Moon in Pisces can severely compromise energetic boundaries and that is why this is an important time to address psychic issues that may be present. People are more open now than during any of the Moon's other transits, but particularly if they are already open to begin with. If necessary, focus on supporting the immune system on a physical level which in turn will help with certain energetic problems. Be extra careful about the company that you keep.

Chapter 14

Protective Remedies for Signs and Transits

Including Herbs, Essential Oils, Flower Essences, Crystals and Resins

There are many tools and methods that can not only help to protect us from psychic dangers but empower us to live harmoniously and express ourselves in authentic ways. The flower essences referenced do not have fragrance but are subtle energy imprints preserved in water and alcohol. They are taken internally to facilitate healthy changes in mental outlook and emotional states. Many of these remedies are not exclusively assigned to any of the signs but examples are given for the ways that they may be particularly suited toward them. One does not necessarily have the Sun in a certain sign to have that sign emphasized in their birth chart. There are also times in life when one may not feel at all like their Sun or Ascendant but rather the sign being progressed by the Sun or Moon, or even by the sign of their Solar Return Moon. During such periods of time, one may find it more relevant to look for the corresponding remedies of the sign of the progressed luminary. There are many ways of approaching the chart, from checking transits and progressions to solar return charts and so much more.

A highly challenged natal planet referenced below shows three or more indications of challenge such as debility of the sign, hard aspects, Retrograde motion, and house placement to name a few. One example would be Venus in Scorpio conjunct Saturn, in the twelfth house, in a square with the Moon in Aquarius. Venus may be especially afflicted in this position and may respond well to the remedies mentioned for Taurus and Libra. Also consider the remedies listed for Scorpio, because Venus is a deeply personal planet that corresponds to emotional states and Scorpio is generally not one of her easy dwellings. All placements have both positive and negative expressions so even in Scorpio there are benefits that Venus bestows.

Some of the stones mentioned are the recommendations specific to Vedic astrology, recognizable by the fact that they are precious gems and as such are much more expensive to purchase. However, I have found certain stones to be equally or more effective for a fraction of the cost of what one would pay for a piece of Vedic jewelry. So much depends on the person, the situation, the time and method of application. That is to say that there is a bit of science and math that goes into the process of using remedial gems. If the idea of using them resonates with you it may wish to consult a Vedic astrologer on the matters of exact gem placements, such as over the heart or a certain finger. Otherwise, you can choose a stone that you sense an intimate healing relationship with and work with it for as long as you sense its relevance in your life. Another method of using gems is by taking an elixir that contains its imprint. Unless you know how to make these yourself, it is best to purchase them from a reputable business because some stones can be toxic. A gem elixir is really just the stone version of a flower essence, which contains not the physical components but rather the energetic imprint of a given crystal, gem or rock. From my experience, the effectiveness of stones is similar to the effectiveness of wellness supplements, which change according to the fluctuations in our bodily chemistry and conditions throughout life. There may well be certain stones that we benefit from for a great length of time without being drawn to others as much.

Aries/Mars

Essential Oils: Those oils and fragrances that help to address haste, impatience, and irritability have calming properties that can help guard Aries against misfortunes. These may include rich grounding oils such as Cedarwood, Patchouli, Sandalwood and Vetiver. Any of these oils may be used to dissolve and protect against negativity and serve as aids in quieting the mind. Any of the Mint essential oils have properties that may help Aries to cool off when they are overly stimulated. Blue oils such as German Chamomile can also be immensely helpful. Lavender can also be helpful for accidents, burns, and infections commonly experienced in this sign.

Flower Essences: One of the most helpful flower essences to address psychic attack relative to Aries themes of imbalance is Impatiens, for the type of impatience which can lead to distractions that scatter the life force energies and leave one vulnerable to unpleasant experiences. The flower essence of Tiger Lily can help Aries to tone down an overly aggressive or competitive attitude that elicits negative responses from others. Dandelion flower essence helps Aries to become aware of their limitations and to avoid overextending themselves. Larkspur is Aries' aid to joyful leadership that helps to inspire others.

Stones: A couple of protective stones to wear or keep close are Ruby, which is known to be a stone of good fortune and protection, and Black Tourmaline, which deflects negativity sent from others instead of absorbing it. Both stones are grounding and support a calm embodiment which also helps to prevent psychic attack. Onyx is traditionally known to be protective for Aries against evil influences. Yellow Sapphire is particularly protective of Aries Sun and Aries Ascendant people. It is believed that Diamond may also be very beneficial for them.

Some of these remedies may also apply to when Mars is in a highly challenged natal position, or when Mars is involved in challenging transits such as squares and oppositions.

Taurus/Venus

Essential Oils: Davana is an essential oil that can support the Taurean desire for security and inspiration drawn from the environment. Frequently used in perfumery and massage oils, it has aphrodisiac and calming qualities. It fights against depressive, dark moods and energies. Myrrh essential oil can support Taurus in guarding against negativity and bringing their dreams to life. Jasmine or Tuberose can help Taurus to release agitation and sink deeper into their well of inner knowing. White Ginger Lily offers another sweet indulgence that staves off negativity.

Flower Essences: A flower essence that Taurus people may find particularly helpful when experiencing psychic interference along with mental and emotional overwhelm is Pink Yarrow, which is available from a company called FES among others. This essence is used to protect the heart and emotions from outside intrusions. This includes situations when people are tugging on the Taurus person because they want something, or to help Taurus release their tight grip on another. It also helps to ease the emotional pain that may have been passed down to them through generations. It can serve as a shield when one feels overly sympathetic or prone to dysfunctional merging patterns with others.

Stones: One stone that Taurus may benefit from wearing and working with includes Rose Quartz, which is very affordable. On the pricier side, Taurus greatly benefits from Pink or White Sapphire. Chrysoprase is bright apple green in color, corresponding to the heart chakra, that may help to uplift and protect Taurus from heartache. The stones Amazonite and Blue Lace Agate both assist them in clear, calm communication. These stones may be used separately or together in helping to revitalize the body's energy field, which in turn helps to defend against and recover from EMF and various forms of psychic attack.

These remedies among the gems, especially the pink, green and white stones may also apply to those with Venus in a highly challenged natal position or when natal Venus is being affected by heavy transits, eclipsed or being transited by Saturn.

Gemini/Mercury

Essential Oils: Ajowan and Eucalyptus are oils that may support Gemini in respiratory health and clear communication. They can also be protective against psychic attack at the throat chakra level. Bay or Laurel leaf essential oil is another highly protective oil that promotes confidence. It can help with mental clarity and focus. Black Spruce can be helpful for Gemini due to its use in lung support. It has also been used in aromatherapy to help ward off infections. Blue Tansy helps with clear, calm communication and protects against panic attacks and negativity associated with thought patterns and nightmares.

Flower Essences: There are several flower essences that can be used to address Gemini's high-strung nature and mental quandaries. One is White Chestnut, for repetitive thoughts that can keep one awake at night. Like hummingbirds, it seems the only time these people slow down or stop doing something is when they are asleep. These flower essences can help Gemini relax and let things unfold instead of going over thoughts and happenings with so much repetition. Heather flower essence can help them to enjoy their own company more easily and to refrain from excess chatter.

Stones: Gemini may benefit from the use of stones that come in pairs, such as Boji stones and Mochi marbles which are said to help balance one's masculine and feminine polarities. These stones are very grounding and may also assist with pain relief and psychic protection. Emerald is often a great astrological remedy for Gemini that targets many problems all at once and provides psychic protection. Consider other green stones of various hues to aid in this regard, until you find exactly the right one.

These remedies may also apply to those with highly challenged Mercury placements or experiencing difficult transits to their third house or natal Mercury.

Cancer/Moon

Essential Oils: Angelica root has a close association with the Archangels and this in part clues us in to its magnificent and protective qualities. When Cancer feels overwhelmed and infringed upon, the essential oil of Angelica can come to the rescue. This is a great oil to use during Full Moons and Eclipses, or when sleep patterns are disrupted by emotional upsets. It can also help to regain energy after draining experiences or being subjected to psychic vampires. Essential oil of Cistus can help to overcome dread, panic and sorrow, and to restore inner peace. Roman Chamomile can act like a charm for cramps and stomach problems that are so common for those of this sign, and to help remove energy cords attached to the solar plexus and navel regions.

Flower Essences: Many varieties of the flower essence of Yarrow may be helpful for Cancer because this flower helps to strengthen the psychic integrity. The Bach flower essence of Chicory can help Cancer to let go of clinging to unhealthy relationships which can be the cause of their own unhappiness and ill fortune. Red Chestnut helps to maintain psychic boundaries and peace of mind when caring for others. Sweet Pea can be a helpful essence for those who don't feel safe at home, in their bodies or on earth or are in search of a new harmonious home.

Stones: Smoky quartz can be very stabilizing for Cancer because it helps with grounding and the release of fear and unhealthy attachments. It can be worn as a protective amulet. Those of this sign may also benefit from the use of the stones White Moonstone and Pearl. Both may help to address overflowing emotions and support intuitive awareness. Pearl is especially useful in helping to overcome deep-set phobias that some Cancerians suffer from. It is a great choice for jewelry. Selenite is a very healing and protective lunar stone. It can help to maintain energetic hygiene; however, it is too delicate to wear as jewelry on a regular basis. It can be held or waved over certain areas of the body to clear stuck energy. Many people place their jewelry on a slab of Selenite overnight to clear it of negativity.

Some of these remedies may be of assistance for those with challenging lunar placements, or during difficult transiting aspects to the Moon, especially those involving Mars, Saturn, Neptune or Pluto.

Leo/Sun

Essential Oils: Many of the Citrus oils are naturally protective against psychic intrusions and they correspond to Leo's ruling planet, the Sun. Lemon oil is purifying and helps to strengthen willpower and resilience. Orange oil brings optimism and protects against dark, heavy energies. Lime is a great oil to use for recovery from stressful situations. The flower oil of Ylang-Ylang may serve as an energy tonic for Leo's caring heart. The bright yellow St. John's Wort flower falls under the rulership of the Sun, and the essential oil produced from it can be uplifting and protective to Leos or any other signs that find resonance with it.

Flower Essences: Buttercup is a flower that can help Leo to feel good about who they are and what they are doing, regardless of the feedback they get from others. Golden Yarrow helps Leos who are uncomfortably in the spotlight or trying to avoid it, and can protect against those who are envious. Another flower that can help address Leo's imbalances regarding their sense of willpower and confidence is that of the bright yellow Sunflower. This essence is used to help highlight a genuine sense of self-esteem and a balanced expression of individuality.

Stones: A highly protective stone for Leo is Malachite, which often appears in a swirl of deep green hues. This stone is believed to protect against evil spirits and bad energy. It may also be used as an aid in creative endeavors and a catalyst for major life changes. Pyrite has a very strong affinity for Leo, as it supports masculine energy, creative expression and business endeavors. Sunstone is a light orange hued stone with streaks of iridescence that can help Leo to combat negativity and stay in their joy. The precious gem for Leo is Ruby, which represents their ruling planet the Sun. This stone can help to protect Leo against various misfortunes.

These remedies may also apply to those the Sun in a highly challenged natal position or during challenging transits to the natal Sun, especially by heavy-hitting planets such as Mars, Saturn or Pluto.

Virgo/Mercury

Essential Oils: Cedarwood can be calming, grounding and protective for Virgos whose nervous systems are on edge. Lemon Balm, also known as Melissa, can help to support their immune system when under stress and may bring both perspective and balance to ruffled emotions. Sagebrush may also be helpful to Virgos who find it difficult to clear their personal space. The oil of Sagebrush can is extremely purifying and protective, but the scent can be overpowering for some people. In a mist bottle it can be used as a substitute for smoking herbs, to help clear the room of earthbound spirits. Lavender oil can help Virgo to relax and unwind after a long day of work and helps to clear psychic debris.

Flower Essences: The flower essence of Apple is one that can benefit many of those who were born under the sign of Virgo. It can have a gently purifying effect on the emotions which helps to highlight the beauty of the soul. The radiance of soul energy automatically deflects a lot of outside negativity that would affect a person's life. The essence of Crab Apple flower produced by Bach can be used as a subtle form of space clearing as well. Manzanita helps Virgo to let go of self-criticism which makes them vulnerable. Red Chestnut can help Virgo to avoid taking on too many of the psychic burdens of others whom they care for.

Mountain Pennyroyal flower essence helps the overwhelmed Virgoan to clear their mental fields of psychic congestion and interference. It also helps to prevent the negative thought forms of others from remaining stuck in their auric fields. Because it addresses the types of energy that may come from the spiritual plane and thus difficult to trace, this essence may also be particularly helpful to those with Neptune in the sixth or twelfth house.

Stones: The green stone Healerite also known as Noble Serpentine can be a good one for Virgo, helping to support their resonance with the wilds of nature and awakening their innate healing abilities. It can be used to help them attune with their animal and spirit allies. Moss Agate is another great choice for Virgo, especially those involved in the medical profession or healing work of some kind. It helps to strengthen the psychic shield against illness. Lepidolite is a sparkly lavender hued stone that Virgo might find especially helpful when experiencing anxiety or insomnia. As with Gemini, Virgo also greatly benefits from Emerald due to its correspondence with the planet Mercury. They might prefer their birthstone Peridot.

These remedies may also apply to those with other challenging planets in Virgo, or during challenging transits or progressions in the natal sixth house.

Libra/Venus

Essential Oils: Anise Seed oil is both protective and motivating, offering that gentle push that Libra needs when feeling stuck, tired and unsure of what to do next. Star Anise has similar properties. The richly sweet essential oil of Geranium is protective against psychic attack, especially for those who are prone to getting caught up in a multitude of trivial concerns. It can help Libra to balance their emotions and hormones. Rhododendron helps Libra to reach higher spiritual states. Celery seed essential oil can be protective of Libra's emotions and aids in the process of elimination. It is an ideal choice for a cleansing bath or for massage when combined with others in a carrier oil.

Flower Essences: The Bach flower essence of Scleranthus can assist that Libra who is unsure of what to do or is torn between two or more decisions to the point that it pains them. This flower helps to clarify what their true values are so they can come to a solid decision. Centaury is another Bach essence that addresses Libra's tendency to conform to others' expectations while slowly and silently growing inner resentment. It dashes the pretense of being nice all the time, supporting their ability to say "No" instead of just agreeing with or overextending toward others to keep the peace. The flower Mountain Pride may help Libra in greater discernment, deciding upon a correct course of action and taking a firm and fair stance when necessary.

Stones: The pink and green crystal Watermelon Tourmaline can be very beneficial for Libra to remain firm in their energetic boundaries without closing their hearts. This stone also offers protection from psychic attack and can help strengthen overall equilibrium. A carefully placed Diamond ring or pendant can help quell emotional disturbances. White Sapphire is a good alternative. Another more affordable option is Danburite, helpful for resolving relationship conflicts and maintaining harmony. Libra may benefit from wearing a fine cut Emerald, a stone which in many old texts is associated with the planet Venus. Regarding the legend and lore of Emerald, Edgar Cayce relayed that it was "used as a deterrent to demons, as an anti-dote to poisons, and endowed its owner with finer intelligence."[1]

These remedies might also apply to those other challenged planets in Libra or during challenging transits or progressions in the seventh house.

Scorpio/Mars/Pluto

Essential Oil: Bergamot has an uplifting aroma that can help Scorpio reverse the direction of a downward spiral and also helps to fight infections. Jasmine can help to lift them up when they've fallen into the pits of despair. Niaouli, which has been used to fight many types of harmful bacteria, fungi and parasites can serve as a great psychic shield to Scorpio. The essential oil of Spikenard has a deep earthy aroma and may serve as a general spiritual protection agent. It has been referenced many times in the Bible as an anointing oil. Spikenard may be used in spiritual emergencies and against psychic attack and entanglements. Deeply rich and mesmerizing scents such as Lotus or Tuberose may serve as aphrodisiacs or may be spiritually uplifting to them.

Flower Essences: One of the flower essences one may use in combating psychic attack is Black Cohosh to help deflect oppressive forces and bring an end to vicious cycles. This essence may be particularly helpful during Scorpio season or while experiencing a heavy transit involving Pluto. This flower essence also helps to recover from various forms of abuse and to ease the fear of death and transitions. Holly flower essence can help those with challenged Scorpio planets to overcome jealousy. Another helpful essence for Scorpio in this regard is Oregon Grape, particularly when they have been so badly hurt that they have developed a thick wall around their hearts and lives that does not allow anyone in.

Stones: Protective stones for Scorpios include Black Tourmaline which deflects rather than absorbs negativity, and Garnet which has been said to strengthen the aura, repel evil and attract prosperity. Labradorite can be very useful as a protective amulet to Scorpio for spiritual work. Onyx is a helpful stone for reserving one's personal energy so that it does not leak out in unconscious ways. White or Yellow Topaz can be a great remedial gem for Scorpio.

Some of these remedies might apply to those with either Mars or Pluto in a highly challenging natal position, or during challenging transits involving Mars and/or Pluto in the natal chart.

Sagittarius/Jupiter

Essential Oils: Rosemary can help to keep Sagittarius focused and motivated. Clary Sage has an expansive and clarifying quality that can be of support during major life changes. It is uplifting but also not over stimulating. It can actually help to quiet an overactive mind and has been used for quelling nightmares and insomnia. Frankincense is a great choice when Sagittarius is engaged in concentration and study. Another wonderfully expansive essential oil is Holy Basil also known as Tulsi, which can serve as an aid in meditation, to enhance a positive outlook and overall well-being.

Flower Essences: The flower essence of Calendula can benefit Sagittarius in the use of kind speech and as an aid to growing compassion for self and others. It can help to calm the mind in a way that still allows for complex studies and communications. Indirectly, this essence can serve as a form of energetic protection by shifting speech patterns that would attract hostility from others. Flower essence of Agrimony addresses the emotional pain masked by a cheerful or detached countenance. Many Sagittarians are found to be Agrimony types in that they may sometimes act tough when they are very unhappy or silently suffering in some way.

Stones: Citrine is a yellow form of quartz which is great for Sagittarius as it helps to support a healthy sense of ego, playfulness, energetic boundaries, digestion and their ideal weight. It naturally deflects negative energy and may help to purify the area it is placed in, held, or worn. Turquoise is one of the stones often associated with Sagittarius and rightly so as it serves as a bridge between the earthly and spiritual realms. The nature of this stone is expansive and supports the quest for truth and justice. It can be highly protective as it aids in clear, kind communication, and self-forgiveness. Sagittarius usually does well with Yellow Sapphire which provides psychic protection and supports overall success.

These remedies might also apply to those with other highly challenged planets in Sagittarius, or during challenging transits involving Jupiter or the ninth house.

Capricorn/Saturn

Essential Oils: Clove can be a great essential oil for Capricorn, offering protection on both the physical and psychic levels. This spice has traditionally been used for the quelling of tooth pain, and Capricorn rules the teeth. The fresh, earthy scent of Plai may be of benefit to the overworked Capricorn to release muscular tension. Energetically both of these oils help to stave off negative forces. Many people have found Plai to be helpful in easing the pain specifically associated with arthritis, which is a common ailment in this sign. Rosemary is a highly protective plant and its aroma can help Capricorn to shift out of negative states, to help alleviate emotional pain and helps to establish a sense of protection in the home.

Flower Essences: The flower essence of purple Trillium can help Capricorn to clear their highly focused and ambitious energy fields from fear and lower energies. It can help to steer them toward the most responsible uses of power. The Bach essence of Vine can help Capricorn avoid conflict with others by softening their approach in certain situations where a domineering attitude elicits resistance rather than cooperation. The Bach flower essence of Gorse can help to lift Capricorn out of dark and depressive moods. Sage flower essence helps to release harmful attachments and to protect against hostile energies.

Stones: Stones that can be particularly protective for Capricorn include Carnelian, which is known to decrease negativity and bring good fortune. Black Garnet can be an excellent choice for the Capricorn who struggles with a sense of futility or depressive thoughts. It dispels evil influences and is highly protective during sleep. Black Obsidian can be used to help overcome destructive habits, and has long been used as one of the most powerful stones against bad luck and curses. This stone may be helpful not only for Capricorn but those of any sign when under heavy psychic attack. Capricorn can gain great benefit and protection from wearing a Blue Sapphire, because it is ruled by their ruling planet Saturn. Blue Sapphire is the stone most regarded with caution when it comes to remedial gems, but of all the signs Capricorn and Aquarius are possibly the most compatible with it.

These remedies may also apply to those Saturn in highly challenging natal position, or during challenging transits involving Saturn or the tenth house.

Aquarius/Saturn/Uranus

Essential Oils: Eucalyptus produces a highly refreshing and energetically protective essential oil that Aquarius may find helpful when life gets too complicated. It is often used to support the lungs and for its antiviral qualities. In a diffuser this or other tree oils such as Cypress can help to clear one's personal space from the energetic imprints left behind by other people, which is useful when Aquarius has overextended in a social sense. Fennel can help to relieve stiffness and spasms so common to those of this sign, while also staving off negative influences. Greenland Moss aka Labrador Tea essential oil may help with circulation issues, nervous anxiety and many other symptoms that may be experienced under stress.

Flower Essences: The flower essence of Goldenrod can help Aquarius in gaining a clear sense of their individuality while also being able to relate to groups in balanced ways. The Bach essence of Rock Water may help Aquarius to become more fluid and open to change, for although they appear to be very open-minded, they can be strict and rigid on many levels. It can also help them to allow their emotions to be expressed rather than repressed or merely intellectualized, and this serves to strengthen the appropriate energetic boundaries instead of rigid ones. Red Clover essence supports calmness despite any hysteria of the masses. Shooting Star helps Aquarius to locate and connect with their soul family, whether in the physical or spiritual realm. Simultaneously, it helps to filter out unwanted spiritual influences.

Stones: The crystal Spirit Quartz, also known as Cactus Quartz, can help Aquarius to maintain their boundaries while engaged in large social gatherings, allowing them to focus on what is important. Grape Chalcedony can help those of this sign to discern the truth about groups and associations, and to understand their place in each situation. Elite Shungite can be a highly protective stone for any sign, but may be especially helpful for the type of Aquarius who is frequently found on their smartphone or engaged with other electrical devices. Aquarius gains protection from Blue or White Sapphire, or Diamond.

Some of these remedies may also apply to those Saturn or Uranus in a highly challenged natal position or during challenging transits involving Saturn, Uranus or the natal eleventh house.

Pisces/Jupiter/Neptune

Essential Oils: Helichrysum essential oil has very healing qualities that can help Pisces to recover or help their clients or loved ones to recover from emotional trauma. This is a great oil to keep in one's medicine cabinet, particularly for its soothing qualities. There are several different varieties of Helichrysum with slightly different properties. Jasmine essential oil is one that Pisces may gravitate to for cultivating compassion and honing their intuition. Its powerful high vibration can dissipate negative energy. They may love the rich earthy scent of Cedar which is known to help to facilitate expanded awareness in meditation. Other rich floral scents such Blue Lotus and Neroli can help the highly sensitive Piscean to overcome depression and to restore hope.

Flower Essences: The Bach flower essences of Elm or Red Chestnut can help Pisces to release the emotional burden of responsibility they may often feel about others under their care, or their attachment to being some kind of savior. This includes situations in which they seem to perpetually martyr themselves. The flower essence of Nicotiana is one that those of this sign may especially benefit from when feeling the need to resist or break away from unhealthy addictions. A supportive essence in combination with this would be Mugwort flower essence, which brings clarity to dreams and visions, which is often what is unconsciously sought after through drug use. Morning Glory flower essence brings the courage and inspiration to face life's challenges more readily, while supporting a balance in overall energy and vitality.

Stones: Aquamarine is associated with Pisces and Neptune due to its calming soft sea-green hues. It is one of the most soothing stones to wear in times of stress and uncertainty as it has been known to help quiet an overactive mind. Larimar is a protective stone that can help Pisces connect with Spirit and it has also been said to connect one with dolphin energy. It has been used in overcoming anxiety and other stress-related states. This stone can also help to speak up for oneself and one's personal values when necessary. Gemstones other than Aquamarine that Pisces gain protection from include Pearl and Yellow Sapphire.

Some of these remedies might also apply to those with Neptune in a highly challenging natal position, or during challenging transits involving Neptune or the natal twelfth house.

Protective Incense for the Signs

The following correspondences are some that make sense to me according to my studies of astrology and aromatherapy, but of course any of these herbs may appeal to those of any of the signs. Use your intuition when selecting resins, herbs and incense for your own purposes. Check to see what kinds of herbs grow wild in your area, or those that you can grow on your property. It is wise to become aware of allergies and avoid those scents and resins that cause any sort of irritation. Many herbs that might not necessarily be considered for use as sweet smelling incense work powerfully for suffumigation purposes.

Aries

Aries people are strong and motivated, and they thrive on the types of incense that support these qualities. Spices such as Black Pepper and Clove may be particularly effective for them to clear their space. They need to balance these stimulating scents with those that are quieting as well, such as German Chamomile and Linden. Frankincense resin can be a great choice for purification and calming.

Copal is a sacred tree sap from Mexico which is considered to be the "blood" of the tree that was traditionally used in offerings to the gods. For this reason, it seems to correspond well with Aries. It is believed to be protective, clearing and uplifting and is perfect for blessing a space and for new beginnings. This resin especially resonates with those of Mexican and South American descent, or when honoring their pantheons.

The herb Chaparral growing in the Southern US and in Mexico has been used in bundles to burn for space clearing. It has a highly potent and purgative aroma, linking it with the energy of Mars.

Saffron is a red spice of the fire element that has long regarded as sacred in many cultures since ancient times. It comes from a purple crocus flower. The dried and powdered stigmas are not only used as a culinary spice but rolled into incense sticks and cones. It has been used as an offering to the gods, as an aphrodisiac, and to sharpen the sixth sense. It can be used as an Arian energizer and protect one from evil influences.

Taurus

Taurus enjoys scents that are rich and sweet such as those of the Rose, Lily-of-the-Valley and many other florals. These are wonderful for putting them at ease, but for effectively clearing their space they may need to first use some herbs that pack a little more punch. Citrus works well for this purpose, especially Orange which is pleasant smelling to a vast majority of people, and has both purifying and uplifting effects.

Cinnamon is a great choice for burning as a purifying incense, due to its sweet aroma and spiritually elevating qualities. This spice has been used since ancient times for many purposes including religious ceremonies. Its bark was used to decorate the temples in Greece and in Rome.

Mullein is an herb that can be burned for promoting calmness, clearing stagnation and supporting the health of the lungs and throat, which can be helpful for Taurus when under stress.

Thyme is a common kitchen herb that was once burned in Greek temples, and in ceremonies to ward off evil spirits and disease. It has come to be associated with Taurus's ruling planet Venus and although used mostly as a flavoring agent these days, it can also be dried and burned as a protective incense.

Gemini

Gemini thrives on incense and fragrances that are uplifting and clarifying such as Lemon, Mint, Rosemary and Sage. All of these happen to be great for space clearing as well. Lemongrass falls under the rulership of Gemini's ruling planet Mercury, and it burns well in the form of dried bundles. Its magickal properties include spiritual purification, production and psychic enhancement. Essential oils from the Fir tree family can be helpful for Gemini in essential oil form for both psychic protection and mental focus.

Hyssop has long been revered as a cleansing and protective herb. It is also used medicinally for clearing the lungs, which are ruled by Gemini. In Biblical times branches of it were used ceremonially to protect the home from evil spirits. It can also be added to waters and oils and for protective purposes. This herb should be handled with care because large quantities have been known to cause convulsions.

Cancer

The sensitivity of Cancer can be eased by incense with soothing qualities. These would include burning of herbs such as Lemon Balm and diffusing essential oils of Jasmine and Yarrow. Catnip is a smoking herb and incense that Cancer may find helpful in clearing negativity and relieving digestive upsets.

Myrrh is a plant that comes under the dominion of the Moon and therefore those with planets in Cancer or strong lunar influences may find resonance with it. It was said to be one of the gifts given to baby Jesus by the three wise men who visited him. Myrrh is often burned along with Frankincense to clear and bless the space. It is one that has long been used in churches of many faiths. It is considered sacred to many Christians, Jews, and Muslims. Its tree is native to Arabia and Northeast Africa. Its resin is healing and protective and helps to clear negative imprints from the environment and was one of the oldest medicines used by the ancient Egyptians.

Sweetgrass is an herb that grows along the edges of marshes, lakes and other wet places both in North America and in Northern Europe. It has long been used as a sacred herb, aka "Holy Grass" by Native Americans as well as used for weaving baskets. The scent of Sweetgrass can be comforting for Cancerians, and when burnt instills an aura of safety and protection.

Leo

Bay Laurel is one of the most ancient herbs that has been used in purification and other ceremonies, especially in Greece. The Bay tree is an evergreen native to the Mediterranean that contains powerful medicinal and spiritual properties. It is believed to correspond to the Sun which is Leo's ruling planet. Burning bay leaves can help to clear negative energy while also increasing psychic perception and discernment. Juniper is another tree compatible with Leo whose leaves are smoked for space clearing. It is sacred to several European cultures and certain Native American tribes.

Rosemary is one of the first herbs recorded for its use as an incense. It is classified as an herb of the Sun, and it does prefer areas with a lot of sun exposure. It was called Incensier by the French, as it was burned as powerful incense to clear the air, including in sick chambers.

Arabic Gum, with its deep golden color corresponds with Leo's ruling planet the Sun. This resin comes from a species of Acacia tree that has been used for thousands of years in food, or as medicine and incense. It is a common ingredient used in adhesives. Though it can be burned alone for protection it makes a great addition to other forms of incense for binding.

Virgo

The types of scents that can help Virgo to release tension and clear their space have a combination of soothing and expansive qualities. One of these is Pine, in the form of needles, resin or essential oil. Both needles and resin can be burned as incense for their protective and cleansing protective qualities. The energy of the pine tree can help to clear emotional heaviness and stress from one's spirit. Pine was sacred to the Druids of ancient times and to the Native Americans.

Dill is an herb steeped in magical traditions that corresponds with Virgo's planetary ruler Mercury. It has been used in love and luck charms but also for protection from negative influences. Feathery dill weed has been used in Europe, Asia and Nordic countries as a culinary spice, to treat stomach upsets, and promote restfulness. It is said that Roman gladiators ate it to boost their courage. Dill makes a great choice as a protective and cleansing herb for those Virgos (and Geminis) who suffer from tension and anxiety, in whatever form they prefer to use it.

Libra

Libra benefits from scents and herbs that simultaneously assist with mental focus and creating an atmosphere of peace. One such plant is Lavender, which is one of the most beloved fragrant herbs of all time. It can be dried in bunches, tied together with string and burned to clear the space. It helps to ease anxiety, bring balance and to regain a clear perspective when life has gotten too complicated. Dried fragrant Rose petals sweeten the air and can be burned alone or along with other herbs such as Lavender.

Linden flowers (from the Lime tree) can produce a sweet incense when burned. Its branches have long been used for protection when hung over doorways. In ancient Europe, ceremonies and tribal council meetings were often held beneath Linden trees, which may associate them with the Libran scales of Justice. It was believed that the tree would unveil the truth.

Skullcap, native to North America, is another calming herb that Libra may burn as incense or combined with other sweet herbs such as Sweetgrass for its purifying qualities. It helps to overcome negative thinking and insomnia. Historically it has been used to treat anxiety and depression, and in spells to ensure fidelity and quell disharmony. In the 19th century it was known as Mad Dog herb and was used to treat rabies.

Scorpio

Helichrysum is an herb native to several warm and dry regions including parts of Asia, Australia, Europe, and South Africa. It has grown in popularity during the past couple of decades. I think of Scorpio as a correspondence, because of its anti-infectious and powerful restorative properties. Known as Impepho in Africa, it has been used by Zulu, Xhosa, and Ndebele tribes for healing purposes and burnt in ceremonies. The essential oil of the flowers or the hydrosols can be used for purification of the aura and environment and to dispel dark energies.

The dark red resin of Dragon's Blood from the rattan palm tree in Southeast Asia has an affinity for the sign of Scorpio. It has long been used by magickal practitioners for space clearing and protection from negative forces. The smoke of this resin can also bring divine inspiration and is of assistance in artistic endeavors and gaining answers to troubling questions.

Sagittarius

In addition to its use as a flower essence, Agrimony may be one of the most powerful herbs for Sagittarius to burn as an incense, although not necessarily due to a particularly pleasant aroma. This herb has many names including Church Steeples, Philanthropos, and Cocklebur and has a long history of usage throughout Europe. It has been used to reverse hexes and to banish goblins and demons. It was assigned to Sagittarius's ruling planet Jupiter by the herbalist Nicholas Culpeper.

Benzoin is heart-warming, protective and elevating resin that Sagittarius may find a deep appreciation for. It is very powerful and can be burned to clear a space of negative imprints, and to help earth-bound spirits or ghosts to move on. It combines well with Frankincense which has often been used as church incense.

Meadowsweet is an herb that was sacred to Celtic cultures and was known as one of the traditional "strewing herbs", indicating herbs that were strewn onto floors for their fragrance, as insect repellents and for their magickal properties. Meadowsweet, ruled by Jupiter, has a sweet aroma and can be combined into herbal incense bundles for happiness, peace and protection in the home.

Capricorn

Capricorns tend to respond well to herbs that grow deep into the soil and work on deep levels. They love richly scented oils and resins that bring good cheer, and are partial to those with a long history of historical usage. One example of such an herb is the Bayberry, whose waxy scented berries have long been used in candles during Yule season. Their usage in holiday candles has been traced back to early colonial settlers in America. They were believed to protect one's home and bring prosperity. Bayberry, also known as Wax Myrtle, has been used for cooking and medicinal purposes, and its fragrant leaves may be dried and burned to clear the air of negativity.

Birch is the traditional tree associated with Capricorn season in the Celtic tree calendar. It is associated with the Norse rune Berkano, which is a symbol of rebirth, wisdom and growth, and it is also the meaning of the first letter of the Ogham alphabet, called Beith. The wood of the Birch tree has a softly sweet aroma when burned, and it has been used in a variety of ways to ward off evil.

Frankincense is an ancient resin with powerful healing properties. It is burned in churches along with myrrh and is protective against negativity. Another wonderful feature of frankincense as an incense or essential oil is that it helps to lift depression and other dark moods. There are different types of Frankincense each with slightly different properties.

Aquarius

Eucalyptus, also known as the Gum Tree, is one of the toughest and most enduring plants on the planet. Its medicine has been used for centuries, and although it has likely been around for millions of years it is difficult to trace back its historical uses. Australian Aboriginal Natives have used it to treat infections, and this is one of the most common uses that Eucalyptus still has. It can be used in aromatherapy for clearing the air, and the leaves can also be burned for this purpose.

Aquarius may enjoy burning dried Marjoram, the herb which translates to "Joy of the Mountain", as a general clearing agent that contains mood-boosting qualities. This herb can be burned as an incense to restore mental calmness, while building a protective field of energy. Medicinally it has been used to soothe the nervous system and support the cardiovascular system among so many other things.

Amber comes in two distinct types. One is that of an ancient tree resin that is hard and lightweight. When rubbed against certain fabrics it creates a spark of electricity. The other is a composition of different resins and herbs used as an incense that is deeply aromatic. Both types of amber are protective and help to clear space.

Pisces

Pisces tends to enjoy those scents that take them just a little bit out of this world or enable them to reach higher states of consciousness. Sandalwood is the base note and fixative used in many perfumes, and one of the most revered plants for spiritual usage. It comes from a tree that grows in India, Indonesia, Nepal, Tibet and different parts of the Middle East. The sweet earthy aroma of Sandalwood bark is highly purifying and protective. The incense repels evil spirits is an aid to meditation.

Marshmallow root is a water element herb that can make a good incense for Pisces, with its sweet scent and soothing properties. It can help support psychic immunity in suppressing the appetite for unhealthy foods. It has been used for space clearing, spell reversal and to attract benevolent spirits. The herb of Marshmallow is native to many parts of Asia and Europe. In ancient Egypt, it was the root that was used to make confection. Today's candy marshmallows do not contain the herb, although originally the confections made from them did.

Note

1. Dan Campbell and Charles Casey, *Edgar Cayce On the Power of Color, Stones and Crystals* (New York: Grand Central Publishing, 1989)

2. Cunningham's Encyclopedia of Magical Herbs by Scott Cunningham, 1985, 1992. Llewellyn Publications, St. Paul, Minnesota.

3. A Modern Herbal by Mrs. M. Grieve, edited and introduced by Mrs. C.F. Leyel. 1931, republished in 1992. Dorset Press, printed in Great Britain by Mackays of Chatham PLC, Chatham, Kent.

4. Crystals for Energy Protection by Judy Hall. Text 2009, 2014, 2020, Hay House, UK.

5. The Encyclopedia of Essential Oils: The Complete Guide to the Use of Aromatic Oils in Aromatherapy, Herbalism, Health and Well-Being by Julia Lawless. Conari Press imprint of Red Wheel/Weiser, 2013 edition, in San Francisco, California.

6. The Complete Floral Healer by Anne McIntyre, 2002. Sterling Publishing Co. Inc. New York.

Chapter 15

Elemental Well-being: Psychic Protection for Body, Emotions, Mind, Spirit

Although we are spiritual beings having a physical experience, it is typically in our best interest to rule out possible physical issues before assuming that the cause of any of our problems are spiritual in nature. With a strong foundation in the physical body and a harmonious living environment, there are fewer chances of psychic invasion and disease, and in most cases quicker rates of recovery if and when problems are experienced.

You can discover your elemental type by examining your natal chart to see what signs you have a predominance of planets in. The Ascendant counts as an elemental influence. Many people have a primary element and a secondary sub-element, or a tie between two elements within their natal chart. They may have half of their planets in air, and the rest in earth, or maybe one in fire. If there seems to be a balance between all the elements, look to the house placements. The elements ruling the houses of the most prominent placements can have major influences in the person's life, in certain cases even more so than the element of the signs involved.

Body

The three earth signs of the Zodiac rule the physical body and its general state of health. These signs are Taurus, Virgo and Capricorn and they rule the Second, Sixth and Tenth Houses. If you are an Earth dominated person, meaning your Sun, Ascendant or three or more of your personal planets fall in these signs you may have strong endurance and an ability to stay focused. As an earth type you are methodical, need active work and thrive under a certain amount of pressure. Natal placements in earth signs reveal certain things about one's physical health and may also indicate what kind of remedies a person responds best to. These would usually involve food, herbs, supplements, and body work such as massage.

Taking care of the body is one of the best things one can do for oneself because it is a lifelong investment. This is true whether they consider themselves to be magical or mundane, and regardless of their occupation. To maintain optimal wellness, we need to start by eating healthy, keeping fit, and getting adequate sleep. Those are the basic top three health factors, but they are not always so easy to reach or maintain. Earth sign or earth type people bring a keen awareness to physical life, and they are often naturally skilled in acquiring what they need and desire in a physical sense.

Earth people can vary between the health-conscious types, the very strict self-disciplinarians and those who are too immersed in sensual delights to pay much regard to their physical health. Earth is a dry element that can cause accumulation of toxins that get lodged in the body, so those with a strong earth influence may benefit from regular whole-body detoxification of some kind. That is because those of us living in modern societies are exposed to a multitude of toxins no matter how healthy we eat. Methods of detoxing include fasting, a temporary vegan diet, and the use of anti-parasitic herbal blends. An overgrowth of parasites throughout the body can affect the way one thinks and feels to an alarming extent. A few indications of parasites may be cravings, irritable bowel syndrome, depression, and weight fluctuations. It might be wise to check in with an experienced health practitioner before beginning a detox or parasite flush to make sure it is the right method for one's body type.

In relation to the physical body, sex is another relevant topic that obviously applies not only to Earth types but all signs of the Zodiac. Having multiple sex partners, especially too soon after the previous partner can not only bring the risk of sexually transmitted diseases but can open one up to all kinds of influences which can leave one drained and vulnerable to psychic disturbances. Who or whatever is allowed to interact with the body temple can either add to the success or stress in one's life. Discernment is key for optimal wellness.

As an earth type, you need good food, physical touch and a stable environment in order to thrive. For those who are alone or single, pets can bring a lot of joy. Keeping a clean space, but not necessarily a large space, is important to your overall well-being and you have the innate ability to harmonize with your environment and accent it with objects of beauty.

Emotions

The three water signs of the Zodiac rule the emotions, spiritual dimensions and many of our spiritual experiences, but particularly those on the astral plane. These signs are Cancer, Scorpio and Pisces and they rule the Fourth, Eighth, and Twelfth Houses. A predominance of planets in water signs can make one sensitive and responsive to others' emotions. If you are a Water type you are both imaginative and psychic, and have a rich inner life. You thrive on quiet reflections and solitude. Placements in water signs indicate where there is an attunement to subtle currents.

Emotions seem to either guide or distract the life of a Water element person. Telepathy or the ability to sense others thoughts and emotions is a bi-product of this person's natural empathy. One cannot hide one's true motives and feelings from water sign people because they can automatically sense what is going on. Occasionally it can be difficult for them to distinguish their own feelings from those of others. They need more rest than those of other elements in order to sort out their moods from their psychic impressions.

Baths can be beneficial for all elemental types but especially water element people, because they are so effective in calming both the body, mind and emotions and can also be directed toward spiritual purposes. Epsom salts can be helpful in some cases but there is the danger of dehydration occurring with too much of it, or by soaking in it for too long. Always drink lots of water afterward. Herbal baths with just a pinch of salt address both the physical and psychic levels. They may help to ease muscular tensions while they clear energy stagnation and certain types of attachments in the aura. Ritual baths are popular with witches because they are so effective at bringing desired changes and manifestations. Remember that you will have the best results in ridding yourself of any problem, be it an attachment, bad habit or other undesirables while the Moon is waning. The same goes for reversing spells and hexes that you know or believe yourself to be affected by. You may wish to have an ephemeris or astrological datebook handy to plan your energy detox bath in alignment with the Moon's placement.

Water people tend to respond well to subtle medicines such as homeopathy and flower essences. Homeopathy can be a highly effective tool for getting to the root of long-standing issues that affect people on all levels, including emotional ones. You may have the best results by working with a practitioner if you don't already know what needs to be addressed or where to start. The results may seem very subtle at first, but by working with these remedies it is possible to experience powerful life changes for the better. Some of the things you might expect to come up while working with appropriate remedies are different forms of physical detoxification, insightful dreams and an improved outlook. At some point, usually over a period of time in working with the correct remedies you may have a visceral experience of the severance of attachments by disease entities from your body and energy field. You may also notice an increase of synchronicity in your daily life.

As a water type you need to be able to cry, vent and express your deep emotions somehow, which eventually allows for a transmutation of lower energies into inspiration and fuel. It can help for you to regularly check in with your feelings and to find ways to "flush" them out, especially if you are caught in a cycle of either self-pity or over-identification with the suffering of others.

Mind

The three Air signs of the Zodiac rule the mental body and its general functioning. These signs are Gemini, Libra and Aquarius and they rule the Third, Seventh and Eleventh Houses. If you are an Air dominated person, meaning your Sun, ascendant or three or more of your personal planets fall in these signs you may have an active mind and are very communicative. Much of your strength lies in your intelligence. As an Air type you are versatile, innovative and like to be on the go. You are solution oriented and bring lots of ideas to others. Natal placements in air signs reveal much about one's mental states and communication methods. They also point toward solutions and activities that decrease stress.

The mind is often taken for granted just as much as the body., if not more so. We've all heard the saying "mind over matter", which indicates the tremendous power of the mind to influence much of our physical experience. Instead of being taught about our amazing mental capabilities, most of us have been barraged by negative reinforcements through our upbringings, in school, and in the media. We've been told we are victims, helpless at defending ourselves in any substantial way, that we are dependent upon outer substances in order to function and that we are at the mercy of those whose rules we must obey. For some of us, at some point in life the eerie realization has crept upon us, that we've been born into a social system of mind control. As disconcerting as it may be, this realization is the first step to freedom.

Meditation can be a very helpful method of gaining clarity, spiritual insights and peace of mind. There are countless methods of meditating, suitable for each type of personality. Some people find that their morning jog is equivalent to daily meditation. In the beginning, five minutes at a time of gentle contemplation or self-guided imagery is going to be much more effective at calming the mind than a whole hour of most likely sitting there fidgeting and trying to stop mental chatter. Accept the fact that this mental chatter is always going to be there for most people but especially for Air signs. The more experienced we become at meditating, the quieter this chatter becomes, and the less engaged we are with it. Ironically, the less we fight it and the more we simply observe it, the less it dominates our psyche.

Protect the mind and psyche by limiting exposure to people and places with negative attitudes, which will only bring you down in time. Avoid spending too much time on social media and watching television, because both these are full of psychic noise. An addiction to social media and the online world must often be kept in check for Air signs more than the others, because of their love of information and communication. Although T.V. can be fun and entertaining at times, it is basically mind control central. Favorite programs and movies are fine, but always know that to some extent you become engaged in a form of hypnosis when watching. Air types need to know when to "snap out of it". Being able to decode the hidden messages within commercials and certain movies is a useful ability that can expand one's awareness of many things.

If you are an Air type it can be helpful to educate yourself and to dig for your own answers to the questions that riddle you the most. Reading books keeps the mind actively engaged, similar to the way crossword puzzles help elderly people stay mentally sound and functional. You need good outlets for sharing your ideas and knowledge with others. When upset, it can be helpful to write in a journal.

Spirit

The three Fire signs of the Zodiac are especially connected to intuition and the spiritual essence of our existence. These signs are Aries, Leo and Sagittarius and they rule the First, Fifth and Ninth Houses. A predominance of planets in fire signs makes one fiery, passionate and energetic, with a strong immune system and a zest for life. If you are a Fire type, you are psychic in a way that is very different from that of the Water signs. You know and sense many things without having to process them emotionally. You thrive on challenging yourself to overcome obstacles. Planets in fire signs indicate areas where there is willpower and spiritual potency.

Fire sign people want to live life to the fullest, no matter what their conditions may be. They tend to be dynamic and physically active. They are the leaders, pioneers and the seekers of wisdom. They are generally drawn to spiritual practices that are broad and holistic rather than exclusive or obscure. Spiritual life has many different expressions and takes on many different forms. For some Fire people a spiritual focus takes precedence over other areas. For the majority it is a part of life but not the main focus. Whatever spiritual path one takes in life, there is a general code of ethics adhered to in most religious and spiritual pursuits. That includes treating others the way that one wishes to be treated, with respect.

The body is a dense extension of the spirit, and it is widely known that many diseases have their origin on the spirit plane. That is why the more a person grows in their overall awareness in life, doing spiritual work becomes a necessity and as critical as the practices of regularly showering, changing socks, washing bed sheets, and getting oil changes for the car. If attention is only given to the physical body and its needs, but emotions and psychic impressions are ignored, then life becomes very sticky, stagnant, and overly dramatic or weak and ineffective. There are as many spiritual practices as there are personality types, which means that different practices are more suitable for some people than others. The important thing is to do them. If you're not religious at all but you know there's more than meets the eye and there must be some kind of Creator, then honor that. A spiritual path doesn't have to be elaborate. It just has to be earnest for beneficial results.

Meditation can be either a mental or a spiritual practice, or both, as is the case in Buddhism, where it is used to discipline the mind and to dissipate negative karma. Some athletes even use meditation before a game or race to prepare them for their best level of performance. They do this by envisioning the entire game and its outcome, in their favor. Just because something is imagined, doesn't mean it isn't real. With strong emotion tied to it and when stretched out over time, that which is imagined becomes more and more a part of our physical reality.

Energy sweeps can be a very helpful exercise to incorporate into both physical and spiritual practices. These are used in many forms of the martial arts, in Qi Gong and in Yoga. You can create your own personal style of energy sweeping, using your arms, fingers, and even legs to clear stagnant energy from your body, aura, and living environment. I like doing this with some of my favorite crystal wands, with what I like to call "crystal chi gung". The more intention going into these motions, the more powerful they become. Using your breath in addition can increase the effectiveness, depending on what it is you are seeking to achieve.

As a Fire person you need to do things your own way, and you thrive in areas that are spacious or wild. The worst thing you could do is to coop yourself up on the couch and seek to control your natural urge to exercise, engage with others, and raise your own bar for success. Avoid pushing yourself too hard because the fire can eventually run out, leaving you with nothing but a weak flicker of light.

Psychic Protection Amulets for Different Environments

There are many different instances where we may become susceptible to psychic intrusions and attacks. These could be work-related, religious, relational, or centered in the home. There are some common settings where psychic protection is frequently needed. Here is a list of them along with how the signs of the four elements may shield themselves and achieve peace of mind by using gemstones, oils, and other objects.

The Bedroom

The bedroom is a place where most of us let down our guard, or should be able to at the end of the day. It is also a place where psychic attacks are very common, particularly at night when we are asleep.

Fire sign people need space in the bedroom, because they are prone toward claustrophobia when too many objects are jammed too tightly together. They might even prefer sleeping outside. Large windows, closets and doors are favored. They love bright colors but should avoid these on the sheets and walls because it can agitate them on a subconscious level. Their bedroom amulet is a soft lit lamp to wind down to, such as a salt lamp or the glow of candles which naturally clear the air of negativity.

Earth sign people need solid, durable structures in the bedroom to feel secure and relaxed. Wood pieces are grounding, but antiques for the bedroom should be selected carefully and cleared before use because they carry old energy. Simplicity is key, and clutter should be avoided because it can add psychic discord if left to grow over time. The bedroom amulet for earth signs is a large stone, plant or painting that reminds them of a favorite place and brings serenity.

Air sign people need access to natural light in the bedroom during the day, and to make sure it's totally dark at night when they lay down to sleep. They should remember to turn off Wi-Fi and remove smart devices. This allows their minds to sink into deeper sleep and for restoration to occur. They should be careful what kinds of decorations or photos they place on the walls, and how many books they allow to pile up, because books in the bedroom are more mentally stimulating than they realize. Their bedroom amulet is a symbol, quote, or deity that represents calmness and healing.

Water sign people need a little pinch of magic or pixie dust in the bedroom to give them that sense that this is where they can leave the rest of the world behind for a while and escape to Neverland. Since they can be the most open and impressionable to psychic influences, it helps them to place a fresh glass or jar of water near their bedside each night before they go to sleep. This is their bedroom amulet. This water is not to drink but should be tossed out in the morning because it soaks up negative energies that may be released in the night. They may also benefit from playing an instrument or listening to soft music an hour before they retire.

The Vehicle

The vehicle that we drive subjects us to large amounts of EMF, but especially for those who live in metropolitan areas. Placing a piece of Shungite anywhere it will safely fit inside the car can help deflect the harmful effects of radiation. However, there are many other stress factors that can arise while driving, such as drastic weather changes, bad drivers and ugly scenery. It is possible for some people to have paranormal experiences while driving because they can enter into a trance or drive into an area where energies are intense, and entities are on high alert.

Fire sign people can sometimes be too hasty and reckless while they are driving. They can easily become impatient or distracted on the road. Avoiding conversations helps them concentrate on their surroundings. Either driving in silence or listening to music with a slow to medium beat and keeping a piece of Crazy Lace Agate or Malachite in the vehicle can help to avoid haste and accidents.

Earth sign people tend to be reasonable drivers although sometimes they wind up in vehicles that are tricky to drive in that they are old, awkward, or packed with too many items. Turquoise, or any type of Jasper in the car can be helpful for them to feel secure and connected to the earth while driving, and to avoid being victimized by reckless drivers.

Air sign people can get spacey or anxious, and easily sidetracked by things they either see or think to themselves while they are driving. Like fire sign people they also tend to speed. They need to keep their car clean to avoid the circulation of dirty air and over-stimulation of their senses. Blue Lace Agate can help them to stay focused and calm, and to avoid multitasking.

Water sign people may get easily stressed out while driving, but especially when traffic is heavy. They may feel edgy or defensive on the road and have a difficult time separating their emotions from other drivers. They could benefit from keeping a piece of Amethyst in their car for protection and calmness. A small aromatherapy pendant with lavender essential oil may help them to relax.

In the Workplace

At work many people are faced with numerous stress factors from the physical to the mental to the energetic. There may be a particularly difficult employer or coworker to deal with, or the mad rush of the public in places with a lot of foot traffic. Mentally putting on your "shield of light" before even entering the workplace is like putting a raincoat on when you have to walk through a storm. Setting this intention in advance helps one subconsciously to be prepared for any challenges that may arise throughout the day.

Fire sign people are often well-equipped to deal with difficult people in the workplace because they have strong, forceful personalities and are not easily swayed. They may need to avoid over-taxing themselves. Some piece of jewelry or other item that can be worn to help remind them of this and instill a sense of calmness can be helpful for them to navigate through the day with greater ease. The stone Labradorite is a good choice, which also helps them to adapt to swiftly changing situations.

Earth sign people are often hard workers who are dedicated, practical and focused. Their greatest challenges may lie in their being overwhelmed by the fast pace and demands of others who may expect them to do things differently. They can ignore their bodily discomforts which eventually catch up with them. Taking "time-outs" to eat, stretch and hydrate are crucial for them to stay energized. They may benefit from wearing stones that serve as deflective shields such as Covellite or Hematite.

Air sign people are the idea people at work and are expert communicators. They may run into arguments a lot or get very riled up about many minor to major issues. Even if they don't say a word, their nerves are often on edge. They may catch themselves holding their breath often, so they need to pause every now and then to take some deep breaths and relax. Stones such as Aquamarine and Blue Kyanite can help them mentally detach when they have become too involved with the drama of others.

Water sign people are the givers and nurturers in the workplace but when they are out of balance their emotions can overflow. Some may become smothering or exhibit controlling behavior. They may sink into a slump of despair due to insecurity, hyper-empathy and hyper-sensitivity. They may need small time-outs to clear their space or regain peace of mind. A piece of Selenite worn or carried can help them to keep their emotional and psychic equilibrium.

Social Media Websites

Although not physical or spiritual in nature, cyberspace accumulates energy and has shown itself to affect our lives in multiple ways. What we post can be helpful or harmful, and what we read and witness online can uplift, amuse, educate or bring us down. Our email accounts can fill up with clutter just the same way that our homes can. They don't seem to have any immediate effect on our lives or psyche but it's interesting to note the mental relief that is experienced whenever we take the time to size down on e-junk. Some things are less obvious to us in the realm of cyberspace, where lurkers and silent stalkers abound. One may or may not know the impact they are having or that is being had on them by way of social media so engaging in a regular form of energy hygiene around it can help to clear energies of negativity and interference. This can be done with strong mental visualizations and making online adjustments. Taking a break from social media periodically can do wonders.

Fire sign people are often enthusiastic, colorful and bold on social media, if they spend time on it. Living life is more important to many of them. What they seek is a deeper sense of meaning, and what they bring is a confident presence. Some of them can be overzealous and go overboard with preaching or posting. In this case, they benefit from taking a stand back periodically to make sure that they are in sync with what they're promoting. For this purpose, Tree Agate can be helpful.

Earth sign people are methodical online, and often make consistent and reliable role models for many people engaged on social media, if they choose to interact. They have a particular style or trademark that is usually easy to identify. They make some of the best salespeople due to their consistency. Negatively, they can get locked into certain viewpoints that cause them to remain stuck. For breaking bad habits, the stone Moldavite seems to be especially helpful.

Air sign people are the walking, talking encyclopedias who are most concerned with education, social events, and justice. They equally enjoy acquiring and sharing information and ideas, making great teachers. They also enjoy things like quizzes and getting to know other people. Some of them can become addicted to the internet while using it as a form of escape from unresolved emotional issues. To address this issue the stone Charoite can be quite useful.

Water sign people are inspirational and creative in their methods of sharing online. They are mainly there for the art, and they come and go based on their moods. They sometimes throw random images, clever words or jokes out there without thinking much of the consequences. However, they can react to things they see with great emotion and sometimes take them personally. Prehnite can help water people to become more detached from unnecessary problems and to gain clarity regarding their feelings.

Energy Vampires and Parasites

Just as physical parasites suck the nutrition from their host, energy vampires and parasites feed off of one's vitality, leaving a trail of waste behind them. We have all had experiences with people who left us feeling drained. They may have done this through a simple handshake, through an intense gaze that bores into you, or through excessive talking and complaining. They may, over a length of time and in disguise, extract from a person their energy, sympathy, and even the fruits of their labors while offering little to nothing in return but grief.

A person of any sign can be a victim of or victimize others through psychic vampirism. This term was made popular in the 60s by Anton LaVey, author of The Satanic Bible. I categorize this particular phenomenon in terms of elemental characteristics, rather than zodiac signs. Those who appear to be the most susceptible to an attack by energy parasites tend to have a predominance of the water element in their birth chart. The water often causes them to care for others, and to absorb and take on too much of the influences of their environment. This can also cause them to become parasitic themselves if they are not mindful of their behaviors with others. As we will see though, all elemental types are capable of becoming energy leeches in their own ways.

In psychic vampirism, fire element people drain others through explosive outbursts, or they could be the victims of such rage. Many Fire element people exhibit what has been described as 'motormouth syndrome'. Some would expect this more from Air element and Air sign people, who are known to be overly talkative at times, but when Fire people are operating in an unconscious way and get heated about a certain subject, they can do a lot more damage. They demand attention and are literally exhausting to listen to. When Fire and Air combine in this negative way, results can be disastrous!

Earth element people can get stuck in parasitic situations that involve money whether they or someone else does the draining of time, money or resources. There is often a blind spot around finances with these types when they maintain their focus solely on a certain area. They might not recognize when they are being taken advantage of, or they might take advantage of those who are unsuspecting or defenseless. Toxic, codependent relationships based on assets, money and survival can go on for many years.

Those of the Air element can get caught up in psychological loops and over-analyzing that drive themselves or others to the brink of insanity. Thoughts don't have to be verbalized to spin out of control. Too much thinking and processing of information can lead to confusion or chaos. Out of the three air signs, the one least likely to engage in psychic vampirism is probably Aquarius because they like to keep things loose and not get too grossly entangled with people. This is definitely not always the case though. They can also be troublemakers who stir up chaos and then leave the scene, forcing everyone who is left behind to suffer the consequences.

Psychic Integrity for the Elemental Types

Fire Type

The Fire Type has a predominant influence in the signs Aries, Leo, Sagittarius and Houses One, Five and Nine

If this is your primary element you thrive where there is some degree of wilderness, heat and light, in areas that enable you to move about freely and challenge yourself in healthy ways. You need physical outlets for personal expression, for it is when your physical drive is suppressed that illness and vulnerability to attacks set in. Inactivity exacerbates many of your problems. If you are in a situation in which you are landlocked or tied down in some way, it is important to at least keep your mind occupied on subjects that are uplifting, funny and affirmative and to continue to engage your psychic senses as much as possible. Open the window, turn on a lamp, let the light in, do breathing exercises.

Avoid overexertion, which is just as bad if not more so than inertia. It is easy for fire element types to take their great reserves of energy and strength for granted and then get slammed hard when they run out of fuel. They move fast, but should learn when to slow down to minimize mistakes.

Earth Type

The Earth Type has a predominant influence in the signs Taurus, Virgo, Capricorn and Houses Two, Six and Ten

As an Earth type you thrive on order and organization. You can only ignore clutter for so long before you either get lost in it all or set about to declutter your environment. You are generally reliable, practical and cautious, while also being easygoing. You are capable of great self-discipline but also like to enjoy the good things that life has to offer. You have a high tolerance level for stress but have your limits, and they sometimes don't reveal themselves until you have already been stretched to the max. Be careful not to internalize your emotions to the point where they become unreachable. Acknowledgment of how you feel makes you more relatable to others and helps you to avoid personal pitfalls.

Avoid overproduction, which could be in a work sense or regarding material goods. Earth element people are naturally industrious and tend to take on more than their share of work at times, or to accumulate more things than necessary. Find temperance and moderation in all things.

Air Type

The Air Type has a predominant influence in the signs Gemini, Libra, Aquarius and Houses Three, Seven and Eleven

You are a mental problem solver and enjoy bringing intellectual pieces together in the puzzling game of life. You need outlets for communication, whether that means with other people or through writing, drawing, or recording your thoughts and impressions for some future use. Your ability to relate to people from all walks of life, although admirable, sometimes draws the wrong types of people to your side. You benefit from developing a stronger sense of discernment when it comes to your associates, saving your breath instead of wasting your time, energy and knowledge on people who don't appreciate or respect you. Building a stronger physique helps to quell your anxiety.

Avoid overthinking, if possible. Air element people get easily pulled into many different directions which causes them to lose their footing. They can find greater peace of mind by simplifying their plans, speaking more slowly, and compartmentalizing things.

Water Type

The Water Type has a predominant influence in the signs Cancer, Scorpio, Pisces and Houses Four, Eight and Twelve

You are a natural channel for life force energy, and you often reflect back to others what they are silently thinking or feeling. Your emotions run deep, and you must find outlets for them, especially if those outlets are somehow artistic. You are very caring, but you need to avoid wallowing for too long in a certain emotion so that it doesn't take hold of your entire life. Keeping yourself physically active also helps you to release pent up feelings through such exercises as swimming, stretching, hiking or dance. Drugs are tempting but beware, you could easily get whisked away into a fantasy world and not wish to return to your earthly responsibilities.

Avoid overexposure, which exacerbates troubling issues in those who are highly sensitive and empathic. Water types thrive best when their privacy is properly maintained and time-outs are honored. These things also help them to prevent co-dependency, wallowing in feelings of despair or internalizing the suffering of others.

Chapter 16

Self-Empowerment Affirmations and Meditations for the Signs

Although these affirmations, meditations and exercises may be useful for Sun signs, those given for the sign of one's Ascendant or Moon sign might be even more pertinent in some cases. We often need some major adjustments around all of these areas.

One can hone in on the influences of their predominant sign by calculating the signature sign of the natal chart. This sign might be the same as that of the Sun, or one that is completely different. This is done by adding one tally for the element and modality of every planet in the chart. If, for example, the Sun is in Capricorn, the element is earth, and the modality is cardinal. Include the element and modality of the Ascendant. Some people also include the Midheaven, which is the sign at the top of the chart that begins the tenth house. If the person with Sun in Capricorn has a predominance of mutable modality and the elements of water in their chart, their signature sign will be Pisces. There are also calculators and software that will do the math for you.

Aries

Affirmation: I am a natural leader who leads with integrity and honor.

Meditation: I joyfully shine my light into the world.

Your possibilities are endless because you have boundless energy to tackle the world and accomplish your goals. Your charisma lights up any place that you enter, and stimulates others on a physical level. When you are tired or run down emotionally, check to see if you are holding in too much of your energy rather than expressing yourself naturally. Also, when you seek too hard for recognition it seems to evade you, but when you follow your joy, it comes to you automatically. If you can accept that others might not be able to keep up with your fast pace, you'll be content to make a positive difference wherever you find yourself, with whoever you meet.

You might check the neighborhood bulletin board or social media pages to see who's in need that you can assist in some way. You can often best take the lead and be the hero or heroine in situations that are not too emotionally close to home. Helping others gives you a great and renewed sense of purpose in your life. You may serve as a light of hope to those in need. As a natural warrior you can help to empower others who are weak or vulnerable, as long as you direct your authority wisely and not in a pushy way.

Taurus

Affirmation: I have access to unlimited abundance.

Meditation: I discipline my senses and attain self-mastery.

Beautiful abundance is yours to enjoy and to share, and you naturally care for living growing beings. While others are busy chasing after riches or the limelight you are quietly tending your own hidden treasures. You love your peace, but you know how to protect your space from intruders and can become furious when crossed.

You may wish to develop a daily or weekly ritual that rewards but simultaneously disciplines your senses. For example, set before yourself and eat something such as a single strawberry or tiny slice of your favorite pie. Savor the bite, and the moment, without reaching out for more. Another example is to put a hundred-dollar bill in your purse or wallet, along with a five-dollar bill. Go window shopping or to a store where you know you'll want to spend, but don't spend over five dollars including tax fees.

This exercise is not about living every single moment of every single day like this. With repetition, your spending and eating habits will become disciplined and will protect you from the problems associated with indulgence. You will know that you have abundance and use it wisely. Nobody can tempt or sway you off your path. You enjoy all good things, but exercise temperance.

Gemini

Affirmation: I direct my thoughts to their highest and best capacities.

Meditation: I cherish this present moment and am filled with gratitude.

You have a multitude of talents to draw from at any given time. Check for resources at your disposal that you might have forgotten or neglected in favor of those that seem more accessible, exciting or special. Take note of your many skills rather than always trying to outdo yourself. Is there one of them in particular that stands out, one that you would like to refine? See if you can dedicate yourself to keeping your skills polished rather than rushing toward developing new ones.

Grass-is-greener syndrome is the belief and sensation that there is always something better to be experienced or acquired than what exists in the present circumstances. What then, is the use of any life experience or relationship if there is always someone else to be with or something greater to attain? If current situations are particularly unpleasant, remember that they will surely pass, for the nature of birth, life and death is impermanence. This is meditation for the soul; to be alert and present to our life circumstances and blessings. Pause to observe your levels of engagement. When there is clarity about oneself, there is clarity moving forward in your endeavors.

Cancer

Affirmation: My emotions are useful barometers, but my intuition is a trustworthy guide.

Meditation: I clear the slates and am relieved of any type of baggage.

Be aggressive in discarding that which is outworn. Examine the things that take up too much space, whether physical, emotional or mental. While there may be reasons for continuing to hold on to them, such as some degree of sentiment, fear of lack, or a sense of familiarity, they are a burden to maintain. This does not pertain to items that are well utilized or enjoyed. They might not be physical objects at all but certain attitudes that need to go. Decipher whether or not you are on a loop of some sort – a type of negative self-talk that does nothing to enhance your life experience or relationships.

Your great sensitivity can seem like either a blessing or a curse, depending on how much power you give to your emotions. Instead of taking every emotion into yourself and churning it over repeatedly, see if you can give yourself permission to observe and ask what it is trying to show you. Often it is your intuition getting filtered through your feelings, which causes a distortion in what you inherently know to be true. Claim your clairvoyance and potent intuitive abilities, allowing them to empower your decisions, health and life overall.

Leo

Affirmation: My willpower is wisely directed.

Meditation: I lead with my heart, not my ego.

Tremendous power is yours to use or abuse. How will you choose to direct it? When you lead from your heart in any given situation, you tend to find your actions affirmed and supported by those around you. Don't wait for drastic occurrences to listen to your heart. Make an exercise of regularly leading with your heart in "light-hearted" scenarios where any known consequences don't bear much weight. Have fun with this, and take note of the results. Your heart is your compass, and shows you where to go, and it even indicates how long you should stay. As long as you take heed, you will always wind up in the right place at the right time. That so-called phenomena of synchronicity will follow you around in mysterious ways.

Sometimes, timing is everything. When you are stressed out or upset, take a deep breath and wait for the appropriate moment to act. Impulsiveness mixed with annoyance leads to unsatisfactory results. Resist the temptation to replace one problematic thing, relationship or job for another due to impatience. Creative expression is your outlet for intense emotions, and you may transform them into beautiful works of art.

Virgo

Affirmation: I offer my service to others with non-attachment to the outcomes.

Meditation: I discover beauty wherever I go.

It is easy for you to spot the things and people in your environment that need all kinds of fixing. It takes a certain eye for seeing the beauty in unlikely places, and you also have that eye. Sometimes clutter must be cleared to showcase its greatest features, or a stone must be chiseled to reveal its sparkle. Sometimes your task is to simplify what has become overly complicated. In your quest for new horizons and experiences, there will always be things that catch your eye and draw you in. You have as much to gain as to share in each place that you visit. To tap into your inner power wherever you may be, meditate upon the healing powers of the Sun, for wherever it lies in your chart it is the source of much hidden treasure in your life.

No matter what your mission or profession may be, remember to keep in touch with the mundane, humble aspects of your existence. You might like to make a weekly or monthly habit of picking up trash at the beach or on the streets. You might also find joy in charity work that involves food. To stimulate new neural pathways, take a trip or a different route to work that you have not yet explored, or do a physical exercise you've never done before. If so inspired, report your findings to share with your community.

Libra

Affirmation: I relate to others and the world with authenticity.

Meditation: I am getting to know and love the face behind the mask.

Many people hide behind a smile or other types of expressions and mannerisms in their daily interactions with others. Sometimes they lose sight of who they are and what they really feel inside. Check in with yourself using a mirror, not to observe your physical appearance but what your spirit is seeking to communicate with you. Ignore bodily details as much as possible. Gaze into your own eyes for at least a minute. What, and who do you see? What emotions come up for you by doing this? What have you been hiding not only from others but from yourself? This is not to judge, but to observe, and come to a new understanding of what is being reflected back to you. Become a fair witness to your own weaknesses and strengths. If you find yourself in negative judgment and repulsion, seek to highlight the positive aspects of your character. If self-glorification is in effect, take note of the lack that you are compensating for. Give yourself a chance to identify and process whatever comes through, whether ugly or beautiful, silly or scary.

Relating to others can take a lot of energy. Take the time to regenerate when needed, but also stimulate yourself to exercise and move your body, even when doing so is not necessarily easy. When you maintain a sense of discipline and order in your life, you achieve an excellent balance of work, rest and play. Saturn is exalted in your sign!

Scorpio

Affirmation: I transform my strong urges into fuel for self-betterment.

Meditation: I maintain my own boundaries and respect those of others.

Through hard work, you attain your goals and many of your heart's wishes in your life. By honoring your own and others' boundaries, you can avoid many pitfalls and mend your wounds. What are psychic boundaries when we cannot see them with our eyes? They are experienced when we have the sensation that either we or someone else has "crossed the line" in some way. When others cross your line, you might become defensive, or you might not even know how to respond. When you cross others' lines, you might not instantaneously recognize your actions until the results catch up with you later. In other words, you might not always know how powerful your effect is upon others. Through your keen perception you quickly see into others' motivations, weaknesses and strengths. Because of this you can either choose to help them or to conquer or take advantage of them. The latter two options always have a way of backfiring.

As an exercise, check in to see where your ambitions or desires do not yet match your levels of capacity, skill or experience. Be honest with yourself about this. This does not mean you should abandon your desires but need to take inventory and see where you need to grow. Make lists of all of your desires and goals and regularly make edits and updates. By making a habit of this you will quickly climb the ladder of success in all your major endeavors.

Sagittarius

Affirmation: I perceive clearly and fully whatever I need to see.

Meditation: I gladly share my greatest gifts with the world.

Your lively, youthful and creative spirit is a blessing to all, but ironically it is not always easy for you to share your unique gifts with others. There might be certain tests, delays or ordeals that you need to work through before you are confident in bringing them to fruition, or out into the world. You might have experienced situations early in life in which you were exploited or taken for granted, and afterward you anticipated that would always happen to you. You can be very psychic, but your impressions sometimes get mixed up with your misconceptions. You might have a tendency to distrust others even when they mean well, and it takes some time to let down your guard.

When you feel inspired, gather around you a few tools for creative expression. They could be markers and paper, natural objects found outside, beads, baking ingredients or other crafting tools. Don't spend more than a couple of hours on your creative work, but pour as much love as possible into it, whatever it is. Now here comes the trickiest part of your task. Take your heart-infused work of art, and release it somewhere into the wild, to dissolve into the earth, scatter into the wind, or melt into the water. Give this offering to Mother Earth as a token of your appreciation for all that she provides for you, unconditionally. Ask that in return, she inspires you with the courage to share your greatest gifts with the world, without reserve or fear of loss. Ask that she help to mend your broken heart.

When you let go of expectations and offer the best possible version of yourself in each situation, miracles begin to unfold. You can make a huge difference in others' lives, bringing clarity and optimism where it is needed most.

Capricorn

Affirmation: I make use of every tool at my disposal.

Meditation: I free myself from self-imposed limitations.

Your resourcefulness combined with your strong sense of responsibility can produce amazing results in your life, admired by many. One of your greatest tests lies in allowing yourself to extract greater joy from your relationships or life experiences. You might find that you "live to work", instead of work to live. When stress levels build up in your body, it becomes important for you to find avenues of release so that various areas, such as your knees and jaws, don't lock up. Stretch and move often, not with speed but with consistency.

See if you can plan for at least one small vacation per year, and at least one adventure per month that takes you completely out of your comfort zone of familiarity and into new terrain, if not physically then mentally. Treat yourself to some much-needed self-care every week, whether you go to a professional or do it all for yourself at home. If your skin is tired or stressed out by the elements, you can revitalize yourself with a DIY facial, using clay or a mashed fruit of your choice that offers skin benefits. For example, avocado is moisturizing, and banana has been used to reduce fine lines and wrinkles. Afterward, spritz yourself with organic rose water. It's often been said that Capricornians tend to age in reverse, and this certainly seems to be true.

Aquarius

Affirmation: I respect others' knowledge as well as my own.

Meditation: I treat my body as the sacred vessel of my soul.

You naturally put your all into your livelihood, and are likely to achieve great success in your life. Your intellect and opinions are usually well pronounced. Allow some room for different viewpoints because sometimes you can come on too strong with your own.

Are you making enough time to stretch, take in adequate nutrients and rest? Maybe you did the best that you could but found yourself struggling with certain health issues anyway. It might have been early life hardships that caught up with you, or some kind of trauma along the way. In any case here is your exercise for recognizing your body as a sacred temple.

If you don't have a bathtub at home, look for a natural body of water somewhere where you can submerge the lower half of your body, at least up to your knees. If this still proves difficult to attain, then perhaps find a spa or visit a local jacuzzi. A tall bucket can also work. Place your feet up to your knees in some clean water. Honor your feet and legs as the pillars of your temple, that keep you upright, keep you going, and allow you to get around and get so much accomplished. Notice how much tension that you hold in these areas of your body, and visualize the water just melting it away. Afterward rub your legs, ankles and feet, applying pressure wherever you sense the need. You could also use an oil, applied to your whole body. This is especially relaxing to do before bedtime. Do something to pamper yourself like this at least twice a month, such as getting a massage. Bring more awareness into your daily movements and intake of food. Know that you deserve to be well, and to feel and look your very best.

Pisces

Affirmation: I gain stability in my worldly affairs.

Meditation: I trust in Divine Providence that there is more to life than meets the eye.

Although sometimes you might feel separate from the rest of humanity, you have a very important role to play in your network of family, friends, and associates. You might struggle with feelings of depression when you are either inactive or overly active and doing too much without allowing yourself to rest. You are well suited to occupations involving travel, environmental causes, or music and the arts. You care deeply about your loved ones, but you also value your space and time to yourself to process things and live your own life on your terms.

Your self-empowerment meditation is something that might be considered to be very dry and left-brained, not at all as your sign tends to be. That is to take stock of what's working and not working in your daily affairs. You may wish to invest in a personal business kit, containing the following items: a daily planner, a filing cabinet, good working ball-point pens, and a desk devoted to your office work. Keep track of your spending and earnings, your personal goals, and your spiritual ideals or wishes for the world. See how all of these things converge and come together in your mind or in your life. Know that you are worth the struggle and the work that it takes to become great, and to attain your desires, and to experience a joyful existence. You don't have to sacrifice everything that you earn for your loved ones. Save something for yourself to enjoy too.

Part Three

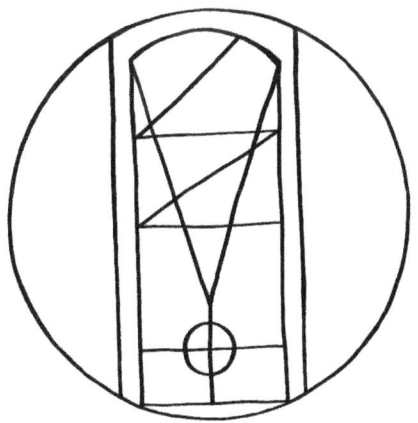

Chapter 17

Adversarial Groups by Sign

"The masses have never thirsted after truth. Whoever can supply them with illusions is easily their master; whoever attempts to destroy their illusions is always their victim."

- Gustave Le Bon, *The Crowd: A Study of the Popular Mind*

Psychic attack does not occur only through individuals but also through groups of every size and category. An overwhelming majority of people on this planet tend to judge what is righteous upon a consensus ideal, which is to say that they base both truth and morality on the dictates of an outer authority rather than an inner assessment of what is wrong and right for them. Because sociopolitical trends are so pervasive in the modern world, breaking free from their clutches entails considering how the group mind operates in contrast to self-reflection and uncommon sense.

Psychic attack by groups can occur in churches, music venues, during political events, between races and in connection with various social causes and gatherings. It can be subtle or obvious and can include physical acts of violence. It is more prominent in some places than others, such as in a part of town where the crime rates are especially high. Group psychic attack may involve physical predators such as in the case of pedophile rings or they can affect victims of circumstance such as in the case of the old neighborhood being haunted by unresolved trauma associated with the land itself. It can stretch far beyond that still, as an idea, fad or doctrine that infiltrates the cultural practices of people all around the world.

The subject of group-affiliated psychic attack merits the exploration of an occult concept known as the egregore, which can be a non-physical entity made up of the collective thoughts of a specific group of people. Such a being is likely to exert a strong influence in religious or occult groups, or those that have a widespread influence, such as political groups. The Book of Enoch made mention of egregorial presences, though they were individual beings known as the Watchers.

The translation of the Greek word egregoros is "wakeful."

Many of us have observed that a certain type of energy that is made up of all of the fears, perversions, and psychic debris of united individuals past or present begins to develop and takes on a more of a mind of its own when too many of the participants in a given situation lack either self-awareness or self-restraint. The more spiritually aware a person is, the greater their recognition of both collective psychic vampirism and worldly oppression. They are capable of identifying their own inner conflicts in contrast to the myriad conflicts that surround them.

Below is a list of certain kinds of groups that correspond in characteristics to the twelve signs of the Zodiac. These groups do not necessarily fall under the signs listed according to natal calculations, but in some cases they do. Some may exude the qualities of more than one zodiacal or planetary influence. There are about three primary influences to each group that can typically be sub-categorized under the influence of one sign.

For example, a group may be predominantly Scorpio-like in nature but have strong Gemini features and a touch of Aquarius at the same time, such as the NSA – the highly secretive and contained intelligence agency of the United States gathering millions of streams of data on everyone outside of itself via the internet.

To discern who in your life belongs to any one of these adversarial groups listed below and how they may negatively impact you is to arm yourself with the knowledge that could save you anywhere from a few minutes to decades of needless annoyance and suffering. A greater understanding of who your adversaries are and who you are better off avoiding interaction with altogether supports your living a happy, healthy and successful life. It also increases the ability to help protect oneself and loved ones from danger. Perhaps the greatest use of a general list such as this is that it may come in handy during important transits through each of the signs. You may be quicker to spot these types of groups and get a head-start on damage control.

There is also a power of divine benevolence when people of like mind gather together for the common good. There are as many if not more groups of loving individuals gathering together to support positive changes in the world as there are negative ones. We just don't seem to hear about them as often because our popular culture has become addicted to drama.

Disclaimer: The material below is not based on ideas that astrologers have agreed upon unanimously. The following information is drawn from a combination of common knowledge, pattern recognition, and personal opinions for people to make of whatever they will. It is not claimed to be absolute truth.

Aries Adversarial Group: The Antagonists

"All violence consists in some people forcing others, under threat of suffering or death, to do what they do not want to do."

- Leo Tolstoy

The Arian adversarial group is outwardly aggressive and easy to identify. Examples include mobs, riot police, school bullies, and street gangs. The quickest way to define them is to say that they appear as armies, but not the ones who are fighting for justice in this world. Their actions are hasty, reckless, selfish and cruel. In most cases their attacks are physical rather than strictly psychic in nature, often having very tangible or bloody effects. Obviously, these groups are more prevalent in certain areas than others, or at certain times.

One recent example of the Arian adversarial group is paradoxically the looters and rioters who have targeted police officers and small businesses in several parts of the world, following the George Floyd murder case. Although racism has long been and continues to be a problem that incites violence in several parts of the world, social engineering is involved in most of today's race-based protests.

Another recent dramatic example of riot police attacking citizens occurred in Ottawa, Canada during a convoy involving truck drivers and other protesters against Covid-19 restrictions. The people began to gather in large numbers during the group-oriented Aquarius season. The protest began in late January of 2022, but as it began to gain momentum in February, many people who were participants in the protest were dragged away, fined, and attacked in various methods by military agents.

Disclaimer: *Military and police only fall under this category when they are acting in senseless violence toward people who have not commit any crimes.*

Taurus Adversarial Group: The Hoarders

"The environment that we call society is created by past generations; we accept it, as it helps us to maintain our greed, possessiveness, illusion."

-Jiddu Krishnamurti

Out of the twelve types, these groups are the most motivated by lust and greed. The Taurean style adversarial group steadily spreads and establishes itself far and wide. This is often done in plain sight but may also to some extent operate behind the scenes. Examples include opportunists, petty thieves, greedy profiteers, such as the ginormous worldwide franchises that promote mass production of genetically modified, highly processed and refined-sugar-laden cheap foods, and countless other items that weaken people's health in some way. Their main objective is profiting from others' poverty and ignorance, and not at all in supporting their wellness.

Politically coordinated and formally engineered mass-migrations with promises of "effortless financial gain" and "guaranteed happiness" is another example. Many of the migrants who partake in this long and hard journey ultimately arrive in Europe, often in bad condition, somewhat disillusioned, and finding themselves incapable or unwilling to integrate into their new cultural environments, due to extreme contrasts in values. Understandably, this causes mutual suspicion and cultural shock. This type of situation has occurred in many parts of the world over many centuries. Directly at the top of the world pyramid scheme are the opportunists who profit from these conflicts and the worldwide divisions that they create. Even as they engage in a tug of war between each other for who wields the most power and influence, all of them are among the most dangerous of the world's hoarders.

The ultimate aim of the world's most powerful hoarders is to create a communistic world, with a world-wide totalitarian government, complete surveillance and dictatorship over the lives of humans. Hoarders rely on Armies (from Arian to Piscean types) to do their dirty work for them while they themselves benefit from the labors of their victims. You sometimes see or hear them speaking from their distant podiums about the types of economic changes that will bring material security to all of humanity (such as eating insects to combat climate change) when their actual agenda can be decoded as exerting total control over the populace. More people are hip to the agenda than ever before, and we have the internet to thank for this recent spread of knowledge.

Gemini Adversarial Group: The Meddlers

"When it comes to gossip, I have to readily admit men are as guilty as women."
-Marilyn Monroe

Geminian adversarial groups are present in everyone's lives to some degree. It can be tricky to get away from these noisy and nosey groups because, although not exactly forceful in nature, they seem to permeate society with their vast numbers of participants. These groups may take the form of gossipy co-workers, busy-body family members who frequently meddle in others' personal affairs, hypocritical religious zealots, unreliable friends who appear and disappear on a whim whenever they want something, and the producers of sensational media and melodrama that is featured on popular tabloids like the National Enquirer. There are lots of these groups on social media websites such as Facebook and Twitter. There are far too many of them to keep up with, but the point is that they are not even worth keeping up with.

These groups are amusing at first, frequently clever and quick-tongued but ultimately toxic. Like fast-moving streamers these groups poke their way into the minds of unsuspecting victims and their infectious thoughts spread out like millions of slithering vines. Do not feel bad about cutting them off because they wouldn't think twice about cutting you up with their words of nonsense. Everything is superficial to them. They only skim the surface and never get to the core of any issue.

"Flying monkeys" is a term used by modern psychologists to describe people recruited by a narcissist to isolate, torment, and spread gossip about a targeted individual. These people are named after the monkeys featured in the story of the Wizard of Oz who did the bidding of the Wicked Witch of the West, while under her evil spell. Similarly, flying monkeys who are loyal to abusive figureheads, charismatic narcissists or leaders are under the spell of mind control, or in their ignorance enable the narcissist to continue to abuse others. These people most often tend to fit under the categories of the Meddlers as well as the Aquarian Cult. When spying or stalking is involved this group would fall under the influence of the Scorpionic Hydra. Dr. Ramani Durvasula shares a great deal of useful information about all things pertaining to narcissism on her YouTube channel, Doctor Ramani.[1]

Meddlers are the enablers of the Taurean Hoarders, because they go around spreading gossip, repeating everything they hear or read on social media and furthering the success of the agenda to seize control of everyone's thoughts, feelings and decisions. Gaslighting (explained in Astrological Cycles and Historical Events) is one method that they use to cause people to doubt their own sanity and discourage them from discovering the truth of any matter.

Cancer Adversarial Group: The Complainers

"This life is not for complaint, but for satisfaction."

- Henry David Thoreau

Cancerian adversarial groups have swiftly grown in numbers over the past decade. Our distant ancestors did not know nearly as many of these kinds of groups as we do today. That is because never before has society known as many privileged individuals as exist in modern times. Our ancestors were too focused on mere survival. Examples include political extremists and pity parties of all varieties. The threat that these modern groups impose on others is based on their cunning ability to convince so many people of their group's collective victimhood, no matter how outlandish their claims may be. These types form pity-party groups, always seeking public sympathy and privileges that are almost never based on positive contributions, but rather external appearances.

Often fixated upon issues such as identity politics, they demand special rights and blow many public concerns out of proportion while ignoring the underlying injustices in society, such as child exploitation, and the ramifications of damages being done to the environment by unnecessary blasts of radiation. As the Moon rules Cancer, many such lunar-based groups seem to exhibit neurotic behavior and will go out of their way to censor or ban other people because of opinions or philosophies that they do not personally agree with. They easily take offense and make it everyone's business when their own feelings have been hurt.

Their political causes are not based on the common good of all people but their own emotional bias and belief systems which they constantly push onto others. They try to monitor and control free speech which has created problems for a lot of people and poses a threat to basic human rights overall. This kind of behavior exemplifies the lower, infantile expressions of Cancer.

The Cancerian Complainers are fueled by the Geminian Meddlers who encourage their emotional outpouring with incessant streams of extremely triggering information and propaganda. The Taurean Hoarders have a lot of money to gain from all the commotion made by both of these groups.

Leo Adversarial Group: The Snobs

"To the elitist hedonist, life is the avoidance of boredom and routine."

- Timothy Leary

The Leonine adversarial group is identifiable by a combination of pride in its own kind and the attempt to dominate others, whether in blatant or subtle ways. This may have racial, religious, social or political connotations or a combination of all of these things. Examples include aristocratic societies and monarchies These groups may be endowed with amazing looks, be of noble birth or have a special combined role in the entertainment industry that brings them great fame and fortune. They are part of a very important club that the rest of humanity is clearly not.

Although there is nothing inherently bad about being a famous entertainer, there are some who are born into fame or came into it at a young age who do not realize the measures by which they are being molded and groomed. Many are trained in using their talents to deceive their fans without even realizing it. Those who are young and seductive tend to serve as role models to the youth of the world in how to dress and behave. A common stage front is showing public charity to Cancerian adversarial groups, as if it is honorable and virtuous to do so. Some seem to be willing to do just about anything for attention, often due to the influence of their managers or parents egging them on.

The pornography industry is a group that manipulates the masses via sexuality, often while degrading its participants in the process. Beautiful women are often chosen to be exploited, who, with their glamour, cause confusion and insecurity in other women, while encouraging men to objectify women. It is not only women who are degraded in these kinds of industries but also men, even children and animals against their will. It is a form of abuse and debasement deceptively labeled as entertainment, and some people defend it, again as if this is an act of charity.

The Leonine Snobs are motivated by their Complainer predecessors to become greater and not to show too much emotion in the process. They are great at congratulating themselves and giving each other pats on the back and all kinds of rewards for all of the great things that they do among themselves and for each other, all while giving off a regal appearance to the world.

Virgo Adversarial Group: The Nitpickers

"The greatest tyrannies are always perpetuated in the name of the noblest causes." -

Thomas Paine

The Virgoan group, just like the Geminian group, is ruled by that swift and crafty character that we call Mercury. Their general external aims appear to be improvement overall, but their methods are more than just a little meddlesome. Some of these groups are merely annoying to others while others are downright dangerous. They have become known as social engineers in the fields of medicine, politics and environmental causes. Examples of such groups include the pharmaceutical industry, and invasive assemblies of micromanagers who claim to be helpful but wind up causing more problems than existed before their involvement.

The pharmaceutical industry or "Big Pharma", falls into the category of the dangerous type of Virgoan group with some strong Scorpionic and Plutonian undertones. They both manufacture and promote drugs of a highly addictive nature that have caused more problems than solutions as a whole, leading to wide scale iatrogenesis. They insist on a universal cure-all for all people, which in reality does not exist. Many of their drugs have not been fully tested as safe, which compounds the problem of medical dependency. For example, pharmaceutical companies such as Pfizer have had to pay large sums of money in lawsuits related to medical violations. Pfizer was founded in 1849, when Neptune was in the early phase of its last transit through Pisces (today Neptune is nearing the end of a transit through this sign lasting from 2011-2025), a planet in its own sign which corresponds with infectious disease, addictions and medical experimentation. Pisces is the opposite sign of Virgo, and these two signs play off each other's themes of focusing on problems and solutions.

On a smaller scale, there are modern day "health nuts" who show aggression in trying to make people feel guilty for eating the wrong types of foods. The problem is not with those who opt for certain diets such as veganism, but in those who impose their beliefs onto others in abusive ways.

These Nitpicker groups pick up where Leonine Snob mobs have left off, believing themselves to be righteous and others in the wrong. They always find ways to let others know how much work they need to do to improve themselves. It's always easier for these groups to project things onto others than to look in the mirror and take stock of their own behavior.

Libra Adversarial Group: The Cliques

"What greater wound is there than a false friend?"

- Sophocles

The Libran adversarial group is best described as provocative in every sense of that word. Smart, savvy and fashionable, they seem to radiate a special kind of collective allure that excites others and simultaneously gets under their skin. Individuals who find them so exciting are frequently audiences or competing performers of some kind. These groups are the socialites who offer great flattery and become high profile "frenemies". They are the fashion police who indicate what looks cool and what's way out of style.

An example of such groups are women in the dance world or those people in the acting profession who resort to superficial gossip and undermining of other team members in an attempt to climb the ladder of success. They may be sexy in appearance and catty in demeanor, pretending to like those that they secretly despise or envy. They live for attention and always seem to know just exactly what to say in social settings to appease their fans and avoid tension, and especially to grow their following. It all depends on what their agenda is, which is usually to win.

Groups engaged in controlled opposition also fall under the Libra Adversarial category. Undercover agents may sometimes work together as a group by hijacking and co-opting other legitimate groups. These are referred to as agent provocateurs. For example, they will join a street protest, disguised as one of the protesters but actually send out a message that conflicts with the original intent and makes the well-meaning protesters look bad. They may also lure people into activities that get them into legal trouble. Many of these groups work together on the internet and they hijack the work of different people by muddying the waters to make their work appear illegitimate. Vladimir Lenin has been quoted as admitting that, "the best way to control the opposition is to lead it ourselves."

Libran cliques have mastered the art of social manipulation to such a degree that deeply satisfies the expectations of Virgoan Nitpickers and lends themselves to the even more devious ploys of the Scorpionic groups that fall under the category of the Hydra.

Scorpio Adversarial Group: The Hydra

"It is a man's own mind, not his enemy or foe, that lures him to evil ways." -

Buddha

The Scorpionic adversarial group is often viewed as the most dangerous and deadly. They could be classified as a sort of group leech or parasite, in that they often succeed in covert methods of draining others' life force energy, money, time and resources. They are very seldom forthright about their identity and intentions, but sometimes they toy with others by hiding everything they are doing "in plain sight". One of the insidious aspects to some of these groups is that the members themselves don't even necessarily know what they are being used for, which is usually to prop up those in much higher positions. Some of them operate on a mundane level while others are very much involved with metaphysics and arcane subjects. Examples of these types of groups include the Mafia, pyramid schemes and certain secret societies.

Some of these groups engage in the occult, some openly and some only in private. It becomes important to distinguish between those such as Goth teens sporting inverted pentagrams as a fashion statement and the low-key looking businessmen and women that could be actual members of an elite group of occult practitioners. The latter is far more dangerous and difficult to spot. There is always some degree of camouflage over their criminal activities. If you happen to come into direct contact with one of these people, you may feel very queasy in their presence and sense something ominous about them that is not visible on the surface.

The Hydra hypnotizes, beguiles and seduces both its members and its victims using occult symbolism, multi-layered power dynamics, and oftentimes sexual energy. Once they have got someone hooked in, they either swoop in to suck the life out of them or manipulate them to do their bidding.

The Scorpionic Hydra often operates in disguise, using Libran Cliques to fulfill its evil and highly elaborate missions, many of which are meant to maim or kill.

Sagittarius Adversarial Group: The Preachers

"I'd like to start a religion. That's where the money is."   -
L. Ron Hubbard

The Sagittarian group may be generally classified as the Preachers because they're always on a mission to indoctrinate others into their own collectivized versions of truth, reality and virtue. They may literally take the form of religious organizations or preachers in a figurative sense. Often these types of groups raise their voices very loudly and say so much so that others cannot help but notice them. They're never subtle and they're always easy to locate. Examples include religious and internet cults. There are many of these types of groups in existence which tend to attract well-meaning individuals who are genuinely seeking for truth, especially truth that is hidden, but who tend to get caught up in a strange combination of magical thinking, political extremism and conspiracy theories. If they stick around in the group long enough, they eventually become convinced that they are right and others (the "sheeple") out there in the world are all wrong – about everything. The group's leaders may be internet figureheads who blend important information with their own personal bias and a lot of non-sense. Facts about the world become convoluted over time making it harder for followers to identify what is actually going on both within and outside of the group they have become affiliated with. All of this warping of the facts contributes to the stigma of the highly ridiculed, tin-foil hat wearing "conspiracy theorist" which downplays the reality that there are indeed conspiracies against humanity. This type of group is one of them.

Several religious organizations in the U.S. are prime examples of how the adversarial Sagittarian groups may manifest. Missionaries who go door to door trying to save souls would fall into this category. They fail to realize how their actions may be considered to be quite presumptuous and invasive, both physically and psychically.

The Sagittarian Preachers gain energy and sustenance directly from underground Hydra without even realizing where their support is coming from. In their arrogance they rather assume it as their own, because their self-aggrandizement knows no bounds.

Capricorn Adversarial Group: The Tyrants

"Does the government fear us? Or do we fear the government? When the people fear the government, tyranny has found victory. The federal government is our servant, not our master
- Thomas Jefferson

Capricorn adversarial groups have long reigned on this planet and their influence has been reaching an absolute pinnacle during the past few years leading up to the conjunctions between Saturn, Pluto, and Jupiter in addition to the recent eclipses involving this sign. They are identifiable by their high-level hierarchies and various degrees of influence over large populations. They manifest as authoritarian government or intelligence operations.

Political figures and the groups they form are some of the most obvious tyrants that affect society. They most often function through a combination of manipulation and forceful dictatorship. However, these political figures are often only the outer front men for those silent ones who operate behind the scenes. The most powerful of these leaders cunningly send their minions forth on world-ravaging rampages through endeavors of ludicrous bureaucracy used to trap millions of people through meaningless rules that drive them into monetary debt. They use red tape to silence those who would oppose their tyrannical rules. Their unwavering dominance is even more pronounced than their obvious greed. They say they want equality and justice for all when what they really care about is power, for themselves. In many instances they are related to each other or at least attend private events together. They have been filmed and photographed kicking up their heels and playing games when they're not overly busy programming public platforms and influencing world affairs.

The communist dictator Joseph Stalin was born under Sagittarius with his Mercury in Capricorn, and demonstrated some of the most radical tyranny in recorded history. To this day there are followers of Stalin's communist ideology who support governmental control systems that impose limitations on peoples' most basic human rights. Furthermore, there are watered down socialist groups who don't realize that the causes they so vehemently defend are directly influenced by leaders who have no interest in their welfare. The end result of un-elected leaders is always dictatorship and never in serving the best interests of humanity.

Capricorn-based tyrannical groups are often propped up by the Scorpionic Hydra and represented by indoctrinated Sagittarian Preachers who believe they are the legitimate leaders.

Aquarius Adversarial Group: The Cult

"The only difference between a cult and a religion is the amount of real estate they own."

- Frank Zappa

Like Cancerian Complainer groups, the Aquarian Cult groups have become very popular over the past few decades. These groups may appear to have a spiritual background or link spirituality with science, but in a way that leans heavily on science, treating it as its own religion. Rather than being driven by emotion they are intellectually oriented, to the point that human emotions and needs are trampled over. They might push the New Age mantra that "ego is the enemy" while promoting world unity and the "highest truth" above all. Those who lean toward atheism may be more likely to orient themselves toward the tech world, nanotechnology and transhumanism.

There are groups of these sorts who lead and those who pride themselves on being free thinkers while following the dictates of their internet authority figures. Those who lead are motivated by a combination of greed and lust for power. They often claim to be philanthropists and are represented by a specific front man or charismatic leader who receives far more publicity than they themselves as a whole.

Those groups who follow cult leaders often engage in the activity of what is called trolling on social media platforms. They frequently post quotes of their beloved figurehead, along with memes and videos that attack and ridicule others who do not adopt the views of the established cult. Typically, those drawn into such groups are intellectually oriented but, in many cases, they are simultaneously unhappy. They may look toward their beloved figurehead as a sort of surrogate parent to help them sort out their unresolved childhood traumas. The figurehead uses various techniques to lure others into their groups that many people fall for hook, line and sinker. Followers begin to believe themselves above the rest of the herd, in this case meaning humanity.

The Aquarian Cult claims to be free from tyranny but is fully backed and funded by Tyrants who enable them to flourish. Their aim is to prevent genuine breakthroughs from taking place on a large scale for humanity.

Pisces Adversarial Group: The Drifters

"Everything in the world displeases me: but, above all, my displeasure in everything displeases me."

- Friedrich Nietzsche

The adversarial Piscean group has its collective head in the clouds like a pack of mumbling vagrants, and yet is as dangerous and difficult to pin down as the most stealthy, underground drug dealers. Some are the seemingly harmless groups who participate in psychotropic ceremonies at different houses on a quarterly basis, recording all of their peak experiences and epiphanies on social media. They organize and regularly attend orgiastic festivals where anything goes, and the only rule is to be as wild and woolly as possible. Their Utopian ideals are compelling to many of their associates.

Drifters often wear an altruistic cover in that they claim to donate to some large cause to alleviate the suffering in the world. Much of what they do is to cause others to view them in a favorable light, while hidden egotism is their primary motivating factor. They may sometimes sacrifice personal pleasure and even legitimate needs in order to fulfill the perceived role of philanthropists.

Altruistic groups are adversarial only when they use deception in their so-called charitable acts. This could mean they pose as saviors of those in need when they are actually collecting money for themselves. They tug on heart strings with both true and fabricated tragedies so that others more easily share their resources. These people serve as reminders to always do your research before donating a large sum of money to a charity, to make sure it's legitimate and that the money is going where it is claimed to be going.

The 60s ushered in the advent of "free love", with its counterculture typically summarized by the slogan "sex, drugs and rock n' roll". In today's internet culture, the belief that everything should be equally free and accessible to all has become popularized in social circles. Some of this stems from the desire to revolt against mass consumerism and greed. A lot of it, however, is the result of a widely promulgated air of entitlement, especially when it comes to spiritual and occult topics. There is a reason why the spiritual initiate was traditionally faced with tests before being granted certain privileges. Each new power attained in life leads to a test of one's character and ability to handle that power wisely. The Piscean concept of "Oneness" has warped itself into a digital conveyor belt of spiritual information, tutorials, and material based on the years of others' research and development, now being doled out lavishly, to "highly online" looky-loos, collectors, plagiarists and preachers of this knowledge (without consent of the authors, teachers, etc.). So little of what is being shared is actually put into action unless it's for the purpose of casting glamour and growing an audience.

Drifter groups find their place in society by way of some type of Aquarian Cult, and they may establish many sub-cults beneath it, thereby spreading their pseudo-spirituality, nihilism, and erosive ideas in many direction

Reference

1. Ramani S. Durvasula, PhD, *Don't You Know Who I Am? How to Stay Sane in an Era of Narcissism, Entitlement, and Incivility.* (New York: Post Hill Press, 2021.

Chapter 18

Astrological Cycles and Historical Events

"That which hath been is that which shall be, and that which hath been done is that which shall be done; and there is nothing new under the sun."

- Ecclesiastes 1:9

Astrology is based on celestial patterns that have repeated themselves for thousands if not millions of years. Below is a selection of historical events with their corresponding astrological transits. Included are the types of themes and challenges that we collectively tend to experience in a cyclical sense, according to the Sun's transit through the twelve signs. Upon thorough examination of world events many astrological configurations reveal themselves to be accurate timeline trackers. However, one reason why history repeats itself is that we as a whole have been lied to about some of the most important events in history, which to this day continue to shape society and world events to our detriment. If only more people knew the truth of our ancestral wars for example, we would never again fall for the same tricks, and we would be better equipped to handle potential future attacks.

Cataclysmic events tend to occur around the Equinoxes, Solstices and their midpoints in the year, and in connection with yearly sets of Eclipses. There is great relevance that these cycles have to psychic attack, both in groups and individuals. Each sign of the Zodiac carries its own set of triggers, and knowing what they are can improve our ability to handle them with greater effectiveness.

In astrology, there is a widely held view that each degree of the zodiac has its own special significance, although exact meanings may slightly vary. Critical degrees are believed to be more challenging and pronounced than others. Two of the most widely used and severe degrees are 0, called the ingress degree, associated with cardinal signs, and 29, called the anaretic degree, which is the final degree of any sign that brings closure to its major lessons. There are a few other critical degrees, relevant to different situations. 18 degrees has been known as a degree that brings sickness and terror. 22 degrees also seems to frequently show up in worldly misfortunes involving death. 15

degrees is more of a keynote degree, that emphasizes the qualities of the sign it happens to be in. A few degrees of significance are referenced below[1]

How to Use this Information for Psychic Self Defense

Although the cycles listed pertain to outer events, their inner ramifications go much deeper in influencing the thoughts, emotions, and beliefs of the masses to which they pertain. The way that I personally make use of historical references is by examining the courses of action that were taken by others that led to major crisis. Each month, each year, and with certain transits we can anticipate that problems of a certain nature may arise, and therefore prepare ourselves accordingly, as one would prepare for a journey. We may do our best to ensure that we have packed the correct types of food, medicine, and tools that will be necessary for this particular journey that is ahead of us, leaving room for the unexpected. It helps to spend some quiet time in meditation that will be of assistance in responding more calmly and rationally to challenges.

Aries Season – The Equinox Kickstarter

Every year, the Sun's entrance into Aries in the tropical zodiac marks the Spring season in the Northern Hemisphere and Autumn in the Southern Hemisphere. It is the true astrological new year. The Sun's transit through this sign lasts from approximately March 21st to April 19th. This equinox has become notorious for signaling massive "attacks" by governments and other establishments.

Political uproars, fatalities, and chaotic events have been noted to occur right before, during and just after the Sun transits Aries. These types of attack are also executed at the other key turning points in the year, which form the cross-wheel of the Zodiac. Countless catastrophic events and natural disasters have occurred like clockwork at these key times. Aries season in particular can highlight accidents and tragedies involving fire, killing and murder. Although false narratives may sometimes be pushed by the media, the violence and damage that occurs is often real. People are further inundated by a combination of fabrications and exaggerations that spread terror through repetition.

One of the most famous incidents that occurred during Aries season involved a religious cult which fell victim to what has been labeled the Waco Texas massacre, on April 19, 1993. This was a Branch Davidians group suspected of stockpiling illegal weapons and who refused to cooperate with an FBI search of their property. As a result, a major gunfight broke out and, whether on purpose or by accident, the entire building that housed these cult members was burned to the ground.

Here are a few other events that have occurred during the season of Aries which served as the mark of some challenging new cycle for the masses.

- The American Revolution was initiated on April 19, 1775, beginning with shots fired at Lexington and Concord in Massachusetts.
- The eruption of the Mount Tambora volcano in Indonesia reached its most violent climax on a New Moon in Aries season, on April 10, 1815. This was reported to be the most powerful volcanic eruption in human history. There were close to 11,000 estimated deaths from direct volcanic deaths and up to 90,000 deaths from post-eruption famine and diseases.
- The American Civil War began on April 12, 1861, and lasted until Taurus season on May 9, 1865. The war began as Confederate forces opened fire on Fort Sumter in South Carolina. Aries is ruled by Mars, the god of war, which hints at the spurring of this event.
- On April 15th of 2019 the famous Notre Dame cathedral caught fire, the cause of which was never publicly determined. Due to the history associated with this cathedral there was a lot of controversy surrounding the fire, which were linked to the arson of several other churches in France and throughout Europe. Fires and explosions are typically associated with fire signs.
- Around the spring equinox in March 2020, a sense of urgency and fear regarding germ invasion was amplified under the influence of Aries. The ruling planet for Aries is Mars, which rules epidemics and infections.

Taurus Season – Silent Wars Set into Motion

Since time immemorial, whenever the Sun has passed through the sign of Taurus many ceremonies have been performed to honor the fecundity of the earth, new beginnings and a soft transition between very active cycles. The bull, which symbolizes Taurus, was held in the highest regard in ancient cultures and originally represented the first and not the second sign of the Zodiac. In ancient Mesopotamia the constellation of Taurus was known as Gu An Na ("Bull of Heaven") and is said to have marked the Spring Equinox.

In these times, using the Tropical Zodiac, this transit occurs between April 20th and May 20th. As with the Sun's transit through Aries, it is also during this time that opposing forces continue to crop up during what seem to be the most inopportune moments and places, when people are more relaxed than usual and have their guards down. This may in some instances be the result of the modern carryover of archaic rituals. For sensitive people, there may arise uncomfortable sensations during this time of year that are hard to trace or pin down to a particular cause. This is an ideal period of time to take enjoyment in life, to lay low in general, to detoxify, tonify, and simplify as much as possible. Although work may be necessary, relaxation and the stillness it implies is equally important. We are reminded to "stop and smell the roses" along the way in the hustle and bustle of things. Beauty, whether its source is tangible or ethereal, helps to elevate thoughts and moods.

The types of attacks that occur during Taurus season tend to relate to finances, property rights violations and the exploitation of natural resources.

Notable historical events that took place during the Sun's transit through Taurus:

- Joan of Arc leading the Dauphin's troops to victory over the English laying siege to Orleans on May 8th of 1429.

- The French Revolution began with the Estates General of 1789 on May 5th, lasting for ten years, six months and four days, until November 9, 1799, ending with the formation of the French Consulate. The causes of this revolution were due to a combination of political, social and economic concerns. There was large-scale resistance to the wealthy elite as the cost of living grew along with the population. Food was becoming too expensive, which is a very Taurean related theme.

- The Spanish American War began in Cuba and Puerto Rico on April 21, 1898, after an explosive attack on the American ship called The Maine. Cuban independence from Spanish rule was the main subject of the conflict. On this day, the Sun was in Taurus with a New Moon to follow.

- On April 24, 1915, the Ottoman empire ordered the arrest and deportation of Armenian intellectuals and leaders from Constantinople (today known as Istanbul, Turkey), ultimately to be killed. These included notable doctors, clergymen, and teachers. The Deportation of Intellectuals was the beginning of the Armenian Genocide. Soon to follow, over a million Armenians were sent on death marches into the Syrian desert between 1915-1916, subjecting them to starvation, robbery, horrific rape and murder. The massacre of Armenians had already been underway in recent years and were a prelude to World War I. In April of 1915, Pluto, the planet of massive expulsion and violence, was 0 degrees of Cancer - the sign of nationality. This was a dark omen of ethnic cleansing.

- It was during Taurus season on May 10th, 1940, that Winston Churchill became Prime Minister of Britain, replacing Neville Chamberlain. Upon meeting his cabinet, he declared: "I have nothing to offer but blood, toil, tears and sweat". That month he established an all-party war government, that escalated in World War II.

- The Russian power plant disaster of Chernobyl occurred during Taurus season, on April 26th, 1986. The Sun was in exact opposition with Pluto in Scorpio (see Scorpio season for more info on Scorpionic influences). Pluto rules toxins, radiation and nuclear waste. Saturn was 8 degrees of Sagittarius, in the degree associated with Scorpio's themes including toxic waste.

- The Deepwater Horizon oil spill in the Gulf of Mexico occurred when the Sun was entering Taurus on April 20, 2010. The Columbine Shooting at a Colorado high school occurred just as the Sun entered Taurus on April 20, 1999. Both of these events took place with the Sun at the critical degree of zero.

Gemini Season – Talking and Circulation

When the Sun transits Gemini, between May 21st and June 20th, many things that were initiated toward the end of the previous year or during March are coming to fruition, finding resolution or closure. That which was stuck may begin moving very quickly, and some of it seems to come out of nowhere. People from the past often reappear, and invitations and opportunities for various occasions tend to arise. Many short trips are made. All kinds of unexpected conversations tend to spring up. The 19th Amendment was passed by congress on June 4, 1919, during Gemini season, giving voice to women who would soon be given the right to vote.

During this time of year, things can move too rapidly, and become overstimulating and chaotic. There can be a lot of agitation and social discord. There may be too much haste, too much cerebral stimulation or many activities and socializing and not enough rest in between. It's easy to get bogged down with the ideas, demands and the energy of others if one is not careful. With that in mind, the solution to such problems should be clear. Be sure not to promise more than you can deliver. It could prove problematic in the future to say yes to everything just because it sounds good in the moment. At this time, it becomes extra important to relax and unwind whenever needed.

Propaganda and gaslighting are two forms of attack that may be particularly noticeable during heavy transits through Gemini or involving Gemini's ruling planet Mercury in aspect to the outer planets Uranus, Neptune and Pluto. In actuality, it happens all year around through the media which targets the general population with information that is meant to constantly confuse and invalidate humanity's own understanding of the world they live in. Gaslighting is a term taken from the old black and white movie Gaslight, in which a house wife notices noises in the house and gaslights dimming for no noticeable reason when her husband is not home. Although he is behind this and other phenomena, he assures her that she must be imagining things, which ultimately leads to her suffering and apparent insanity. Saturn and Uranus happened to be transiting the sign of Gemini at the time of this movie's release, on May 4, 1944. Today this word is commonly used as a verb and used to define a form of psychological manipulation that slowly diminishes the confidence of the individual or group under attack. The person who attacks repeatedly chooses words that invalidate the experiences and feelings of the other, causing them to doubt their own sanity or even their precise memory of certain events. This type of behavior seems most common under heavy influence of any of the four mutable signs of Gemini, Virgo, Sagittarius and Pisces. I theorize that this is due to mutable signs bringing so much flexibility to various viewpoints, changeability in demeanor, quickness in letting go and dismissal of that which would cause great upset in cardinal and fixed signs.

If the majority of people are saying, displaying and doing the same things, such as changing the background of their online profile photo to being covered in red polka dots or blue stripes, it often means they are under a kind of media spell. They want to make sure others approve of their opinions, and to be seen as virtuous. They are being guided by a hidden agenda that they don't even remotely suspect because the subject matter on display appeals to their deepest emotions, fears and desires to be accepted. Meanwhile, those who are being done tremendous damage to are blamed for things that other people did to them.

Scandals are exposed. The types of attacks most commonly experienced during this season are verbal in nature. They come through the media. Lies, mind games and double-speak are profuse. Some of the things that occur during this time can come across as ridiculous. Others are intriguing. Here are a few examples:

- The grand opening day for cable cars in Los Angeles was on June 8, 1889. Gemini relates to city travel and small trips verses long voyages.[2]

- The world's first commercial electronic computer, the Univac 1 was introduced on June 14, 1951, in the United States. It was an elaborate piece of equipment with numerous knobs, lights and dials. Who knew how quickly computer technology would advance in the decades to come?

- The first publication of the Pentagon Papers by the New York Times occurred on June 13, 1971. These were a collection of top-secret documents exposing U.S. strategy in the Vietnam War. Information is something that becomes increasingly available during Gemini season, whether trivial or large-scale in nature.

- NASA's project "Gemini 4" was launched in Gemini season on June 3, 1964. There were two featured astronauts, James McDivitt and Ed White on this mission who are found in a "goofy looking" photograph together, giving off a symbolic representation of "The Twins". [3]

- Criminal charges were filed against whistleblower and former computer intelligence consultant Edward Snowden on June 14, 2013.

- On June 7, 2021, Vice President Kamala Harris handed out cookies in her likeness, only faceless, to Air Force Two reporters on her way to Guatemala. This odd, cryptic gift had many media reporters perplexed. The random nature of Gemini was in full effect.

Cancer Season – The Power of Nationhood and Location

The sign of Cancer is transited by the Sun between approximately June 21 and July 22. The Sun's entrance into Cancer in June marks the Summer Solstice in the Northern hemisphere where the sun reaches its highest position in the sky, producing the longest day of the year. On this day, and in the days just leading up to and after it, many peak psychic experiences may occur ranging from the ghostly to the ecstatic to the terrifying. In particular it may become easier to make contact with or be contacted by ethereal beings of the nature realm, such as the fairies and gnomes referred to in many cultures as the "Little People".

During the month of Cancer, finding safety and refuge become paramount issues on a collective level. The power of location, for better or worse, is something that becomes very pronounced. Due to the weather, people tend to take their vacations or get married during this time period. The whole world seems to become more sentimental, emotional, and quieter overall. The issues that spring up tend to involve family, loved ones and familiar places. There is a noticeable overhaul of outdated systems taking place as people look to improve the conditions of their environments. The Moon is Cancer's ruling planet and the famous yet much-debated Moon landing on July 20th, 1969, took place during Cancer season.

The sign of Cancer rules the bloodline and nationality. Its placement in your natal chart will tell you something about your feelings toward your ethnicity or place of birth. The United States and Canada are two of the world's largest and most influential nations who were legally "born" or gained their great status under the sign of Cancer. This explains why both are known to have sympathy for the underdog, but both get themselves into a lot of trouble by taking on too many responsibilities outside of their own country. Canada has the influence of Uranus in a conjunction with its Sun, which makes a huge difference in its Cancerian expressions. To other nations Canada's citizens may seem rather unorthodox as many of them are strong individualists and activists. America wants to take care of others but leaves much to be desired in taking care of its own land and people. The more material goods this country accumulates to quell its growing anxieties the more spiritually impoverished it seems to be. Its debt has grown into a bottomless pit. Both America and Canada are emotionally dominated nations.

In general, the major types of attacks that occur during Cancer season often relate to nationalism and homeland security. They also sometimes relate to the food industry and environmental issues.

- The July Crisis was a chain reaction of events among European powers in 1914 that are said to have led to World War I. The crisis began during Cancer season on June 28, 1914, and led to diplomatic and military escalations.

- World War I began on July 28, 2014, when Pluto was in the very early phases of its twenty-five-year transit through Cancer. The first war lasted until November 11, 1918. Shortly after this transit, Pluto entered Leo and World War II began. The Sun in Leo was moving into opposition with impactful Uranus. Mercury was just stationing Direct at the dreadful 18th degree in the sign of homeland focused Cancer, near the fixed star Wasat which is associated with destruction.

- The Russian Imperial Romanov family was brutally massacred in the basement of their own home, on July 17, 1918, by Bolshevik revolutionaries. This event was soon followed by the rise of communism in Russia.

- On July 18, 1936, Spanish troops began the revolt against the Republican government that led to the Spanish Civil War.

- The U.S Navy technical research ship USS Liberty was attacked by Israel on July 8, 1967. This occurred on the Sinai Peninsula in Egypt.

- On July 2, 2012, the pharmaceutical group GlaxoSmithKline pled guilty to promoting prescription drugs and failing to report safety information. There was a settlement of $3 billion for their criminal and civil violations. Cancer season tends to highlight safety concerns. Mars at 29 degrees of health-conscious Virgo was also "laying down the law" that day.

- On June 24, 2020, the pharmaceutical and biotechnology company Bayer agreed to pay $10.9 billion to settle lawsuits regarding the link between Roundup weedkiller and cases of cancer. This was after a very long and drawn-out series of disputes. Venus (which rules money) Retrograde was collecting her dues while stationing to turn direct.

- On July 6, 2022 a granite monument called the Georgia Guidestones was intentionally damaged by bombing, and subsequently dismantled that same day. The motives around this were not clear, and identity of the bomber was uncertain. This structure, sometimes referred to as the "American Stonehenge" had been unveiled at the Equinox of March 22, 1980, and over the years had become a source of great controversy. The monument contained a set of its own new version of the Ten Commandments that were intended to serve as a guide for coming humanity. One remarkable feature of this monument was a hole in the center column through which the North Star could be seen. The entire structure was also aligned with the Equinoxes and Solstices, and its four outer stones were oriented to mark the limits of the 18.6 lunar declination cycle. On the date of the bombing, the Sun was in Cancer (one of the cross-signs in the year) which highlights powerful locations. Explosive Mars had just entered into earthy Taurus at 0 degrees, quickly destroying all of the labor that went into the creation of this moment, while Jupiter was in the fire sign of Aries.

Leo Season – Laws Broken and Established

The Sun transits the sign of Leo between approximately July 21 to August 22. Every year when the Sun passes through the sign of Leo, people's passions in general run higher and they long for love or outlets for creative expression. This is an optimal time of year for performances and presentations of all kinds, as attention is more easily captivated than at other times. There are also more visible allies, and more strength available to meet various challenges.

Since Leo is a fire sign, tempers can flare up during the Sun's transit through it. Extreme pride and revenge are the dark side of Leo's fiery energy. Leo is a fire sign, which indicates events involving fire and explosives. This goes for all three of the fire signs.

- The convicted child sex offender Jeffrey Epstein was proclaimed dead during Leo season on August 10, 2019, apparently due to a suicide while in prison. This is the sign that relates both to sex as enjoyment and to children as offspring. The subject of Epstein's death has been a subject of debate and controversy ever since then, and many of his female victims have continued to speak out about his crimes.

- The founding of the CCP (Chinese Communist Party) occurred in Beijing on July 23, 1921. The result was the surveillance and dictatorship of millions.

- Operation Gomorrah is one of the most horrific yet least known historical events to have taken place in Europe. The first air raid bombing attack of Hamburg, Germany was on July 24, 1943, at around midnight. It is known to have killed 40,000 civilians and wounded approximately 180,000 more. The flames reached three miles high and fifteen hundred degrees Fahrenheit. The resultant overwhelming heat of burning asphalt caused countless people of all ages, as well as animals to burn to death and liquefy into black grease. Under the command of prime minister Winston Churchill of the UK and President Roosevelt of the US, the US and UK air forces dropped several surprise bombs over Hamburg and several other cities Germany when no one was prepared for what was coming. On the night of this first attack, the Sun in Leo was at the critical zero degree of Leo, conjunct Jupiter, Pluto (which rules bombs), and Mercury in Leo, while the North Node was also in Leo. These all formed a fixed square with Mars in Taurus, indicating the massive destruction and violence inflicted upon the German people. Neptune was at 29 degrees of crisis prone Virgo. This crime was justified by many by saying that all Germans were evil.[4]

- The first atomic bombs using Plutonium were used during World War II in the year 1945 when Pluto, the planet presiding over nuclear explosions, was in the early degrees of Leo.

- The atomic bombings of Hiroshima and Nagasaki occurred from August 6th to the 9th in 1945. The United States was responsible for detonating two nuclear weapons in these Japanese cities, instantly killing thousands of civilians. The Moon was conjunct Saturn at 18 degrees of Cancer. This degree was said by Nikola Stojanovic to be "diabolical". 18 degrees of Cancer specifically is the degree of the fixed star Wasat, having many malevolent connotations.

- The Berlin wall was established during Leo season, on August 13, 1961. The Communist government of the German Democratic Republic began to build a barbed wire and concrete between East and West Berlin. This was called *Antifascistischer Schutzwall* or antifascist bulwark.

- The Forsmark failure of Sweden took place during a New Moon in Leo on July 25, 2006. This event involved a short circuit in the electrical switchyard just outside of the Forsmark power plant, and several other issues that would lead to nuclear disaster if left unchecked. It was automatically shut down which prevented massive environmental shocks, although it raised a lot of fear.

- On August 8, 2023, the island of Maui broke out in a huge fire, killing over a hundred people and forcing thousands to evacuate the city of Lahaina. It was said to be the deadliest U.S. wildfire in more than a century, burning an estimated 2,170 acres of land. Tragically, the sirens that were designed for emergencies such as this were not even activated during the onset of this massive fire, but instead alerts were sent to people's cell phones, TVS, and radios, with the assumption that all residents had cell phones, TV, and internet service. Ironically, Hawaii had previously been known for having the largest system of outdoor alert sirens in the world after a tsunami that occurred in 1923.

- In mid-August of 2023, "Hurricane Hilary" born from the Southwest coast of Mexico began to violently sweep the Pacific Coast, resulting in flooding and mudslides in various regions. It was during a New Moon in Leo on the 16th of that month that the hurricane formed. This particular New Moon was in a square with Uranus in Taurus, which brought about many shocking events in general that week. Although hurricanes are more water element in nature than fiery, they move with great force causing so much damage in their paths. Brush fires were fanned by the furious winds, displacing many California residents.

Virgo Season - Chaos, Cures and Crisis-Staged Events

During the Sun's transit through Virgo from approximately August 23rd to September 22nd there is an overall sense of busyness, socializing and multi-tasking that seems to pervade in nature and human endeavors. It is a time for reaping the fruits of our labors, although there is still some work to be done. This work often entails purification, organization and making dietary changes. Some seeds that were planted previously in the year grow into fullness and much that was initiated comes into manifestation, both positive and negative.

Virgo season is one of those times of year when many key figures are placed in the public eye as a way of possibly distracting the masses from things taking place behind the scenes. With this sign, the "devil is in the details" which are often deliberately scrambled and intensified so that people are challenged in distinguishing the real from the unreal. Virgo season reveals fault-finding in many things, people and situations, which ultimately creates wider gaps and divisions, potentially weakens teamwork and generates panic.

In the United States of America, voting becomes a pressing issue as it gets closer to Election Day. Politicians suddenly have a lot more to say. There are apparently so many problems and things to address that some of the most important things underlying them are neglected. On the positive side it can bring people together toward a common goal, especially one that relates to health or finances.

- World War II began on September 1, 1939, and lasted for six years. Britain and France declared war on Germany during Virgo season, on September 3, 1939.

- The Soviet Union invaded Poland from the east on September 17, 1939, sixteen days after Germany's entry into Poland from the west. The Sun was in exact conjunction to Neptune, hiding the details of what had happened during and after the wars had occurred.

- The 9-11 World Trade Center Attacks occurred on September 11 of 2001. To this day there has not been a collective agreement as to what exactly took place in the collapse of the Twin Towers. Those who pull up details counter to the main narrative are automatically labeled as "conspiracy theorists." Coincidentally, on June 1st of 2001 a joint task counterterrorist and field training exercise was carried out in Tyndall Air Force Base in Florida. The name of this exercise was *Operation Amalgam Virgo*.

- The Occupy movement began September 17th of 2011 and into 2012. This was a socio-political movement of uprising against social and economic inequality around the world.

Libra Season - The Lull Before the Storm

The Sun transits Libra between approximately September 23rd and October 22nd and its entrance into this sign marks the beginning of a new season which is Autumn in the North, and Spring in the South, occurring six months from the first Equinox in the year. Since this is a turning point in the year, many large-scale ordeals tend to occur, but most of these do not become obvious until the Sun has entered the following sign of Scorpio. Such ordeals brew beneath the surface of things, people, and relationships, taking their toll inwardly or privately before becoming an outward expression. Mass manipulations are conducted through deceit, to be revealed later.

Whether an issue is centered on work, health or love, Libra season will turn it over on its side, upside down and toss it around to see what it's really made of. "Passing the test" will allow someone to graduate to the next level of whatever their troubled subject matter involves. A person may decide to keep their job or leave it with dignity and respect. They may honor their contracts or break them. They may discover the cure for their illness and apply it. If not, then things may progressively worsen.

Instead of the new beginnings associated with spring, Libra season generally tends to emphasize closures and releasing of things and ideas from the past. The negative aspects are that some might slip into depression or give up on their hopes and goals. There may be less vital energy to draw from and this makes some people more vulnerable to psychic attack. On a lighter note, people often become a bit more relaxed and willing to listen, or to take a step back and observe in order to learn and grow.

Over the years I have noticed a few mass fires that have taken place not only during Libra season, but when the Moon is passing through this sign. These are the types of fires spread by wind that create a lot of traveling smoke. One example of this was the Northern California fires in early October of 2017. I remember the very evening that they occurred, when I had just landed at San Francisco airport from Ireland. Even though the fires were almost a two-hour drive away from where I landed, the air was thick with the stench of burning rubber. This was not an ordinary forest fire. Entire neighborhoods were being swallowed in flames!

- The most devastating forest fire in American history was the Peshtigo fire in Wisconsin, which occurred on October 8, 1871. The number of deaths were estimated to be approximately 2,000 people. On that very same day, another fire, called the Great Chicago fire, occurred killing approximately 300 people. The Sun was 15 degrees of Libra that day, and Uranus, planet of sudden upsets and reversals was at the critical degree of zero in the sign of fiery Leo.

- The Kyshtym nuclear explosion occurred during Libra season, on September 29, 1957. This is regarded as one of the top three worse nuclear disasters in history, in addition to Fukushima and Chernobyl. The explosion took place at a secret plant that was producing atomic weapons.

- On October 2, 2013, Chinese president Xi Jinping officially announced the launch of the Belt and Road Initiative in a speech he gave in Jakarta, Indonesia. About a month prior, on September 7th, he had given a speech describing his plans, in Kazakhstan University in Russia. It was during Libra season that the initiative took hold and became more publicized. This belt and road, also known as the maritime silk road, has been a route for China to pass through Russia and Europe for the purpose of easier and more widespread infrastructure strategy that is intended to eventually reach every part of the world. The initiative was presented in a manner that would be perceived as peaceful, tactful, very Libran, with a "win-win" incentive. The end-goal is a Eurasian super state that would eventually push everyone into smart cities. As the road expands and lengthens, there are many countries struggling to become free of debt, with the fear of being overrun by China's influences. In addition, the road has paved the way for more installations of 5G+ technology, which continues to increase the amount of human and animal exposure to EMF. The Belt and Road Initiative is supported by the United Nations.

- *Event 201* was conducted in New York on October 18, 2019. The CHS (John Hopkins Center for Health Security) partnered with the World Economic Forum and the Bill and Melinda Gates Foundation to host this pandemic tabletop exercise in New York City. The event was designed to simulate the effects and responses to a severe pandemic. Those who took part in this exercise reject the notion that it had anything to do with the pandemic that took place immediately after it, with the first outbreak making headlines in Wuhan, China. Mercury was 18 degrees of Scorpio, dealing with hidden operations.

Scorpio Season – Poisons, Power Trips and Purification

The most infamous season of all is that of Scorpio season, taking place between October 21 and November 21. Just like those born under this sign are often looked upon with suspicion, this time of year has a bad rap in general. The U.S. Elections that occur in November have many times been the cause of mass hysteria and anxiety.

Halloween occurs on October 31 during Scorpio season, when the veil between the worlds becomes thin. This day celebrates souls who have crossed over to the other side of existence. Due to thinning veils and ghostly encounters, people also become more vulnerable to vampiric entities both human and non-human. It is during this time and season that many of us require heavy duty protection methods to remove sticky and stubborn energy, parasites, and leeches from our personal space. When either the Sun or Moon transits through Scorpio there may be more cases of sexual abuse and misconduct than usual, but sometimes they are brought to light rather for the purpose of reparation, class action lawsuits or imprisonment.

Preparation for what may come may be key to successfully overcoming it. For example, one may expect that there will be a certain amount of fearmongering by the media. In that case, staying informed of what's going on but keeping one's own council can be an effective method of maintaining energetic integrity. People might knowingly or unknowingly try to draw you into their webs of fear and intrigue. Resist the temptation to engage in their subconscious games. Keep your salt lamps on and light a white candle or two. Amethyst can be a great source of psychic protection and can be helpful placed next to a bedside to help protect you from psychic intrusions and nightmares while you sleep. Remember to say your prayers or a mantra that helps to elevate your mind and spirits. This is often the time of year when people's immunity begins to lower so it can help to take immune-boosting herbs, avoid excess sugar and eat foods that are very nourishing and grounding.

- Red October, also known as the October Revolution, began on November 7, 1917, and lasted until 1923 in Russia. It was also known as the Bolshevik Revolution led by Vladimir Lenin and was a precipitating event of the Russian Civil War. This was the mark of the Bolshevik's rise to power in establishing the Soviet Empire. This occurred at 15 degrees in the middle of the sign of Scorpio, the tail end of a stretch of the zodiac that has been called Via Combusta[4] (the "burning way" in Latin), which lies between 15 degrees of Libra and 15 degrees of Scorpio. These degrees were long considered to be highly malefic in their influences due to the presence of certain fixed stars. Many astrologers still take Via Combusta into consideration as it relates to misfortune or notable occurrences.

- The Vietnam War began on November 1, 1955, and ended in Scorpio's polar opposite Taurus season on April 30, 1975. What had started as an anti-colonial war against the French became an extremely long and costly war involving the communist government of North Vietnam against South Vietnam which had partnered with the United States.

- The Berlin Wall stood until one Scorpio season, on November 9, 1989, when the East German Communist Party announced that citizens of the GD could cross the border whenever they pleased. That same night the walls were swarmed by crowds. Some of them crossed into West Berlin and others chipped away at the wall with hammers. The remainder of the Wall serves as a reminder of the Cold War. This is one example of how Scorpio's influence can remove things that no longer belong in our lives.

- The assassination of John F. Kennedy occurred on November 22, 1963, at 12:30 pm in Dallas, Texas when the Sun was at the very end of very last degree of Scorpio, which is the sign of death. The 29th degree is significant in astrology, known as the anaretic degree, and as such on this day it signaled a major culmination that would become the subject of intrigue and speculation for decades.

- The Yellow Vest Movement began in France during Scorpio season, on November 17, 2018. It consisted of weekly grassroots protests in favor of economic justice in the face of encroaching government policies. The movement grew as a result of the rise in crude oil prices, Austerity measures, fuel taxes and forced immigration.

- The Patriot Act was signed into being by U.S. President George W. Bush on October 26, 2001. Initially a reaction to the attack on the World Trade Center buildings, the "War on Terror" (and the many new laws that came with it) have become an intrusive, prying and "paranoid" government program that spans throughout the United States and beyond, rendering every citizen a potential terrorist until proven innocent.

Sagittarius Season – Dreams, Schemes and Setting Sail into the Unknown

The Sun passes through the sign of Sagittarius between November 22nd and December 21st. This time of year is considered to be mid to late fall in the Northern regions, as trees begin shedding their colorful leaves and the temperature cools considerably. For such a vital Sun sign, it would seem fitting that most people are vital and well during the period of its transit but quite the opposite is often true. Those born under it may be strong and vital, but others who come under its influence are often challenged by its influences. I think maybe this has something to do with the manner in which those in Western society indulge themselves on so much unhealthy food at this time of year. Part of the problem could be due to the mutable nature of the sign, which is unpredictable in nature. People are torn in different directions, scattering their energies.

This time marks both the peak of the frenzied "holiday season" when many people come down with common cold or flu symptoms that seem to easily take hold when the weather gets cold and dark and people are under a great deal of stress, especially related to family matters.

Freedom is the battle cry of Sagittarius, who refuses to be pinned down in any way. Here are a few examples of historical events that occurred during the Sun's transit through this sign. It seems that during this time many fiery arrows of attack fly out of nowhere. In cases of opposing Communism people were reclaiming their sovereign rights. Many attacks during this season involve international affairs. Some of the attacks highlighted during this time of year involve the internet.

- On December 4, 1872, the seaman John Johnson of the Dei Gratia ship spotted a vessel adrift off the islands of Portugal with only three sails set. The ship, called Mary Celeste, was abandoned with signs of minimal damage, containing a six-month supply of food. No one could figure out what had happened to the crew.

- On November 25, 1936, Nazi Germany and Imperial Japan signed the Anti-Comintern Pact in an agreement to collaborate in opposing the spread of Communism.

- On November 30, 1939, Soviet troops launched a series of assaults on Finnish territory. This was called the Winter War. Although initially the Finns put up great resistance, they were too few in numbers to defeat the Soviets. In 1949 they wound up ceding 11 percent of their territory to the Soviet Union.

- The attack of the U.S. Naval base at Pearl Harbor occurred on December 7, 1941. The next day, the U.S. and Britain declared war on Japan. On December 9, 1941, China issued a formal declaration of war against Japan, Germany and Italy. Japan invaded and seized control of Hong Kong on December 18, 1941.

- The Battle of Changjin, in connection with the Korean war, turned out to be one of the most unusual and shocking battles in all of history. It took place after the People's Republic of China entered the conflict and infiltrated the northeastern part of North

Korea. On November 27, 1950, a blizzard fell, and the temperature dropped to extremes. The battle lasted for 17 days, ending on December 13th. Over a hundred soldiers died, not of gunshot wounds but of frostbite. It has been said they were literally frozen into ice sculptures. Sagittarius season can sometimes bring us in touch with aspects of nature that were previously unfathomable. When the battle began, Saturn had just ingressed into Libra at 0 degrees, while Sagittarius' ruling planet Jupiter was 29 degrees of Aquarius, the coldest sign of the zodiac. Mars was 15 degrees of Capricorn, accentuating the severity of environmental conditions. The Moon was in Aquarius, approaching a very cold degree (15 degrees) when the battle ended. An unforgettable impression had been made.

- On November 29, 1989, forty-one years of Communist rule came to an end in Czechoslovakia. This followed a twelve-day revolution that was sparked by the beating of protesters.

Capricorn Season – A Turn of the Wheel and Currency

Capricorn season begins on approximately December 21 and lasts until approximately January 19. Capricorn, being ruled by Saturn, brings an attitude of seriousness to interactions and endeavors. Suddenly, many become more goal-oriented and aware of their finances. Work becomes a priority and travel is often centered around business. In many cases this is true even if a trip is for some kind of vacation. The world of trade and commerce takes center stage. The monetary system becomes a highlight, and it is during this time that significant changes can be observed in the stock market.

Although December 25 is celebrated as Christmas and January 1 as the first day of the New Year, these are two days of the year when the energy is often the heaviest on a collective level. Both occur during Capricorn season, when the forces of nature in the Northern hemisphere tend to be at their most severe. Capricorn's ruler, Saturn, is also the bringer of fate, and of death. Death may come into prominence during this time.

- The Battle of New Orleans occurred on January 8, 1815, between British and US armies, with General Andrew Jackson and American troops defending themselves against a British attack. There were over 2,000 casualties recorded. Tragically, participants in the battle were unaware that peace had been declared two weeks prior, with the Treaty of Ghent, to end the War of 1812.

- The Coal Industry Nationalisation Act was enacted on January 1, 1946, by the Parliament of the United Kingdom. This act was to establish public ownership and control of the coal-mining industry and certain allied activities.

- The Third Battle of Seoul took place between December 30, 1950 and January 7,

1951 in South Korea, both beginning and ending during Capricorn season. Communist forces attacked and took control of the city.

- On January 1, 1999, eleven European nations began using a new single European currency. The Euro was launched, and in the beginning only used for electronic payments and business purposes. Coins and banknotes were launched on January 1, 2002. Many people were very unhappy with their change in currency, which literally left them feeling shortchanged.

- During Capricorn season health becomes a struggle for many, especially in the Northern hemisphere where temperatures drop. Outbreaks of the Coronavirus (Covid-19) were first reported in late December of 2019 in Wuhan, China, coincidentally just after 5G (fifth generation of telecommunication) was installed there. It seems like an uncanny coincidence that is worth investigating.

- An attack on the United States capitol occurred on January 6, 2021, that led to a lot of controversy. The chaotic scene followed the defeat of President Donald Trump in the 2020 election. A mob of his supposed supporters attacked the White House in Washington D.C. in defense of their former president Trump. Some people suspect that these people were paid actors and part of a controlled opposition ploy. Many people were said to have been injured including police officers. The riot mob was linked with the group known as Q-Anon and among the rioters was a man known as the Q-Anon Shaman, wearing horns and a painted face with patriotic colors and symbols. The Sun was at the critical 15th degree of Capricorn, heightening government-related drama. That very day Mars was making its exit from Aries and entering into the sign of Taurus, the Bull. Many astrologers noticed that this made for an odd parallel with the guy wearing those large horns.

Aquarius Season – Technological Advancements and Massive Attacks

Aquarius season occurs between January 20 and February 18. For many cultures this is when the New Year actually begins. There is a focus on coming out into the open after a period of withdrawal, large-scale social events and interacting with others. Aquarius is ruled by Uranus which in turn rules technology, and not surprisingly it is during this time of year that many types of technical experiments have been conducted on humans and animals, often without their knowledge or consent.

Explosive events can occur at this time that seem to come out of nowhere. These events may involve electronics, or they may involve warfare.

- The Bombing of Dresden occurred between February 13th to 15th in 1945. British and American aircraft bombed the German city of Dresden, killing an estimated 25,000 – 30,000 people. The incendiary devices used caused huge firestorms that destroyed much of the city.[5]

- DARPA (Defense Advanced Research Projects Agency), an agency responsible for the developing of technologies used by the military was founded on February 7th, 1958, by Dwight Eisenhower. It was DARPA that gave rise to the digital protocols that eventually led to the creation of the Internet. The problem of excess EMF and radiation from 5G cell-towers, the Fukushima nuclear disaster, and wide use of smart devices has reportedly led to a multitude of health complications in the modern world.

- The Irish massacre known as Bloody Sunday occurred on January 30, 1972. British soldiers shot twenty-six unarmed civilians during a protest march in Derry of Northern Ireland. Fourteen of these people died and others were injured. All of them were Catholics. The purpose of the protest was against imprisonment without trial. A group of people (Aquarius rules groups as well as activism and protests) were attacked for voicing their human rights. Mars was in Aries, which is a sign that relates to bloodshed and military attacks.

- The very first scientific handheld calculator, called the HP-35 (by Hewlett-Packard) was released on February 1, 1972. It sold for $395.00.

- Coinciding with the spring equinox, on March 21, 2020, the planet Saturn, associated with tests, limitations and fear entered into the sign of Aquarius, associated with groups and humanity at large. Quarantines were mandated in the USA, soon followed by quarantines in several other parts of the world. For the following two years social distancing was enforced in most major cities. Many people lost or quit their jobs, and some chose to work at home via the internet.

Pisces Season – Leaks, Spills and the Collective Sea of Consciousness

The Sun transits Pisces between February 19 and March 20 of the year. During this time the Piscean themes escalate and there is a sort of glamour in the air, which is great for creative endeavors. Negatively, it is common to witness the sweeping effects of mass deceptions, addictive habits, the phenomena of thinning boundaries and contagion. When any of the so-called outer planets transit this sign, the effects are even more noticeable on a collective level.

Have you ever noticed how a couple of days before getting sick you began to feel heavy or depressed, or simply didn't feel like your normal self? You might not have even been aware that you were coming down with a sickness, likely due to accumulated stress and toxic overload. This is very common, and most people don't put together the reason why they are feeling so low on energy until they've already become symptomatic. Many types of illness operate in an insidious way, invisible to the naked eye. Covid-19 was declared a "global pandemic" by the World Health Organization on March 11th, 2020, during Pisces season.

- The first stock market crash of the United States occurred in early March of the year 1792. It was known as a central bank crisis that occurred just following the new taxation policies in the US Congress that were granted to pay off debts in 1787-1789. This all caused a great stir in the financial systems.

- The first documented case of the Spanish flu was in March of 1918

- On March 5, 1946, Winston Churchill warned of an "iron curtain" descending across Europe. His speech on that day came to be known as an incitement for the Cold War.

- March 20, 1995, the highly toxic nerve gas sarin was released in a subway in Tokyo, Japan by terrorists. The attack resulted in the deaths of twelve or more people and the injury of thousands. Pisces rules gases.

- Fukushima nuclear disaster March 11th, 2011. This was a massive disaster triggered by an earthquake and tsunami in Japan. This was during Pisces season, the day before Uranus transited from Pisces to Aries. Uranus is the planet of major shocks, reversals, electrical energy and explosions and it was shifting from watery Pisces to fiery Aries where it would be entering into a cataclysmic square with Pluto that lasted approximately between 2012 and 2015. Huge amounts of water contaminated with radioactive isotopes were released into the Pacific Ocean after the power plant explosion.

- On March 16, 2016, the bust of the "world's largest internet pedophile ring" was announced from the Netherlands. This was during the waning square between Uranus (ruling the internet) and Pluto, still ripping the lids off of corrupt power structures.

- Russia engaged in a full-scale invasion of Ukraine on February 24, 2022. Although war is more of an Arian theme, this particular war has carried a lot of confusion, intrigue and controlled opposition around it, which are all Neptunian in nature (Neptune has been given rulership over Pisces). This war was actually an escalation of a conflict and that began on February 20, 2014. The fact that many nations have relied upon Russia's supply of oil and gas is relative to the sign of Pisces, as are nuclear explosions and widespread unrest. In April of 2022, a Russian warship was said to sink after being shot by Ukrainian missiles. This event occurred during a conjunction between Jupiter and Neptune in the sign of Pisces. It was reported that the weapons used to sink the ship were the aptly named "Neptune" cruise missiles. All of these details considered, this was the kind of event to cause people to scratch their heads and wonder more.

General References:

https://www.historyplace.com/

https://militaryhistorynow.com/

https://www.history.com/

Endnotes

1. Information on degrees can be found in the book *The Degrees Theory*, [Nikola Stojanovic, The Degrees Theory (Novi Sad: Nine Horses Journey, 2018)]

2. https://calisphere.org/item/0f98937a2ba3f312dc678e9d81e63143/

3. https://en.wikipedia.org/wiki/Gemini_4

4. Sepharial's New Dictionary of Astrology, by Sepharial. Galahad Books, 1963.

5. The book *Hellstorm* by Thomas Goodrich contains eyewitness accounts [Thomas Goodrich, *Hellstorm: The Death of Nazi Germany, 1944-1947* (Sheridan, CO: Aberdeen Books, 2010)]

Conclusion

In adapting to a rapidly shifting paradigm, it has become highly challenging to maintain a sense of personal integrity despite the inundation of both degeneracy and general negativity that permeate popular culture. The ability to do so is to "hold on to our humanity" so to speak, in an age where the inherently natural roles of humans appear to be systematically replaced by robots, clones, and highly influential narcissists. Rotten behavior seems to be the most rewarded across the board while acts of virtue are frequently punished as though vices. Therefore, it is no easy feat to remain civil in a society where terrible experiences either accumulate or escalate over time.

After I had written this book, another war began to erupt in the Middle East, relative to a war that has actually been going on for centuries in that area. Although there were astrological influences leading up to this explosive series of events, it seems as though there is never a long stretch of time where there is not some huge conflict occurring, affecting not only targeted groups, but the masses in some way or another. Understanding the cycles that affect the collective can be helpful in dealing with issues that arise, but we still must put in the work to build our vitality and preserve our own sanity. There are certain challenges that are very unique to us as individuals, and others that are universal in nature. Astrology is the map, but we must still navigate our own ships through the storms of life.

To remain objective despite whatever happens to be going on around us is so much easier than it sounds. It requires discipline, including what may be termed a form of mental martial arts that hones our intuitive faculties to see through deceit, and to disengage from all that we have been tricked into to relying upon for our every seeming need, as well as entertainment. With maturity comes the recognition of our responsibility and impact in the world. We reject participation in sensational media, gossip, and petty smear campaigns. Energy is instead directed toward meaningful activities and relationships, or self-defense when that is necessary. Rather than random people being bullied for inconsequential matters such as their views, the real criminals are exposed and held accountable for their actions. True spiritual warriors only go to war when they need to, and they never waste time picking fights just because their ego is bruised or their anger is aroused. Acts of charity, as with notable accomplishments, tend to speak for themselves and are not mere props designed for public social media posts.

Those who can manage to escape from the monstrously addictive programming that promises to slake every ounce of boredom that might be experienced without its glamorous aid will gain something far more significant, powerful and long-lasting, that nothing or no one can take away. That is the gift of self; in this case meaning a state of being that brings conscious awareness of one's connection to the infinite creator, allowing the gates to limitless creativity and abundance to open themselves up effortlessly. Life becomes a magical adventure, and rather than being strung along in endless, artificial challenges that have been cunningly orchestrated for us cradle-to-grave by power hungry psychopaths, we fight our own demons, overcome our own obstacles, cry our own tears, and travel a heroic journey. We rejoice in our victories and in so doing, uplift those around us who are scarred and weary from battle.

If this sounds like a tall order, that is mainly because most of us have been taught to suppress our gut instincts. Also, what we can take from Stoic and Buddhist philosophies is how to make the best of what we know and have, thus growing more enlightened overall. Instead of chasing after fleeting moments of happiness that repeatedly leave us disappointed, we experience a quiet, yet genuine undertone of joy that remains constant with us throughout life.

If you've read through every chapter, by now you may have learned how to more quickly spot crazy-makers, or recover from abusive relationships with individuals, groups, and worldly trends, all of which are too easy to lose oneself in these days. You might have gained insight into spiritual antagonism, or identified the causes of certain paranormal experiences, all relative to the positions of the heavenly bodies above us. Perhaps you have discovered how to empower yourself based on the knowledge of your planetary placements. This is psychic self-defense as it relates to the zodiac.

Appendix

Quizzes for Psychic Self-Evaluation

There are many indications of psychic ability that may be hinted at in a natal chart. Common factors include accents in any of the three water signs and houses, and any major aspects between either of the two major luminaries and the planets Jupiter, Uranus, Neptune and Pluto. These planets are especially pronounced when they are found on any of the four angles.

When it comes to psychic indicators in the natal chart, it's not as simple as something like being a Scorpio or having the Sun conjunct Neptune. These factors may or may not manifest in psychic abilities as most of us define them. They bring about very different sorts of results in different people. Whole charts should be taken into consideration. Check for multiple testimonies - the more of them there are the better. The strength and number of aspects between "psychic planets", "psychic signs" and "psychic houses" can increase the likelihood of psychic ability being utilized.

Examples include having a water sign Ascendant, the Moon in a water sign or house (especially in house eight or twelve), strong aspects between the Moon and Uranus, Neptune or Pluto, Jupiter in a water sign or house, and any strong emphasis in house eight or twelve. For special abilities related specifically to astrology, look for a prominent Jupiter or Uranus, strong placements that emphasize house nine or twelve, and strong aspects between the Moon and Uranus.

A psychic person with the Earth element pronounced in their chart experiences the energy of a thing, entity or place in a physical way. They see, smell, taste and experience sensations of a spiritual nature that are as real to them as anything that is tangible. Water psychics react more emotionally to energy and tend to take on the feelings of a place, entity or person nearby. Air element psychics process their perceptions on a mental level, analyzing what they hear and sense in order to translate it to others. They can easily detach themselves from their observations. Fire psychics are quick to perceive, and they do not necessarily experience related emotions or prolonged thoughts regarding their perceptions. Both Air and Fire psychics are often capable of shifting the energy of a space with their intentions, while Earth and Water psychics tend to sponge up the energy of their environment.

All signs possess their own particular sets of psychic skills, and their various methods tend to be expressed through the element that they are ruled by. Here is just a quick guide to how certain psychic abilities may be emphasized according to the elements.

Fire signs:

- Claircognizance – ability to know without prior knowledge
- Clairsentience – ability to sense on multiple levels

- Pyrokinesis – ability to manipulate fire with intentions
- Telekinesis – ability to move objects with intentions

Earth signs:

- Clairalience – ability to sense spiritual energy through smell
- Clairgustance – ability to sense spiritual energy through taste
- Clairtangency – ability to sense energy through touch
- Synesthesia – ability to connect psychic sounds with sights and vice versa

Air signs:

- Clairaudience – ability to hear beyond ordinary human perception
- Telepathy – ability to read minds and communicate on the psychic level
- Precognition – ability to predict future events
- Prophecy – ability to see into major world events (Water and Air signs often share this ability)

Water signs:

- Clairvoyance – ability to see spirits, auras and spiritual energies
- Empathy – ability to sense and feel others' emotions
- Mediumship – ability to communicate with spirits
- Retrocognition – ability to see into the past

How Psychic are You?

Here are a few questions to help you to figure out your level of psychic ability, if you have any doubts.

Number scale:

- 0 – Does not apply
- 1 – Seldom
- 2 – Sometimes
- 3 – Often
- 4 – Always

___My dreams are sometimes filled with images, words or happenings that bear very close relevance to occurrences that take place the following day.

___I receive strong visual, auditory, emotional, or physical impressions through each person I meet and each new place that I enter. My impressions give me additional information about things that are not evident on the surface.

___I have had physical symptoms along with a strong emotional uneasiness with no known cause before something bad happened, such as a misfortune that affected my entire family, neighborhood, or city. In other cases I woke up and just knew it was going to be a fantastic day, and sure enough it was.

___Many people have validated things that I told them would happen for them later down the line. I accurately predicted their outcomes in myriad situations.

___In old spaces or in the presence of very old jewelry, furniture or other items, I get strong impressions of what and who occupied them previously. I can feel or picture the lives that they lived.

___I get these random sensations like someone is touching me, usually on the face, arm or shoulder. This seems to coincide with the sense that I am not alone, or someone is trying to contact me from afar.

___I know when someone is lying to me because multiple things begin to fire off in my mind or surroundings that indicate something isn't right. My hunches in these situations have proven right.

___I often see orbs of light and other non-physical moving shapes that other people do not see. Some of these take recognizable forms, such as human ghosts.

___Just as our other human senses can become overwhelmed and overstimulated, I have experienced times when my sixth sense was so overworked that I felt exhausted from all that I was perceiving on invisible levels.

___I can sense what another person is feeling or thinking overall even when they are not saying anything. When they finally speak, it usually confirms what I thought was on their mind.

___I have visited a place that felt very familiar to me and brought up memories of experiences that I never had in my current life.

___Sometimes I have smelled things in the air that were in no way physically present. The smell reminded me of a certain person or thing, whether good or bad.

___Electrical appliances often malfunction or act strangely around me, especially when I'm excited. My computer, phone or other electronic devices experience more glitches than most people that I know. Light bulbs may also flicker frequently or burn out rapidly in my presence.

Score Key

38-52

You are highly psychic in many ways and most likely already had some prior knowledge of your abilities. You were born with these abilities even if something else heightened them later in life. Most children are born psychic and become less so the older they get due to conditioning. In your case, you only become more skillfully psychic over time. Other people have acknowledged this in some way, because of your being able to validate their experiences, warn them of danger or help them make wiser choices. Whether or not you choose to put your gifts toward a particular vocation is another subject.

24-37

You have certain psychic abilities that are more noticeable or activated at certain times than others. You might not always understand why you are having these impressions or why strange things are happening to you, but over time they begin to make more sense. You can further develop your psychic gifts if you so desire. You will probably find that certain methods of psychic work come more naturally to you than others.

0-10

You may not be particularly psychic, but you still have intuitive flashes about things now and then. You lean on your intellect and your instincts rather than inexplicable hunches about things. You basically prefer to stick with what you know rather than go exploring the hidden side of life, unless your interest is set upon a subject such as psychology or archeology. It is also possible that you are psychic but not allowing yourself to have psychic experiences because they make you uncomfortable. There is nothing wrong with that. This can be a personal choice.

Are You Under Psychic Attack?

It is difficult for most people to be fully objective with themselves when they are under a lot of stress because emotions color the perspective regarding whatever may be taking place. At some point we have each been blamed for something we didn't do, have been projected at and have experienced others being nasty toward us for no justifiable reason. We have all experienced a dark night of the soul. Some of us have feared we would be destroyed by it.

Many astrological factors can validate a person's experience of being heavily impacted by challenging influences. There are a few things to be aware of and to look out for if you suspect that you are under psychic attack. Attacks can commonly be traced to transits involving Mars, Saturn,

Neptune or Pluto. They also tend to involve houses eight and twelve in the natal chart, by birth or triggered by transits. A person might even be the cause of their own suffering, and struggle with severe depression as a result of subconscious patterns that are very difficult to break.

The Moon's placement by birth is a very important thing to consider when psychic disturbance is prevalent in a person's life. The sign alone will not indicate this, not even in its detriment or fall. There are many factors that can debilitate the Moon and make one vulnerable to many types of interference, both physical and spiritual. This problem can be solved but is typically not a quick fix unless the person in question is still a very young child. The Moon's energy imprints itself upon each of us from the moment we are born and continues to exert a strong influence until we have grown into adulthood or maturity which everyone arrives at differently.

The quiz below is meant to help someone better discern whether or not they are truly under psychic attack. If you are taking these quizzes, be very honest with your answers to get any use out of them. They need not be shared with anyone else unless you score high and choose to seek counsel and assistance with your issue.

Number scale

0 – Does not apply

1 – Seldom

2 – Sometimes

3 – Often

4 – Always

___I often feel drained after being around other people.

___Nightmares cause me to wake up and are so exhausting I feel as though I barely sleep. In them I am being attacked or chased by monsters, or I see them hovering beside me when I am awake.

___I frequently get disoriented for no apparent reason, and then my senses return to normal.

___I have not been diagnosed with any serious health problems and yet I frequently feel lethargic and debilitated.

___There is at least one person in my life that I don't owe anything to but feel obligated to give time and energy to even though they give nothing of equal value in return.

___Sometimes I get a sudden pressure on my chest that weighs me down. At the same time, I feel emotionally heavy without knowing why.

___Every time I am about to overcome a major life challenge, despite my best efforts, something beyond my control throws me right back where I started. I feel thwarted.

___I feel like sometimes I am suddenly not myself at all but someone else is inhabiting my body. It also sometimes feels like I'm literally beside myself, having been pushed out of my own body. Other times I feel that I am above myself, looking down, disengaged.

___Random scratches or bruises appear on my body, and disappear just as quickly as they came. Or, physical symptoms with no known medical cause rapidly come and go, leaving me very disconcerted.

___I keep meeting people who insist on helping me in some way but instead they always seem to make things worse.

___I can't shake off this feeling that people are not being honest with me. Someone close to me is lying. At the same time, it's hard to trust my own intuition about people. Am I crazy?

___I have recurring flashes of dark thoughts and violent images that make me feel like I'm spinning out of control.

___I am having a string of bad luck and cannot figure out why this is happening.

Score key

38-52

It is highly probable that you are under severe psychic attack by either a person or non-physical entities, or both. Something most likely happened to you at a young age that weakened your boundaries and made it difficult for you to stand up for yourself. The first step to healing is recognizing where you have been hurt and having compassion for yourself. The second step is to put your foot down and refuse to accept psychic vampirism in your life in any way, shape or form. Check your living arrangements and either make changes or relocate if necessary. Make a conscious choice to rid yourself of negative influences and self-talk that you might be engaged in. Remove and/or avoid all recreational drugs and alcohol. Seek professional help if you need it. Take extra good care of yourself and make this your top priority until you have seen the desired changes in your life.

24-37

You may be experiencing a temporary setback that includes mental instability or psychic attack. You might have been surrounded by certain negative influences and are experiencing the results. As soon as you pull yourself away from them you tend to immediately begin to recover. Any existing health issues may or may not be related to psychic phenomena. Seek medical help if you suspect a chemical imbalance. You may benefit from purifying the energy of your home with sacred herbs or stones, and taking all of the necessary precautions when it comes to psychic exposure and activity. Practicing daily visualizations for self-empowerment could also be helpful. Gold is a protective color and metal that you can incorporate.

0-10

You have strong psychic immunity. Paranormal problems are not regular occurrences for you. You are grounded in earthly reality for the most part and are probably in good health overall, and if not, there are obvious causes for your ailments. You have a buoyant disposition overall and are not prone to superstitions, even if occasionally curious and interested in the supernatural. Others' bad vibes just bounce off of you and don't stick. After encountering them you simply go on with your life as before.

Are You Subconsciously or Consciously Attacking Others?

It seems to be widely agreed upon that most people don't like to think of themselves as being the villain in any scenario. It's always easier to point a finger at someone else than to take responsibility for things that go wrong in our lives or in the lives of others. Everyone has their moments of being short-tempered, but that doesn't make them bad people. When meanness, using and abusing others becomes a way of life, then it becomes a major problem.

Some argue that some signs are more evil than others, and certain stars have long been known to have evil influences. There are many clues that can point toward domineering, parasitic or cruel tendencies. In the modern age it has become too easy to take these ideas and run with them, even when the total assessment is off base. There are countless short and superficial articles claiming to categorize signs and other astrological factors according to their merits. Jumping to conclusions based on stereotypes is lazy and all too common. For a clear and objective analysis, the total picture should always be taken into consideration. This is something that experienced astrologers should be able to understand and accomplish.-

In the rare event that someone who is attacking others on a regular basis decides to come clean and change their ways, I have provided the following quiz for reflective purposes.

Number scale

0 – Does not apply

1 – Seldom

2 – Sometimes

3 – Often

4 – Always

___Other people always know when I am having a problem because I immediately vocalize or demonstrate it.

___In conversations I enjoy speaking so much that I hardly remember what the other person said.

___Given the opportunity, I tell others, in detail, about how miserable I feel and all of the bad things going on in my life. Their "helpful" advice to me is only annoying.

___I use every chance I get to gossip about others because it takes my mind off my own issues.

___I frequently think about people who make me very angry, and I would like to see them suffer.

___I am often jealous of my friends who are well off instead of happy for them.

___When someone says no to my requests, I get very annoyed at them.

___When I'm upset with people, I talk behind their back rather than confront them directly with what's bothering me.

___I often call people funny names and make derogatory remarks about them. I expect they will understand my jokes instead of getting offended. Otherwise, they have issues.

___I do what I want, whenever I want, conditions around me be damned. I tend to make good excuses for my mistakes.

___I believe that it's my job to take people down a notch when they have become too popular, well-liked, successful, etc. Somebody's got to do it and it might as well be me.

___I make it a point to prop myself up in social settings, no matter who is ignored or affected in the process. People should know about my achievements whether or not they have inquired about them.

___I do many great things for people and am extremely generous so that they will owe me and be there for me when I need them. They will also tolerate me at my worst.

Score key

38-52

You have got a major attitude problem, and everyone who knows you knows it. If you're not basically alone in life, it's because you push your way into others' space when you're unwanted. That's the only way you know how to receive the attention that you crave. For far too long you have been trying to make other people do your own dirty work for you. You blame others for your own failures and your own unhappiness. If you want real love, then learn how to become more loving. Your actions have ripple effects, and you have a choice to make about how you wish to make your mark in the world. Nobody can change it but you.

24-37

You could be on a negativity spree lately due to high amounts of stress. Maybe people have been pushing your buttons and bringing out the worst in you. You are probably unhappy with who you think you've become and want to go back to normal. Take a deep breath, and realize that this too shall pass. There is a better way to cope with challenges and in each new moment there is an opportunity to shift gears. Remember who loves you, who is counting on you and who is being affected by your behavior the most. If you want to keep your loved ones in your life, you will stop pushing them away and start by becoming more appreciative today.

0-10

You are basically a positive person by nature. Though you may have an occasional outburst or in the past have acted out of accordance with your own moral standards you have genuine respect for both others and yourself. You are aware of your effects on others and aim to harmonize with them. You are conscious of your mistakes, and you seek to learn from them, because that is how we as humans grow spiritually. You are choosing to make the best of your life, whatever your conditions may be

Angels, Demons and Spirits of the Elements

The following correspondences are based on the characteristics and archetypal energy of each spirit. They are not necessarily limited to specific categories. Those with a predominance of a certain element in their natal chart often experience an affinity with the spiritual beings associated with it. However, spirits are not limited to elements in the way that we typically perceive them to be.

Paracelsus described a set of spirits that fell into four distinct categories relative to the four elements. They were literally named the "elementals", and each were said to serve various functions. He named the fire spirits Salamanders, earth spirits Gnomes, air spirits Sylphs, and water spirits Undines. Since then, many authors over time have continued to attribute spirits to the elements as a way of trying to create order, or as a way to gain control over them. These elementals have long been invoked in ceremonial magic. Here, the spirits are categorized loosely, knowing that they will not be bound by human reason or rules. Some of the beings listed below are benign, some neutral, and others being quite malignant should be regarded with utmost caution, preferably avoided at all costs.

Times that spirit beings are most likely to appear to a larger percentage of humans include the Equinoxes and Solstices, their cross-quarter days, during eclipses, at dusk and at dawn. These cross-quarter days are celebrated by pagans, and they hold astrological significance as well. They are part of what has been termed the Wheel of the Year, and in addition to the Equinoxes and Solstices include Beltane (a European celebration of the flowers of spring season) on May 1st, Lughnasadh (Gaelic celebration of the Sun god, Lugh) on August 1st, and especially Samhain, also known as Halloween. There are eight Sabbats of the year, celebrated from sundown to sundown the next day. The Sabbat of Samhain begins on October 31st and ends on November 1st. This holiday is celebrated by Americans on October 31st. Originally this was a day that celebrated the lives of those who have crossed over. In Mexico, the Day of the Dead is celebrated at the same time of year.

It is common for people to fall under psychic attack at 3:00 am, known as the Witching Hour, or the Devil's hour. This hour, observed in many cultures worldwide is believed by some to be the opposite hour of the death of Christ, and three is also the number of the Holy Trinity. True stories of horror, murder and paranormal phenomena that have occurred between 3 and 4 am abound. I have lost count of my own paranormal experiences that have occurred during this hour. Another meaning of waking up at this time is found in traditional Chinese medicine, which connects 3:00 am to the functioning of the liver. The liver is considered to be the warehouse of negative emotions. A traditional acupuncturist would say that if a person has repeated nightmares, especially that occur close to 300 am, one's liver chi (energy) is disturbed and in need of support. In order to restore equilibrium, alcohol, stimulants, refined sugar and hard drugs of any kind should be eliminated, and adding more fresh greens into the diet may be helpful. To be clear, a liver-related issue does not invalidate a paranormal experience, but it can definitely exacerbate it, making it more challenging to overcome. Outer spiritual disturbances are often the reflection of internal ones that have not been resolved and healed.

Spirits of Fire (Aries, Leo, Sagittarius)
Associated Archangel: Michael

Djinn: A spirit that holds prominence in the folklore of Islam. Its name is sometimes spelled as genie, but genii (genius) is a also the name of a different group of spirits in ancient Roman, Etruscan, and Assyrian mythology who served as the guardian spirits of each human from birth onward. The Middle Eastern djinn is known to take any shape and size, beautiful or ugly, beastly or human. It can also remain invisible. The djinn primarily inhabit remote areas of the desert, but some are found by rivers, wells and other bodies of water. Their most famous descriptions are found in the *Thousand and One Takes of the Arabian Nights*. Djinn are very protective of the areas in which they dwell, and will attack when they take offense to certain activities in their presence. Although some have been said to grant favors and be helpful, such beings are generally dangerous and should be regarded with caution. Djinn have been known to mate and reproduce with humans.

Dragon: Tales of fire-breathing dragons abound in many parts of the world. Although Christians have associated the dragon with evil, it is not an evil creature by nature. Dragons are associated with weather changes and control of the weather. There are dragons that specifically dwell in the water, and the tops of waterfalls are known to be their gateways. Dragons have come to symbolize power, prosperity and good fortune. Some dragons have been known to be protective and others formidable foes. They basically appear as gigantic reptiles with superpowers, used for good or evil purposes.

Gryphon: The gryphon or griffin is an ancient hybrid beast that is half lion and half eagle. It tends to make itself known through thunder and lightning. It is usually known to serve as a guardian.

Michael: Michael is known as the "dragon slayer". The literal Hebrew translation of his name is "who is like God" and he was ranked as the greatest of all angels in heaven. He is the angel who is most often invoked for protection against the forces of evil in this world. One of my grandmothers relayed a story to me of her childhood, when she was around five years of age. She had just been tucked into bed and a few minutes later, a large male form appeared in her doorway. His height reached all the way to the ceiling, glowing with white light and he had a piercing gaze. In one hand he held a sword, pointed downward. She screamed in fear at the top of her lungs and when her mother showed up he had disappeared. Her mother's response was one of joy and excitement, for to her this was a sign from God, perhaps as a manifestation of the Archangel Michael. Although this is not certain, it seems possible since my great-grandmother was a very pious woman who prayed daily and was a strong believer. Children have greater clairvoyance than most adults in today's world, and spirits more readily reveal themselves to them.

Phoenix: The Phoenix is a majestic bird with golden feathers that represents rebirth; in Egypt it was associated with the Sun. It resembles the peacock but it is much larger and has great longevity. It is a symbol for the highest attainment of the sign of Scorpio, after the stinging defensiveness of the scorpion and the shedding phase of the snake. The Phoenix has come to symbolize transformation and immortality. It shares many similarities with the Thunderbird that is sacred to Native Americans.

Will o' the Wisp: This being is known in the British Isles for leading wanderers astray, often to their death. It takes the form of a glowing light, especially in the evening when sight is dimmed by the darkness. Other British names for this being include Jack-a-lantern, Hobby-lantern, and Ignis Fatuus which means 'the foolish fire', among others. This type of beings exist in many parts of the world and are given different titles. I believe that I caught a glimpse of one of these while out on a walk one fall evening, and it looked like an odd-shaped orange light crossing the road into a ditch. It was a baffling sight, but I knew better than to follow it.

Spirits of Earth (Taurus, Virgo, Capricorn)
Associated Archangel: Uriel

Centaur: Centaurs are a hybrid creature, half man and half horse that feature prominently in Greek mythology. Chiron, known as the "wounded healer" was the most celebrated centaur of them all, known for being wise and just. It is not common to encounter centaurs on the spiritual plane, but when they do appear it may well be to aid with healing of some kind, particularly when it comes to healing from sexual abuse or trauma, or in overcoming a crippling fear.

Elf: The "elf", just as the "fairy", has been diminished in both size and significance over the centuries. Now when people hear the term elf, they tend to think of Santa's little helpers at Christmas time, preparing presents for all the good little boys and girls in the world. Santa Claus is the modern-day archetype of a being that was known in Europe and Western Asia by many names, including the Holly King of Britain and Sinter Klass of the Netherlands. His true identity has been traced back to the Norse god Odin and his flying horse. As for elves, I tend to think of them as more closely resembling those described by the author J.R.R. Tolkien. Such beings are of European and Scandinavian origin, commonly as tall or taller than humans, often with pointy ears. They are stronger, more intelligent and more skilled in every way than ordinary humans.

Dryad: A tree spirit identified in Greek mythology as female nymph that presides over a forest or a particular tree. Some dryads are bound to the tree itself and cannot move far beyond it. Their body is the same color and contains the same characteristics of the tree they inhabit. Dryads, dryad-like beings and other tree spirits in general have different personalities that resemble the qualities of their tree. Some have a liking for humans and others are wary of them. We tend to take trees for granted when they do so much for us. One may appeal to tree spirits by showing respect to the trees, asking for direct permission before altering or taking anything from the tree. Otherwise "bad luck" may soon follow. One may also leave offerings for them, in the form of coins, small desserts, or special stones. Be especially careful around any of the three sacred Fairy trees: Oak, Hawthorne and Rowan, native to the British Isles.

Dwarf: Germany is the origin of the dwarf, a man found in the mountains who is a skilled smith. He is typically depicted as being very short, carefully watching over his treasures and jewels. The original dwarves may have been taller in size than they are usually portrayed.

Goblin: A malicious spirit, diminutive and grotesque in appearance. Goblins are not always mean but are at least mischievous in their behavior. They are more kind toward children than adults. They have been known to stir up trouble in the household.

Leprechaun: This being originated in Ireland, and is known as the shoemaker spirit. He is often depicted as a little bearded man wearing green, guarding a pot of gold at the end of an elusive rainbow. Leprechauns are known to be male, and they tend to live in caves and tree hollows. He is a trickster so anything he says or promises should be regarded with a grain of salt.

Satyr: This type of being is known to be mischievous and lustful and is usually male in appearance. The most prominent satyr in Greek mythology was Pan, the god who appeared half man and half goat. Another well-known satyr is Robin Goodfellow, of English folklore. Satyrs may be classified as a type of devil, and are generally not to be trusted.

Skinwalker: A malevolent being associated with Navajo culture that is known to take the shape of animals. One can only encounter this particular being in the Southwestern region of United States, because this is its native land. There are similarities in this being with the djinn of Middle Eastern culture in that they are both shapeshifters who dwell in remote, rugged, hot regions. Skinwalkers tend to be tall and somewhat humanoid in stature, but extremely swift. They mimic the sounds of animals, but there is always something strange and offbeat in these sounds. They feed on any type of negativity and have the power to possess the weak. They have been been known to cause nightmares and even to kill, but this is usually only when one is unfortunate enough to be caught alone among them in the wild. They tend to attack people while they are driving at night and may cause accidents. They may be further provoked by non-Native people who use Native medicines. If you are being attacked by this creature and you are not Native, do NOT use White Sage to protect yourself. This will only make matters worse. Instead, pray or find other ways to clear your space. You may effectively use salt or your own cultural herbs if you have access to them.

Troll: The troll is native to Germany, Scandinavia, Scotland and Italy. It is known to be shorter than humans but bipedal, hairy and extremely ugly. Their behavior is bullying toward other beings and creatures. They are highly antisocial and prefer not to have contact with humans.

Unicorn: The unicorn is the horned horse which holds magical significance and has captured the human imagination unlike any other creature in world mythology. It is one of the four auspicious creatures known in Chinese folklore, including the Dragon, Phoenix and Tortoise. Sometimes unicorns are pictured with wings in addition to a golden horn protruding from their forehead. Then they become more like Pegasus, which was a white stallion of Greek mythology. Unicorns were featured on medieval tapestries and in heraldry. Today they are found adorning everything from children's toys to adult clothing items. Sadly, the symbol of the unicorn has been grossly distorted and cheapened due to greed and misunderstanding. The actual presence of a unicorn spirit is exceedingly rare, but if one should be fortunate enough to encounter or even to dream of one, it may serve as an omen of profound spiritual purification and healing.

Uriel: One of the four great archangels, whose name means "fire of God". Somewhere along the way, this angel came to be associated with the element of earth. He is also associated with the month of September. It has been said that the sacred art of alchemy was brought to earth by Uriel, and that he also gave the knowledge of the mystical Qabalah to humankind.

Spirits of Air (Gemini, Libra, Aquarius)
Associated Archangel: Raphael

Harpy: The Harpies were wind spirits in classical Greek and Roman mythology that appeared during storms, hurricanes and whirlwinds. They had the lower bodies of large birds and the heads of ugly, animal clawed women, but could morph themselves into terrifying demons. They were foul smelling, as is typical of many types of demonic entities, and were known to contaminate all that they touched.

Sprite: Most closely resembles the popular idea of a dainty little female fairy with gossamer wings. They can be tiny or quite large compared to humans. There is no specific gender assigned to sprites, as they can appear either male, female or a combination of both. They can be neutral or mischievous, but never malicious in demeanor. Their natural habitat is usually wild and sprinkled with flowers.

Raphael: One of the four great archangels of Chaldean origin, Raphael's name means "God has healed". He was known in the Book of Enoch to be a guide in the Underworld. Although taking various forms and roles, this archetypal being has come to be associated with all forms of healing in general, including healing of the earth.

Trooping Fairies: These beings are described in the British Isles as fairies who always travel in groups. They can be small or large in size, and they may be dangerous or playful in a non-threatening way. There are many different types of trooping fairies, each with different habits.

Tuatha de Danaan This is an ancient race of beings described as having "descended from the clouds from the east and settling on a mountain in the west of Ireland, causing a great eclipse of the sun as they did so". Note – The Truth About the Leprechaun by Bob Curran (listed below), page 66. Their name means "People of the Goddess Danu", linking them with the most revered goddess of the Emerald Isle. They came from the Four Cities of the North, bringing with them their advanced skills in magic and the arts. Eventually they descended into the earth, where they are now said to dwell in the underworld.

Zephyrus: Zephyrus is the name of the god of the West wind in Greek mythology. Some people refer to spirits of the wind as zephyrs, as the word zephyr has also come to describe a gentle breeze or the west wind itself.

Spirits of Water (Cancer, Scorpio, Pisces)
Associated Archangel: Gabriel

Gabriel: Gabriel is one of the four great archangels, and along with Michael is the only other angel mentioned by name in the Old Testament. He is the angel known to have brought glad tidings to Mary, before she knew that she would give birth to Jesus. Gabriel is known as the messenger angel and his name means "God is my strength". Somewhere along the way he came to be associated with the element of water, and many modern day magickal practitioners invoke Gabriel to assist them in their work with water, understanding hidden messages and emotional currents.

Mermaids and Merfolk: The beautiful, long-haired mermaid has come to be an iconic symbol of the magic, mystery, and sensuality of the natural world and its copious waters. Usually the half-fish, half-human hybrid is depicted as female, but mermen also exist on the spirit plane. Merfolk have been seen worldwide, in various forms, sizes, and apparent ages from very young to very old, and from hauntingly beautiful to outright hideous.

Naga: Naga are a type of serpentine spirit native to India that are associated with the god Vishnu. Nagas, which inhabit the waters, have the upper body of a human and the lower body of a snake. Although the Buddha was said to be protected by a Naga king, the relationship that these beings have to humans is generally ambivalent and they can be mischievous in nature.

Nereid: These are the sea nymph of classical Greek mythology whose name means "wet one". Nereids appear as beautiful young women who inhabit the sea, sometimes leading humans into muddy waters by deception. The Nereids, along with the Tritons were attendants to the god

Neptune, and his wife Amphritrite.

Selkie: Selkies are seaside beings native to Scotland and the Orkney islands, and the same kind of being is called Roane in Ireland. They appear as seals in the water but can shed their skin to become beautiful and humanoid in shape. They have been known to lure and mate with humans but find it difficult to remain on land and eventually return back to the sea.

Siren: Sirens are a type of half-bird, half woman island creature, who in Greek mythology bewitched sailors with sweet songs, leading them toward chaos or death.

Water Dragons: Water Dragons are dragons who inhabit the seas. They may be monstrous or magnificent, helpful or harmful. They tend to take on the shape of a giant serpent. The beloved goddess Quan Yin of China is often depicted riding upon the back of a dragon across the sea.

Ether (All Elements, All Signs)

Familiar: A familiar is the attending spirit of a good witch, good wizard, or sorcerer of the black arts. The familiar is native to cultures worldwide, always as a servant that may take on the appearance of a small animal of some kind. Its purpose is to give protection, warnings or advice to its keeper.

Ghost: These are disembodied humans and animals, found in every land known to humankind. These are the remnant spirits of those who have passed on, lingering on in a state of either unrest or attachment to their previous life and location.

Grey: The Grey is widely believed to be an extraterrestrial being that is often unfriendly toward humans and animals. They are described as misshapen, lanky, and barely humanoid, with grey skin, oversized heads and bulging black eyes. I personally think it's possible that greys are actually a type of demon or shapeshifter. Some people think there are benevolent greys, but from my point of view, none of them are to be trusted.

Hag: The hag, or crone woman appears in many parts of the world as a hideous old woman with evil powers. The modern concept of a wicked witch with a crooked nose and warts is derived from this archetypal image. However, in much older times, in certain regions of Europe and the British Isles, she was a kind and helpful spirit. Some evil spirits indeed take on the shape of a hag, or may be the astral projection of an actual sorceress. You will know her intentions by the way you feel in her presence. The benevolent hag may help to heal injuries or grant wishes.

Imp: An imp is a miniature devil. The name imp means "offshoot" or "cutting". An imp tree was grafted, grown from a cutting rather than from a seed. "Imp properly means a small devil, an off-shoot of Satan" - [*Encyclopedia of Fairies* by Katherine Briggs, page 232]. These beings are mischievous and childlike pests who taunt and play pranks on their victims, simply because it is fun for them.

Lwa: The lwa or loa spirit is a being of African descent, serving as intermediaries and guardians of the Voodoo religion. They are also the allies of practitioners of Santeria. Unless these religions are part of one's own personal lineage, it is wise not to invoke loas.

Poltergeist: German name for a household spirit, who name means "noise spirit". Such beings may go by different names and can manifest in homes all over the world. They are known to shuffle objects and furniture around, make creaking sounds, tapping on the walls and ceilings. These beings often seem to become active in the presence of adolescents. Some people theorize that they are not actual entities, but bursts of unconscious energy emitted from the child.

Shapeshifter: Describes a spirit that changes into specific shapes, such as a werewolf, or a spirit that can take any shape it chooses. There are different types of shapeshifters, but they are so called by the fact that they do not have one single form. They tend to take on the characteristics of the environment that they inhabit. They may be benevolent or malevolent. One will usually be able to tell this from their actions.

Incubus: A male demon identified in medieval Europe that descends upon women to have intercourse with them while they sleep. The Latin translation of incubus is "that which lies upon". This spirit often takes on the appearance of the husband, lover or familiar man. In some cases, the incubus may appear as the Devil himself. He transfers fear into her soul, or may whisper lies into her ears while she is being raped.

Succubus: The succubus is a type of female demon also known as the lamia who copulate with men during their sleep, sucking the life from their souls, through their semen. She may cause men to dream of erotic experiences with women, which also causes ejaculation, allowing the succubus to procreate a new spirit. Incubi and succubi can only descend upon those who are already compromised by excess negativity and stress. It is not uncommon for one to become physically ill or go insane after being attacked by one.

Further Reading

1. *How to Talk with Spirits: Seances, Mediums, Ghost Hunts* by June Ahern. San Francisco, 2017.

2. *An Encyclopedia of Fairies* by Katherine Briggs. Pantheon Books in New York, 1976.

3. *The Truth About the Leprechaun* by Bob Curran. Wolfhound Press in 2000.

4. *A Dictionary of Angels* by Gustav Davidson. The Free Press in New York, 1971.

5. *Great Encyclopedia of Faeries* by Pierre Dubois. Simon & Schuster in New York, 1996.

6. *Mermaids: Nymphs of the Sea* by Theodore Gachot. Collins Publishers in San Francisco, 1996.

7. *Angels: An Endangered Species* by Malcolm Godwin. Simon & Schuster in New York, 1990.

8. *Faery Healing: The Lore and the Legacy* by Margie McArthur. New Brighton Books in Aptos, California, 2003.

9. *Good and Evil in Myth and Legend* by Anthony S. Mercante. Barnes & Noble Books in New York, 1978.

10. *Spirits, Fairies, Leprechauns, and Goblins: An Encyclopedia* by Carol Rose. W.W. Norton & Company, New York and London, 1996.

11. *The Woman's Encyclopedia of Myths and Secrets* by Barbara Walker. Harper & Row Publishers in San* Francisco, 1983.

A Few Fixed Stars

When the Sun, Moon, any of the four angles, either Node or a planet is in a conjunction with a fixed star, the star can make a special impact. This topic can fill several volumes, but the following information is included just to offer a glimpse into the importance of degrees and how they may be influenced by certain stars. About a two-and-a-half-degree orb is allowed for most of them to count as an influence in the natal chart or by transit. Many of the fixed stars that are known to be primarily negative in their effects tend to be more favorable when in conjunction with Jupiter. Although generally only the conjunctions to fixed stars are considered to exert their influence, I have noticed that the oppositions to some of them are equally intense in their effects.

Most of the stars listed below belong to a group of fifteen Behenian stars, which have been selected by Medieval astrologers for their use in magical applications. The traditional gemstones and plants associated with them are listed. Fomalhaut, Betelgeuse, and Vertex are not Behenian stars. The others not included here are Alcyone, Algorab, Capella, Alphecca, and Procyon. There are well over a hundred fixed stars that some astrologers take into account[1,2]

Algol — 26 degrees of Taurus
Gemstone: Diamond — Plant: Black Hellebore

Algol, an Arabic name meaning "Head of the Ogre", has long been considered to be one of the most malign and unfortunate fixed stars of all. It is also known as the "demon star." If you have anything at 26 degrees of Taurus or within a couple of degrees from it, that planet, Node or other important spot may be affected by the so-called evil influence of Algol. This star is most widely known as the harbinger of cruelty, violence, morbidity, or misfortune. This doesn't mean you're destined for doom, but rather that special effort may be needed to counteract these negative influences. In self-aware individuals, its energy is directed is positive ways. Algol is connected with the mythology of snake-headed Medusa in Greek mythology who was said to turn men into stone with a mere glance. One may possess the feminine power of Medusa before her transformation into a gorgon. Sensuality may be noticeably heightened but can be creatively channeled or harnessed for personal growth.

ALGOL also happens to be an abbreviation of Algorithmic Language in computer programming, that was developed in 1958 by European and American scientists. Today's Internet algorithms (artificial intelligence) are both an aid and an intrusive development for people on social media. This has become the leviathan in cyberspace where the screen is always "staring back" at you.

Aldebaran — 9 degrees of Gemini
Gemstone: Ruby — Plant: Milk Thistle

Aldebaran is one of the four Royal Stars, in the Left Eye of the Bull, in the constellation of Taurus. Ptolemy considered it to be of the nature of Mars, and it has often been associated with the military and war. As the Guardian of the East, this giant orange star was seen in ancient Persia to mark the vernal equinox. This star is not necessarily negative in its influences, as much depends on the planet making contact with it, and the other conditions around it. It is actually usually seen as more of an empowering kind of influence, bringing honors, wealth, and fame. With the Sun it is believed to give great energy and stamina, but with the danger of losing them. Aldebaran is known to produce riots led by revolutionaries, but sometimes success in war.[3]

Alkaid — 26 degrees of Virgo
Gemstone: Magnet — Plant: Chicory

Fixed star Alkaid, also known as Eta Ursae Majoris, is a white star on the tail of the Great Bear, Ursa Major, constellation. It was once utilized in magical ritual as one of the Behenian stars, and was one that was mentioned by Cornelius Agrippa[4] Its influence is likened to that of Mars, and it has been associated with revenge, natural disasters and violent death. It is also associated with mourning and funeral services.

Antares — 9 degrees of Sagittarius
Gemstones: Sardonyx and Amethyst
Plants: Birthwort and Saffron

The Greek translation of Antares is "anti-Ares", indicating its influence as the rival of Mars. It is a bright red and green star located in the heart of the Scorpion, known to bring mighty success in war, and also known as a powerful aid in the driving away and binding of evil spirits. As the Guardian of the West, Antares was known in ancient Persia to mark the autumn equinox. In some cases, Antares has been known to bring malevolent influences of violence, sickness and destruction. There can sometimes be a strong religious influence connected with Antares. This large star, along with Aldebaran, which are both in the tenth degrees of the polar opposite signs Sagittarius and Gemini were believed by Sepharial to produce terrible periods of stress to which a person may be subjected in life, when either is directed to the angles of the horoscope [5]

Arcturus — 24 degrees of Libra
Gemstone: Jasper Plant: Plantain

Arcturus is considered to be one of the more fortunate and the fourth brightest of the fixed stars, situated in the left knee of Bootes, the Herdsman. Its name is derived from an ancient Greek term meaning Bear Guardian or Bear Watcher. Arcturus and Spica are very close together and they are both known as benign in their effects. Arcturus has the more mature and industrious influence of the two. Having the nature of Jupiter and Mars, it is said to give riches and high renown, but also can produce folly and extravagance.

Deneb Algedi — 23 degrees of Aquarius
Gemstone: Chalcedony Plant: Marjoram

Deneb Algedi is a binary star system in the tail of the Sea-Goat, and its Arabic name literally means "tail of the goat". According to Ptolemy it is of the nature of Saturn and Jupiter. Misfortune, sorrow and destructiveness are often attributed to this star, but sometimes beneficence and happiness. It is said to have rulership over the blood vessels and nerve channels surrounding the vertebrae. Challenges are implied with every planetary conjunction. Its most fortunate position of all appears to be the Midheaven, where it is said to bring fame and wealth, as well as dignity and authority by the aid of an old clergyman or influential person.

Fomalhaut — 3 degrees of Pisces

Fomalhaut is a white star, in the "mouth of the Southern fish". It has been said to be of the combined nature of Mercury and Venus. It's influences are primarily considered to be both fortunate and spiritual in nature. It is not so helpful for mundane or political purposes. As the Guardian of the South, Fomalhaut was known in ancient Persia to mark the winter solstice. With either the Sun or Mars it is said to bring danger of the bite of venomous creatures. Being associated with Archangel Gabriel, Fomalhaut has been known to bring good news, prophecy, and messages from the Divine.

Betelgeuse — 28 degrees of Gemini

This is a super-giant red star located in the right shoulder of Orion, said to be of the nature of Mercury and Mars. It is known to give martial honor, wealth, and a keen interest in occult and mystical subjects. It is also associated with danger, violence, and untimely death. It often gives athletic and leadership abilities, except, when in conjunction with Venus, it is more reserved. With Saturn it is considered to be particularly unfortunate.

Regulus — 29 degrees of Leo
Gemstone: Garnet Plant: Mugwort

Regulus, Latin for "little king" is one of the four Royal Stars, of the nature of Mars and Jupiter according to Ptolemy, and of the proud nature of the Lion. As the Guardian of the North, Regulus was known in ancient Persia to mark the summer solstice. It is associated with Archangel Raphael, the angel of healing. This star can either appear as highly benefic or violent and destructive in its influences. It is known to give a regal and generous disposition, but is also associated with imprisonment, scandal, and injuries to the head and face. Overall, it is considered to be one of the most fortunate and protective of the fixed stars. At the Midheaven, for example, Regulus has been known to give prosperity in business.

Sirius 14 — degrees of Cancer
Gemstone: Beryl Plant: Juniper

Sirius, also known as the Dog Star, is known to be the brightest star in the heavens. According to Ptolemy it is of the nature of both Mars and Jupiter, indicating high ambitions and lust for power. Positively, it is said to bring honor and fortune, but negatively it is believed to give resentment, a violent temper, and the danger of dog bites. In some cases it has been known to cause violence. As with all other fixed stars, much depends on the conjunction being made. Its natives have also been known to become curators, custodians and protectors. Sirius has been observed to bestow lasting fame when it is well connected. In many cases, fame comes after death or toward the end of life, and is carried beyond the grave.

Spica — 23 degrees of Libra
Gemstone: Emerald
Plants: Sage, Periwinkle, Trefoil

Spica is a giant blue star in the ear of wheat of Virgo. According to Ptolemy it is of the nature of Venus and Mars, indicating a tendency for self-indulgence in its natives. It is known to grant success, riches, and a sweet disposition, but also injustice to the innocent. Although it seems benign in many respects, Spica is not always a particularly fortunate star. It is known to be of great assistance to artists, authors and musicians, as well as to scientists. It can be an especially helpful influence for any occupations dealing with grains, for construction and real estate.

Vega — 15 degrees of Capricorn
Gemstone: Chrysolite
Plants: Winter Savory and Fumitory

Vega is considered one of the more fortunate fixed stars, being of a pale sapphire hue and located in the handle of the Lyre. Its name stems from an Arabic word meaning "falling eagle". According to Ptolemy it is of the nature of Venus and Mercury. It is known to bestow idealism, loyalty and musical ability. Also, it has been connected with criminal activity, fraud, pretentiousness and torture. It may relate both to fame and the dreams of becoming well-known, but may lead to disappointment in these areas. With Vega featuring prominently, there are many talents, and perhaps much power and influence, but challenges accompany them.

Vertex — 27 degrees of Aries

This fixed star is not to be confused with the Vertex point referred to in astrology as a calculated spot on the western hemisphere of the chart. The Vertex point is considered to be an area that indicates personal fate, especially regarding relationships. In contrast, the fixed star Vertex is one of the so-called unfortunate stars, associated with punishment, murder, and sickness. Located on the thigh of the Chained Woman, Andromeda, it is actually connected with the head and eyes, and when poorly connected is said to weaken the vision.

References

1. Vivian Robson, *The Fixed Stars in Astrology* (London: The Aquarian Press, 1969)

2. Joseph E, Rigor, *The Power of the Fixed Stars* (Hammond: Astrology and Spiritual Publishers, 1979)

3. Ptolemy, *Ptolemy's Almagest*, translated by G.J. Toomer (Princeton: Princeton University Press, 1998)

4. Henry Cornelius Agrippa, *Three Books of Occult Philosophy*, modern translation by James Freake (Llewellyn Sourcebook Series, 1992)

5. Sepharial, *Sepharial's New Dictionary of Astrology* (New York: Galahad Books, 1963) p. 42

Glossary

Affliction: A planet is said to be afflicted when it forms a poor aspect or several poor aspects, especially when the aspects involve malefic planets.

Angle: The cusps of houses 1, 4, 7 and 10. Planets on the angles are called "angular planets" and they have a cardinal quality, and a particularly pronounced effect in the natal chart.

Aspect: An angle made between planets to each other or other important areas. There are "major" and "minor" aspects. Among the aspects of top importance (major) are the conjunction, the square, the sextile, the trine, and the opposition. Many astrologers find minor aspects to be no less important than major ones. A conjunction is two or more planets within 10 degrees of each other. In some cases, the orbs must be tighter, such as 6 degrees or less to be considered valid. Conjunctions emphasize the coming together of these planets for better or worse. The sextile is a sixty-degree angle between planets, and considered to be a positive aspect that brings opportunity. A square is a ninety-degree angle between two points or planets, or between a planet and conjunction, etc. This aspect is known to be one of tension, conflict, and action. The trine is a one-hundred-and-twenty-degree angle between planets that brings harmony and ease. An opposition is a one-hundred-and-degree angle between opposing planets. It is known to be stressful and to come from other people or outside forces.

ASC = Ascendant: The beginning of the first house of the natal or other astrology chart. It rules the outer appearance, general health and the most obvious personality traits.

Benefic: Refers to the benefic qualities of the planets Jupiter and Venus, which are known to have inherently beneficial or fortunate influences, unless they are somehow afflicted.

Cadent: Houses 3, 6, 9 and 12 are cadent houses. Cadent is linked with the Latin word *cado*, which means "fallen" in Latin, as the cadent houses have fallen from the angles. Planets in these houses have mutable qualities, and are subject to conditions related to service, subordinance or simply a lot of contemplation rather than definitive action.

Cardinal: The signs that begin the four seasons – Aries, Cancer, Libra, Capricorn. These signs set things into motion. The associated cardinal directions are: the *Ascendant* which corresponds to the East (Spring), the *Nadir* which corresponds to the South (Summer), the *Descendant* which corresponds to the West (Autumn), and the *Midheaven* which corresponds to the North (Winter).

Detriment: A planet is believed to be distressed or uncomfortable in the sign of its detriment.

Dignity: Planetary dignities refer to signs where planets function naturally, at their best, or where they are challenged. Planets have what is called *essential* dignity when they are in the sign of their rulership or domicile, or where they are in the sign of their *exaltation*, *fall* or *detriment*. A planet is in detriment when it is in the sign opposite of the sign that it rules. Likewise, a planet is in its fall in the sign opposite of the one where it would be exalted. Planets in their fall or detriment were traditionally believed to be weakened in some way.

Descendent (DC): The beginning of the seventh house, directly opposite of the Ascendant. This rules marriage and partnerships, including business. It can also describe open enemies.

Fixed: The fixed signs are Taurus, Leo, Scorpio, and Aquarius. They are known as the 'foundation' signs and are known to aid in stability and resourcefulness.

Dispositor: The planet that is the ruler or "lord" of the sign where another planet is located. For example if Venus is in Aries, Mars is the dispositor of Venus. The planet being disposited draws additional energy from the dispositor.

Divisions: Use of the divisions of the days, hours, and minutes are all important in modern astrology. The 2nd century Greek astronomer Hipparchus is credited with having discovered the division of the day into 24 hours, based on 12 hours of daylight and 12 hours of darkness observed on equinox days. This division fits perfectly into wheel of the Zodiac. Previous astronomers such as Eudoxus, Timocharis, and Aristillus had already divided the ecliptic into 360 degrees, of which make up the wheel or circle. They learned this from the ancient Babylonians and Sumerians who used a sexagesimal system which divided a circle into 60 arcminutes. From this mathematical system of division and time tracking, 60 seconds makes a minute and 60 minutes make an hour.

Domicile: A planet's domicile is the sign which has rulership over it. For example, Saturn is in domicile in the sign of Capricorn.

Exaltation: The sign where a planet is said to function at its peak of awareness and capacity.

Fall: A planet in its fall is traditionally said to be weak in its expression, as it is opposite its sign of exaltation.

Feminine and Masculine Signs: Each of the twelve signs are considered to be either feminine (yin) or masculine (yang) in their expression, which are known as the polarities, but these do not necessarily relate to sex. These polarities are masculine Aries/Libra, feminine Taurus/Scorpio, masculine Gemini/Sagittarius, feminine Cancer/Capricorn, masculine Leo/Aquarius, and feminine Virgo/Pisces. Feminine signs are generally emotional, reactive, pensive and receptive and include the elements earth and water. Masculine signs are generally active, enthusiastic, intellectual, and passionate and represent the elements fire and air.

Fixed Stars: The stars that do not appear to move but have been observed to have particularly powerful effects when they are situated on angles of the horoscope, or in conjunction with any of the planets.

Horary: "Of the hour", horary refers to the chart of a moment in which a question is asked. This chart may be used to gain a simple yes or no answer, or may offer specific clues into the nature of a more detailed question.

Horoscope: May refer to the astrological chart or an astrological forecast that is based on transits.

Imum Coeli (IC): The lowest part of the chart, which is the beginning of the fourth house, directly opposite the Midheaven. It rules one's family, private life, and the conditions of life's ending.

Luminaries: Generally refers to the Sun and Moon.

Malefic: Traditionally refers to the malefic qualities of the planets Mars and Saturn, which are known to bring sickness, strife and hardship. Today, the planets Uranus, Neptune and Pluto may also be categorized as malefic planets when their troublesome influences are more pronounced than their beneficial ones.

MC = Midheaven: The degree at the top of the chart, ruling the career, public image and impact on society.

Mutable: The mutable signs are Gemini, Virgo, Sagittarius, and Pisces. They are known to be changeable, fluid, and unstable.

Natal: A natal chart relates to one's time or place of birth, or both. Some astrologers regard the nativity as the moment that an infant takes its first breath, while others consider it to be the moment the umbilical cord is severed. Many people do not have a record of their time of birth, while others may have a record that is a few minutes up to an hour from the actual moment of birth. Even a minute could sometimes make a difference in one's Ascendant or other planets if they are in the midst of transitioning from one to another, although they can only be in one or the other. This may explain why some natal charts do not make sense.

Orb: Refers to the distance allowed between planets in order to qualify as an aspect.

Polarity: Describes the opposing signs and their corresponding houses.

Quadruplicity aka Modality: Three different groupings of signs based on their qualities, being Cardinal, Fixed, or Mutable.

Rectification: This is a method for determining the true time of birth, by tracking specific major life events going as far back into childhood as possible. This can be a very complex, lengthy, and tricky process, with no absolute guarantees. However, when conducted by a skilled astrologer it can shed much light into a previously unknown or inaccurate natal chart.

Rulership: Refers to planets in domicile, or refers to the planets that rule particular signs.

For example, Mars is the ruler of Aries. The ruler of the natal or horary chart is the planet that has rulership over the sign of the Ascendant.

Solar Calendar: One of the earliest calendars designed for a year based on the sun's position in relation to the stars was developed by the Egyptians, in which the fixed star Sirius was the annual sunrise marker in the eastern sky. Its appearance coincided with the annual flooding of the Nile River. Their calendar consisted of 365 days, 12 months and 30 days each, with 5 days added to the end of each year. Over time the calendar has shifted and today's Gregorian calendar months are skewed. The Julian calendar followed the traditional sun calendar and the Latin names of the months clue us in to its cycles. The year began with Martius or March (ruled by Mars/Aries), which is the astrological beginning of the year due to the equinox. The following months were Aprilis, Maius, Junius, and Quintilis. Sextilis Augustus was the 6th month rather than the 8th (connected with the beginning of the 6th sign Virgo), September was the 7th month (the 7th sign Libra begins here), October was the 8th month (Scorpio's month), November the 9th month (Sagittarius), and December the 10th month, coinciding with the tenth sign of the Zodiac, Capricorn, marking a solstice. Ianuarius or January was named after the Roman god of doorways and passages, Janus. Februarius or February was the month of purification, appropriately linked with the final sign, Pisces.

Succedent: The succedent houses 2, 5, 8, and 11 follow the angles. Planets in these houses have a fixed quality which may grow in strength over time. These houses especially relate to personal attainments, desires and finances.

Synastry: The comparison of two natal charts to determine their compatibility. A synastry chart is a biwheel of one chart upon the other to show the interactions of planets. Two different biwheels should be made to see how each person influences the other.

Transit: The passage of a planet through a particular sign or house, as it forms aspects to other planets.

Triplicity: The grouping of signs based on their same element, each of which form the trine aspect.

Zodiac: A celestial band that is divided into 12 equal parts that are called signs, each of which contain equal sections of 30 degrees through which the sun, moon and planets make their way in a cyclic fashion. The word zodiac stems from the Greek word *zodiakos,* meaning "circle of little animals"